D1095400

OFFICIALLY WITHDRAWN

PHILOSOPHY OF THE PRACTICAL

ECONOMIC AND ETHIC

MACMILLAN AND CO., Limited
LONDON · BOMBAY · CALCUTTA
MELBOURNE

THE MACMILLAN COMPANY
NEW YORK · BOSTON · CHICAGO
DALLAS · SAN FRANCISCO

THE MACMILLAN CO. OF CANADA, Ltd.
TORONTO

PHILOSOPHY OF THE PRACTICAL

Economic and Ethic

BENEDETTO CROCE

Translated from the Italian
by
Douglas Ainslie

BIBLO and TANNEN
NEW YORK
1967

ORIGINALLY PUBLISHED 1913
REPRINTED 1967
BY
BIBLO and TANNEN BOOKSELLERS and PUBLISHERS, INC.
63 FOURTH AVENUE   NEW YORK, NEW YORK 10003

Library of Congress Catalog Card Number: 66-30790

917227

NOTE

CERTAIN chapters only of the third part of this book were anticipated in the study entitled *Reduction of the Philosophy of Law to the Philosophy of Economy*, read before the Accademia Pontaniana of Naples at the sessions of April 21 and May 5, 1907 (*Acts*, vol. xxxvii.); but I have remodelled them, amplifying certain pages and summarizing others. The concept of economic activity as an autonomous form of the spirit, which receives systematic treatment in the second part of the book, was first maintained in certain essays, composed from 1897 to 1900, and afterwards collected in the volume *Historical Materialism and Marxist Economy* (2nd edition, Palermo, Sandron, 1907).

B. C.

NAPLES,
19th April 1908.

TRANSLATOR'S PREFACE

"A noi sembra che l' opera del Croce sia lo sforzo più potente che il pensiero italiano abbia compiuto negli ultimi anni."— G. DE RUGGIERO in *La Filosofia contemporanea*, 1912.

"Il sistema di Benedetto Croce rimane la più alta conquista del pensiero contemporaneo."—G. NATOLI in *La Voce*, 19th December 1912.

THOSE acquainted with my translation of Benedetto Croce's *Æsthetic as Science of Expression and General Linguistic* will not need to be informed of the importance of this philosopher's thought, potent in its influence upon criticism, upon philosophy and upon life, and famous throughout Europe.

In the Italian, this volume is the third and last of the *Philosophy of the Spirit*, *Logic as Science of the Pure Concept* coming second in date of publication. But apart from the fact that philosophy is like a moving circle, which can be entered equally well at any point, I have preferred to place this volume before the *Logic* in the hands of British readers. Great Britain has long

been a country where moral values are highly
esteemed ; we are indeed experts in the practice,
though perhaps not in the theory of morality, a
lacuna which I believe this book will fill.

In saying that we are experts in moral practice
I do not, of course, refer to the narrow conventional morality, also common with us, which so
often degenerates into hypocrisy, a legacy of
Puritan origin ; but apart from this, there has
long existed in many millions of Britons a strong
desire to live well, or, as they put it, cleanly and
rightly, and achieved by many, independent of
any close or profound examination of the logical
foundation of this desire. Theology has for
some taken the place of pure thought, while for
others, early training on religious lines has been
sufficiently strong to dominate other tendencies
in practical life. Yet, as a speculative Scotsman,
I am proud to think that we can claim divided
honours with Germany in the production of
Emmanuel Kant (or Cant).

The latter half of the nineteenth century wit-
nessed with us a great development of materialism
in its various forms. The psychological, antihistorical speculation contained in the so-called
Synthetic Philosophy (really psychology) of
Herbert Spencer was but one of the many power-

ful influences abroad, tending to divert youthful minds from the true path of knowledge. This writer, indeed, made himself notorious by his attitude of contemptuous intolerance and ignorance of the work previously done in connection with subjects which he was investigating. He accepted little but the evidence of his own senses and judgment, as though he were the first philosopher. But time has now taken its revenge, and modern criticism has exposed the Synthetic Philosophy in all its barren and rigid inadequacy and ineffectuality. Spencer tries to force Life into a brass bottle of his own making, but the genius will not go into his bottle. The names and writings of J. S. Mill, of Huxley, and of Bain are, with many others of lesser calibre, a potent aid to the dissolving influence of Spencer. Thanks to their efforts, the spirit of man was lost sight of so completely that I can well remember hearing Kant's great discovery of the synthesis *a priori* described as moonshine, and Kant himself, with his categoric imperative, as little better than a Prussian policeman. As for Hegel, the great completer and developer of Kantian thought, his philosophy was generally in even less esteem among the youth ; and we find even the contemplative Walter Pater passing him by with a polite

b

apology for shrinking from his chilly heights. I
do not, of course, mean to suggest that estimable
Kantians and Hegelians did not exist here and
there throughout the kingdom in late Victorian
days (the names of Stirling, of Caird, and of Green
at once occur to the mind); but they had not
sufficient genius to make their voices heard above
the hubbub of the laboratory. We all believed
that the natural scientists had taken the measure
of the universe, could tot it up to a T—and consequently turned a deaf ear to other appeals.

Elsewhere in Europe Hartmann, Haeckel, and
others were busy measuring the imagination and
putting fancy into the melting-pot—they offered
us the chemical equivalent of the wings of Aurora.
We believed them, believed those materialists,
those treacherous neo-Kantians, perverters of
their master's doctrine, who waited for guileless
youth with mask and rapier at the corner of every
thicket. Such as escaped this ambush were
indeed fortunate if they shook themselves free of
Schopenhauer, the (personally) comfortable philosopher of suicide and despair, and fell into the
arms of the last and least of the Teutonic giants,
Friedrich Nietzsche, whose spasmodic paragraphs,
full of genius but often empty of philosophy,
show him to have been far more of a poet than a

philosopher. It was indeed a doleful period of transition for those unfortunate enough to have been born into it: we really did believe that life had little or nothing to offer, or that we were all Overmen (a mutually exclusive proposition!), and had only to assert ourselves in order to prove it.

To the writings of Pater I have already referred, and of them it may justly be said that they are often supremely beautiful, with the quality and cadence of great verse, but mostly (save perhaps the volume on *Plato and Platonism*, by which he told the present writer that he hoped to live) instinct with a profound scepticism, that revelled in the externals of Roman Catholicism, but refrained from crossing the threshold which leads to the penetralia of the creed.

Ruskin also we knew, and he too has a beautiful and fresh vein of poetry, particularly where free from irrational dogmatism upon Ethic and Æsthetic. But we found him far inferior to Pater in depth and suggestiveness, and almost devoid of theoretical capacity. Sesame for all its Lilies is no Open Sesame to the secrets of the world. Thus, wandering in the obscure forest, it is little to be wondered that we did not anticipate the flood of light to be shed upon us as we crossed the threshold of the twentieth century.

It was an accident that took me to Naples in 1909, and the accident of reading a number of *La Critica*, as I have described in the introduction to the *Æsthetic*, that brought me in contact with the thought of Benedetto Croce. But it was not only the *Æsthetic*, it was also the purely critical work of the philosopher that appeared to me at once of so great importance. To read Hegel, for instance, after reading Croce's study of him, is a very different experience (at least so I found it) to reading him before so doing.

Hegel is an author most deeply stimulative and suggestive, but any beginner is well to take advantage of all possible aid in the difficult study.

To bring this thought of Hegel within the focus of the ordinary mind has never been an easy task (I know of no one else who has successfully accomplished it); and Croce's work, *What is living and what is dead of the Philosophy of Hegel*, as one may render the Italian title of the book which I hope to translate, has enormously aided a just comprehension, both of the qualities and the defects of that philosopher. This work appeared in the Italian not long after the *Æsthetic*, and has had an influence upon the minds of contemporary Italians, second only to the *Philosophy of the Spirit*. To clear away the débris of Hegel, his false conception of art and of religion, to demonstrate his erroneous application of his own great discovery of the dialectic to pseudo-concepts, and thus to reveal it in its full splendour, has been one of the most valuable of Croce's inestimable contributions to critical thought.

I shall not pause here to dilate upon the immense achievement of Croce, the youngest of Italian senators, a recognition of his achievement by his King and country, but merely mention his numerous historical works, his illuminative study of Vico, which has at last revealed that philosopher as of like intellectual stature to Kant ; the immense tonic and cultural influence of his review, *La Critica*, and his general editorship of the great collection of *Scrittori d' Italia*. Freed at last from that hubbub of the laboratory, from the measures and microscopes of the natural scientists, excellent in their place, it is interesting to ask if any other contemporary philosopher has made a contribution to ethical theory in any way comparable to the *Philosophy of the Practical*. The names of Bergson and of Blondel at once occur to the mind, but the former admits that his complete ideas on ethics are not yet made known, and implies that he may never make them entirely known. The reader of the *Philosophy of the*

Practical will, I think, find that none of Bergson's explanations, "burdened," as he says, with "geometry," and as we may say with matter, from the obsession of which he never seems to shake himself altogether free, are comparable in depth or lucidity with the present treatise.   The spirit is described by Bergson as memory, and matter as a succession of images.   How does the one communicate with the other ?   The formula of the self-creative life process seems hardly sufficient to explain this, for if with Bergson we conceive of life as a torrent, there must be some reason why it should flow rather in one channel than in another.   But life is supposed to create and to absorb matter in its progress ; and here we seem to have entered a vicious circle, for the intuition presupposes, it does not create its object.   As regards the will, too, the Bergsonian theory of the Ego as rarely (sometimes never once in life) fully manifesting itself, and our minor actions as under the control of matter, seems to lead to a deterministic conception and to be at variance with the thesis of the self-creation of life.

As regards Blondel, the identification of thought and will in the philosophy of action leads him to the position that the infinite is not in the universal abstract, but in the single concrete.   It is through matter that the divine truth reaches us, and God must pass through nature or matter, in order to reach us, and we must effect the contrary process to reach God. It is a beautiful conception; but, as de Ruggiero suggests, do we not thus return, by a devious and difficult path, to the pre-Hegelian, pre-Kantian, position of religious platonicism?[1]

This, however, is not the place to discourse at length of other philosophies. What most impresses in the Crocean thought is its profundity, its clarity, and its *completeness,—totus teres atque rotundus.* Croce, indeed, alone of the brilliant army of philosophers and critics arisen in the new century, has found a complete formula for his thought, complete, that is, at a certain stage; for, as he says, the relative nature of all systems is apparent to all who have studied philosophy. He alone has defined and allocated the activities of the human spirit; he alone has plumbed and charted its ocean in all its depth and breadth.

A system! The word will sound a mere tinkling of cymbals to many still aground in the abstract superficialities of nineteenth-century scepticism; but they are altogether mistaken. To construct a system is like building a house: it requires a

[1] G. de Ruggiero, *La Filosofia contemporanea*, Laterza, Bari, 1912.

good architect to build a good house, and where it is required to build a great palace it requires a great genius to build it successfully. Michael Angelo built the Vatican, welding together and condensing the works of many predecessors, ruthlessly eliminating what they contained of bad or of erroneous : Benedetto Croce has built the Philosophy of the Spirit. To say of either achievement that it will not last for ever, or that it will need repair from time to time, is perfectly true; but this criticism applies to all things human ; and yet men continue to build houses—for God and for themselves. Croce is the first to admit the incompleteness, the lack of finality of all philosophical systems, for each one of them deals, as he says, with a certain group of problems only, which present themselves at a definite period of time. The solution of these leads to the posing of new problems, first caught sight of by the philosopher as he terminates his labours, to be solved by the same or by other thinkers.

And here it may be well to state very briefly the basis on which rests the *Philosophy of the Spirit*, without attempting to do anything more than to give its general outline. The reader should imagine himself standing, like bold Pizarro, on his "peak of Darien," surveying at a great distance the vast outline of a New World, which yet is as old as Asia.

The Spirit is Reality, it is the whole of Reality, and it has two forms: the theoretic and the practical activities. Beyond or outside these *there are no other forms of any kind.* The theoretic activity has two forms, the intuitive and individual, and the intellectual or knowledge of the universal: the first of these produces images and is known as *Æsthetic*, the second concepts and is known as *Logic*. The first of these activities is altogether independent, self-sufficient, autonomous: the second, on the other hand, has need of the first, ere it can exist. Their relation is therefore that of double degree. The practical activity is the *will*, which is thought in activity, and this also has two forms, the economic or utilitarian, and the ethical or moral, the first autonomous and individual, the second universal, and this latter depends upon the first for its existence, in a manner analogous to *Logic* and to *Æsthetic*.

With the theoretic activity, man understands the universe, with the practical, he changes it. There are no grades or degrees of the Spirit beyond these. All other forms are either without activity, or they are verbal variants of the above, or they are a mixture of these four in different proportions.

Thus the Philosophy of the Spirit is divided into *Æsthetic, Logic, and Philosophy of the Practical* (Economic and Ethic). In these it is complete, and embraces the whole of human activity.

The discussion of determinism or free will is of course much more elaborated here than in the Æsthetic, where exigencies of space compelled the philosopher to offer it in a condensed form. His solution that the will is and must be free, but that it contains two moments, the first conditioned, and that the problem should be first stated in terms of the Hegelian dialectic, seems to be the only one consonant with facts. The conclusion that the will is autonomous and that therefore we can *never* be obliged to do anything against our will may seem to be paradoxical, until the overwhelming argument in proof of this has been here carefully studied.

Croce's division of the practical activity into the two grades of Economic and Ethic, to which Kant did not attain and Fichte failed fully to perceive, has for the first time rendered comprehensible much that was hitherto obscure in ancient history and contemporary history. The "merely economic man" will be recognised by all students of the *Philosophy of the Practical*, where his characteristics are pointed out by the philosopher; and a few years hence, when Croce's philosophy will have filtered through fiction and journalism to the level of the general public, the phrase will be as common as is the "merely economic" person to-day.

For indeed, all really new and great discoveries come from the philosophers, gradually filtering down through technical treatises and reviews, until they reach the level of prose fiction and of poetry, which, since the *Æsthetic*, we know to be one and the same thing with different empirical manifestations.   In truth, the philosophers alone go deeply enough into the essence of things to reach their roots.   Thus some philosophy, generally in an extremely diluted form, becomes part of every one's mental furniture and thus the world makes progress and the general level of culture is raised.   Thought is democratic in being open to all, aristocratic in being attained only by the few—and that is the only true aristocracy : to be on the same level as the best.

Another discovery of Croce's, set forth in this volume for the first time in all the plenitude of its richness, is the theory of Error.   The proof of the practical nature of error, of its necessity, and of the fact that we only err because we will to do so, is a marvel of acute and profound analysis.   Readers unaccustomed to the dialectic may not at first be prepared to admit the necessary forms of error, that error is not distinct, but opposed to truth and as such its simple dialectic negation, and that truth is thought of truth, which develops by conquering error, which must always exist in every problem.   The full understanding of the Crocean theory of error throws a flood of light on all philosophical problems, and has already formed the basis of at least one brilliant study of contemporary philosophy.

To the reduction of the concept of law to an economic factor, which depends upon the priority and autonomy of Economic in relation to Ethic, is devoted a considerable portion of the latter part of the *Philosophy of the Practical*, and it is easy to see that an elaborate treatment of this problem was necessary, owing to the confusion as to its true nature that has for so long existed in the minds of thinkers, owing to their failure to grasp the above distinction.   In Great Britain indeed, where precedent counts for so much in law, the ethical element is very often so closely attached as to be practically indistinguishable from it, save by the light of the Crocean analysis. In the *Logic as Science of the Pure Concept* will be found much to throw light upon the *Philosophy of the Practical,* where the foreshortening of certain proofs (due to concentration upon other problems) may appear to leave loopholes to objection. Thought will there be found to make use of language for expression, though not itself language ; and it will be found useless to seek logic in words, which in themselves are always æsthetic. For there is a duality between intuition and concept, which form the two grades or degrees of theoretic knowledge, as described also in the *Æsthetic.* There are two types of concept, the *pure* and the *false* or *pseudo-concept,* as Croce calls it. This latter is also divided into two types of representation—those that are concrete without being universal (such as the cat, the rose), and those that are without a content that can be represented, or universal without being concrete, since they never exist in reality (such are the triangle, free motion). The first of these are called empirical pseudo-concepts, the second abstract pseudo-concepts : the first are represented by the natural, the second by the mathematical sciences.

Of the *pure concept* it is predicated that it is

ineliminable, for while the pseudo-concepts in their multiplicity are abolished by thought as it proceeds, there will always remain one thought namely, that which thinks their abolition. This concept is opposed to the pseudo-concepts : it is ultra or omni-representative. I shall content myself with this brief mention of the contents of the *Philosophy of the Practical* and of the *Logic* upon which I am now working.

Since the publication of *Æsthetic as Science of Expression and General Linguistic,* there has been some movement in the direction of the study of Italian thought and culture, which I advocated in the Introduction to that work. But the Alps continue to be a barrier, and the thought of France and of Germany reaches us, as a rule, far more rapidly than that of the home of all the arts and of civilization, as we may call that Italy which contains within it the classical Greater Greece. A striking instance of this relatively more rapid distribution of French thought is afforded by the celebrated *Lundis* of Sainte-Beuve, so familiar to many readers ; yet a critic, greater in depth than Sainte-Beuve, was writing at the same period— greater in philosophical vision of the relations of things, for the vision of Sainte-Beuve rarely rose above the psychological plane. For one reader acquainted with the *History of Italian Literature* of De Sanctis, a hundred are familiar with the *Lundis* of Sainte-Beuve.

At the present moment the hegemony of philosophical thought may be said to be divided between Italy and France, for neither Great Britain nor Germany has produced a philosophical mind of the first order. The interest in Continental idealism is becoming yearly more keen, since the publication of Bergson's and of Blondel's treatises, and of Croce's *Philosophy of the Spirit*. Mr. Arthur Balfour, being himself a philosopher, was one of the first to recognise the importance of the latter work, referring to its author in terms of high praise in his oration on Art delivered at Oxford in the Sheldonian Theatre. Mr. Saintsbury also has expressed his belief that with the *Æsthetic* Croce has provided the first instrument for scientific (*i.e.* philosophical, not "natural" scientific) criticism of literature. This surely is well, and should lead to an era of more careful and less impartial, of more accurate because more scientific criticism of our art and poetry.

I trust that a similar service may be rendered to Ethical theory and practice by the publication of the present translation, which I believe to be rich with great truths of the first importance to humanity, here clearly and explicitly stated for the first time and therefore (in Vico's sense of the word) "created," by his equal and compatriot, Benedetto Croce.

Then leaning upon the arm of time came Truth, whose radiant face,
Though never so late to the feast she go, hath aye the foremost place.

DOUGLAS AINSLIE.

ATHENAEUM CLUB, PALL MALL,
January 1913.

CONTENTS

FIRST PART

THE PRACTICAL ACTIVITY IN GENERAL

FIRST SECTION

THE PRACTICAL ACTIVITY IN ITS RELATIONS

I

II

action and succession or event—Volition and event—Successful
and unsuccessful actions : critique—Acting and foreseeing :
critique—Confirmation of the inderivability of the value of
action from success—Explanation of facts that seem to be at
variance.

VI

Practical taste and judgment — Practical judgment as historical
judgment—Its Logic—Importance of the practical judgment—
Difference between practical judgment and judgment of event
—Progress in action and progress in Reality—Precedence of
the Philosophy of the practical over the practical judgment—
Confirmation of the philosophic incapacity of the psychological
method.

VII

Justification of the psychological method and of empirical and
descriptive disciplines—Practical Description and its literature
—Extension of practical description—Normative knowledge or
rules : their nature—Utility of rules—The literature of rules
and its apparent decadence—Relation between the arts (collections of rules) and philosophic doctrines—Casuistic : its nature
and utility—Jurisprudence as casuistic.

VIII

First form : tendency to generalize—Historical elements that persist
in the generalizations—Second form : literary union of philosophy and empiria—Third form : attempt to put them in close
connection—Science of the practical, and Metaphysic : various
meanings—Injurious consequences of the invasions—1st, Dissolution of empirical concepts — Examples : war and peace,
property and communism, and the like—Other examples—
Misunderstandings on the part of the philosophers—Historical

Good as freedom and reality, and evil as its opposite—Critique
of abstract monism and of dualism of values—Objections to
the irreality of evil—Evil in synthesis and out of synthesis—
Affirmative judgments of evil as negative judgments—Confirmations of the doctrine—The poles of feeling (pleasure and
pain) ; and their identity with the practical opposites—Doctrine
relating to pleasure and happiness : critique—Empirical concepts relating to good and evil—To have to be, ideal, inhibitive,
imperative power—Evil, remorse, etc. ; good, satisfaction, etc.
—Their incapacity for serving as practical principles—Their
character.

III

The multiplicity of volitions and the struggle for unity—Multiplicity
and unity as good and evil—Excluded volitions and passions or
desires—Passions and desires as possible volitions—Volition
as struggle with the passions—Critique of the freedom of
choice—Meaning of the so-called precedence of feeling over
the volitional act—Polipathicism and apathicism—Erroneity of
both the opposed theses—Historical and contingent meaning of
these—The domination of the passions, and the will.

IV

Passions and states of the soul—Passions understood as volitional
habits—Importance and nature of these—Domination of the
passions in so far as they are volitional habits—Difficulty and
reality of dominating them—Volitional habits and individuality
—Negations of individuality for uniformity and criticism of them
—Temperament and character—Indifference of temperament
—Discovery of one's own being—The idea of "vocation"—
Misunderstanding of the right of individuality—Wicked individuality—False doctrines as to the connection between virtues and
vices—The universal in the individual, and education.

V

Multiplicity and unity : development—Becoming as synthesis of
being and not-being—Nature as becoming. Its resolution in
the Spirit—Optimism and pessimism : critique—Dialectic

CONTENTS

THIRD SECTION

UNITY OF THE THEORETICAL AND THE PRACTICAL

CONTENTS

theoretical or of the practical reason—New pragmatism : Life conditioning Philosophy—Deductive confirmation of the two forms, and deductive exclusion of the third (feeling).

SECOND PART

THE PRACTICAL ACTIVITY IN ITS SPECIAL FORMS

FIRST SECTION

THE TWO PRACTICAL FORMS : ECONOMIC AND ETHIC

I

The utilitarian or economic form, and the moral or ethical form— Insufficiency of the descriptive and psychological distinction— Deduction and necessity of integrating it with induction—The two forms as a fact of consciousness—The economic form—The ethical form—Impossibility of eliminating them—Confirmations in fact.

II

Exclusion of materialistic and intellectualistic criticisms—The two possible negations—The thesis of utilitarianism against the existence of moral acts—Difficulty arising from the presence of these—Attempt to explain them as quantitative distinctions —Criticism of it—Attempt to explain them as facts, either extraneous to the practical or irrational, and stupid—Associationism and evolutionism. Critique — Desperate attempt : theological utilitarianism and mystery.

III

The thesis of moral abstractionism against the concept of the useful —The useful as means, or as theoretic fact—Technical and

VI

VII

SECOND SECTION

THE ETHICAL PRINCIPLE

I

CONTENTS

II

THE ETHICAL FORM AS ACTUALIZATION OF THE SPIRIT IN UNIVERSAL

III

HISTORICAL NOTES

THIRD PART

LAWS

I

LAWS AS PRODUCTS OF THE INDIVIDUAL

CONTENTS

Exclusion of the character of constriction : critique of this concept—Identical characters of individual and social laws— Individual laws as the sole real in ultimate analysis—Critique of the division of laws into judicial and social, and into the sub-classes of these. Empiricity of every division of laws—Extension of the concept of laws.

II

The volitional character and the character of class—Distinction of laws from the so-called laws of nature—Implication of the second in the first—Distinction of laws from practical principles —Laws and single acts—Identity of imperative, prohibitive, and permissive laws—Permissive character of every law and im-permissive character of every principle—Changeability of laws —Empirical considerations as to modes of change—Critique of the eternal Code or natural right—Natural right as the new right—Natural right as Philosophy of the practical—Critique of natural right—Theory of natural right persisting in judicial judgments and problems.

III

Law as abstract and unreal volition—Ineffectuality of laws and effectuality of practical principles—Exemplificatory explanation —Doctrines against the utility of laws—Their unmaintain-ability—Unmaintainability of confutations of them—Empirical meaning of these controversies — Necessity of laws — Laws as preparation for action—Analogy between practical and theoretical Spirit : practical laws and empirical concepts—The promotion of order in reality and in representation—Origin of the concept of plan or design.

IV

Transformation of principles into practical laws : legalism—Genesis of the concept of the practically licit and indifferent—Its con-

V

JUDICIAL ACTIVITY AS GENERICALLY PRACTICAL ACTIVITY

VI

HISTORICAL NOTES

TRANSLATOR'S NOTE

THIS translation of Benedetto Croce's *Philosophy of the Practical* (Economic and Ethic) is complete.

FIRST PART

THE PRACTICAL ACTIVITY IN GENERAL

FIRST SECTION

THE PRACTICAL ACTIVITY IN ITS RELATIONS

I

THE PRACTICAL ACTIVITY AS A FORM OF
THE SPIRIT

A GLANCE at the life that surrounds us would *Practical and theoretic life.* seem more than sufficient to establish, without the necessity of special demonstration, the existence of a circle of practical activity side by side with the theoretical. We see in life men of thought and men of action, men of contemplation and of action, materially distinct, as it were, from one another: here, lofty brows and slow dreamy eyes; there, narrow brows, eyes vigilant and mobile; poets and philosophers on the one side; on the other, captains and soldiers of industry, commerce, politics, the army, and the church. Their work seems to differ as do the men. While we are intent upon some

3

discovery just announced, in chemistry or in physic, or upon some philosophy that comes to shake old beliefs, upon a drama or a romance that revives an artist's dream, we are suddenly interrupted and our attention is called to spectacles of an altogether different nature, such as a war between two states, fought with cannon or with custom-house tariffs ; or to a colossal strike, in which thousands upon thousands of workmen make the rest of society feel the power of their numbers and of their strength, and the importance of their work in the general total ; or a potent organization which collects and binds together the forces of conservative resistance, employing interests and passions, hopes and fears, vices and virtues, as the painter his colours, or the poet his words, sometimes making like them a masterpiece, but of a practical nature.   The man of action is from time to time assailed as it were with nausea at his orgies of volitional effort and eyes with envy the artist or the man of science in the same way as polite society used to look upon the monks who had known how to select the best and most tranquil lot in life.   But as a general rule they do not go beyond this fleeting feeling, or if they do resolve to cease their business on the Ides, they return to it on the

Kalends. But the contemplative man in his turn also sometimes experiences this same nausea and this same aspiration ; he seems to himself to be idle where so many are working and bleeding, and he cries to the combatants : " Arms, give me arms,"[1] for he too would be a miner with the miners, would navigate with the navigators, be an emperor among the kings of coal. However, as a general rule, he does not make more out of this than a song or a book. Nobody, whatever his efforts, can issue from his own circle. It would seem that nature supplies men made precisely for the one or for the other form of activity, in the same way as she makes males and females for the preservation of the species.

But this mode of existence with which the *Insufficiency of descriptive distinctions.* practical activity manifests itself in life, as though physically limited, has no certainty, when separated from the theoretical life, nor is it, as might be believed, a fact that imposes itself. Facts never impose themselves, save metaphorically: it is only our thought which *imposes* them upon *itself*, when it has criticized them and has recognized their reality. That existence and that distinction, which seem so obvious that

---

[1] Allusion to a verse of Leopardi in *Canzone all' Italia.*

one can touch them with one's hand, are at
bottom nothing but the result of primary and
superficial philosophic reflection, which posits as
essentially distinct that which is so only at a
first glance and in the mass.   Indeed, if we
continue to meditate with the same method and
assumptions as in the first instance, we shall find
that those very distinctions, which reflection had
established, are by reflection annulled.   It is not
true that men are practical or theoretical.

The theoretical man is also practical; he
lives, he wills, he acts like all the others.   The
so-called practical man is also theoretical; he
contemplates, believes, thinks, reads, writes,
loves music and the other arts.   Those works
that had been looked upon as inspired entirely by
the practical spirit, when examined more closely,
are found to be exceedingly complex and rich
in theoretic elements—meditations, reasonings,
historical research, ideal contemplations.   Those
works on the other hand that had been assumed
to be manifestations of the purely artistic or
philosophic spirit, are also products of the will,
for without the will nothing can be done; the
artist cannot prepare himself for his masterpiece
for years and years, nor the thinker bring to
completion his system.   Was not the battle of

Austerlitz also a work of thought and the
Divine Comedy also a work of will? From
such reflections as these, which might be easily
multiplied, arises a mistrust, not only of the
statement first made, but also of the inquiry
that has been undertaken. It is as though one
had filled a vessel with much difficulty and were
then obliged to empty it anew with a like effort,
to find oneself again facing the vessel, empty
as before. Or one adheres to the conclusion
that neither the theoretic nor the practical exists
as distinct, but that they are one single fact,
which is one or other of the two, or a third to
be determined, manifesting itself concretely in
infinite shades and gradations, which we arbitrarily
attempt to reduce to one or more classes,
separating and denominating them as distinct
in a not less arbitrary manner.

By describing this process of ordinary reflec- *Insufficiency of*
the psycho-
tion, in relation to reality and by demonstrating *logical method*
in philosophy.
its philosophic impotence, has at the same time
been demonstrated the nature and the *impotence*
of the *psychological method*, applied to philosophical
problems. For psychological philosophy, though
contained in ponderous treatises and in solemn
academical lectures, does not really achieve more
than ordinary reflection, or rather, is nothing

but ordinary reflection. Having classified the images of the infinite manifestations of human activity, placing, for instance, will and action side by side with thought and imagination, it looks upon this classification as reality. But classes are classes and not philosophical distinctions: whoever takes them too seriously, and understands them in this second sense, finds himself eventually obliged to admit that they possess no reality. Thereupon he declares with shouts and protestations the non-existence of the *faculties of the soul*, or rather their existence as a mere mental artifice, without relation to reality. He may do more than this and throw overboard the criterion or distinction itself, together with those false distinctions, proclaiming that all spiritual manifestations are reducible to a single element. This element turns out in the end to be precisely one of the rejected classes; hence the attempt to show that facts of volition are nothing but facts of *representation*, or that those of representation are nothing but facts of *volition*, or that both are nothing but facts of *feeling*, and so on.

Necessity of the philosophical method.   We must then remain perfectly indifferent to the affirmations or negations of this psychological philosophy. If it affirm the existence

of the practical activity, we must not put faith
in it until we have recognized its existence by
the philosophical method, and equally so in case
it should deny it. The philosophical method
demands complete abstraction from empirical data
and from their classes, and a withdrawal into the
recesses of the consciousness, in order to fix
upon it alone the eye of the mind. It has
been affirmed that by this method the individual
consciousness is made the type and measure of
universal reality, and it has been suggested, with
a view to obviate this restriction and danger,
that we should extend observations, so as to
include the soul of other individuals, of the
present and of the past, of our own and of other
civilizations, thus completing (in the accustomed
phrase) the psychological with the historical and
the ethnographical methods. But there is no
need to fear, because the consciousness which is
the object of the philosophical inquiry is not that
of the individual as individual, but the universal
consciousness, which is in every individual the
basis of his individual consciousness and of
that of other individuals. The philosopher who
withdraws into himself is not seeking his own
empirical self: Plato did not seek the son of
Aristo and of Perictione, nor Baruch Spinoza

the poor sickly Jew; they sought that Plato and that Spinoza, who are not Plato or Spinoza, but man, the spirit, universal being. The remedy proposed will therefore seem not only useless, but actually harmful; for in an inquiry whose very object is to surpass the empirical itself, is offered the aid of a multiplicity of selves, thus increasing the tumult and the confusion, where there should be peace and silence; offering, in exchange for the universal that was sought, something worse than the individual, namely, the *general*, which is an arbitrary complex of mutilated individualities.

Constatation and deduction. It may seem, however, that the result of such an inquiry as to the form and the universality of consciousness would merely possess the value of a statement of fact, not different from any other statement, as when we say, for instance, that the weather is rainy, or that Tizio has married. If these two last facts be indubitable, because well observed, in like manner indubitable, because likewise well observed, will be an affirmation concerning the universal consciousness. And since both affirmations are true, there is certainly no difference between them, or between truth and truth, considered as such. But since single and contingent facts, like the two adduced in the example, are single and contingent, precisely because they have not their own reason in themselves, and because the universal is the universal, precisely because it is a sufficient reason to itself, it clearly results that we cannot assume that truth has been definitely established from the universal standpoint of consciousness, save when the reason for this also has been seen, that is to say until that aspect has been simply enunciated and asserted, as in the case of a single fact.　To affirm the existence of the practical form of activity, side by side with the theoretical, means to deduce the one from the other, and both from the unity of the spirit and of the real.　We do not intend to withdraw ourselves from this duty and exigency; and if we limit ourselves here at the beginning to the assertion of its existence and to the demonstration that the arguments brought against it are unfounded, we do so for didascalic reasons, certain that in due course we shall be able to free this assertion from what it may contain of provisional, that is to say, from the character itself of assertion.

The doctrines which deny the practical form of the spirit are and cannot but be of two fundamental kinds, according to the double

Theories which deny the practical form of the spirit.

possibility offered by the proposition itself which they propose to refute. The first doctrine affirms that *the practical form is not spiritual activity*; the second that although it be spiritual activity, *yet it is not in any way distinguishable from the already recognized theoretic form of the spirit.* The second, so to speak, denies to it specific, the first generic character.

The practical as a fact of unconsciousness. Those who maintain the first of these theses say :—We are unconscious of the will at the moment of willing and during its real development. This consciousness is only attained after one has willed, that is to say, after the volitional act has been developed. Even then, we are not conscious of the will itself, but of our representation of the will. Therefore the will, that is to say the practical activity, is not an activity of the spirit. Since it is unconscious, it is nature and not spirit. The theoretic activity which follows it is alone spiritual.

Critique. Were we, however, to allow this argument to pass, the result would be that none of the activities of the spirit would belong to the spirit, that they would all be unconscious and all, therefore, nature. Indeed, the activity of the artist, at the moment when he is really so, that is to say in what is called the moment of artistic

creation, is not conscious of itself: it becomes
conscious only afterwards, either in the mind
of the critic or of the artist who becomes critic
of himself. And it has also often been said of
the activity of the artist, that it is unconscious;
that it is a natural force, or madness, fury, divine
inspiration. *Est Deus in nobis*; and we only
become conscious of the divinity that burns and
agitates us when the agitation is ceasing and
cooling begun. But what of the activity of the
philosopher? It may seem strange, but it is
precisely the same with the philosopher. At the
moment in which he is philosophizing, he is
unconscious of his work; in him is God, or
nature; he does not reflect upon his thought,
but thinks; or rather the thing thinks itself in
him, as a microbe living in us nourishes itself,
reproduces itself and dies: so that sometimes
the philosopher has also seemed to be seized
with madness. The consciousness of his philosophy is not in him at that moment; but it is in
the critic and in the historian, or indeed in himself a moment after, in so far as he is critic and
historian of himself. And will the critic or the
historian at least be conscious? No, he will not
be so either, because he who will afterwards
criticize the historico-critical work is conscious

of it, or he himself, in so far as he criticizes himself, and by objectifying himself occupies a place in the history of criticism and of historiography. In short, we should never be conscious in any form of the spiritual activity.

But this negation is founded on a false idea of consciousness: spontaneous is confused with reflex consciousness, or that which is intrinsic to one activity with that which is intrinsic to another, which surpasses the first and makes of it its object. In such a sense we can certainly not be conscious of the will, save in the representation which follows it, as we are not conscious of a poem, save at the moment of criticizing it. But there is also consciousness in the act itself of him who reads or composes a poem, and he "is conscious" (there is no other expression) of its beauty and of its ugliness, of how the poem should and of how it should not be. This consciousness is not critical, but is not therefore less real and efficacious, and without it internal control would be wanting to the formative act of the poet. Thus also there is consciousness in the volitional and practical act as such: we are not aware of this act in a reflex manner, but we feel, or, if you will, we possess it. Without it there would be no result. It is

therefore developed in moments or alternatives
of happiness and of unhappiness, of well-being
and of malaise, of satisfaction and of remorse,
of pleasure and of pain.   If this be unconsciousness, we must say that unconsciousness is
consciousness itself.

The practical activity may appear to be nature *Nature and*
in respect of the theoretical, but not as some- *activity.*
thing without the spirit and opposed to it, but as
a form of the spirit opposed to another form.
Æsthetic contemplation has in like manner, as
has already been mentioned, appeared to be a
natural force creating the world of intuition,
which the philosophical activity of man afterwards
understands and recreates logically.   Hence art
can be called nature (and has indeed been so
called), and conversely philosophy has been
called spirituality.   This gives rise to the
further problem : whether it be correct to consider nature (it is convenient so to call it) that
which has afterwards been recognized in substance as spiritual activity ; or whether the
concept and the name of ~~spirit~~ should not be
reserved for that which is truly altogether outside
the spirit, and whether this something placed
altogether outside the spirit truly exists.   This
point does not concern us here, although we

are much disposed to admit that one of the mainstays of that absurd conception of nature as of the extra-spiritual is precisely the practical or volitional form of the spirit, so conspicuously different from the theoretical form and from the subforms of the same. We do not therefore hold those philosophers to have been so completely in the wrong, who have identified nature and will, for they have thus at any rate discovered one aspect of the truth.

Reduction of the practical form to the theoretical.

Passing to the second thesis, which does not place the will outside the spirit, but denies to it the distinction between practical and the theoretical forms and affirms that the will is thought, there is nothing to be objected to it, provided that, as is often the case, " thought " be taken as synonymous with " spirit." In this case, as in that where it is affirmed that art is thought, we need only inquire, what form of thought is the will, as in the other what form of thought is art. It is not, for instance, logical or historical thought, and the will is neither imaginative, logical nor historical thought: if anything, it must be *volitional thought.*

But we have the genuine form of this thesis in the affirmation that the will is the intelligence itself, that to will is to know, and that action practically well conducted is truth. This thesis would not have arisen, had it not found support in the real situation of things (and what this support is will be seen when studying the relation of the practical with the theoretic activity, and the complicated process of deliberation). But, when tested here independently, it proves to be unsustainable.

We must not oppose to it the usual observa- *Critique.* tions as to the lack of connection between great intellectual and great volitional development, or the cases of those theoreticians who are practically quite ineffectual, of philosophers who are bad governors of States, of the "very learned" who are not "men" and the like; for the reason already given, that an observation is not a philosophical argument, but a fact which itself has need of an explanation, and when this has been done, it may serve as proof of the philosophical theory, but can never be substituted for it. But it is well to recall to memory the quite peculiar character of the will and the practical activity in respect of knowledge. Intellectual light is cold, the will is hot. When we pass from theoretic contemplation to action and to the practical, we have almost the feeling of generating, and sons are not made with thoughts and words. With

c

the greatest intellectual clearness, we yet remain inert, if something does not intervene that rouses to action, something analogous to the inspiration that makes run a shiver of joy and of voluptuousness through the veins of the artist. If the will be not engaged, every argument, however plausible it may seem, every situation, however clear, remains mere theory.

The education of the will is not effected with theories or definitions, æsthetic or historical culture, but with the exercise of the will itself. We teach how to will as we teach how to think, by fortifying and intensifying natural dispositions, by example, which suggests imitation, by difficulties to be solved (practical problems), by rousing energetic initiative and by disciplining it to persist. When an act of will has taken place, no argument will extinguish it. As an illness is not to be cured with reasons, so an affective and volitional state cannot be altered by these means. Reasoning and knowledge may and certainly do assist, but they do not constitute the ultimate and determining moment. The will alone acts upon the will, not in the sense that the will of one individual can act upon that of another (which is merely a fact among the facts perceived by him), but in the sense that the will of the individual himself, causing the previous volition to enter upon a crisis, dissolves it and substitutes for it a new practical synthesis, with a new volition.

The evident paradox of the thesis which *The practical as thought* identifies without any distinction thought and *which realises itself. Recog-* will, theory and practice, has caused it to be *nition of its autonomy.* modified and to be produced in another form, expressed in the definition; that the will is thought in so far as it *is translated into act*, thought in so far as it is *imprinted* upon nature, thought when *held* so *firmly* before the mind as to *become action*, and so on. Now it remains to determine what may be the relation between thought and will, and when this has been done, we shall see what is exact and what inexact in the above formulæ, of translating, imprinting, and holding fast. These formulæ are all logically vague, however imaginative they may be. But what is important to note here is that with the new turn given to the thesis that denies the peculiarity of the practical activity, this same peculiarity is unconsciously affirmed, because that transforming, that imprinting, that holding fast, which did not exist in the simple theory, conceal precisely the will. Thus the ultimate form of the negation comes to join hands with that of the affirmation, and we can consider undisputed the existence of a particular form of the spirit, which is the practical activity. We must now examine the relation of this form with the other from which it has been distinguished.

II

NEGATION OF THE SPIRITUAL FORM OF FEELING

In affirming the existence of the practical form *The practical activity and* of activity, we have had in view only the theoretical *the so-called third spiritual* form and have demonstrated that the one cannot *form: feeling.* be absorbed and confused in the other, and we have referred only to the theoretic form, when announcing our intention of determining the relations of the practical with the other forms of the spirit. This seems but little correct, and in any case not exhaustive, because there are or may be other non-theoretical forms of the spirit, into which the practical form could be resolved. Of these it would be necessary to take account. And not to beat too long about the bush, that of which in this case it is question, is the form of *feeling*, the last or intermediary of the three forms into which it is customary to divide the spiritual activity : representation, feeling, tendency ; thought, feeling, will. Attempts have not been wanting to reduce tendency or will to feeling, or, as is said, to a sentimental reaction from perceptions and thoughts. In fact there is hardly a treatise of philosophy of the practical without a preliminary study of the relations between the will and feeling. We cannot, then, escape from the dilemma; either we must recognize the omission into which we have fallen and hasten to correct it, or else make explicit the supposition that may be contained in that omission (which would thus be intentional and conscious), that *a third general form of the spirit, or a form of feeling, does not exist.* We have adopted precisely this last position, and it therefore becomes incumbent upon us briefly to expose the reasons for which we hold that the concept of feeling must disappear from the system of the spiritual forms or activities.

Various meanings of the word feeling, as a psychological class.   Feeling may and has been understood in various ways, some of which do not at all concern our thesis. In the first place, the word " feeling " has been used to designate a class of psychical facts constructed according to the psychological and naturalistic method. Thus it has happened that, with various times and authors, all the most rudimentary, tenuous, and evanescent manifestations of the spirit have been called " feelings," slight intuitions (or sensations as they are called), not yet transformed into perceptions, slight perceptions, slight tendencies and appetites, in fact all that forms, as it were, the base of the life of the spirit. The name has thus, on the other hand, also been given to psychical processes and conditions, in which various forms follow one another or alternate in relation to a material empirically limited. Such are what are called feelings of " fatherland," " love," " nature," "the divine." Nothing forbids the formation of such classes and the use of that denomination, but as has already been declared in relation to the psychological method, they are of no use to philosophy, which not only does not receive them within its limits, but does not occupy itself with them at all, save to reject them when they present themselves, as philosophical psychology or psychological philosophy. To classify is not to think philosophically, and philosophy on the one hand does not recognize criteria of small and great, of weak and strong, of more and of less, and a small or smallest thought, a small or smallest tendency, is for it thought and tendency and not feeling at all; on the other, it does not admit complicated processes without resolving these into their simple components. Thus the feeling of love or of patriotism, and the others

made use of in the example, are revealed to
philosophy as series of acts of thought and of
will, variously interlaced.   Let the psychologists,
then, keep their classes and sub-classes of feeling.
We, for our part, not only do not dream of dis-
possessing them of such a treasure, but shall
continue to draw from it, when necessary, the
small change of ordinary conversation.

Feeling as a state of the spirit.   There also exists another meaning of the
word "feeling," of which, at present at any rate,
we do not take account.   This appears when the
word is used to designate *the state* of the spirit or
of one of the special forms of the spirit ; we should
indeed term these more correctly the *states*, since
the spirit in this case, as is known, is polarized
in two opposite terms, usually denominated
pleasure and pain.   Indubitably these two terms
can also be taken as psychological (and are thus
included in the preceding case).   Hence it results
that pleasure and pain are represented by psychologists as the two extremes of a continuous series,
in which there is a passage from the one to the
other term by insensible increases and gradations.
But we must also recognize that this psychological representation is not the only one possible,
and indeed is not truly the real one, and that the
two terms have their place and their proper

meaning in the philosophy of the spirit. They are, as has been said, *opposites*; and are differentiated, not only by a more and a less, by a greatest and a least, but also by the special character of distinction that opposites possess. The doctrine of opposites and of opposites in the practical activity of the spirit does not, however, appertain to this part of our exposition. In denying feeling, we do not here deny the doctrine of opposites, and that psychology of the *states* of the spirit which is founded upon it, but the doctrine of feeling considered as a particular *form* of *activity*.

The conception of feeling as a spiritual activity has answered to a want of research, which may be described as *provisional excogitation*. Whenever thought has found itself face to face with a form or subform of spiritual activity, which it was not possible either to eliminate or to absorb in forms already recognized, the problem to be solved has been endorsed with that word "feeling." With many this has passed for a solution. Feeling, in fact, has been the indeterminate in the history of philosophy, or rather the not yet fully determined, the *half-determined*.

Function of the concept of feeling in the History of philosophy: the indeterminate.

Hence its great importance as an expedient for the indication of new territories to conquer, and as a stimulus against remaining obstinately shut up in old and insufficient formulæ. But hence also its fate : the problem must not be exchanged for its solution, the indeterminate or semi-determinate must be determined. Whenever the determination of the forms and subforms of the spirit has not been given in a complete manner, the category of feeling will reappear (and it will be beneficial) ; but at the same time will reappear the duty of exploring it and of understanding what is concealed beneath it, or at least what unsolved difficulty has caused it to reappear afresh.

Now we have already met with the concept of feeling on more than one occasion, when investigating the philosophy of the theoretic spirit, as something supplying a theoretical need outside the theoretic forms generally admitted, or as a special form of theoretic activity. Every time that we have done this, an attentive examination has caused it to disappear before our eyes, and has generally helped us, either to discover something previously unknown, or to confirm the necessity of contested categories.

Feeling as herald of the æsthetic form ; Thus it happened that when a special *æsthetic* function was not recognized and it was attempted to explain it, either intellectualistically, as nothing but an inferior form of philosophy, or historically, as a reproduction of the historical and natural datum, or almost as the satisfaction of certain volitional wants (hedonistic theory), the view of art as neither a form of the intellect nor of perception nor of will, but of *feeling*, was an advance, as also was the appeal to men of *feeling* to recognize and to judge it. As a result of this insistence, it was eventually discovered that art possessed an absolutely simple and ingenuous theoretic form, without either intellectual or historical contents, the form of the pure intuition which is that of the æsthetic and artistic activity. Whoever returns to treat of art as a product of feeling, after this discovery of the pure intuition, falls back from the determinate to the semi-determinate, and is at the mercy of all the dangers which arise from it.

The theory of historiography owes its progress in like manner to the demonstration that it is impossible to deduce the historical statement from concepts, but that we must deduce it in final analysis from an immediate *feeling* of the real, that is to say, from the *intuitive* element, which inevitably exists in every historical recon-struction, as in every perception. On the other hand, and in altogether another sense, reacting

As herald of the intuitive element in Historio-graphy.

against the false idea of an extra - subjective historical objectivity, to be found in the mere reproduction of the datum, it was made evident that no historical narration is possible without the *reaction of feeling* in respect to the datum. Thus was discovered the indispensability of the *intellective* element in the historical affirmation. Whoever has recourse to feeling as a factor in historiography, after this complete constitution of the historical judgment, returns from the clear to the confused, from light, if not to darkness, then to twilight.

Feeling as herald of the pure concept in philosophical Logic.

The concept of feeling has also been of capital importance in the progress of the Logic of philosophy. For how could we begin to explain that philosophy is constructed with a method altogether different from that of the exact disciplines (natural sciences and mathematics), without denying to those sciences the capacity of conquering the supreme truth, the true truth, full reality, and recognizing such capacity on the other hand to a special function called *feeling* or *immediate* knowledge? That function was void, that is to say, undetermined, because defined in a negative and not in a positive manner : feeling was something different from the abstract and arbitrary procedure of the exact sciences, from the abstract intellect, but its true nature was unknown. When this was at last known it was discovered that it was not a question of " feeling " or of " immediate knowledge," but of the intellect itself, in its genuine and uncontaminated nature, its pure and free activity, of intellect as *reason*, of thought as *speculative* thought, of that " immediate knowledge," which is true, intrinsic, perpetual *mediation*. Whoever henceforth returns to feeling, after the discovery of the pure or speculative concept, and believes it to be the creator of philosophy and of religion, fighting with it against the natural and mathematical sciences, behaves as he who should wish to return to-day to the flint-lock, for the excellent reason that it was an advance upon the bow and the catapult. Thus those who invoke feeling in philosophy are henceforth a little ridiculous. This does not imply that they were not at one time to be taken seriously, for this concept has been of great provisional assistance and has been as it were the compass of the new idea of philosophy.

The same will be the case in the investigation *Analogous function in* that we have begun of the practical form of the *the Philosophy of the practical.* spirit and of the problems to which it gives rise. This concept of feeling has been mingled with them all, and propositions have been formed, of which we shall indicate the true significance in the proper places. Beginning at once and limiting ourselves solely to the question of the existence of a peculiar practical form, it is easy to understand why it has so often been maintained against the intellectual and theoretical exclusivists, that the will consists, not of knowledge, but of feeling; that the principle of action, far from being an intellectual principle, is sentimental emotion; that in order to produce a volition, reason, ideas, and facts perceived do not suffice, but that it is necessary that all these things be transformed into feelings, which must take possession of the soul; that the base of life lived, that is, of practical life, is not thought, but feeling, and so on. With these formulæ was recognized the peculiarity of the practical activity. The theory of feeling in respect of the practical represents progress as compared with the intellectualistic theory, because the appearance of indeterminateness is progress as compared with bad determinateness, and contains in itself the new and more complete determinateness.

Negation of feeling.

But in this very way of ours of understanding the value of these formulæ, is implied their resolute negation, when they tend to persist, after having accomplished their function, and to maintain side by side with the theory of the practical a third general form of the spirit, namely feeling. No spiritual fact or manifestation of activity can be adduced, which, examined without superficiality, is not reducible to an act of fancy, intellect and perception, that is, of theory (when it is not at once revealed as an abstraction or as a merely psychological class of these acts); or to an act of utilitarian or ethical volition (when it is not here too a psychological class, variously designated as aspirations, passions, affections, and the like). Let him who will search his spirit and attempt to indicate one single act, differing from the above, as something new and original and deserving of the special denomination of feeling.

This "constatation" of fact (we repeat the *Its deductive exclusion.* warning) is but the first step in the complete philosophical demonstration, which demands that we show not only that a third form does not exist, but that *it cannot exist*. This demonstration will be given further on, and will coincide with that of the demonstration of the necessity of the two forms, theoretical and practical; a duality that is unity and a unity that is duality.

Recognizing the legitimacy of the demand for a philosophical deduction of the forms of the spirit, and therefore of a deductive exclusion of those that are spurious and wrongly adopted, it seems that if it be somewhat delayed, such a mode of exclusion will also yield clearer results.

III

RELATION OF THE PRACTICAL TO THE
THEORETIC ACTIVITY

FREED from the equivocal third term, which is *Precedence of the theoretical activity.* feeling, and now passing to the problem of the relation between the theoretical and the practical activity enunciated, we must in the first place declare the thesis that *the practical activity presupposes the theoretical.* Will is impossible without knowledge; as is knowledge, so is will.

In recognizing this precedence of knowledge *The unity of the spirit and the co-presence of the practical.* to will, we do not wish to posit as thinkable a theoretical man or a theoretical moment altogether deprived of will. This would be an unreal abstraction, inadmissible in philosophy, which operates solely with real abstractions, that is, with universal concretes. The forms of the spirit are distinct and not separate, and when the spirit is found in one of its forms, or is *explicit* in it, the other forms are also in it,

but *implicit*, or, as is also said, *concomitant*. If
theoretical and "cognoscitive" man were not at
the same time volitional, he would not even be
able to stand on his feet and look at the sky,
and, literally speaking, if he were not alive, he
would not be able to think (and thinking is
both an act of life and an act of will, which
is called *attention*). Were he not to will, he
would be unable to pass from waking to sleep,
and from sleep to waking. Thus in order to be
purely theoretical, it is necessary to be at the
same time in some degree practical; the energy
of pure fancy and of pure thought springs from
the trunk of volition. Hence the importance
of the will for the æsthetic and intellectual life;
the will is not theory, nor is it the force that
makes grain to grow or guides the course of
rivers, but as it assists the culture of grain or
restrains the destructive impetus of rivers, so it
assists and restrains the force of fancy and of
thought, causing them to act in the best way,
that is, to be as they really ought to be, namely,
fancy and thought in their purest manifestation.
The practical activity, therefore, acts in this way,
and as it drags the man of science from his study
and the artist from his studio, if it be necessary
to defend his country or to watch at the bedside

of his sick father, so it commands the artist and
the man of science to fulfil their special mission
and to be themselves in an eminent degree.

All the arguments that have been used in the *Critique of*
pragmatism.
past and that are used in the present, to maintain
the dependence of the theoretical upon the
practical activity, are of value for what of truth
they contain, that is, only to demonstrate this
unity of the spiritual functions that we have
recognized, and the indispensability of the volitional force for the health of the cognoscitive
spirit. But the passage from this thesis to the
other, that the true is the production of the will,
is nothing but a sophism, founded on the double
signification of the word " production." It should
be clear that to *assist* the work of thought with
the will is one thing and that to *substitute* the
will for the work of thought is another. To
claim to substitute the will for the work of
thought, is equivalent to the negation of that
force that should be assisted ; it is the most
open proclamation of scepticism, the most complete distrust of the true and of the possibility
of attaining to it. This attempt is now called
pragmatism, or is at any rate one of the meanings
of the word, with which the school of the
greatest confusion that has ever appeared in

philosophy adorns itself in our day. This school
mixes together the most divergent theses—that
of the stimulating effect that the will has upon
thought, that other of the volitional or arbitrary
moment, by means of which perceptions and
historical data are reduced to abstract types in
the natural disciplines, or postulates laid down for
the construction of mathematical classes. The
third form, which might be called the Baconian
prejudice, maintains the exclusive utility of the
natural sciences and mathematics for the well-
being of life. The fourth thesis is positivistic :
here it is maintained that we cannot know anything save what we ourselves arbitrarily com-
press into the formula and classes of mathematics
and of naturalism. The fifth thesis is a romantic
exaggeration of the principle of creative power
in man, substituting the caprice of the individual
for the universal spirit. The sixth, something
between silliness and Jesuistry, recommends the
utility of making one's illusions and believing
them to be true. The seventh is superstitious,
occultist and spiritistic—and there are others that
we omit. If pragmatism has had and preserves
any attraction, it owes this to the truth of its first
and second theses and to the half truth of the
fifth. All the three are however heterogeneous

in themselves and unreconcilable with the others, which are most fallacious. But we repeat with the old philosophers that whoever in thinking says, "Thus I will it," is lost for truth.

Certain reservations that are made to the *Critique of psychological objections.* above truth from the point of view of that philo- sophy, which we have called psychological, are scarcely deserving of brief mention. We find in treatises of Psychology that knowledge does pre- cede the practical act, but only in the higher forms of volition, whereas in its lower forms are found only impulses, tendencies, appetites, al- together blind of any knowledge. Thus they are able to talk of involuntary forms of the practical activity, of a will that is not a will, when once the true will has been defined, as precisely appetition illumined by previous know- ledge. The *blind will* of certain metaphysicians is derived from such excogitations of psycho- logists, who make of it a practical act without intelligence. They have here attributed the value of reality to a crude concept of class, a thing that happens not infrequently. A blind will is however unthinkable. Every form of the practical activity, be it as poor and rudimentary as you like (and let as many classes and gradations as you will be formed), presupposes knowledge

of some sort. In animals too? will be asked.
In animals too, provided they be, and in so far
as they are centres of life, and so of perceptions
and of will. This is also true of vegetables and
of minerals, always with the above hypothesis.
We must banish every form of *aristocracy* from
the Philosophy of the practical, as we have
banished it from Æsthetic, from Logic, from
Historic, esteeming it most harmful to the
proper understanding of those activities. The
aristocratic illusion is closely allied to that one
which makes us believe that we, shut up in the
egotism of our empirical individuality, are alone
aware of the truth, that we alone feel the beautiful,
that we alone know how to love, and so on. But
reality is democratic.

From the psychological point of view yet
another objection has been raised. Knowledge
(it is affirmed) cannot be the indispensable base of
the will, if, as is the case, the ignorant are often
far more effective than many learned men and
philosophers. These latter, they say, although
possessing very great knowledge, and no less a
stock of good intentions, yet do not know how to
direct their lives successfully. But it is evident
that in these cases the so-called ignorant possess
just that knowledge which is necessary for the

purpose and is lacking to the learned and to the philosopher, who would themselves be the ignorant in such a case. Nicholas Macchiavelli was ignorant as compared with Giovanni dalle Bande Nere, when he kept the spectators waiting two hours in the sun, while he was attempting to dispose three thousand infantry according to the directions that he had written. This he would never have succeeded in doing, had not Signor Giovanni, with the help of drummers and in the twinkling of an eye caused them to execute the various manœuvres and afterwards carried Master Nicholas to dine, who, save for him, would not have dined at all that day.[1]

The knowledge required for the practical act is not that of the artist, nor of the philosopher, or rather, it is these two also, but only in so far as both are to be found as elements co-operating in that ultimate and complete knowledge which is *historical.* If the first be called intuition, the second concept, and the third perception, and the third be looked upon as the result of the two preceding, it will be said that the knowledge required for the practical act is *perceptive.* Hence the common saying that praises the sure eye of the practical man ; hence, too, the close bond

Nature of the theoretical precedence of the practical : historical knowledge.

[1] Bandello, *Novelle,* i. 40, intro.

between historical sense and practical and political sense ; hence, too, the justifiable diffidence of those who, unable to grasp effectual reality, hope to attain to it by force of mere syllogisms and abstractions, or believe that they have attained to it, when they have erected an imaginary edifice. They prove by so doing that they can never be practical men, at least in the sphere of action at which they are then aiming.

Such knowledge is not of itself the practical act. The historian as such is a contemplative, not a practical man or politician. If that spark which is volition, do not spring forth, the material of knowledge does not catch fire and is not transformed into the material of the practical. But that knowledge is the condition, and if the condition be not the conditioned, yet one cannot have the conditioned without the condition. In this last signification, it is true that action is knowledge, will, and wisdom, that is to say, in the sense that willing and acting presuppose knowledge and wisdom. In this sense, and considered solely in the stage of the cognos-citive investigation which will form the base of action, the deliberation is a theoretical fact. The customary expressions of logical, rational, judicious actions, are metaphors, because action

may be weak or energetic, coherent or incoherent; but it will not have those predicates
which are proper to theoretical acts that precede
actions, on which the metaphors aforesaid are
founded. As are these acts, so originate the
practical act, will, and action. We can act in so
far as we have knowledge. Volition is not the
surrounding world which the spirit perceives; it
is a beginning, a new fact. But this fact has its
roots in the surrounding world, this beginning is
irradiated with the colours of things that man
has perceived as a theoretical spirit, before he
took action as a practical spirit.

It is important to observe, as much to pre- *Its continual*
vent an equivoke into which many fall, as *changeability.*
because of the consequences that will follow from
holding it, that we must not look upon the
perceptive knowledge of reality that surrounds
us as a firm basis, upon which we act, by translating the formed volition into act. For were
this so, we should have to assume that the
surrounding world, perceived by the spirit, stops
after the perceptive act, which is not the case.
That world changes every second, the perceptive
act perceives the new and the different, and the
volitional act changes according to that real
and perceived change. Perception and volition

alternate every instant; in order to will, we must touch the earth at every instant, in order to resume force and direction.

No other theoretic precedent.   Continuous perception and continuous change, that is the necessary theoretic condition of volition. It is necessary and unique. No other theoretical element is needed, because every other is contained in it, and beyond it no other is thinkable.

Critique of concepts and practical judgments.   But if this be true and no other theoretic element save that precede the volition, then we find in the aforesaid theory the criticism of a series of other theories, generally admitted in the Philosophy of the practical, not less than in ordinary thought, none of which can be retained without alterations and corrections.

Or better, there are not so many various theories to criticize ; there is rather one theory, which presents itself under different aspects and assumes various names. This theory consists substantially in affirming that with the complex of cognitions, of which we have hitherto treated (all of which are summed up in the historical judgment), we do not yet possess that one which is necessary, before we can proceed to volition and action. A special form of concepts and judgments which can be called *practical*, must, it is said,

appear; these render the will possible, by interposing themselves between the previous merely
historical judgment and the will. Is it not
indubitable that we possess practical concepts, that
is, concepts of classes of action or of supreme
guides to action, concepts of things *good, of ideals,
of ends*, and that we effect *judgments* of value by
the application of those concepts to the image of
given actions? Is it not indubitable that those
judgments and those concepts refer, not to the
simple present fact, but to the future? How
could we will, if we did not know what is good
to will, and that a given possible action corresponds to that concept of good?

Now it is undeniable that we in fact possess *Posteriority of*
the above-mentioned concepts and judgments. *judgments to the practical*
But what we must absolutely deny is that they *act.*
differ in any respect from other concepts and theoretical judgments, and that they deserve to be
distinguished from these as practical and that
they have the future for their object. The future,
that which is not, is not an object of knowledge;
the material of the judgment, whether it concern actions or thoughts, does not alter its
logical and theoretical character; the concepts
of modes of action are concepts neither more nor
less than those of modes of thought. With this

negation we at the same time deny the possibility
of their interposing themselves between knowledge and will. Those judgments, far from being
anterior to the will, are posterior to it.

Let us state a simple case and observe the
course of analysis on the lines of the theory here
criticized. It is winter-time; I am cold; there
is a wood close by, and I know that by cutting
wood one can light a fire and that fire gives heat :
I therefore resolve to cut wood. According to
that theory, the spiritual process would be expressed in the following chain of propositions :
I know the actual situation, that is to say, that I
am cold, that wood gives fire and fire heat, and
that there exists wood that can be cut ; I possess
the concept that it is a good thing to provide for
the health of the body ; I judge that with heat I
shall procure health during the winter, and that
in consequence heat is a good thing and the
cutting of wood, without which I cannot procure heat, is also good. Having made all these
constatations, I set in motion the spring of my
will, and I *will* to cut the wood.—The process
as above described seems real and controllable by
every one ; but it is, on the contrary, illusory. The
practical judgment : " I shall act well in cutting
the wood " really means, " I will to cut the

wood ; " " this is a good thing " really means, " I
will this."   I may change my will a moment after,
substituting for this volition one that is different or
contrary, that does not matter.   At the moment
that I formed that judgment, I must have seen
myself in the volitional attitude of a man cutting
wood; the will must have come first.   Otherwise
the judgment would never have existed.   Given
the first actual situation and its complete expression in the judgment, no other judgment can arise,
if the actual situation do not change and nothing
new supervene.   This new thing is always my
will, which, when the situation changes (as in the
example, if I walk from the house to the tree,
or if I simply move my body in an imperceptible
manner in the direction of the action willed),
by adding to the actual reality something that
was not there before, provides material for a new
judgment.   This judgment is called practical,
but it is theoretical, like the others that precede
it ; a judgment believed to precede the volition,
whereas in reality it follows it ; a judgment
believed to condition a future act of will, whereas
it is in reality the past act of will looking at itself
in the glass; a judgment that is not really
practical but *historical.*

The illusion that things happen differently is

caused by the fact that we possess judgments
concerning our past volitions, which are afterwards collected into abstract formulæ, such as
that "it is well to cut wood." But, on the one
hand, those formulæ and judgments are in their
turn formed from previous volitions, and on the
other, those formulæ do not possess any absolute
value in the single and concrete situation, so that
they can be modified and substituted for others
that affirm the opposite. The question is not
whether cutting wood has been as a rule a good
thing for me in the past, nor whether I have
generally willed it in the past : the question is to
will it at this moment, that is, to posit the cutting
of wood at this moment as a good thing.

Posteriority of
the practical
concepts.
As is the case with the pretended practical
judgments and concepts of classes formed upon
them, so the concepts that they imply, of *things*
good, of ideals, of ends, of actions worthy of being
willed, and so on, do not precede, but follow the
volition that has taken place. These concepts
are the incipient reflection, scientific and philosophical, upon the spontaneous acts of the will,
and we cannot practise science nor philosophize
save about facts that have already taken place :
if the fact do not precede, there can be no
theory. Certainly theory does not do other than

seek out the already created and give the real principles of actions in the form of thought principles, in the same manner as Logic discovers those principles that live and operate in logical thought. But since the formula of the principle of contradiction is not necessary for thinking without contradiction, but presupposes it, so the concepts of ends, of things good, and of ideals are not necessary for volitions, but presuppose them.

The thesis of the will as knowledge draws support from the mistaken belief in the practical principles and judgments that precede volition, as also does the proposition that he who knows what is good for him also wishes it, and that he who does not wish it does not know it. This thesis is to be inverted, because to know what is good for one means that one has willed it. From the opposite point of view, the other thesis, of the impossibility of volition unless *feeling* be interposed between what is known and the will, is to be attributed to a like mistaken belief. Feeling is held to give, as it were, a particular value to facts, and to cause them to be felt as they should be felt, or to be changed. The customary merit possessed by theories of feeling is to be recognized in this thesis: that is to say, it has awakened or

Origin of intellectualist and sentimentalist doctrines.

reawakened consciousness of the peculiarity of the practical act in respect to intellectualistic reductions and identifications. This merit is not altogether lacking to the general theory of practical judgments itself. These, although called judgments, were classified differently to all the others, precisely because they were *practical*.

The concepts of end and means.

Having thus shown that it is not true that man first knows the end and then wills it, it is possible to establish with greater precision what is to be understood by *end*. The end, then, in universal, is the concept itself of will. Considered in the single act, as this or that end, it is nothing but this or that determinate volition. Hence is also to be derived a better definition of its relation to the *means*, which it is usual to conceive empirically and erroneously as a part of volition and action at the service of another part. An act of will is an infrangible unity and can be taken as divided only for practical convenience. In the volitional act, all is volition ; nothing is means, and all is end. The means is nothing but the actual situation, from which the volitional act takes its start, and is in that way really distinguished from the end. Distinction and unification take place together, because, as has been remarked, the volition is not the situation,

yet, on the other hand, as the volition, so the
situation : the one varies as a function of the
other.   Hence the absurdity of the maxim, that
the end justifies the means.   This maxim is of
an empirical character and has sometimes been
employed to justify actions erroneously held to
be unjustifiable, and more often to make pass as
just actions that were unjustifiable.   As the end,
so the means, but the means is what is given
and has no need of justification.   The end is
what has been willed and must be justified in
itself.

The idea that we generally have of finality is *Critique of*
the end as plan
to be eliminated, owing to the continual change- *or as fixed*
design.
ability of the means, that is, of the actual situation,
which would posit the end as something fixed,
as a *plan* to be carried out.   The difference
between the finality of man and that of nature
has recently been made to reside in nature : which
has seemed to act upon a plan which she changes,
remakes, and accommodates at every moment,
according to contingencies, so that the point of
arrival is not for her predetermined or predeter-
minable.   But the same can be said of the human
will and of its finality.   The will too changes at
every moment, as the movement of a swimmer
or of an athlete changes at every moment,

E

according to the motion of the sea or of the rival athlete, and according to the varying measure or quality of his own strength in the course of the volitional process. Man acts, case for case and from instant to instant, realizing his will of every instant, not that abstract conception which is called a plan. Hence also arises the confirmation of the belief that there do not exist fixed types and models of actions. He who seeks and awaits such models and types does not know how to will. He is without that initiative, that creativeness, that genius, which is not less indispensable to the practical activity than to art and philosophy.

The will and the unknown. It will seem that the will thus becomes will of the unknown and is at variance in too paradoxical a manner with the sayings, so clearly evident, that *voluntas quae non fertur in incognitum* and *ignoti nulla cupido*. But those sayings are true only so far as they confirm the fact that without the precedence of the theoretical act, the practical act does not take place. Apart from this significa-tion, it should rather be maintained that *noti nulla cupido* and that *voluntas non fertur in cognitum*. What is known exists, and it is not possible to *will the existence* of what *exists*: the past is not a content of volition. The will is the

will of the unknown, that is to say, is itself,
which, in so far as it wills, does not know itself,
and knows itself only when it has ceased to will.
Our surprise when we come to understand the
actions that we have accomplished, is often not
small ; we realize that we have not done what we
thought we had done, and have on the contrary
done what we had not foreseen. Hence also the
fallacy of the explanations that present volitional
man as surrounded with things that he does or
does not will ; whereas things, or rather facts
are the mere object of knowledge and cannot be
willed or not willed, as it is unthinkable to will
that Alexander the Great had not existed, or that
Babylon had not been conquered. That which
is willed is not *things* but *changes* in things, that
is to say, the volitions themselves. This fallacious
conception also arises from the substitution of
abstractions and classes of volitions for the real
will.

It is to be observed, finally, that the erroneous
concept of a form of science called the *practical*
or *normative* has its roots in the concept of *the
end, of the good, of concepts and judgments of
value* as original facts. When practical concepts
and judgments, as a special category of concepts
and judgments, have been destroyed, the idea of

*Critique of
the concept of
practical
sciences and
of a practical
philosophy.*

a practical and normative science has also been destroyed. For this reason, the *Philosophy of the practical* cannot be *practical philosophy*, and if it has appeared to constitute an exception among all philosophies and that above all others it should preserve a practical and normative function, this has arisen from a verbal misunderstanding that is most ingenuous and most destructive. For our part we have striven to dissipate it, even in the title of our treatise, which, contrary to the usual custom, we have entitled not *practical,* but *of the practical.*

IV

INSEPARABILITY OF ACTION FROM ITS REAL BASE AND PRACTICAL NATURE OF THE THEORETICAL ERROR

THE connection between the actual situation and will, means and end having been made clear, no distinction that it may be desired to establish between general and concrete volition, ideal and real volition, that is to say between *intention and volition*, is acceptable. Intention and volition coincide completely, and that distinction, generally suggested with the object of justifying the unjustifiable, is altogether arbitrary in both the forms that it assumes.

Coincidence of intention and volition.

The first form is that of the distinction between abstract and concrete, or better, between general and particular. It is maintained, that we can will the good in the abstract and yet be unable to will it in the concrete, that we may have good intentions and yet behave badly. But by our reduction of the thing willed to the volition,

Volition in the abstract and in the concrete: critique.

53

to will the abstract is tantamount to *willing abstractly*. And to will abstractly is tantamount to *not willing*, if volition imply a situation historically determined, from which it arises as an act equally determined and concrete. Hence, of the two terms of the pretended distinction, the first, volition of the abstract, disappears, and the second, concrete volition, which is the true and real volition and intention, alone remains.

Thought volition and real volition : critique.

The second form abandons, it is true, the abstract for the concrete, but assumes two different volitional acts in the same concrete : the one real, arising from the actual situation, the other, thought or imagined, side by side with the former : this would be the volition, that the intention. According to such a theory, it is always possible to *direct the intention*, that is, the real volition can always join with the volitional act imagined and produce a nexus, in which the volition exists in one way, the intention in another ; the first bad and the second good, or the first good and the second bad. Thus the honourable man approved by the Jesuit, of whom Pascal speaks, although he desire the death of him from whom he expects an inheritance and rejoice when it takes place, yet endows his desire with a special character, believing that what he wishes to attain is the prosperity of his affairs, not the death of his fellow-creature. Or the same man may kill the man who has given him a blow; but in so doing he will fix his thought upon the defence of his honour, not upon the homicide. Since he is not able to abstain from the action, he at least (they say) purifies the intention. The worst of this is that the real situation, the only one of which we can take account, is the historical, not the imaginary situation. In the reality of the consequent volition, it is not a question of his own prosperity and nothing more, but of his own prosperity coupled with the death of another, or of false prosperity. It is not a question of his own honour and nothing more, but of his own honour in conjunction with the violation of the life of another, that is, of false honour. Thus the asserted fact of prosperity and honour is changed into two qualified bad actions, and what was honourable in the imaginary case, becomes dishonourable in the real case, which is indeed the only one of which it is question. It is of no use to imagine a situation that differs from reality, because it is to the real situation that the intention is directed, not to the other, and therefore it is not possible to direct, that is to say, to change the intention, if the actual situation do not change.

The antipathy that has been shown for good-hearted and well-intentioned men in recent centuries, and for practical doctrines with intention as their principle (the morality of intention, etc.), arises from the sophisms that we have here criticized. But since it is henceforward clear to us that those so-called well-intentioned and good-hearted people have neither good hearts nor good intentions and are nothing but hypocrites, and because we do not admit any distinction between intention and will, we are without fear or antipathy in respect to the use of the word "intention," understanding it as a synonym for "volition."

Critique of volition with base either unknown or imperfectly known.

But it will be said that we have here considered the case, in which, while the real situation is known, there is a hypocritical pretence of not knowing it, in order to deceive others and maybe oneself, and that we have justly here declared that in such a case the will and the intention were inseparable. But there is another case, in which, though the situation of affairs be not known, yet it is necessary both to will and to act at once. Here the concrete will is separated at the beginning from the intention: the will is what it *can* be, the intention is as the action *would wish* to be.

But this instance is equally or even more inconceivable than the preceding. It has been clearly established that if we do not know, we cannot will. Before arriving at a resolution, man tries to see clearly in and about him, and so long as the search continues, so long as the doubt is not dissipated, the will remains in suspense. Nothing can make him resolve, where the elements for coming to a resolution are wanting; nothing can make him say to himself "I know," when he does not know; nothing can make him say "it will be as if I knew," because that "as if I knew" would introduce the arbitrary method into the whole of knowledge, and would cause universal doubt to take the place of doubt circumscribed. This would disturb the function of knowledge itself, against which an act of real felony would be committed. From nothing nothing is born.

There are no exceptions to this law, and those *Illusions among the cases that are cited.* that are adduced can be only apparent. A man is cautiously descending the dangerous side of a mountain, covered with ice: will he or will he not place his foot on that surface, of which he does not and cannot know the resistance? How-

ever, there is no time to be lost: he must go on
and take the risk.   It seems evident that in a case
like this he wills and operates without complete
knowledge.   But the case is not indeed unique
or of a special order: every act of life implies
risk of the unknown, and if there were not in us
(as they say) *potestas voluntatem nostram extra
limites intellectus nostri extendendi*, it would be
impossible to move a step, to lift an arm, or to
put into one's mouth a morsel of bread, since
omnia incerta ac periculis sunt plena.   What must
be known in order to form the volition is not that
which we should know if we were in a situation
different from that in which we are (in which case,
also, the volition would be different), but that
which we can know in the situation in which we
really find ourselves.   The man on the glacier has
neither time nor means to verify the resistance of
the surface of the ice; but since he is obliged to
proceed further, he does not act in a rash, but in
a very prudent manner, in putting his foot trust-
fully on the ice that may be unfaithful to him.
He would be acting rashly if, having the means
and the time, he failed to investigate its resistance, that is to say, if he were in *another and
imaginary situation*, not in that real and present
situation, in which he finds himself.   If I knew

the cards of my adversary, as the cheat knows
them, I should play differently, but it cannot
be argued that because, as an honest player,
I know only my own, I am therefore playing
inconsiderately : I am playing as I ought, with
the knowledge that I possess, that is, with full
knowledge of the real situation in which I find
myself.

With this very simple observation is also
solved an old puzzle of the theory of volition.
How does it happen that a man can choose
between two dishes of food at an equal distance
and moving in the same manner,[1] or between two
objects altogether identical, offered for sale to
him at the same time, at the same price, by the
same individual ? First, we must correct the
hypothesis, for as two identical things do not
exist in nature, so the two objects in question
and the two possible actions of the example are
not identical.

Indeed the refined connoisseur always discovers some difference between two objects,
which to the ignorant, the absent-minded, and
the hasty seem to be the same. The question,
then, is not of identical objects and actions, but
of those as in which there is neither time nor

---

[1] This was an example used by the Schoolmen and by Dante.

mode (*majora premunt*) of recognizing the difference. For this reason, therefore, we take no
account of this difference, or, as is said, they are
looked upon as equal in this respect. But the
adiophora, the indifferent, do not exist, and owing
to that abstraction, we do not take account of
other differences that always exist in the real
situation, owing to which my volition becomes
concrete in a movement that causes me to take
the object on my right, because (let us suppose)
I am wont to turn to the right, or because, owing
to a superstition that is not less a matter of habit,
I prefer the right to the left, or because, through
sympathy due to dignity, I prefer the object that
is offered to me with the right hand to a similar
object offered with the left, which, if only for this
reason, is, strictly speaking, not the same, but
different, and so on. These minute circumstances
are absent from consciousness and are not felt by
the will, not because they escape as a rule reflection. If we neglect them in analysis as non-
existent, this always occurs, because we substitute
for the real situation another unreal situation
imagined by ourselves. Thus it has also been
remarked, as a proof of the irrationality believed
to exist in our volitions and to be the cause
of our acting without precise knowledge, that

no reason nor any theoretic precedent can be adduced as to why, when fixing legal punishments, or in the application of sentences, we give forty and not forty-one days' imprisonment, a hundred lire fine instead of a hundred and one. But here, too, it is clear that the detailed facts are not wanting, the knowledge of which causes us to will the punishment to be so and so. This knowledge is to be found in traditions, in the sympathy that we have for certain numbers, in the ease with which they can be remembered or calculated, and so on.—To sum up, man forms the volitional act, not because he possesses some portentous faculty of extending his will outside the limits of the intellect, but, on the contrary, because he possesses the faculty of circumscribing himself within the limits of his intellect on each occasion and of willing on that basis and within those limits. That he wills, knowing some things and ignorant of infinite other things, is indubitable. But this means that he is man and not God, that he is a finite and not an infinite being, and that the sum of his historical knowledge is on each occasion human and finite, as is on each occasion the act of will which he forms upon it. Psychologists would say that this arises from *narrowness* of consciousness, but Goethe, on the contrary, remarked with metaphor more apt and thought more profound, that the true artist is revealed in *knowing how to limit himself.* God himself, as it seems, cannot act, save by limiting himself in finite beings.

Impossibility of volition with a false theoretic base.

If the intention cannot be separated from the volition, because this belongs to the real and not to the imaginary, and proceeds from the known and never from the unknown, there yet remains a third possibility, which is, that the will results differently from the intention, owing to a *theoretical error*; as when we are said to err *in good faith* as to the actual situation, that is, we do not indeed substitute the unknown for the known, nor do we substitute the imaginary for the known, but we simply make a mistake in enunciating the historical judgment to ourselves: intending to perform one action, we perform on the contrary another.

This third possibility is also an impossibility, because it contradicts the nature of the theoretical error, which, precisely because it is a question of error and not of truth, cannot be in its turn theoretical and must be and is practical, conformably to a theory of error of which many great thinkers have seen or caught

sight and which it is now fitting to restore and
to make clear.

We have elsewhere amply demonstrated how *Forms of the theoretical error and problem concerning its nature.*
theoretical errors arise from the undue trans-
ference of one theoretical form to another, or
of one theoretical product into another distinct
from it. Thus, the artist who substitutes for the
representation of the affections, reasoning on
the affections, mingling art and philosophy, or he
who in the composition of a work, fills the voids
that his fancy has left in the composition, with
unsuitable elements taken from other works,
commits the artistic error, ugliness. Thus too,
the philosopher, who solves a philosophical
problem in a fantastic way, as would an artist,
or, instead of a philosopheme, employs the
historical, naturalistic or mathematical method,
and so produces a myth, or a contingent fact
universalized, or an abstraction in place of concreteness, that is to say, a philosophical error.
It is also a philosophical error to transport
philosophical concepts from one order to another
and to treat art as though it were philosophy,
or morality as though it were economy. This
also happens in an analogous manner with the
historian, the natural scientist, and the mathematician, all of whom are wrong, if they interweave

extraneous methods with those that are their own, and with the views, conceptions, and classification of one order, those of another.— But if this be the way in which particular errors and general forms of theoretical error arise, what is the origin of the theoretical error in universal? We have not asked this question explicitly elsewhere, because only now can it receive the most effective reply.

Distinction between ignorance and error: practical genesis of the latter.

Error is not ignorance, lack of knowledge, obscurity or doubt. An error of which we are altogether without consciousness is not error at all, but that inexhaustible field which the spiritual activity continues to fill to infinity. True and proper error is the affirmation of knowing what we do not know, the substitution of a representation for that which we do not possess, an extraneous conception for the one that is wanting. Now affirmation is thought itself, it is truth itself. When an inquiry has been completed, a process of cogitation closed, the result is the affirmation that a man· makes to himself, not with a new act added to the foregoing, but with the act itself of thought that has thought. It is therefore impossible that in the circle of the pure theoretical spirit error should ever arise. Man has in himself the fountain of truth. If it be true that on the death-bed there is no lying, because man transcends the finite and communicates with the infinite, then man who thinks is always on his bed of death, the death-bed of the finite, in contact with the infinite. We may know that we are ignorant, but this consciousness of ignorance is the cogitative process in its *fieri*, not yet having attained to its end, certainly not (as has been said) error. Before this last can appear, before we can affirm that we have reached a result, which the testimony of the conscience says has not been reached, something extraneous to the theoretical spirit must intervene, that is to say, a practical act which simulates the theoretical. And it simulates it, not indeed intrinsically (one does not lie with the depth of oneself or on one's death-bed), but in taking hold of the external means of communication, of the word or expression as sound and physical fact, and diverting it to mean what, in the given circumstances, it could not mean. The erroneous affirmation has been rendered possible, because something else has followed the true affirmation, which is purely theoretical, something that is improperly called affirmation in the practical sense, whereas it is

F

only *communication*, which can be substituted in a greater or less degree for the truth and falsely represent it. Thus the theoretical error *in general* arises, as do its particular forms and manifestations, from the substitution for, or the illegitimate mating of two forms of the spirit. These cannot be both theoretical here, but must be the theoretical and the practical forms, precisely because we are here in the field of the spirit in general and of the fundamental forms of its activity. We are ignorant, then, because it is necessary to be ignorant and to feel oneself ignorant, in order to attain to truth ; but we err only because *we wish to err*.

Proofs and confirmation. Like all true doctrines, this of the practical nature of the theoretical error, which at first sight seems most strange (especially to professed philosophers), is yet found to be constantly confirmed in ordinary thought. For all know and all continually repeat that (immoderate) passions and (illegitimate) interests lead insidiously into error, that we err, to be quick and finish or to obtain for ourselves undeserved repose, that we err by acquiescence in old ideas, that is to say, in order not to allow ourselves to be disturbed in our repose that has been unduly prolonged, and so on. We do not mention those cases in which it is a question of solemn and evident lies, the brazen-faced manifestation of interests openly illegitimate. Let us limit ourselves to the modest forms of error, to the venial sins, because if these be proved to be the result of will, by so much the more will this be proved of the shameless forms, the deadly sins. It is also said that we err in *deafening* ourselves and others with words, with the verse that sounds and does not create, with the brush that charms but does not express, with the formulæ that seem to contain a thought but contain the void. In this way we come to recognize that will has been rendered possible, owing to the communication being a practical fact, of which a bad use can be made by means of a volitional act. For the rest, if this were not so, what guarantee would truth ever possess? If it were possible to err even once in perfect good faith and that the mind should confuse true and false, embracing the false as true, how could we any longer distinguish the one from the other? Thought would be radically corrupt, whereas it is incorrupt and incorruptible.

It is vain, therefore, to except the existence or the possibility of errors of good faith, because truth alone is of good faith, and error is always

in a greater or less or least degree, of bad
faith. Were this not so, it would be incorrigible, whereas it is by definition corrigible.
Consequently, the last attempt to differentiate
intention from volition fails, since it posits an
intention that is frustrated in the volition, as the
effect of a theoretical error, a good intention
that becomes, through no fault of its own, a
bad volition. The intention, being volition, takes
possession' of the whole volitional man, causing
the intellect to be attentive and indefatigable
in the search for truth, the soul ready to accept
it, whatever it be, pure of every passion that is
not the passion for truth itself, and eliminates
the possibility, or assumes the responsibility of
error.

A proof of this is afforded by the fact that
to exquisite and delicate souls, to consciences
pure and dignified, even what are called their
theoretical errors are a biting bitterness, and they
blame themselves with them. On the other hand,
in the presence of the foolish and the wicked,
one is often in doubt as to whether their folly
and wickedness come from the head or from the
heart, whether it be madness rather than set
purpose. The truth is that all this evil, which
seems to arise from defective vision, comes really

from the heart, for they have themselves forged those false views with their sophisms, their illegitimate internal affirmations and suggestions, that they may be more free in their evil inclinations, thus obtaining for themselves and for others a false moral *alibi.* We must applaud the former and exhort them to continue to persevere in their scruple, the condition of theoretical and practical health : we must inculcate to the second a return to themselves and the removal of the mask that they have assumed as a disguise from themselves, before assuming it towards others.

A consequence of the principle established is the justification of the use of practical measures to induce those who err theoretically to correct themselves, castigating them, when this is of assistance, for admonition and example. It will be replied that these are measures of other times, and that we are now in an epoch of liberty, when their use is no longer permissible, and that we should now employ only the persuasive power of truth. But those who say this are without eyes to look within upon themselves. The Holy Inquisition is truly *holy* and lives for that reason in its *eternal* idea. The Inquisition that is dead was nothing but one of its contingent historical incarnations. And the Inquisition must have

Justification of the practical repression of error.

been justified and beneficial, if whole peoples invoked and defended it, if men of the loftiest souls founded and created it severely and impartially, and its very adversaries applied it on their own account, pyre answering to pyre. Thus Christian Rome persecuted heretics as Imperial Rome had persecuted Christians, and Protestants burned Catholics as Catholics had burned Protestants. If certain ferocious practices are now abandoned (are they definitely abandoned, or do they not persist in a different form?), we do not for that reason cease from practically oppressing those who promulgate errors. No society can dispense with this discipline, although the mode of its application is subject to practical, utilitarian and moral deliberation. We begin with man as a child, whose mental education is at once and above all practical and moral education, education for work and for sincerity (and no one has ever been seriously educated who has not received at the least a provident slap or two or had his ears pulled). This education is continued with the punishments for culpable negligence and ignorance threatened in the laws, and so on until we reach the spontaneous discipline of society, by means of which the artist who produces the ugly and the man of science who teaches the false are

rebuked by the intelligent, or fall into discredit
with them.   Such illegitimate and transitory
applause as they may sometimes obtain at the
hands of the unintelligent and of the multitude
is but a poor and precarious recompense for them.
Literary and artistic criticism always has of
necessity, and the more so the better it understands its office, a practical and moral aspect
reconcilable with the purest æstheticity and
theoreticity in the intrinsic examination of works.

We certainly have good empirical reasons *Empirical*
for distinguishing between errors of bad faith *distinctions of*
errors and
and errors of good faith, errors that are avoidable *philosophical*
distinctions.
and errors that are unavoidable, pardonable and
unpardonable, mortal and venial.   No one would
wish to deny that there is a wide difference between a slight distraction that leads to a wide
erroneous affirmation, and such malice as gives
rise to a small and almost imperceptible error,
to a lie, which, externally considered, is almost
harmless.   We should be as indulgent in respect
to the former as we are severe in respect to
the latter.   And from the empirical standpoint
we should recommend in certain cases tolerance
and indulgence in respect to the theoretical error,
which should be looked upon rather as ignorance
than as sin.   We cannot but take count of all

those affirmations, which, while they do not re-present the firm security of the true, are yet offered as points of support, or as provisional affirmations, like those *tibicines*, props or stakes, those bad verses that Virgil allowed to remain in the *Aeneid*, with the intention of returning to them again.   But it was needful to record the true bases of the theory of error against the illusions arising from empiricism, the more so since the general tendency of our times (for reasons that we need not here inquire into) has led to their not being recognized.   Those bases are in the practical spirit, and the practical theory of error is one of the justified forms of pragmatism, although perhaps it be that very truth against which the pragmatists sin.

V

IDENTITY OF VOLITION AND ACTION AND DISTINC-
TION BETWEEN VOLITION AND EVENT

SUCH are the relations between the practical *Volition and*
action :
activity and the theoretical, which precedes and *intuition and*
expression.
conditions it.

Asking ourselves now, what are the relations
of this same activity with that which seems to
follow it and to be outside the spirit, in company
with corporeality, naturality, physic and matter
(or however else it may be called)? we find
ourselves face to face with a problem which we
have already treated and solved in another part
of the system of the spirit, and which we shall
solve here in an analogous manner. What we
may now designate as the problem of the relation
between *volition and action,* formerly appeared in
the theoretical philosophy as the problem of the
relation between *intuition* and *expression.*—Are
then volitions and actions two distinct terms that
may appear now together, now separate? Can

volition remain for its part isolated from action, whereas action is not able to separate itself from volition, or is the opposite true?—We reply, as we did on the former occasion, by denying the problem itself and by identifying intuition with expression, in such a manner that effective intuition became at the same time expression, and it was declared that a so-called expression, which was not at the same time intuition, was declared to be non-existent.—We reply in like manner on this occasion, that *volition and action* are *one*, and that volition without action or action without volition is inconceivable.

Spirit and nature.   Indeed, the relation between spirit and nature (which is a general relation, including the other particulars between intuition and expression, or between volition and action), understood in the way that it is here, is a relation, not between two entities, but only between two different methods of elaborating one unique reality, which is spiritual reality : thus it is not truly a relation. Nor are the two modes of elaboration two co-ordinated modes of knowledge, for that would lead back to a duplicity of objects, but the first is cognoscitive elaboration and true science, or philosophy, in which reality is revealed as activity and spirituality, while the other is an abstract elaboration for practical convenience, without cognoscitive character. When this has been posited, the spiritual act of volition has not another reality face to face with it, with which it must join or combine, in order to become concrete, but is itself full reality. That which is called matter, movement, and material modification from the naturalistic point of view, is already included in the volitional spiritual act, of which it might be said without difficulty (as was once said amid much scandal of the Ego) that it is heavy, round, square, white, red, sonorous, and, therefore, physically determinable. The volition is not followed by a movement of the legs or arms ; it is those movements themselves that are material for the physical, spiritual for the philosopher, extrinsic for the former, at once intrinsic and extrinsic for the latter, or better, neither extrinsic nor intrinsic (an arbitrary division). As poetry lives in speech and painting in colours, so the will lives in actions, not because the one is in the other as in an envelope, but because the one is the other and without the other would be mutilated and indeed inconceivable.

We cannot affirm the distinction between *Inexistence of volitions* volition and action, save in force and as a proof *without actions and vice versa.* of a dualistic metaphysical view, of an abstract

spiritualism, with matter as being and substance
for correlative term. But this point of view is
eliminated by the idealist view, which recognizes
only one unique substance, and that as spirituality
and subjectivity. Without, however, now basing
ourselves upon such considerations, and according
to the order that we follow, applying ourselves
to the examination of the facts of consciousness,
we affirm that it would be impossible to adduce
one volitional fact that should not be also a
movement called physical. Those volitional
acts, which according to some philosophers are
consumed within the will and are in that way
distinguished from external facts, are a phantasm.
Every volition, be it never so small, sets the
organism in motion and produces what are called
external facts. The purpose is already an
effectuation, a beginning of combat; indeed,
simple desire is not without effects, if it be
possible to destroy oneself with desires, as is
in effect maintained On the other hand, it is
not possible to indicate actions without volitions.
Instinctive or habitual acts that have become
instinctive are adduced; but these too are not
set in motion, save by the will, not one by one,
in their particulars, but as a whole, in the same
way as a single hand sets in motion a most

complicated machine which a thousand hands have previously constructed. There cannot then be volition without action, nor action without volition, as there cannot be intuition without expression or expression without intuition.

It is well, however, to indicate one among the many sources from which is derived the illusion of this distinction and separation, effectively inexistent. A volitional act, which is a process of some duration, may be interrupted and substituted for other volitional acts; it may declare itself again and again begin its work (although this will always be more or less modified), and this may give occasion to new interruptions and new beginnings. It seems that in this way the will stands on one side, as something formed and definite, and that on the other execution pursues its way and is subject to the most varied accidents. But volition and execution proceed with equal and indeed with one single step. What we will we execute; the volition changes as the execution changes. In the same way, when we are engaged upon a work of art, on a long poem for instance, the illusion arises of an abstract conception or plan, which the poet carries out as he versifies. But every poet knows that a poem is not created from an abstract plan, that the initial

Illusions as to the distinction between these terms.

poetical image is not without rhythm and verse, and that it does not need rhythm and verse applied to it afterwards. He knows that it is in reality a primitive intuition-expression, in which all is determined and nothing is determined, and what has been already intuified is already expressed, and what will afterwards be expressed will only afterwards be intuified. The initial intuition is certainly not an abstract plan, but a living and vital germ ; and so is the volitional act.

Distinction between action and succession or event. When, therefore, it is affirmed that a volition is truly such, only when it produces effects, or that a volition is to be judged by its results, it is impossible not to assent, as we assent that an unexpressed expression or an unversified verse is neither an expression nor a verse. But in this signification only, because those propositions have sometimes assumed another, which on the contrary it is needful resolutely to reject. This is that in them action (will-action) has been confused with *succession or event.* Now, if volition coincide with action, it does not and cannot coincide with *event.*

Volition and event. It cannot coincide, because what is action and what is event? Action is the act of the one event is the act of the whole : will is of man, event of God. Or, to put this proposition in a less imaginary form, the volition of the individual is as it were the contribution that he brings to the volitions of all the other beings in the universe, event the aggregate of all the wills and the answer to all the questions. In this answer is included and absorbed the will itself of the individual, which we have taken and contemplated alone. If, then, we wished to make the volition depend upon event, action upon succession, we should be undertaking to make one fact depend upon another fact, of which the first is a constituent part, placing among the antecedents of action what is its consequence, among things given those to be created, the unknown with the known, the future in the past.

The concepts of actions that are successful and of those that are unsuccessful, of actions that become fully concrete in the fact, and of those that become concrete only in part or not at all, are therefore inexact. No action (not even those that are empirically said to be most successful, not even the most obvious and ordinary) succeeds fully, in the sense that it alone constitutes the fact : every action diverges by necessity and by definition from succession or happening. If I return home every day by the usual road, my return home is every day new

Successful and unsuccessful actions : criticism.

and different from that which might have been
imagined. This often amounts to a diversity of
particulars which we may call of least importance,
but which yet are not for that reason the less
real. On the other hand, no action, however
vain it be held (if it be action and not velleity
of action and intrinsic contradiction, or by as
much as it is action and not imagination and
contradiction), passes without trace and without
result.

If any action could be rendered altogether vain,
this same rendering vain would invade all other
actions and no fact would happen.

Action and foresight : critique. The current proposition that we cannot act
without *foreseeing* is also incorrect. Since the
conception of foreseeing is contradictory, and
since we cannot know a fact if it be not first a
fact, that is, if it have not happened; if the
contradictory hypothesis held, it would be impossible to act. But the truth is that what is
called foreseeing is nothing but seeing; it is
to know the given facts and to reason upon
them with the universals. That is to say,
it is the invariable theoretical base of action,
already illustrated. When we will and act, what
we will and do is *our own action* itself, not
that of others or of all the others, and so is

the resulting event. *Voluntas fertur in incognitum*, but the all intent upon itself does not take count of the unknown, which is in this case relatively unknowable and, therefore, relatively non-existent. The individual is aware that when he acts, he does not aim at anything but the placing of new elements in universal reality. He takes care that they shall be energetic and vital, without nourishing the foolish illusion that they must be the only ones, or that they alone produce reality. A popular little tale tells how God, who had at first granted to men to know their future lives and the day of their death, afterwards withdrew this knowledge from them altogether, because He perceived from experience that such knowledge made them lazy and inert. The new ignorance, on the other hand, revived and impelled them to vie with one another in activity, as though it had been granted them to obtain and to enjoy everything.[1] How can we doubt that our good and energetic work can ever be rendered nugatory in the event? That is unthinkable, and the saying *fiat justitia et pereat mundus* is rectified by that other saying: *fiat justitia ne pereat mundus*. Bad is not born from good, nor inaction from action.

---

[1] *Arch. p. lo st. d. trad. pop.*, of Pitré (1882), pp. 70-72.

Every volitional man, every man active in goodness, is a contradiction to that one-sided attitude in which the will is suppressed to give place to happening, a world unmade is believed to be already made, arms are crossed or the field deserted. But it also contradicts the fatuous security that the future world will conform to the ends of our individual actions taken in isolation ; saying with the good sense of the Florentine statesman, that we ourselves control one half of our actions, or little less, Fortune the other half. Hence our trust in our own strength ; hence, too, our apprehension of the pitfalls of Fortune, continually arising and continually to be conquered. This constitutes the interior drama of true men of action, of the political geniuses who have guided the destinies of man. While the unfit is all anxiety, or bewilderment and depression, the fatuous is all over-confidence or expectation of the impossible, also losing himself in bewilderment when he finally discovers that the reality is not what he imagined. Hence also the serenity of the sage, who knows that whatever happen there will always be opportunity for good conduct. *Si fractus illabatur orbis*, there will always be a better world to construct. Hope and fear are related to action itself in its becoming, not to its result and succession.

We can illustrate the fact that no one seriously *Confirmation of the inderiva- bility of the value of action from its success.* thinks of valuing an action according to its success, but that all value it at its intrinsic value as action, from the circumstance that no one recognizes any merit to the action of a marks-man who hits the bull's-eye, when shooting at the target with closed eyes; whereas no little merit is recognized to him who, after having taken careful aim, does not hit the mark but goes very near it. We are certainly often deceived in our practical judgments, and fortunate men are continually praised to the skies as men of great practical capacity, while the unfortunate are hurled into the mire as incompetent; for we do not distinguish exactly between action and success. This is not only so as to judgments of the present life : it is also true of the life of the past, of the pages of history, where imbeciles are made heroes and heroes calumniated; to the worst of leaders is attributed the honour of victories, ridiculous statesmen credited with ability. On the other hand, the sins of madmen are attributed to the wise, or they are accused of faults that are nobody's fault, but the result of circumstances. In vain will the Pericleses of all time ask, as did the ancient Pericles of the people of Athens, that the unforeseen misfortunes

of the Peloponnesian war should be attributed
to him, provided that by way of compensation
he might have praise for all the fortunate things
that should also happen παρὰ λόγον.[1]   All this
depends upon an imperfect knowledge of facts
more than upon anything else : hence the necessity of criticism.   Just as the work of the poet and
of the painter is not materially to be laid hold
of in the poem or in the picture, but requires
a re-evocation that is often very difficult, so the
work of the man of action, which is in part fused
in events and partly contained in them, as a
bud that will open in the future, asks a keen eye
and the greatest care in valuation.   The history
of men of action and of their deeds is easily
changed into *legend*, and legends are never
altogether eliminable, because misunderstanding
or error is never altogether eliminable.

Explanation
of apparently
conflicting
facts.
On the other hand, certain commonplaces
seem to be in opposition to the criterion itself :
for example, that men are judged by success and
that it matters little what we have willed and
done, when the result is not satisfactory.   There
are also certain popular customs that make
individuals responsible for what happens outside
their own spheres of action, not to mention the

[1] Thuc. ii. 64.

well - known historical examples of unfortunate leaders crucified at Carthage and guillotined at Paris, for no other cause in reality than that of not having won the victory. And there is also the insistence of certain thinkers upon the necessity of never distinguishing the judgment of the act from that of the fact. But such insistence is nothing but a new aspect of the implacable struggle that it has been necessary to conduct against the morality of the mere intention and against the sophisms and the subterfuges that arise from it ; an insistence that has expressed itself in paradoxical formulæ, as are also paradoxical the trivial remarks of ordinary life that have been mentioned. As to the customs and condemnations narrated by history, these were without doubt extraordinary expedients in desperate cases, in which people had placed themselves in such a position that it was impossible or most difficult to verify intentions and actions, and to distinguish misfortunes from betrayals ; and as all expedients born of like situations sometimes hit the mark, that is to say, punish bad faith, so will others increase with irrationality the evil that they would have wished to diminish, since in those cases there has not been any bad faith to punish and to correct.

VI

THE PRACTICAL JUDGMENT, THE HISTORY AND THE PHILOSOPHY OF THE PRACTICAL

WITH these last considerations, we are conducted to the theory of practical judgments, that is, to those judgments of which we have demonstrated the impossibility, when their precedence to the volitional act was asserted; but their conceivability as following it, indeed their necessity, is clear, by the intrinsic law of the Spirit, which consists in always preserving or in continually attaining to full possession of itself.

Practical taste and judgment. But we must not confound the practical judgment with what has been called *practical taste, or the immediate consciousness of value, or the feeling* of the value of the volitional act. None can doubt that such a taste, consciousness, or feeling is a real fact. The practical act brings with it approbation and disapprobation, joy and sorrow, and like facts of consciousness that are altogether unreflective. By these we explain the immediate sympathy that certain actions afford us, and the enthusiasms that are often spread through wide circles of society, and the force of example, which is most successful in arousing imitative efforts. Thus at certain moments the soul of all seems to vibrate in unison with the soul of one, and the actions of many to be prepared and carried out, as though with one accord, without its being possible to say at those moments what is willed, what abhorred and what admired. That taste, or consciousness, or feeling is not, however, distinct from the volitional act, and is, indeed, the volitional act itself. It is that internal control of which we have already spoken, that immediate feeling of oneself, that immediate consciousness, which makes of it a spiritual act. Abstract it from the volitional act and the volitional act itself disappears from before you.

If it can take place, not only in the individual who is acting, but also in him who contemplates the action, that is because the individual who contemplates becomes unified in that moment with the individual who acts, he wills imitatively with him, with him suffers and enjoys, as the disc-thrower watches with his eye and with his whole person the disc that has been thrown,

follows its rapid and direct course and the dangers
in the form of obstacles that it seems to be about
to strike, its turns and deviations, and seems to
become himself a running turning disc. The
denomination "practical taste" is very well
chosen, because the analogy with the theoretic
activity and with æsthetic taste is here most full.
But since æsthetic taste is not æsthetic judgment,
as the mere reproduction of the æsthetic act is not
the criticism of it, as the listener to a poem who
sings within himself with the poet, must not be
confused with the critic, who analyses and understands it, any more than the contemplator of a
picture, of a statue, or of a piece of architecture,
who paints with the painter, sculptures with the
sculptor, or ideally raises airy masses with the
architect; so we must distinguish practical taste
and sympathy (or antipathy) from the practical
judgment. Without taste (æsthetic or practical),
judgment (æsthetic or practical) is not possible;
but taste is not judgment, which demands a
further act of the spirit.

The practical judgment as historical judgment.   The practical judgment is, as has already been
observed, a *historical* judgment; so that to judge
practical acts and to give their history is really
the same thing. What occurs here is analogous
to what was demonstrated of the theoretic and

æsthetic act, when we illustrated the coincidence of literary and artistic criticism with literary and artistic history. Criticism, be it practical or theoretic, cannot consist of anything but determining whether a spiritual act has taken place and what it has been. The differences between the one and the other criticism arise only from the diversity of content present in each case, asking different categories of judgment, but not of logical procedure, which is in both cases the same. Every other conception of the judgment, which should make it consist, not of a historical judgment, but of heaven knows what sort of measurement upon transcendental models, separated from the real world by a measurement of which the measure is extraneous to the measured, indeed (as though it were something of the other world) extraneous to the real itself, runs against insuperable contradictions, and makes judgment arbitrary and history grotesque ; history would thus have value, not in itself, but outside itself, enjoying it as a loan from others, a gracious concession. But even these contradictions cannot appear in all their crudity, nor the opposite theory in all its unshakable truth, save from what will be seen further on, and we must here be satisfied with the enunciation.

Its logic. In order to avoid repetition, we must refer to the analysis of the single or historical judgment already given and assume its result, namely, that it is the only judgment in which there is a true and proper distinction between subject and predicate, and that it is composed of an intuitive element (subject) and of an intellectual element (predicate). In like manner the practical judgment is not possible without a clear representation of the act to be judged and a conception not less clear of what the practical act is in its universality and in its particular forms, and so on, specifying in its various subforms and possibilities of individuation. The judgment is the compenetration of the two elements, the historical synthesis which establishes : Peter has accomplished a useful act in tilling a piece of land of such and such dimensions; Paul has accomplished an action that is not useful in opening a new manufactory of boots, more costly and not better than those already on the market ; —Pope Leo III. acted wisely, as custodian of the universal character of the Church of Rome, in consecrating Charles the Frank emperor, thus restoring the empire of the West ;—Louis XVI. acted foolishly in not deciding upon a prompt and profound change of the French political constitution, and in allowing himself to be afterwards dragged unwilling whither he had not known how to go of his own will. And so on. There are therefore two ways of sinning against the exactitude of the practical judgment: either by not having exact information as to the content of the volitional act to be judged and understood, or by not having an exact criterion of judgment. The first of these errors can be exemplified by those judgments that are so frequently pronounced, without knowledge as to the true sequence of events or without placing oneself in the precise conditions in which the person to be judged found himself. Hence it happens not less often, that when the facts are really known, the precise conditions understood, and the defence of the accused has been heard, the judgment must be altered. A cause of the second error is the substitution (likewise a very common occurrence) of one category of judgment for the other, as when a moral act is praised and admired for its cleverness, or the gestures and the felicitous utterance of a practical man are praised, as though it were a question of judging an actor or reciter. As in art, so in life, differences of judgment arise, not so much from difference of understanding, as from these oscillations and undue transpositions of judgments and concepts.

It is likewise superfluous to enter into disputes as to the absoluteness or relativity of the practical judgment, because these have been superseded by the concept of the historical judgment, which is *both absolute and relative* : absolute for the categories that it applies, relative for the matter, always new, to which it applies them.

Importance of the practical judgment. The importance of the practical judgment for practical life is of the greatest, and when we are warned : *nolite judicare* or *noli nimium judicare*, what are meant are not true acts of judgment, but certain psychical conditions, which reveal slight spiritual seriousness.   And the importance is of the greatest, precisely because the nature of the judgment is historical, and as we know already, historical knowledge, knowledge, that is, of actual situations, is the basis of future actions. For this reason every man who is strongly voli-tional is continually submitting himself and others to judgment ; for this reason we feel the need of talking to others about our own actions, in order to be upheld by the spirit of others in forming a just judgment.   This is the origin of such social institutions as the confessional, or of poems such as the *Divina Commedia*.   The only

judgment without meaning is that *final judgment*
made in the valley Jehoshaphat,• because what
object can there be in giving oneself the trouble
of judging a world looked upon as ended? We
judge in order to continue to act, that is, to live,
and when universal life is at an end, judgment
is vain (vain praise or paradise, vain cruelty or
hell).

The value of the volitional act is therefore, *Difference*
between the
as has been demonstrated, in the act itself, and *practical*
judgment and
we must not expect and derive it from succession *the judgment*
of the event.
or event. The practical judgment always concerns the volitional act, the intention, the action
(which are all one), and never the result or
happening. With this distinction we annul one of
the most disputed, intricate, and difficult questions:
if it be possible to judge, or as they say, to try
history. Since we know well that judgment and
historical narrative coincide, we must reply in
general, as we have replied, in the affirmative.
We must in consequence deny all the absurd
claims of an objectivity, which is the irrealizable
aspiration to the abstention from thought and
from history itself. We must also deny to the
historian that frivolous privilege by which he
is allowed to judge, almost tolerating in him an
original sin or an incorrigible vice, provided

he clearly distinguish between the serious and the facetious, · between the narrative and the judgment, as though the distinction were ever possible. But the prejudice against those who make out a case against history on the ground that it should have happened in a manner different from what actually took place, and describe how this should have been, is well justified. Whoever possesses historical sense, or even simple good sense, cannot but agree to this. The question should in reality be asked differently, and in this manner : Is it correct to apply to history the categories of judgment that we apply to volitions and single acts? Is it correct to judge in a utilitarian or moral manner historical events and the whole course of history ? Rectified in these terms, the question becomes clear, and requires a negative answer. When we narrate artistic or philosophical, economic or ethical history, we place ourselves at the point of view of the individual activity. As we expose æsthetic or philosophical products, useful or moral actions, we judge them at the same time æsthetically, philosophically, economically, morally, and we know in every case if the action has been such as it ought. Who would hesitate to affirm that (at least as an affirmative method) the *Africa*

of Petrarch was not what he wished it to be,
a poetic work; or that Emmanuel Kant did
not succeed in establishing from his practical
postulates, according to his intention, the existence of a personal God and the immortality of
the soul; or that Themistocles behaved in an
undecided manner as regards Xerxes, not knowing how to resolve to sacrifice his ambitions to
the safety of Greece, nor to inflict a grave loss
upon his country, in order to satisfy his desire
for vengeance; or that Napoleon ignored the
rights of man, and behaved as one without
scruples, when he ordered the arrest and shooting
of the Duc d'Enghien?   But what can be the advantage of asking if the arrest of the Persian
expansion in Europe were a bad thing or a
good? if the creation of the Roman Empire
deserve blame? if the Catholic Church were
wrong in concentrating Western religion in herself? if the English revolution of the seventeenth
century, the French of the eighteenth, or the
Italian of the nineteenth, could have been
avoided? if Dante could have been born in our
day and have sung the Kantian rather than the
Thomist philosophy? if Michael Angelo might
have painted the victories of the modern industrial world, which Manzotti has made into a

ballet in his *Excelsior*, instead of the visions of the Last Judgment? Here we have before us, not individual spirits, whose work we examine in given circumstances, but facts that have happened, and these are the work, not of the individual, but of the Whole. They are (as has already been said) the work of God, and God is not to be judged, or rather He is to be judged, but not from the visual angle at which individual works and actions are to be judged. He is not to be judged as a poet or as a philosopher, as a statesman or a hero, as a finite being working in the infinite. The contemplation of His work is at the same time judgment. *Die Weltgeschichte das Weltgericht*: the history itself of the world is the judgment of the world, and in recounting the course of history, while not applying the judgment of the categories above indicated, which are inapplicable, we do, however, apply a judgment, which is that of necessity and reality. That which has been had to be; and that which is truly real is truly rational.

But we cannot give the justification of this supreme judgment, of this world-embracing judgment (we repeat the refrain), until further on. Let it suffice for the present that in discussing the practical judgment we have limited it to all that part of history which contemplates actions, that is, to individual activity, to biography and to the biographical element, which is the material of all history.   In it, the practical judgment is active and energetic, but is silent before the event, and every history is like an impetuous river of individual works, which flows into a sea, where it is immediately restored to calm serene.   The rush of actions and of their vicissitudes, of victory and of defeat, of wisdom and of folly, of life and of death, are set at rest in the solemn peace of the " historical event."

As we have distinguished the practical judg- *Progress of action and* ment from the judgment of the event, the *progress of Reality.* historical-individual from the historical-cosmic, so we must distinguish the concept of progress, as the progress which belongs to the volitional act and that which belongs to the event.   The concept of progress (according to the explanations given elsewhere) coincides with the concept of activity.   There is progress whenever an activity declares itself, whenever (not to leave the circle of the practical) we pass from irresolution to resolution, from conflict to the volitional synthesis, from suspense to action.   But the event, which is no longer action but result, that is to say, is action, not of the individual but of the Whole, is not to be judged with that concept of progress, and in it progress coincides with the fact.   That which follows chronologically, if it be truly real, represents a progress upon what precedes.   Even illness is progress, if there were a latent crisis of health, and getting over it gives rise to more vigorous health.   Even apparent regression (invasion of barbarians) is progress, if it lead to the ripening of a wider civilization. What is death for the individual is life for the Whole.—Hence the insipidity of the question, often proposed and still discussed by writers of treatises, whether there be practical progress, or as is said when limiting the question, moral progress.

From the individual point of view, at every new volitional act, practicality and the relative impulse of progress are once more born, and they are extinguished with that act, to be born again in a new one, and so on in a circle of infinite changes.   As to cosmic reality, we must declare, as in the previous example of the course of history, that it is itself progress (which is also confirmed by the positivist philosophy, when it declares that reality is evolved), but this is progress of reality and therefore progress without adjective, or at least without practical or moral adjective.

The intellectual element, which is constitutive in the practical judgment as in every other historical judgment, can also be called the philosophical element. Hence the consequence that a philosophy of the practical activity is a necessary condition of every practical judgment. This is another thesis of paradoxical appearance, which, however, it is not difficult to make plausible with suitable reflections, plausible at least to those who do not refuse to reflect. For what is philosophy but the thinking of the concept, and in this case the concept of the practical? The conclusion, then, that a philosophy is necessary for a judgment is irrefutable. The difficulty in admitting it comes from the false association of ideas, for which the sound of the word "philosophy" suggests the disputes of the schools, the treatise, the manual, or the academic lecture, whereas we should think of philosophy in all its extension and profundity, inborn in the human spirit (we have elsewhere called this *ingenuous philosophy*) before its more complicated forms. Every man has his own philosophy, more or less developed or rudimentary, more or less defective; no one is without any philosophy. The first judgment on the practical activity is already guided by the light of a philosophical concept,

Precedence of the philosophy of the practical over the practical judgment.

which, if it does not give a light, gives at least a glimmer, if not straight and certain, at the least undulating and tremulous, producing therefore tremulous and undulating judgments. Ingenuous philosophy and philosophy in the specific sense are not, therefore, separable from one another with a clear-cut distinction, and if there exist a disability in pronouncing a judgment as to many people and to many actions, that arises from difficulties consequent upon the philosophy of the time, which must first of all be solved, before passing to the effective judgment. Hence long researches into doctrine are sometimes necessary. Thus it is difficult to do justice to the work of a rebel or of a revolutionary, without first clearing away prejudices and understanding what a revolution is, and the relative value of what is called obedience to the existing order of things. Thus it would be naïve to condemn as faithless the Saxon regiments which deserted Napoleon on the field of Leipzig, or Marshal Ney, who returned to the service of Napoleon from that of Louis XVIII., unless we previously make clear the meaning and the limits of the political treaty and of the military oath, which cannot be the only unconditioned things in a world where nothing is unconditioned save the world itself.

From the recognized precedence of philosophy *Confirmation of the philosophical incapacity of the psychological method.* over the practical judgment arises the confirmation of the impossibility of the psychological method as the foundation of a Philosophy of the practical. Descriptive psychology is based upon practical facts historically ascertained, or upon practical judgments. Hence, by proceeding from particular to particular, it is not only incapable of exhausting the infinite and of attaining to the real universal, but by the very choice of particular examples, which should be the foundation of philosophical research relating to the practical, it is under the necessity of first possessing a concept of the practical. Hence it stands between Scylla and Charybdis, between a vicious *progressus ad infinitum* and a not less vicious circle.

In this way is eliminated the problem, monstrous from whatever point of view it may arise, as to the historical origin of the practical activity (economy or morality). If these activities be categories, which constitute fact and judge it reflected in the spirit, they cannot have arisen historically, as contingent facts. When we prove the historical origin of anything, with that very proof we destroy its universal value. The fears of certain moralists lest, with the indication of the historical origin of morality, its value should come to be denied, have therefore been wrongly mocked. Certainly, if morality had a historical origin, it would also have an end, like all historical formations, even the most grandiose, the Empire of the East or the Empire of the West, the Hunnish Empire of Attila or the Mongolian Empire of Gengiskhan. The fear manifested by the moralists in question was then an instinctive horror of the incorrect method of philosophical psychology, which now presupposes, now destroys the categories that it would wish to establish.

VII

THE PRACTICAL METHOD, RULES AND CASUISTRY

IN repeatedly rejecting the psychological method, *Justification of the psycho-logical method and of empirical and descriptive disciplines.* as at the end of the last chapter, we have been very careful to make use of a cautious phrase-ology. Thus we have employed such expressions as "psycho-philosophical method," "speculative-descriptive method," and the like, in order to make it quite clear that our hostility is directed against that mixture, or rather against its intro-duction into Philosophy, but is not directed against Psychology itself, that is, descriptive psychology. This psychology has always been practised, since the world was world, and we all practise it at every instant, and could not propose to banish it from the spirit, save at the risk of going mad.

If indeed we know that the true and proper knowledge of theoretical philosophy is resolved into the cycle of art, philosophy, and history, and that we possess no other means of knowing the individual, both ingenuous and reflective, outside the knowledge of the universal given by philosophy, then we also know that the spirit needs to arrange and to classify the infinite intuitions and perceptions given to it by art and history, and to reduce them to classes, the better to possess and to manipulate them. We also know that the method called *naturalistic or positive* performs this function, and that hence arise natural disciplines or sciences. These do not, as is the popular belief, deal only with so-called inferior reality (minerals, vegetables, and animals), but with all manifestations of reality, including those most strictly termed spiritual.

Thus we can at this point reduce to a more correct meaning a claim that has been usually maintained by those who have treated of the Practical and of the Ethical in our day. They demand that a science of the practical and of morality should be preceded by a wide historical inquiry and have a great mass of facts as its foundation. If such science be understood as a Philosophy of the practical and as an Ethic, such a demand is an irrational pretension, because the true relation is exactly the opposite : from philosophy to history, not from history to philosophy. But if, on the other hand, this science be understood as a naturalistic and empirical discipline, the claim is rational, because it is not possible to construct a discipline of that sort, save with material that has been historically verified.

The practical discipline that arranges in groups *Practical description* and classifies the spiritual facts concerning man, *and its literature.* is *Psychology*. But the writer or the professor is not the only psychologist. Man himself is a psychologist; even the savage constructs in some sort of way his psychology of types and classes. And to remain within the circle of volitional acts, their psychology or description by types has always existed. A conspicuous example of this was the Comedy of Menander or the New Comedy in Greece. This partly received and gave artistic form to the results of the observations of the moralists and partly served as material for the elaboration of treatises, to such an extent that the *Characters* of Theophrastus have been looked upon as a repertory or summary of theatrical types. In the *Rhetoric* of Aristotle, a whole book is devoted to a description of affections, passions, and habits. In modern times, Descartes lamented the insufficiency of ancient treatises on the subject, and presented as quite a new thing his *Traité des passions.* In this treatise, six *primitive* passions being distinguished (admiration, love, hate, desire, joy, and sadness), he maintained that all the others were derived from them: esteem, contempt, generosity, pride, humility, baseness, veneration, disdain, hope, fear, jealousy, certainty, desperation, irresolution, courage, hardihood, emulation, cowardice, terror, remorse, mockery, piety, satisfaction, repentance, favour, gratitude, indignation, anger, glory, shame, and so on. Spinoza, following the example of Descartes and correcting his theories, devoted the third part of his *Ethic* to the affections or passions, considering them *perinde ac si quaestio de lineis planis aut de corporibus esset.* Let it suffice to mention the *Anthropologia* of Kant among the other most celebrated treatises upon the argument.

Extension of practical description. But although we have recorded as examples these general treatises on the passions, it would be impossible to continue the enumeration, because descriptive psychology is carried out, so to speak, with the widest divergences and is infinitely subdivided. An ample bibliography would not suffice to catalogue all the books dealing with this discipline. These are sometimes arranged in chronological divisions (Psychology of the Renaissance, of the eighteenth century, of the Middle Ages, even including prehistoric man!). Sometimes they contain geographical divisions (Psychology of the Englishman, of the Frenchman, of the Russian, of the Japanese, and so on), with subdivisions according to regions. Sometimes they combine the two methods (Psychology of the ancient Greek, of the Roman of the Decadence), and sometimes according to their psychical content (Psychology of the priest, of the soldier, of the politician, of the poet, of the man of science), and so on. And when the treatises that bear a title of the kind above mentioned had been catalogued, it would be also necessary to trace a great mass of descriptive psychology (and of the best sort) in the books of historians, novelists, dramatists, in memoirs and confessions, in maxims and advice for the conduct of life, in the sketches of satirists and caricaturists. And when all these had been catalogued (a very difficult task), it would be necessary to take account of all the other psychology, which, formed in the spirit of individuals who are not writers, is poured forth in speech. This is found, but in small part, in collections of proverbs. It would also be necessary not to neglect (an altogether desperate enterprize) everything that each one of us does and forgets and substitutes continually in life, according to his own needs and experiences. *Tantae molis* would be a complete account, precisely because psychological construction, having for its object actions and individuals in action, is of such common use.

Normative knowledge or rules: their nature.

There is another class of mental forms intimately connected with Psychology, and of this also we have denied the justification in the foregoing chapters, but only in the philosophical field, and not at all outside it. These are the *norms*, or *normative* knowledge and science, *maxims*, *rules*, *and precepts*. In truth, if philosophy, which commands and wills and judges, when its task is on the contrary to understand willing and commanding, and to make possible correct judgment — if such a philosophy be a contradiction in terms, there is yet nothing to prevent our taking the psychological classes, of which we have indicated the formation, and separating them from one another, according as they do or do not lead to certain other classes, which are called *ends* and are *abstract ends*. This is done when those classes are selected which are more efficacious for practical action. Psychological classes and rules are therefore the same, save that in the second the character possessed by knowledge as prior to action is placed in relief, that is to say, its *technical* character.   This is proved by the easy convertibility of rules into psychological observations, and of the latter into the former.   It suffices to add the imperative to the first and to remove it from the second.   " Do everything so as to seem good, for that helps in many things ; but since false opinions do not last, you will have difficulty in seeming good for a long period, if you are not so in reality."   That is a rule of Francesco Guicciardini[1] (or rather of the father of Guicciardini, quoted by him).   Now if we transfer this proposition from the imperative to the indicative mood and remove the predicate of exhortation, we have a mere psychological observation : " To seem good helps in an infinite number of things ; but since false opinions do not last, it is difficult to seem good for long, unless one really be so."   Here is a psychological observation of Vico upon seeming and being : " It happens naturally that man speaks of nothing but what he affects to be and is not."[2]   This can be turned into a maxim : " Watch yourselves, in

---

[1] (ɪ) *Ricordi politici e civili*, n. xliv. (in *Opere inedite* (2), Firenze, 1857 ; p. 97).

[2] *Scritti inediti*, ed. Del Giudice, Napoli, 1862, p. 12.

order that by talking too much of a given advantage, you may not let it be seen clearly that you do not possess it." Or in relation to moral classes it can be turned thus: "Try to be that which you would like to appear to others," and so. on.

Usefulness of rules.   Of rules it can be said that they do not possess absolute value. This is to be found written at the beginning of one of the best books of rules: *Peu de maximes sont vraies à tous égards* (Vauvenargues), and he might have said, "no maxim"; for if it were ever possible to produce one that was absolutely true, by that alone would it be demonstrated not to be a true maxim. But criticism prevails against the distortion of empirical rules into philosophical principles, or against the confusion between the psychological and the speculative methods, to which attention has already been drawn. If this distortion be not committed, then rules are altogether innocuous. Not only are they innocuous, they are indispensable. Each of us is constantly making them for use in his own life. To live without rules would be impossible. Certainly, the man of action makes no practical rule, nor does he indicate how we should will and act in definite circumstances, nor does the poet make any rule of Poetic. Guicciardini himself, whom we have just quoted, and who formulated stupendous maxims, warns us : " These memories are rules that can be written down in books ; but special cases, which, since they have a different cause, ask a different treatment, can ill be written down *elsewhere than in the book of discretion.*" Action depends upon the quickness of the eye, upon the perception of the situation historically given, which has never occurred before, and never will occur again, precisely identical. But it is useful to possess these types of actions to encourage and of actions to avoid, in order to sharpen the attention and to find one's way in the world of action, to facilitate and to discipline the examination of the concrete fact. If, therefore, individual rules are more or less transitory, the formation of rules is immortal.

The condition of literature in recent times would seem to be in disagreement with this affirmation, since as a fact there is a great falling off in the appearance of books of rules, compared with the enormous mass that remains in our libraries as an inheritance of the past. At one time rules of conduct were compiled for everything, not only for the moral life, in

The literature of rules and its apparent decadence.

the multiplication of treatises relating to vice
and virtue, to merits and to sins, to things good
and evil, to duties and to rights, dividing these
and entering into minutiae, and again, summaries,
catechisms, and various "decalogues," relating
to every part of life. The literature of the
Cinquecento gives rules even for the procuress
and the courtesan, in most elegant little books,
which bear the names of Piccolomini and of
Aretino. In this same century, too, Ignatius
of Loyola formulated rules for "tying up"
the will, and for the reduction of the docile
individual *perinde ac cadaver*, for the ends of
"sanctity." We must further remark that all
rules, including those on poetry and the arts,
have at bottom a practical character. That
is to say, they are directed to the will, if
only as intermediary. Thus it is necessary to
add to the great mass of practical rules the un-
numbered and innumerable treatises of Grammar,
Rhetoric, Poetry of the figurative arts, of music,
of dancing, and so on. But it is a fact that
there are now hardly any treatises containing
rules, either for morality, politics, or for the arts.
Has the world by chance become learned on the
subject, through inherited aptitude, or rather has
the inutility of rules been discovered?

Neither the one nor the other. The rules still live in books and treatises; they have only changed their literary form. In literature they have reabsorbed that imperative which they used at first to display and to boast of, not only mentally but literally. That has been made possible by the already established convertibility of rules into psychological classes. Hence in modern times the literary form of the psychological observation is preferred to that of rules. This was indeed redundant, pedantic, and at the same time ingenuous, as for instance in the Italian Seicento. It is difficult to restrain a smile when reading the many books on what was called the *reason of State*, elaborated by the Italians of that day and imitated by foreigners, especially Spaniards and Germans. Those *arcana imperii*, those "secret strokes," those impostures, mysteriously inculcated on the printed page, are a true and real æsthetic contradiction. The eighteenth century therefore began to give up this form of treatise, and as it happens that men are accustomed to attribute to moral virtue that which is necessity or virtue of another kind, the writers of that century boasted of the moral progress which had set them free from the pernicious and immodest maxims of the "reason of State."

It is very amusing to assist at the acts of repulsion and of exorcism, which a man like the Abbé Galiani believes himself obliged to make in his treatise *Dei doveri dei principi neutrali* (1782). When, having amply discussed this matter from the point of view of morality, he goes on to discuss it from the point of view of politics and of the reason of State, he despatches it in a few pages, abhorring, as he says, that "insidious and wicked science" which formed "the delight, first of Italian and then of almost all European minds of the fifteenth and seventeenth centuries." He protests at every step that he is "tired of repeating and of developing teachings of cunning and wickedness." But what the Abbot Galiani really abhorred was the robed scholastic treatment of a matter that he who was termed *Machiavellino* by his French friends, and declared that he did not admit in politics anything but *le machiavélisme pur, sans mélange, cru, vert, dans toute son âpreté*,[1] handled with very different ability and elegance in his conversations in Parisian *salons* and in his witty letters to Madame d'Épinay. The rules of the eighteenth century are to be sought in the speeches, essays, political opuscules, tragedies,

---

[1] Letter to the d'Épinay, 5th September 1772.

plays dealing with the life of citizens, fiction, history, and books of memoirs. If Aretino and Piccolomini provided for the necessities of the respectable courtesans and procuresses of the Cinquecento, in the Settecento, Giacomo Casanova constructed the type of the perfect adventurer. He began with the rules to be followed as a system of life, the *se laisser aller au gré du vent qui pousse,* and passed to those that were more special and yet fundamental, such as that one should have no scruples *de tromper des étourdis, des fripons et des sots,* because they *défient l'esprit* and *on venge l'esprit quand on trompe un sot.* There should be still less scruple in deception in affairs of love, for, *pour ce qui regarde les femmes, ce sont des tromperies réciproques, qu'on ne met pas en ligne de compte; car, quand l'amour s'en mêle, on est ordinairement dupe de part et d'autre.*[1] Let us leave to the reader to investigate, if he please, the rules of life that are concealed beneath the most modern forms of literature; these are a continuous, if not always beneficent, guide for daily life.

Another circumstance that has led to the belief *Relation between the arts (collections of rules) and philosophical doctrines.* in the disappearance of books of rules is the observation that from those books dealing with

[1] *Mémoires,* ed. Paris, Garnier, s.a., i pp. 3-4.

the so-called *arts*, there has come to be a treatment of the philosophy of their subject-matter, in which those treatises have been dissolved. Thus from Poetics and Rhetorics has come Æsthetic, from Grammatic the Philosophy of language, from the Art of teaching and of reasoning Logic and Gnoseology, from the historical Art, Historic, from the Arts of economic government, the Science of Economy, from the treatises on Natural Law, the Philosophy of Law.

When such philosophies, then, had appeared, treatises upon the Arts seemed to have become superfluous, and to this is attributed the cause of their diminution or disappearance. But although it be impossible not to recognize the historical process above described from books on the arts to books of systems, it is necessary to be careful to interpret it exactly and not to confuse it with a passing from empiria to philosophy. Thus it will be seen that the part absorbed and dissolved in philosophy has been precisely those philosophical attempts that were mingled with such collections of rules and precepts. For it was very natural that the writers who put them together and had ideas as to what should be done and what avoided, were often led to investigate the principles from which sprung the particular rules. Believing that they were strengthening, they really came to surpass them, that is, they passed unwittingly from one form of treatment to another, from Psychology to Philosophy. But not even here has empiricism been refined into philosophy (a refinement which, strictly speaking, is impossible), but a more perfect philosophy has been substituted for one less perfect. The dissolution, then, has not been of the rules, but of that imperfect philosophy, a chemical process which has left the rules in what they possess of original as residuum. Hence their persistence, and indeed the impossibility that they should not persist, side by side with the most pure and perfect of philosophies.

Casuistic has had the same fate as the rules, and was also at one time responsible for a very copious literary production. Now it is cultivated as literature only by a few Jesuits, who carry on the glories of Escobar and of Sanchez, read only by priests preparing themselves for the post of confessor, whose studies are based for the most part upon old books (such as the *Theologia moralis* of the Neapolitan Sant' Alfonso de' Liguori). At one time Casuistic was not confined only to profane or theological morality, to the *casus conscientiae*. There were also books of

Casuistic: its nature and utility.

casuistry composed for all aspects of life, for
politics, for the life of the courtier ("the Wise Man
at Court"), for the art of love. When the literary
form of rules fell into discredit, that of Casuistic
fell with it. But this does not mean that it is
dead; it lives and will live as long as rules live.
For Casuistic is nothing but the process of reasoning by which rules are made always more precise,
passing from more general cases to those more
particular, so that no one will ever be able to
do without them.—If we take for rule of life this
maxim : to avoid scientific polemics, because they
constitute a waste of time, adding little to the
progress of knowledge; in what way must we
behave if a polemic be such that it enables us
to gain on the one hand the time it makes us
lose on the other? Shall we maintain the
general rule, or shall we waive it on this occasion,
if for no other reason than to give variety to our
occupations? And how shall we behave if not
only we retrieve the time lost but avoid losing
more time in the future? Shall we wish to enter
upon the polemic at once? But if our future be
looked upon as uncertain, if we be far advanced
in years or in bad health, will it not be better to
renounce the uncertain gain of the future for the
certain gain of the present?—This is a very

simple example of Casuistic, which a critic and
writer (let us suppose that he is the writer of these
pages) is obliged to propose to himself and to
solve.   Naturally, no Casuistic will ever furnish
the concrete solution (which is the only one that
counts), since, as has been said, no rule can ever
furnish it.   Rules and casuistry do not reach
the individuality *omnimodo determinata*, which is
the historical situation ; yet if Casuistic aid my
action, this will always differ from that, as concrete from abstract ; or better, my action will
always truly possess the form, the definiteness
that abstract casuistry cannot possess.   Woe to
practical men who rely upon collections of maxims
and casuistical reasonings, and woe to those who
rely upon them.   Those who argue at length
upon practical matters and draw subtle distinctions, are to be avoided in the world of affairs and
in the world of action.   If they have not yet provoked some disaster, they are on the road to
doing so now.   This, at least, is a good rule ;
like the supreme rule (which is not a rule
but philosophical truth), namely, that we must
abandon rules, that is, face the individual case,
which, as such, is always irregular.

But if a further proof be wanted of the neces-   *Jurisprudence*
sity and perpetuity of maxims and of casuistry,   *as casuistry.*

observe how these also persist in literary form, as laws, where this form is not eliminable. *Laws*, as we have seen, are not simple rules, but are based upon *formulae of rules*, and must of necessity make explicit in them decisions as to doing and not doing. Jurisprudence is the Casuistic of law, or all the labour of so-called interpretation, which is at bottom the excogitation of new rules. All know that not only is Jurisprudence not of itself legislative, but that it cannot even determine the volitional act of the Statesman, nor the sentence, or decision upon the particular case, a decision which the judge creates upon each occasion. But no one would seriously think of suppressing the work and the function of those *casuists*, or judicial experts, a function which, since it has always existed and continues to exist, cannot but answer to a social need. It is possible to predict a form of social life, less complicated and weighty, in which that function would have less scope, but whatever be the case as regards this prediction, the casuistry of judicial experts will continue so long as there are laws and rules, that is to say, always.

VIII

CRITIQUE OF THE INVASIONS BY PHILOSOPHY OF THE DOMAIN OF PRACTICAL DESCRIPTION AND OF ITS DERIVATIVES

In demonstrating the legitimacy and necessity of practical description and of its derivatives, Regolistic and Casuistic, we have not fulfilled, as it were, our whole knightly duty, which binds us to that discipline, which we have been obliged to maltreat so exceedingly, and shall further maltreat, when it has been or shall be presented as a philosophical method. It is now necessary to defend its existence against the invasion of philosophy, or rather of philosophers. We must make it obvious that if the empiricists and psychologists, who swell themselves out to philosophers, are bunglers, those too are bunglers who claim to solve empirical questions philosophically. Perhaps they are bunglers less worthy of pardon, because it is part of philosophy to know itself clearly, and consequently its own limits.

First form: tendency to generalize. The first bad effect that philosophy has upon practical description is the tendency to change it from description and collection of particular descriptions into something that has the air of generality and comprehensiveness. Because, if practical description be closely connected with the historical conditions of definite individuals and societies and with their wants, the more specific and near to the concrete it is, the better it will be, and the more useless by as much as it goes wandering toward the general. We owe to the evil influence of philosophy those verbose treatises upon psychological classes, such as virtue, duties, things good, affections, passions, and human types, to read which nourishes less than fresh water, which at least refreshes.

Let him who wishes to be convinced compare the books of rules and observations that we owe to men of experience and to men of the world, such as the *Ricordi* of Guicciardini, the *Maximes* of Larochefoucauld, and the *Oraculo Manual* of Balthazar Gracian, with the *Traité des passions* of Descartes, with that section of the *Ethica* of Spinoza that relates to this matter, with the *Anthropologia* and the *Doctrine of Virtue* of Kant (we prefer to record great names). He will then see on whose side is the advantage, an advantage of originality, of importance, and even of style, which is in this case a revelation. Those books by philosophers contain for the most part definitions of vocabulary and of words which there is no need to define, because everybody knows them to such an extent that the definitions, rather than make them more clear, make them obscure. Who, for example, can resist the philosophical triviality of the *Aphorisms for the Wisdom of Life* of Arthur Schopenhauer? Take the trouble to open a book to learn that good things are to be divided into personal, wealth and imagination, or reputation, and that the first (such as good health and a gay temperament) are pre-eminent over the others. Do we not learn more and with greater rapidity and efficacy from such proverbs as "God helps the merry man"? It is superfluous to observe that those books, in so far as they generalize, can never attain to philosophy. They remain at bottom more or less historical.

The good and generous wine of the born psychologists and precept-makers is diluted in a great deal of water, but that water, however much there be of it, never becomes pure and is always discoloured and of an unpleasant taste. Thus in classifications of ancient Ethic the

Historical elements persisting in generalizations.

idea of "virtue" or of "good" was announced
as the most important, in Christian Ethic that
of "duty," in the same way as in ancient Ethic
the political character was dominant, in the
modern the individualistic, according to the
different character of the corresponding civilizations. Historical elements differentiate the Ethic
of Aristotle, impregnated with sane Greek life,
from that of the Stoics, in which is foretold
the decadence of the antique world and the
germs of the future discovered (for instance,
cosmopolitanism, which precedes the Christian
idea of the unity of the human race). The four
Platonic virtues retain the name, but are filled
with a new content, in the four cardinal virtues of
the Christian Ethic ; the seven deadly sins are
not to be explained in all their settemplicity
without the ascetic ideal of the Middle Ages.

Among the various writers of treatises, the
foreground is filled, now with the idea of effort
or of duty, now with that of enjoyment and satisfaction ; ideas are now despotic masters, now
smiling friends ; the dominant idea is in turn
that of justice, of benevolence, of enthusiasm, and
so on. In the systems of Catholic Ethic are
reflected political absolutism and semi-feudal
economy ; in those of Protestant Ethic, constitu-

tionalism, liberalism, the industrial and capitalistic
world; a strict probity, not indeed without
utilitarianism, and a hardness of heart, not indeed
without austerity. Modern Ethic is concerned
with property, with the struggle of classes, with
proletarianism and communism. These are all
historical facts and as such most worthy of
attention, but for that very reason they should
be examined in all their force and value and
not through the medium of the pale categories
of a universal doctrine, which they disturb and
falsify and by which they are very often disturbed
and falsified. Whoever undertakes to write
general treatises upon the passions, upon the
virtues, and upon the other practical classes,
will always show the signs of his time in the
categories that he establishes, and the result will
be at once banal and empirical, that is to say,
badly empirical.

But hitherto the chief ill has been that useless *Second form:*
literary
and tiresome books are written. Matters begin *union of*
philosophy
to look graver when an approach is attempted *and empiria.*
between philosophical theories and empirical
classifications and they are united in one treatise,
as the *general* part and the *particular* part, the
abstract and the *concrete* part, the *theoretical* and
the *historical* part. We do not wish to refuse

recognition to an occasionally just sense of the
intimate relations between philosophy and history
as among the motives that lead to such unions,
the first of which flows into the second, revives
it and is by it in turn revived.   But the history,
to which philosophy applies the torch, is all
history in its palpitating reality; it is history
represented by all histories that historians have
written and will write, and also by those that
they have not written and will not write.   The
history offered by these empirical descriptions
is only a very small part of history and (what
is worse) abstract and mutilated.   This would,
however, be an injury of not too grave a nature,
even at this point, provided the incongruity were
limited to literary unfitness; in which case, it is
true, would be added to inutility the ugliness of
a union capricious and artificial, but fortunately
extrinsic.   But by means of that extrinsic
approach, the way is opened to the attempt
at an intrinsic approach, and thus to the third
form of the undue invasion of practical description by philosophy, which constitutes the *morbus
philosophico-empiricus* in all its harmfulness.

Third form:
attempt to
place them in
intimate
connexion.
The attempt at intrinsic approach takes place
when empirical classes are placed in connection
with the philosophical concepts or categories,

with pure thought. Nearly all philosophers
have fallen into this error, since it is very
natural that they should not have wished to
leave a *hiatus* between the first and second
parts of their books of Philosophy of the practical, between the general and particular parts,
and that they should have striven to connect
the one with the other by passing logically from
the concepts of the first to those of the second.
The mistake was indubitably increased owing
to their small degree of clearness as to the
logical nature of the two orders of concepts
(concepts and pseudo-concepts), which is funda-
mentally diverse, and we shall not further insist
upon this matter.

Rather let us note that sometimes there has *Science of the*
practical and
been something rational in the minds of those *Metaphysic :*
various
who have required the Science of the practical *significations.*
or Ethic to be constructed independently of
all Metaphysic. In truth, that programme of the
independence of the Science of the practical or
Ethic of Metaphysic has had various meanings
that it will be well to enumerate briefly. The
first meaning was that the Science of the
practical, in so far as it was philosophy, should
be independent of the *aggregate* of the philosophical system (Metaphysic). In this case

the claim was not acceptable, as we shall see, because it was at variance with the nature itself of philosophy, which is unity. The second meaning was that the Practical, as science, should be kept remote from every form of faith, or feeling or fancifulness (which has sometimes been called "Metaphysic"); and in this case the proposition was inexpugnable, however contestable may have seemed the opportuneity of the meaning given to that word. The third meaning was that the Science of the practical, in so far as it was descriptive, should stand by itself, in order to afford a base for philosophical induction. Use was here made of the erroneous idea, already rejected several times, of philosophy as an intensification of the psychological method, or as a carrying of it on. But in a fourth sense, it was desired finally to withdraw practical description from the perilous care of the philosophers, and it seems to us that with this fourth meaning was expressed a very just demand.

Damaging consequences of the invasions. What are, in fact, the consequences of the care that philosophers have bestowed upon practical description? We would not wish to use an over-coloured simile, but what happens is very much what would happen if a man were given a baby to suckle. He would press it violently against his dry and arid breast, incapable of nourishing, but well capable of tormenting it. Philosophy, when it approaches the empirical classes, will either begin to criticize their distinctions and abolish them, reducing several classes to one, and then reducing the reduced classes in their turn to a less number, until none are left at all and it finds itself in company with the universal philosophical principle alone, or alone with itself;—or it will contrive to preserve them as classes, deducing them philosophically, and will thus make them rigid and absolute, removing from them that elasticity and fluidity which they derive from their historical character, and converting them from useful classes that they were, into bad philosophemes, concepts contradictory in themselves.

Both these consequences have occurred, for the books of philosophers are full of examples, now of destruction, now of corruption of the empirical classes of the Practical. The treatment of the doctrine of the virtues or of so-called natural rights affords examples of destruction. Striving to distinguish courage from prudence, or justice from benevolence, or on the other hand, egotism from wickedness, they ended by

ɪa. Dissolution of the empirical concepts.

K

recognizing that true courage is prudence, true prudence courage; that benevolence is justice, justice benevolence; that egotism is wickedness, wickedness egotism, and so on. In this way, all the virtues became one, the virtue of being virtuous, the will for the good, duty. In like manner, by giving philosophical form to the natural rights of life, of liberty, of culture, of property, and so on, they ended by recognizing that all rights merge in one single right, which is that of existence; which latter, indeed, is not a right, but a fact. The passions were reduced from seventy or eighty classes to six or seven fundamental, but these six or seven were in their turn reduced to two only, pleasure and pain, and of these two it was finally discovered that they constituted one only—life, which is pleasure and pain together. But virtues, rights, passions, possess value in practical description only in so far as they are multiplicity —their value is always plural, never singular. To reduce them to a single class signifies to annul them, as to blow upon a candle signifies to extinguish it and to remain in darkness; darkness is to be understood as without empirical light. Now the philosopher should certainly destroy empirical ideas, but only in so far as

they present themselves as philosophical distinctions, that is, in so far as they are empirico
philosophical: and in that case it suffices him
to show that they are empirical, without
pretending to annul them in their own domain
also: *debellare superbos*, but *parcere subjectis*;
that is, he should spare strangers who remain
quietly in their own house.

It might seem desirable to pass in review *Examples:*
all these empirical distinctions and questions *war and peace, property and*
which the philosophers have thought that they *communism, and the like.*
had satisfactorily solved, when they had, on the
contrary, passed beyond them. But the theme
is inexhaustible, and we cannot here give even
a rich selection, comprising the most frequent
and important cases. We must limit ourselves
to brief mention.—People discuss every day:
whether war be an evil, and if it be possible
to abolish it; if community of goods should
take the place of private property; if rational
government be that of liberty or of authority,
of democracy or aristocracy, of anarchism or state
organization; whether the State should be in
the Church or the Church in the State, or side
by side and independent; if freedom of thought
should be admitted or restrained; if instruction
should be free or undertaken by the State;

and other similar problems. Now behold the
philosopher applying himself to the study of these
ideas. Having tested them, he is astonished that
people can find in them opposing terms, and
make them argument for dispute. In truth (he
says), war is intrinsic to reality, and peace is
peace in so far as by making an end of one
war it prepares another; as Socrates demonstrated
in the *Phaedo*, when, scratching his leg in the
place where it had been pressed by the chain,
he realized that he could not have experienced
that pleasure had he not previously experienced
the pain. Nor is property different from communism : the individual declares himself by an
individual taking possession of things and
becoming their owner; but by so doing he
enters into relations and into communion with
other individuals, and does business with them.
And liberty excludes subjection the less, since
sub lege libertas; nor does aristocracy exclude
democracy, since the true aristocrat is the bearer
of those universal values that are the substance
of democracy ; hence the more we are aristocratic
the more we are democratic, and inversely.
Nor does anarchism exclude State organization,
because a collection of men, however free we
suppose it to be, must nevertheless govern

itself according to some laws, and these laws are the State. Then, the ideal State, being the best government of men for their perfectionment, both material and spiritual, accomplishes the work of the Church itself, which is neither above, nor below, nor beside the State, because it is the State. Thus in like manner, no one can grant or abolish freedom of thought, since thought is by definition freedom, and the restraint is thought itself, because liberty coincides with necessity. And finally State instruction cannot but correspond with rational demands, and the free instruction of citizens, if it be really so and not arbitrary and capricious, will be the same as that of the State, or will be changed into the instruction of the State.

Passing to other orders of fact that are less political, but are also argument for practical *Other examples.* discussions, we shall refer to the so-called conflicts between duty or interest, as symbolized in the legendary Titus Manlius, when offered the alternative *aut reipublicae aut sui suorumque obliviscendi*;—or to the so-called question of the two moralities, private and public, in support of which the not legendary Camillo Cavour said in 1860, that if he had done in his private interest what he had done for Italy, he would have deserved the galleys ;—or we can refer to questions of classification, and ask whether the kind of man who is socially harmless should be placed side by side with the criminal ;—or to those others, famous in Casuistic, relating to capital punishment, homicide, suicide, lies, whether and when they should be permitted, and other similar questions. Here, too, the philosopher will smilingly observe that duties and interests can never be in conflict, because in every given case duty is always one only, and interest is always one only, that of the given case ;—he will deny that there is one public and one private morality, because in man, the private person and the citizen, family relations, or those of friendship, and those of political life, are inseparable and indistinguishable ;—that every man is bad and good, inoffensive and criminal, and that in the so-called criminal there must also be the non-criminal, if he be given the name of man ;—that every punishment is a punishment of death, that is, it causes something to die, and that it is impossible to find a clear distinction between shutting a man up in prison and thus taking from him a more or less large slice of physical life, and taking it from him altogether by hanging or shooting

him; — that homicide, as such, is so little a
crime that in war it is a duty to commit it;
— that a lie, which is silence as to what one
knows, is in itself so innocent that no one in the
world, save a foolish prater, tells all he knows,
and that if it be admitted that one can and
should be silent, that is to say, let others be
deceived by our silence (though this is eloquent),
there is no reason for not admitting that we
can also betray them with speech (often less
eloquent), as is done with children in order
to send them to bed, and with sick persons
in order to comfort them ;—that, finally, culpable
suicide is not the material act of depriving
oneself of physical life (a thing done without
incurring blame, and indeed with praise and
glory, by those who sacrifice themselves for
others in war, in epidemics, in dangers of all
sorts, and by every one who consumes his own
vital strength in a worthy cause), but the killing
of the moral life in oneself.

In all these answers to questions, we have *Misunder-*
standing on
not made our imaginary philosopher commit *the part of*
philosophers.
any blunder; we have indeed put into his mouth
things that we believe to be all of them most
true and irrefutable, because we believe them
ourselves. And we hold that it is necessary

to profess them against those who arbitrarily make questions philosophical whose terms are not philosophical. But when the philosopher offers those solutions to the empirical disputants, he behaves like him who, hearing a speech in a language of which he knows little, makes a reply that is in itself most reasonable, but without relation to the previous speech. The empiricist, if he have studied philosophy, will be able to reply, as did King Theodore, worn with misery, in the old *opéra bouffe* of the Abbé Casti, to him who recalls to him the miseries suffered by Marius, Themistocles, and Darius :—

> Good my son, I know them well,
>> For I have heard these tales before ;
> But just at present, truth to tell,
>> 'Tis money interests me more.

Historical significance of the aforesaid questions.

Money, that is, ready money to spend in definite situations historically given, in order to find one's way in them ; for all those questions are without universal signification, but have arisen from political and individual problems, to which they do and must belong. Certainly they are insoluble in the abstract, and this is the defect, or rather the nature of empirical questions, which, if they admitted of rigorous solution, would not be any longer empirical. Therefore it is a foolish thing to discuss them philosophically, as is seen in the conspicuous example of certain casuistical enquiries (the homicide of the unjust aggressor, the lie, incest, etc.) which have been treated by nearly all philosophers and have been dragged about for centuries in discussions on Ethic, although every century has left them at the same point as they were in the one preceding.

But if it be not possible to solve, we can at least *state* them in abstract terms, in the same way as drill and the sham-fight are abstract, though certainly of use when the battle is really fought. We can and we should bear in mind these abstract solutions, in order that we may be the better able to solve a series of concrete cases, which are not identical, certainly, because identical cases do not exist, but more or less similar, and therefore require solutions that are more or less similar.—Can war be done away with? This question refers not to the elimination of the category "war," but to the possibility or the reverse of avoiding in the twentieth century and in European countries that empirical war which is waged with cannons and cruisers, that costs milliards when it is not waged, and tens of milliards when it is waged, and out of which the conqueror comes conquered. It is well understood that some form of war will always continue, because war is inherent to life.—Can private property be done away with? This does not mean to ask if it be possible to prevent man from taking possession of things, of his food, or of the material that he requires for dress, or from inhabiting a house; but whether it be possible to alter, to the advantage of mankind, the proportion that now obtains between production with private capital and production with collective capital, giving the preference to the latter.

And so on, for it would be tiresome to continue to state the historical problems that are grouped beneath each of the recorded formulæ, which indeed are easily to be found. Thus when we absolutely forbid the telling of lies, as indecorous and degrading, as that which severs the ties of human community and of reciprocal faith, as the vice (said Herbart) that has the special faculty of stirring up against it all the five moral ideas—justice, benevolence, equity, perfection, and internal liberty—the intention is to forbid what is usually called lying; but it is certainly not intended to institute a speculative enquiry as to the relation between knowing and making known, between the theoretic act of thought and the practical act of its communication to other individuals. Thus again, the prohibition of suicide has in view suicide through egoism, which is the most frequent form, and it is therefore useless to identify this with the universal relation between death and life, and with the proposition that life is preserved by means of death. Thus too, finally, the conception of the delinquent has been a beneficent rectification of common prejudices relating to the efficacy of certain laws and penalties applied to certain classes of individuals who are led to crime as though through unrestrainable natural tendency. For the rest, the wisdom of life teaches us usually to take individuals as we find them, with their virtues and vices, and without claiming to set them violently right, and to remake them from top to bottom. We should rather adapt them in the best way possible for our own ends, or for those of society. This does not, however, imply that they are fixed beings, and that each of those classes is heterogeneous in respect of the others. If, with the help of a foolish positivist philosophy, we make of the idea of the delinquent something necessary, a natural being, as it is called, confounding naturalistic with natural and incorrectly hypostasizing gnoseological procedure, then, and then alone, are we right in reacting and in denying.

2a. False deduction of the empirical from the philosophical.

And yet those solutions of philosophers, who think that they are solving empirical questions by annulling or ignoring them, do not yet represent the worst that happens when philosophy usurps the function of empiria. Such misunderstanding, such hardness of hearing, may be proof of a spirit so energetically directed to universals that it is unable to see anything else, and may even for that reason possess some sympathetic quality. The worst of the worst is the entering upon empirical questions, not in order to annul, but to take sides in them and to solve them philosophically.

Affirmations relating to the contingent changed into philosophemes.

This cannot be done, save by supporting empirical concepts with rigorous and philosophical concepts, confounding the one with the other by a trick of thought, and sometimes of words, making use of synonyms and homonyms, and pronouncing in the name of philosophy arbitrary solutions suggested only by caprice or self-interest. This is the complete corruption, alike of philosophy and of empiria. Not satisfied

with making practical classes follow philosophical
concepts of the practical, it is then sought to
deduce the former from the latter, and behold
them now deriving virtues and duties from
the universal concept of practical moral activity,
by means of the divisions of internal and
external, of part and whole, of individual and
society. These are concepts of relations, not
susceptible of division, and therefore incapable
of serving as base for empirical divisions.
Or they have recourse to the triad of thesis,
antithesis, and synthesis, which is the universal concrete itself, constituting unity, and
therefore incapable of serving as basis for
division. Or they will deduce the moral virtues
according to the three faculties, as virtues of
representation, feeling and thought, or according
to the two of the will and the intellect, as
dianoetic and ethical virtues; as though the base
of the division of the *practical* could be that of
theoretical and *practical*. Empirical concepts
become in this way all false, whereas, in their
real nature, they are neither false nor true.

There is no thesis, however absurd, which
cannot be defended with such a method. All
know that there are aristocratic and democratic philosophers, libertarian and authoritarian,

anarchical and organicist, socialistic and anti-
socialistic, bellicose and pacific, feminist and
antifeminist; and there are others who maintain
the right to lie, the right to suicide, the right
to prostitution, the right to incest, to making
of themselves caterers for the scaffold, the
right to the penalty of death. These solutions
can be morally and politically justified in certain
definite and particular cases. There are other
solutions rationally unjustifiable in the individual
case and put forward only through passion,
wickedness, or prejudice, but in both hypotheses,
they are outside philosophy and within it so false
as to be odious, as that is odious which is maintained, not by means of intrinsic reason, but by
imposition altogether extrinsic and external.

Reason of the rebellion against rules. Such hatefulness explains the rebellion against
moral rules and concepts that has often taken
place. This, together with that against literary
classes and rules and others of the same sort,
forms part of the vast movement of rebellion
against empirical or empiricized philosophy. In
truth, when those rules and ideas are taken by
themselves, no rebellion is possible, because they
do not exert any pressure and obey the orders
of the man who has made them. But it happens
otherwise, when they become rigid and philo-

sophical, and as is said, absolute, claiming to substitute themselves as such for philosophy and to provide a base for judgments. In addition to this, from the enforced union of philosophemes with rules, has arisen the false idea of philosophizing about the practical (about an Ethic, for example), which showed itself to be *practical*, or, as is said, *normative*.

Philosophy, by taking part in empirical ques- *Limits between* tions, ruins both itself and them, because it *empiria.* loses the serenity, the dignity, and the utility that are intrinsic to it. In like manner, the empirical disciplines ruin themselves and philosophy when they claim to philosophize with their classes, which are not categories, with their pseudo-concepts, which are not concepts, with their *generalia*, which are not *universalia*. Here too, safety lies in distinction : the observation of distinction alone makes possible beneficent co-operation.

IX

HISTORICAL ANNOTATIONS

A HISTORY of the general theories relating to the practical activity is still to write, although we have several relating to particular theories of Ethic. The mode in which such a historical narration should be conducted results from the historical explanations themselves, which we have exposed and shall continue to expose. Here we cannot even offer a rapid summary. We shall limit ourselves to making a few remarks on the subject, and we shall give some historical account of certain problems of the philosophy of the practical, that have had, to some extent, profound treatment, or have at least been sufficiently discussed (for not a few others are virgin, or almost so), with the sole object of serving as a guide.

I. Distinction between history of the practical principle and history of the liberation from the transcendental.   I. A first warning to bear in mind concerns the historical inquiry as to the varying *recognition of, or failure to recognize* the *practical reason* in respect to the other forms of the spirit.

This series of thoughts is not to be confounded with that *other historical process*, so long and so intricate, which had its origin in the debate between St. Augustine and Pelagius (or perhaps rather in the opposition between Platonic mysticism and Aristotelian humanism), and through analogous debates, arising afresh during the Middle Ages and onward to modern times, culminating in the strife for the independence of morality and the practical reason in general from religion, which took place in the seventeenth century. The account of the various incidents of that debate perhaps occupies a larger space and a different place in the special histories of Ethic than it deserves. For it is not concerned with an entirely ethical or practical problem, but with that general philosophical movement which produced the progressive elimination of the transcendental and founded the " immanentistic " consideration of the real: a necessary condition for the conceivability of philosophy itself. In this lay the great importance of the affirmation that the practical and the moral spirit of man reveals itself as constant in the midst of the most various and opposed religious beliefs. This amounts to saying that it is independent of religion and knowable naturally and humanly, without the

L

necessity of having recourse to the authority of revelation and of making shipwreck in mystery. It is customary to say that in the seventeenth century free-thought definitely won the victory upon the point most ardently contested, and in this connection are recorded the names of Charron, Grotius, Spinoza, and Pierre Bayle. To these could be added that of G. B. Vico, who conceived of Providence as immanent and considered that morality arose from "a sense common to all men," from a judgment "without any sort of reflection," foundation of the natural rights of man. But should the word "definite" be really used here? Whenever the idea of the transcendental reappears, even in the timid form of agnosticism, the autonomy of the practical reason is denied, or at least again put in doubt (and with it that of the whole human spirit).

Two examples only of this must suffice, but they are conspicuous. Emmanuel Kant, not having been able to surpass the mystery that he had formulated—the principle of the practical reason—the categoric imperative remained suspended in the void, and in that void it invokes in relation to itself faith in a personal God and in a transcendental future life, which shall conciliate virtue and happiness, at variance in the life lived upon earth. This scrap of mystery which Kant allowed to remain in his system, suffices to obscure that autonomy of the practical reason and that concept of spiritual productivity which he had affirmed with so much energy. Another example, perhaps even more characteristic, is furnished by the Ethic that was prevalent for three centuries in the English School. It was a utilitarian Ethic and therefore incapable of truly founding moral reason. What was the consequence of that incapacity when recognized as such? Nothing but the renewed introduction of mystery, the explanation obtained by means of the idea of a personal God, assuming that most extravagant form known as "theological utilitarianism." By this theory, moral actions that in this life do not receive adequate recompense and seem to be unjustified from the utilitarian point of view, are rewarded by God in another life, thus finding their economic motive for being carried out in the present life. In our theoretic treatment of the subject, we do not concern ourselves with the controversy, already mooted in the *Eutyphron*, as to whether sanctity be loved by the gods as sanctity, or whether it be sanctity because it is beloved by the gods [1]—a

---

[1] *Eutyphron*, 10.

question that in the Middle Ages was transformed into that other one, differently solved by Abélard, Thomas Aquinas, Duns Scotus: whether the moral law be given by divine decree, or whether the idea of God does not of necessity coincide with the idea of moral law. We do not treat of this, since we are occupied with the practical, not with theology or antitheology, and consider that the contest between philosophy and theology has been already solved and surpassed in the theory of knowledge. For the same reason, it seems to us that we should not trace its history in the History of the Philosophy of the Practical.[1]

II. The distinction of the practical from the theoretical.

II. The true and proper history of the practical principle, conceived as autonomous, and of the problem concerning the identity or the distinction of the practical from theory, has a different line of development. As a rule this problem is referred back to the celebrated sayings of Socrates, that virtue is knowledge and vice ignorance, and to the corrections that Aristotle, while accepting, proposes in them, when he takes note of the part that belongs to the non-cognoscitive element. But, as often happens,

[1] The history of the enfranchising of Ethic from Religion has been done with especial care by Jodl, *Gesch. d. Ethik als philos. Wissensch.* vol. I[2]. (Stuttgart—Berlin, 1906). For Vico, cf. my book, *The Philosophy of G. B. Vico* (Bari, 1911).

those sayings and those corrections have been taken as being more profound than they genuinely were and could be. This, if it have not aided the exactness of historical interpretation, has nevertheless stimulated and fecundated thought. On reading without prejudice the parts of the *Memorabilia*, of the Platonic dialogues, of the *Nicomachean Ethics*, and of the *Magna Moralia* that relate to it, it appears evident that what is treated of in them is the altogether empirical question of the importance that mental development has for practical life, and whether knowledge suffices for this, or natural dispositions and discipline of the passions be not also necessary. Aristotle replied to Socrates, who had insisted upon the element of knowing, conceiving virtue as knowledge (λόγος), by modifying the statement with the assertion that virtue is not indeed simply knowledge, but is *with* knowledge (μετὰ λόγου). In these very ingenuous considerations is to be found at the most implicitly, but certainly not explicitly, the problem that was only stated later on ; and it would be rash to classify Socrates as an intellectualist and Aristotle as a voluntarist. It is certain that the Aristotelian philosophy, in accordance with good sense, preserved the distinction between the two forms of the spirit, the theoretical and the practical, the reason and the will, a distinction that has also passed into the scholastic philosophy (*ratio cognoscibilis, ratio appetibilis*) and into that of the Renaissance. But it remained always vague, sometimes brought into prominence, sometimes, on the other hand, attenuated. Almost dissipated in those who conceive the principles of the practical as something similar or analogous to mathematical truths (Cudworth, Clarke, Wollaston, etc.), it always reaffirms itself when importance is given to the affections and passions, as is the case with many thinkers of the seventeenth century (Bacon, Descartes, Spinoza, Vico); and the doctrines of the Scottish school of sensationalists contributed not a little to keep it alive.

It seems indubitable that Emmanuel Kant is to be connected to some extent rather with this last tradition than with that of the intellectualists : with Kant the practical reason possessed a domain of its own altogether distinct from and almost antithetical to the domain of the theoretical. But it is erroneous to present the successors of Kant as forgetful of the practical reason and as resolving every spiritual manifestation in the theoretical form of the spirit. For instance, Fichte, who had a very strong consciousness of the peculiarity of the practical activity, did not do this, nor did Hegel, though as commonly as unjustly accused of being a cold intellectualist. It should suffice to recall how Hegel always opposed that view of Plato and of other thinkers (for example Campanella) who assigned the government of the State to philosophers, a view in which the resolution of the practical into the theoretical spirit and of the will into knowledge seemed to become concrete. For Hegel, on the contrary, the domain of *history* is different from that of *philosophy*; history is indeed the idea, but the idea that shows itself in a *natural and unconscious* manner, and *philosophical* genius is not *political* genius. Nor must we forget the importance that he accorded to passion, to custom, to what is called the heart and is wont to be opposed to the brain and to argument. For Hegel, the will is not thought, but a special kind of thought, that is to say, thought which translates itself into existence, the impulse to give oneself existence. Whereas in the theoretical process, the spirit takes possession of the object and makes it its own by thinking, that is

by universalizing it, in the practical process a
difference is also stated and determined, which
on the other hand consists of its own determinations and ends. The theoretical is contained in
the practical, since there cannot be will without
intelligence ; but, on the other hand, the
theoretical contains the practical, since to think
is also to act. Hegel, in short, distinguishes the
practical from the theoretical and unifies them,
while retaining the distinction.[1] What is not
perhaps altogether clear to him, notwithstanding his view that history is the idea in a
natural and unconscious mode, is the unreflective
character of willing. To have given relief to
this character, although in the exaggerated and
inacceptable form of the will as blind and unconscious, is the merit of Arthur Schopenhauer,
who is indeed far from standing alone in assigning an eminent place to the will, but connects
himself with all the Kantian and post-Kantian
philosophy, and in the first place with Fichte
and Schelling.

III. The mixtures of philosophy of the practical and description.

III. The mixture of philosophical concepts
with empirical concepts and with rules is a vice
common to nearly all treatises of the Philosophy
of the practical, beginning with the *Nico-*

[1] *Phil. d. Rechts*, § 4, Zus. ; *Gesch. d. Philos.* ii. pp. 66, 169.

machean Ethic, which, although in certain places loftily philosophical, should be placed in greater part rather at the head of the history of the works of the moralists and of writers on the practical, than of Ethic. The author himself recognized this practical character when he wrote, πᾶς ὁ περὶ τῶν πρακτῶν λόγος τύπῳ καὶ οὐκ ἀκριβῶς ὀφείλει λέγεσθαι.[1] And in this appears the prejudice that practical philosophy should be occupied with the practical : ἐπεὶ οὖν ἡ παροῦσα πραγματεία οὐ θεωρίας ἕνεκά ἐστιν ὥσπερ αἱ ἄλλαι (οὐ γὰρ ἵνα εἰδῶμεν τί ἐστιν ἡ ἀρετὴ σκεπτόμεθα ἀλλ᾽ ἵν᾽ ἀγαθοὶ γινώμεθα, ἐπεὶ οὐδὲν ἂν ἦν ὄφελος αὐτῆς), κτλ.[2] Even the greatest thinkers of modern times are not exempt from that characteristic. Emmanuel Kant, while recognizing that the division and treatment of duties do not belong to the Critique of the Sciences (he should therefore have excluded them from philosophy, which is always *criticism*), finally relegates them to what he calls the "system" (and is in truth the anti-systematic)[3] and writes the *Metaphysic of Customs,* divided into the doctrines of law and of the virtues. Fichte, in his *System of Ethic,* makes the applied follow the theoretical part. Hegel gives the doctrine

---

[1] *Eth. Nicom.* 1103.   [2] See above.
[3] *Kritik d. prakt. Vern.,* ed. Kirchmann, pp. 7-8.

of duties in the third part of his *Philosophy of Law*, which is entitled Of Ethicity (*Sittlichkeit*). The Ethic of Herbart is intrinsically descriptive, for the author himself professed to wish simply " to describe the ideal of virtue,"[1] and the five practical ideas that he takes as principles were at bottom nothing but classes of virtue refined into ideas. Treatises of to-day are overflowing with empirical elements, as can be seen from those in English by Ladd and Seth, and by those in German of Paulsen, Wundt, and Cathrein. Sometimes a more concrete historical element is coupled in those treatises with the empirical classification of practical examples and institutions: as, for instance, in Cathrein, a modernized Jesuit, who exposes at length the moral views, not only of civilized people, ancient and modern, but also of the savages of Oceania, of Asia, of Cochin China, of the Hottentots and Boschimans, of the Botocudis, and so on. Questions of casuistry also survive in these treatises, such as whether and on what occasions it is permissible to tell a lie ; this question is notably represented in the history of ideas, from the Socrates of the *Memorabilia* to Kant and Schopenhauer.[2] Kant added

---

[1] *Allg. prakt. Phil.*, ed. Hartenstein, p. 107.

[2] *Memor.* iv., c. 2, §§ 14-16. Schopenhauer also exhaustively, *Grundl. d. Moral*, in *Werke*, ed. Grisebach, iii. pp. 603-607.

questions of casuistry to the various sections
of the *Metaphysic of Customs*, as scholia to
the system and examples of the way in which
the truth of particular questions should be
sought.[1]

But the efforts of ancient and modern philosophers rigorously to define empirical concepts
afford more interest than the external form of
treatment, as do their efforts to modify or to
simplify, or indeed finally to deduce them
rationally. The Platonic dialogues, such as the
Charmides, the *Lachetes*, the *Protagoras*, are
most instructive in this respect. Here it is
sought to define sophrosune, andreia and the
other virtues, without arriving at any precise
result, or rather arriving at the contradictory one,
that each of these virtues is *the whole of virtue*,
whereas it should only be a *part* of it. In the
Republic is sought the relation of the four
virtues, or rather of three of them, prudence,
temperance, and fortitude, with justice, which
forms as it were the foundation and unity of the
whole. From such discussions arose the affirmation, to be found also in Cicero, that the
virtues are inseparable from one another:
virtutes ita copulatae connexaeque sunt, ut omnes

*Vain attempts
at definitions
of empirical
concepts.*

---

[1] *Metaphys. d. Sitten*, ed. Kirchmann, p. 248.

participes sint, nec alia ab alia possit separari.[1]
The difficulty of the Platonic inquiry is renewed
with all those who have given definitions of the
virtues and of the other empirical concepts,
because, when they have achieved with much
labour a definition which appears satisfactory,
it is afterwards always found to be too narrow
or too wide. Thus the definition given by
Kant and by others (Fichte, Schopenhauer)
of egoism, consisting in their view, of considering other individuals as means and not
ends, is the definition, not of egoism, but of any
form of immorality which debases the Spirit that
should be the end, by means of its own
caprices. The same is to be said of the definitions given by Fichte as to the duties inherent
to this or that condition and state : the duties, for
instance, of the learned, who should love truth,
communicate it to others, rectify errors, promote
culture,[2] and so on. These are all things that
form part of the duty, not only of the learned,
but of every man. The simplifiers are not more
fortunate in their attempts to reduce the number
of empirical concepts, for the concepts excluded
by them have neither more nor less right to

---

[1] *De Finibus*, v, c. 23.
[2] *System der Sittenlehre*, § 29, in *Werke*, iv. 346-347.

recognition than the others that they have accepted. Schopenhauer, for instance, when he rejects the class of duties toward oneself,[1] should also reject that of duties toward others. For others and ourselves are correlative terms, and we cannot be benevolent to others and malevolent to ourselves, just to others and unjust to ourselves. If this be met with the objection that the empirical self is not the object of duties, we must reply that neither are the empirical "others," but only that Spirit which is in all and constitutes all. In reacting against these unifiers and simplifiers, other philosophers (as for example Herbart) have maintained the indeducibility of the virtues or duties from a single principle, which means that they have received those concepts into their philosophy atomistically, and left them there as something not digested and not digestible, an extraneous element. If they had openly admitted this and drawn from it the legitimate consequence, and for that reason excluded those concepts from philosophy, they would really have contributed toward simplifying and unifying, by making it homogeneous. But Herbart, if he have no other merit, has at any rate declared that the Philosophy of the practical is not

[1] *Grundl. d. Moral*, ed., cit., iii. pp. 506-508.

capable of solving all the problems that occur in life, and that we must always rely upon the answer of the heart, upon the delicacy of individual tact. And, therefore, while Kant still preserved casuistic questions in Ethic and professed to solve them rationally, Herbart showed that they lack the determinations that are of true importance in real cases, and that such questions are therefore as a rule either without meaning or insoluble (*entweder gar keiner Fragen, oder im Allgemein unauflöslich*).[1]

Attempts at deduction. As concerns the attempt to connect and to deduct the empirical part of treatises from the philosophical, the first example is the Aristotelian division of the virtues into the dianoetic and ethic, with their consequent determination by means of the concept of mediacy (μεσότης) between two extremes. But this Aristotelian method, which was continued by the Scholastics, seemed to others (as for example Schleiermacher) nothing but "a heap of virtues," without any rule and without any certainty ; hence he made constant attempts at new classifications and new deductions. Kant recognized that the ethical obligation, that is, respect for the law, is something unique and indivisible, and that to attain

[1] *Allg. prakt. Philos.*, ed. Hartenstein, pp. 29-30.

from that to duties or *ethica officia*, which are
many, it is necessary to introduce the consideration of objects.[1]   Here he should have stopped,
because objects have infinite determinations, are
infinite.   Hence the enumeration, division and
deduction of duties, should be simply pronounced
impossible.   Instead of doing this, he passed at
a bound, how far logical we know not, from the
general ethical obligation, to the division of duties
into two great classes: of man toward man, and
of man toward beings that are not human.   He
divided the first into duties toward oneself and
duties toward other men, the second into that of
the duties toward beings beneath man (animals)
and those toward beings above him (God).[2]   The
strangeness of these divisions, which sometimes
verge on the comic, can already be seen, though
abridged, in the first class of the duties toward
oneself, subdivided in its turn into duties toward
oneself as an animal or physical being, and duties
toward oneself as a moral being; as though
human duties are not always to be referred to
spirituality and can ever concern physicality or
animality.   In their first aspect they receive a
tripartite division, into the duty of self-preserva-

[1] *Metaphys. d. Sitten*, pp. 247-248.
[2] *Op. cit.* p. 251.

tion, which is violated by suicide, by allowing oneself to be castrated (in order to sing soprano, as used to be done at that time at the San Carlo of Naples and at the Opera of Berlin), by allowing a healthy tooth to be pulled out in order to sell it (as does poor Fantine in the story of the *Misérables*); into the duty of preserving the species (violation: unnatural use of the sexual impulse);—into the duty of preserving the use of one's own strength (violation: gluttony). The duty of preserving the dignity of man is contained beneath the second heading (violation, lying, covetousness, abjection, etc.[1]). The fact is that the duty of preserving the dignity of man comprises in itself, not only the class that stands first, of duties toward oneself, but also all the other duties toward men, animals, or gods. Fichte feels the difficulty, because he sees that conscience is that which determines our duty on each occasion; but he adds: "This is not enough for science: either we must be able to determine *a priori* that which our conscience will affirm in universal, or we must admit that an Ethic, as a pure applied science, is impossible."[2] The second horn of the dilemma was precisely that

[1] *Metaphys. d. Sitten*, p. 255 *sqq.*
[2] *System d. Sittenlehre*, pp. 208.

of the truth, but Fichte, like Kant, bowed to the supreme power of tradition and clung to the first. He divides duties into mediate and conditioned (toward oneself) and immediate and unconditioned (toward others), and into general and special (those of various states and conditions), deducing from this the fourfold division, resulting from the meeting of general conditioned duties, particular conditioned, general unconditioned, and particular unconditioned. Hegel, who in his youthful writings had denied absolute value to the virtues, and consequently the possibility of collisions between the virtues (for example, in the *Life of Jesus*, recently published), well defines the altogether empirical character of that treatise, calling it, by reason of its natural element and of the quantitive considerations upon which it is founded, " a natural history of the spiritual world " (*eine geistige Naturgeschichte*); but since he did not perceive the identity of the concept of duty with that of virtue, he believes in the possibility of a philosophical theory of duties.[1] This is developed by him, as has been said, in the section of Ethicity, applying to it the dialectical rhythm proper to the philosophical universal, and distinguishing in it three moments: of the

[1] *Philos. d. Rechts*, §§ 148, 150.

M

immediate natural spirit, which is the family, of the dissension from which arises civil society, and of conciliation, whence arises the State. But notwithstanding the external dialectical form, there is to be found in all this section of the Ethicity at every point, not so much the philosopher properly so-called, as the historian who describes and narrates, the acute and well-balanced politician and moralist. The merit of such a treatise resides precisely, therefore, in the abhorrence of a sham philosophy; with but slight modifications of literary form, it could be developed into a series of excellent historico-political essays. Certain of the propositions of the writing on *Natural Law* (1802-3)[1] would tend to show that Hegel inclined to look upon the treatment of duties and institutions as nothing more than a provisional classification of historical and changeable material, a thought that is in any case suggested by his whole system. Schleiermacher was among the philosophers of that time who laboured, perhaps, with the greatest tenacity upon the empirical classes, with a view to reducing them to philosophical form; but the results were unhappy, only revealing, by their contradictions persisting after such efforts, the

[1] *Werke*, i. 323-423.

impossibility of the task. In fact, Schleiermacher sees and does not see the unity of the
three spheres of things good, of duties, and of
virtues ; hence they appeared to him to be three
aspects of the same object, and he strangely
placed them in analogical connection with three
spheres of the natural world, the mechanical,
the chemical, and the organic. He, too, starting
from a double division and a double antithesis,
ideal and temporal, of knowledge and exposition
(*Darstellen*), arrived at a quadruple division of
the virtues, into wisdom and love, discretion and
perseverance, which seemed to him to coincide
with the four Platonic virtues, of φρόνησις,
δικαιοσύνη, σωφροσύνη, and ἀνδρεία, or with the four
cardinal virtues derived from them, to which
would correspond the four duties : of right,
of vocation, of love, and of conscience.[1] After
this, it would be superfluous to proceed to
enumerate the ethical systems of contemporary
philosophy, noteworthy neither for the ingenuity
of their artificial deductions nor for the grandeur
of their paradoxes.[2]

IV. The very copious empirical element that *IV. Various*
questions.
fills the books on the Philosophy of the practical

[1] In the *Entwurf e. Systems d. Sittenlehre* (in *Werke*, sec. iii. vol. v.),
and cf. the collected writings in *Werke*, iii. 1.

[2] For example, F. Paulsen, *System der Ethik*, Leipzig, 1906,

and the attempt to treat it philosophically have also had the injurious effect of distracting their authors from entering deeply into the problems of true and proper philosophy, to which the practical activity gives rise. Thus a history of the aforesaid aberrations would be as rich as a history of the speculation as to the will would be poor. The problem of the theoretic element in the volitional act, or of the theoretic phase of deliberation, has not been developed as it deserved, and as the important pages of the third and seventh books of the *Ethica Nicomachea* seemed to augur. The question, too, of the priority of the will over the concepts of the useful and of the good and of the practical judgments, is hardly touched by a philosopher here and there, and the Herbartian theory of practical judgments failed to excite any fervour of examination, criticism, or opposition. The concept of good will and of good intention, to which Kant gave a prominent place, is not discussed profoundly, save by Hegel, who goes deeply into the difficult problems of abstract and concrete intention in the introduction and in the second section of the *Philosophy of Law*. The other problem, as to the possibility or impossibility of willing without full knowledge, was not adequately treated after Descartes and Spinoza.

In Descartes are also to be found the most *The practical nature of error.* acute observations as to the practical nature of error. After having stated that it is impossible that God should have given to man any faculty that was not perfect of its kind, he asks himself: "*D'où est-ce donc que naissent mes erreurs? C'est à savoir, de cela seul que la volonté, étant beaucoup plus ample et plus étendue que l'entendement, je ne la contiens pas dans les mêmes limites, mais que je l'étends aussi aux choses que je n'entends pas; auxquelles étant de soi indifférente, elle s'égare fort aisément, et choisit le faux pour le vrai et le mal pour le bien: ce qui fait que je me trompe et je pèche.*" Errors arise from the concourse of two causes, the faculty of knowing and the faculty of choice: "*car pour l'entendement seul je n'assure ni ne nie aucune chose, mais je conçois seulement les idées des choses que je puis assurer ou nier.*"[1] For Descartes the affirmation was an act of the will, and here perhaps lies his mistake and the mistake of those who have followed him in this theory (Rosmini for example); that is to say, they have *mistaken* the *affirmation*, which is theoretical,

---

[1] *Médit.* iv. ; and *Réponses aux 3mes et aux 5mes object.*

for the *communication*, which is practical, or they have taken as being of the same degree the general will that is in affirmation through the unity of the spirit, and the particular will that is in error. Spinoza opposes Descartes' theory of error, but in conformity with the deterministic nature of his. philosophy, his criticism relates only to the point as to whether the will can be the cause of error when it is not more than a mere abstraction or *ens rationis*; hence errors or the *particulares volitiones* can be determined, not indeed by the will and by liberty, but *a causis externis*.[1] The consciousness of the introduction of the will into the theoretical spirit as production of error has been affirmed by Schleiermacher as well as by Rosmini:[2] "It is the will (he writes) that conceals men from themselves: the judgment cannot err if it turn its gaze really upon itself."[3] Baader frankly reduced incredulity to ill-will and moral corruption.[4]

Practical taste. As to the concept of an immediate form of practical discrimination, independent of the

---

[1] Epist. in *Opera*, ed. Gfrörer, p. 523.

[2] Cf., among other places, *Logica*, §§ p. 278 *sq.*; *Fil. d. diritto* (Napoli, 1844), I. p. 50.

[3] *Monologen*, in *Werke*, i. 363.

[4] Cf. Jodl, *Gesch. d. Eth.* ii. pp. 131-132.

intellectual judgment, it is to be remarked that the faculty of *taste* in Gracian and in other thinkers of the seventeenth century[1] has a practical rather than a theoretical origin, and that the sentimentalists of Ethic (Shaftesbury, Hutcheson, and others) were led to posit a moral tact or sense. Before Herbart talked of a *moral taste* (*sittlicher Geschmack*[2]) Jacobi, who saw better than others the analogy between practical and æsthetic facts, had written: "The science of the good, like the science of the beautiful, is subject to the condition of *taste*, without which nothing can be decided, and beyond which nothing can be carried. The taste for the good, like that for the beautiful, is formed by means of models of excellence, and original acts are always the work of genius. By means of genius, nature gives laws to art, both as regards the good and the beautiful. Both are *liberal* arts; they do not allow themselves to be lowered to the level of mechanical arts and placed at the service of industry."[3]

V. With the mention of a few facts and names, it can be proved that the function of the term "feeling" in the history of philosophy

V. The doctrines of feeling.

[1] *Estetica* 4, p. 222.
[2] *Allg. pract. Phil.* pp. 9-22.
[3] *Woldemar* (1779, 1794-95), in *Werke*, v. p. 78.

has been as shown above. We have already
said that the peculiarity of the practical form
has been asserted by the use of the word "feeling" or similar denominations ("moral sense,"
"conscience," and the like), especially by the
Scottish School, in opposition to intellectualist reductions. Jacobi appealed to the feeling of duty
(*Gefühl der Pflicht*) or conscience in his ethical
discussions. In our day, too, it has been affirmed
(by Simmel [1] and others), in opposition to abstract
and imperative Ethics, that the practical decision
is the product of feeling and is not definable by
theoreticians. But the principal cause of the
importance attached to feeling in the eighteenth
century was the æsthetic problem. This is seen
in Dubos's book, in the English sentimentalists
(who approach the ideas of virtue and of beauty,
treating of the moral sense and of the beautiful),
and, finally, in the doctrines of Leibnitz himself
and of his school, as to *confused cognition*, which
led to the *Aesthetica* of Baumgarten. We owe

The Wolfians. the word and the concept of *feeling* (*Gefühl*
and sometimes also *Empfindung*) principally to
the Leibnitzian - Wolfians and to the German
thinkers under the influence of Wolff (Mendelssohn, Tetens, Sulzer, Riedel). By means of the

---

[1] *Einleitung in die Moralwissenschaft*, Berlin, 1892-93.

speculation of Jacobi, on the other hand, feeling *Jacobi and Schleier-* was called upon to fulfil the functions of a true *macher.* and proper metaphysical organ. He had demonstrated in a rigorous and irrefutable manner that the form of the empirical sciences and of the abstract intellect, since it proceeds by nexus of cause and effect, is incapable of attaining to the infinite, and had assigned the affirmation of God to the "sense of the supersensible," to "immediate knowledge," and to "feeling." After Jacobi, the same position was assumed by Schleiermacher, who maintained that it was impossible to know God by means of the intellect and to treat Him as an object, since He is indifference of thought and being. He can be known only by feeling, which is indifference of all determinate functions of ideal and real, of thought and being. The neocriticists and agnostics of to-day, with their appeal to feeling in all truly philosophical questions, are followers, often unconscious and certainly less coherent, of Jacobi and Schleiermacher.

The concept of feeling in the Kantian philo- *Kant.* sophy can be said to derive its importance from the meeting of two unsatisfied wants, namely, that which sought a concept for the æsthetic activity and that which sought a *forma mentis* proper to philosophy. Indeed, the *Critique of Judgment* corresponds to feeling, the first part of which consists of an inquiry into the nature of the beautiful and of art. The second part (critique of the theological judgment) is an anticipation of the *concrete concept*, or of that organ of speculative thought which the *Critique of Pure Reason* had not discovered.

Hegel. Feeling, therefore, cannot but lose importance in the Hegelian philosophy, which makes of art a form of knowledge, and of the teleological judgment the logic of the idea or philosophical logic, resolving also in it the demand of Jacobi, whose feeling or immediate knowledge is shown to be logical knowledge and supreme mediation. In Hegel feeling is nothing but a class of spiritual facts, the lowest of all, that in which theory and practice are still indistinct. But this class has a merely psychological value in his system, not philosophical and real (which is not clearly recognised by him). Indeed, feeling, which was absolute knowledge for Jacobi and for Schleiermacher, is placed, not in the sphere of the absolute spirit, nor in that of the objective or practical spirit, but in the subjective spirit, or Psychology. The " doctrine

of the three faculties" (*Dreivermögenslehre*),
as was called that elaborated from Mendelssohn
to Kant and promulgated in the Kantian philosophy, did not, however, remain without opponents in the nineteenth century; from Krug
(1823) to the youthful Fichte, and in more *Opponents of the doctrine*
recent times Brentano (1874). Krug's confuta- *of the three faculties.*
tion is wrongly combated by Hamilton and *Krug.*
discredited by Brentano, for it proceeds with
perfect correctness, and is founded on the
correct philosophical principle that there are
no other activities of the spirit conceivable,
save those directed either inwardly or outwardly
(immanent or theoretical and transcendent or
practical), and that therefore there is no place
for feeling, which would be a mixture of the
two activities, and consequently a failure of
direction or inactivity, nothing, therefore, but
a poor, rudimentary knowing or willing, that
is, a psychological class, not a philosophical
category.

Brentano, returning in a measure to Descartes, *Brentano.*
constructs the doctrine of the three faculties
in a different way, determining them as representation (to which he makes art and the æsthetic
activity correspond), judgment (to which corresponds science), and love and hate (to which

corresponds the practical). Feeling, therefore, does not find a place of its own in the psyche, and that which is wont to be called feeling is either representation, or love and hate. Brentano shows himself inferior to Krug in the philosophical demonstration of the inconceivability of this form of the spirit, but he has the merit of having substituted certain positive elements for the indeterminate word "feeling," although the function exercised by feeling in the development of philosophical thought is more important than Brentano succeeds in perceiving, for among other things he ignores and fails to recognize the relation of the concept of feeling to the demands of speculative thought.[1]

---

[1] For the doctrine of feeling see, chiefly, Volkmann, *Lehrb. d. Psychol.* (Cothen, 1885), ii. pp. 301–311 ; F. Brentano, *Psychol.* (Leipzig, 1874), i., ii. c. 5 ; cf. *Ursprung sitt. Erkennt.* (Leipzig, 1889) pp. 51-55 ; A. Palme, *Sulzer's Psychol. u. d. Anfänge d. Dreivermögenslehre* (Berlin, 1905). Cf. also Croce, *Estetica*, pp. 226-228, 4th ed.

SECOND SECTION

THE PRACTICAL ACTIVITY IN ITS DIALECTIC

I

NECESSITY AND LIBERTY OF THE VOLITIONAL ACT

THE relations of the practical form with the *The problem of freedom.* other forms of the spirit having been examined, it is now necessary to re-enter, so to speak, the interior of the volitional activity, and enclose ourselves within it, that we may study its mode of development, its rhythm, its dialectic. We shall no longer ask, therefore, whether the practical activity precede or follow knowledge, or exactly what knowledge it follows and what it precedes, what the volition is in relation to events, what the practical concept or judgment, and the like. But we shall ask what are good and evil, the passions and the forces that dominate them, desires and aspirations; and in the first place (this being the problem that opens the series and gives the key for the solution of the others) what are the *freedom and necessity* of the volitional act.

173

This problem of freedom and necessity (that is to say, whether the will be free or determined) has seemed to be and is, from a certain point of view, most weighty and complicated, and we shall soon see why this is so. But at this point, owing to the premises that we have already laid down in our preceding treatises, and also in the part of the present treatise that has already been developed, it will be convenient to solve it with relative expedition.

Freedom of willing and freedom of action : criticism of such distinction.

First of all, we have been able to eliminate the distinction that is wont to be made between freedom of willing and freedom of action, with the duplicity of the problem thus entailed. Indeed we know that volition and action coincide, and that it is impossible to conceive either a volition which is not at the same time action, or an action which is not at the same time volition, and that in consequence there cannot be freedom of willing on the one hand and freedom of action on the other. All the instances of the one that are brought forward can be reduced to the other, provided that the word " freedom " be not used in an improper and metaphorical manner. For example, a paralytic (they say) wills to get up and run ; his spirit is free, but his action is restrained ; he has freedom of willing, but not of action. But in reality the paralytic does not seriously will to get up and run; that is, he does not really will anything at all. Were he really and seriously to will, that might happen to him which happened to a paralytic gentleman in the Neapolitan revolt of 1547. This gentleman had himself carried into the square on the arms of his servants, but he was found, after the tumult, to the great astonishment of all, on the top of the campanile of San Lorenzo, whither he had climbed with his own legs; such had been his terror and such his will to be saved.[1] As a rule, on the other hand, the paralytic does not will, because he knows that he cannot; at the most, he *would wish* or desire to find himself in different conditions to those in which he finds himself, in order that he may be able to will otherwise than he does now, which is to remain quiet. This confirms the identity of volition and action, and proves that the two supposed freedoms are one only. Thus, he who is threatened and yields to the threat declares that he is deprived of freedom of action, but that this is not exact is already affirmed in the formula: *coacti tamen volunt.* Enforced actions not only do not exist, but are not even conceivable. The

---

[1] Summonte, *Historia di Napoli*, ed. 1675, iv. 205, "Miracle caused by fear."

demand for greater freedom of action, such as new political liberties, is nothing but the demand for certain *new conditions of fact* for future volitions and actions. But it is a question of more or less, since, as we know, no countenance of imminent tyrant can extinguish the freedom of the soul; no ruler, be he ever so strong and violent, can prevent a rebellion, or, when all else fails, a fine death that affirms externally the freedom within. "The will that wills not cannot be subdued." [1]

The volitional act: both free and necessary.

The question that we have here to treat is, then, single, and concerns only the will, which, as such, includes in itself action. In replying, however, we cannot accept the dilemma, that the volitional act must be free or determined, and cling to one of the two horns: we must on the contrary deny the form of the question itself and say that the volitional act is *at once free and determined.*

Volition, in fact, as has been seen, does not arise in the void, but in a definite situation, in unchangeable historical conditions, in relation to an event, which, if it be, is necessary. The volition corresponds to that situation and it is impossible to separate it: when the situation changes, the volition changes; as the situation,

[1] Dante, *Parad.* iv. 76.

so the volition. This amounts to saying, that it is *necessitated* or always conditioned by a situation, and precisely by that situation in which it arises.

But this also means that the volition is free. Because if the actual situation be its condition, the volition is not the condition, but the conditioned, for it does not remain fixed in the actual situation, nor repeats and makes a duplicate of it, which would be superfluous and therefore impossible in the effective development of the real, which does not allow of superfluity. The volition produces something different, that is, something new, something that did not exist previously and that now comes into existence: it is initiative, creation, and therefore act of *freedom*. Were this not so, volition would not be volition, and reality would not change, would not become, would not grow upon itself.

And since without necessity there cannot be liberty, because without an actual situation there cannot be volition, so without liberty there cannot be necessity, the actual situations are not formed, which are always new and always necessary in respect to the new volitions. Actual situations are events, and events are the result of the concourse of individual volitions. The two terms cannot be separated, for if one be removed, so is the other ; but neither can they be looked upon as identical or synonymous. They are the two moments of the volitional act, distinct and united, which act is the *unity* of both, and therefore, as was said, is at once free and determined.

This consciousness of necessity and liberty inseparably united is found in all men of action, in all political geniuses, who are never inert or reckless : they feel themselves at once bound and unbound ; they always conform to facts, but always to surpass them. The fatuous, on the other hand, oscillate between the passivity of the given situation and the sterile attempt to overleap it, that is, to leap over their own shadow. They are consequently now inert, now forward. They do not therefore fix or conclude anything, they do not act ; or, if they do, it is always according to what of the actual situation they have understood, and what of initiative they have displayed.

Comparison with the æsthetic activity. The best comparison is afforded on this occasion also by the æsthetic activity. No poet creates his poem outside definite conditions of space and time, and even when he appears to be and is proclaimed "a soul of other times," he belongs to his own time. The historical situation is given to him. The world of his perceptions is such, with those men, those customs, those thoughts, those works of art. But when the new poem has appeared, there is in the world of reality (in the contemplation of reality) something that was not there before, which, although connected with the previous situation, yet is not identical with it, is indeed a new form, and therefore a new content, and so the revelation of a truth previously unknown. So true is this, that in its turn the new poem conditions a spiritual and practical movement, becomes part of the situation given for future actions and for future poems. He is a true poet who feels himself at once bound to his predecessors and free, conservative and revolutionary, like Homer, Dante, and Shakespeare, who receive into themselves centuries of history, of thought and of poetry, and add to those centuries something that is the present and will be the future: *chargés du passé, gros de l'avenir.* The false poet, on the other hand, is now a blind follower of tradition and imitator, now a charlatanesque innovator, and if in the vacuity in which he labours he sometimes does produce a fragment of poetry, this happens only when he is made to look into himself and to have a vision, be it great or small, of a world that arises.—But the comparison instituted is rather an analogy than a comparison, for that which happens in the practical sphere happens in that of poetry and in all the other spheres of the spiritual activity. The Spirit is freedom, and in order to be so, not in the abstract, but in the concrete, it must also be necessity.

Critique of determinism and of arbitrarism.

This indissoluble connection of necessity and liberty confutes both the partial theories which dispute the field in the problem of freedom : the *deterministic* theory and that of *free will.* The determinists do not see in the volitional act anything but the actual situation ; the followers of the theory of free will see nothing but the moment of freedom. These conceive a volition that is as it were a duplication, triplication, quadruplication of the given fact, and so on to the infinite ; those a volition that bursts forth from nothing, or rains down from above and then inserts itself, no one knows how, into the course of the real. Both exaggerate, and since exaggerations are called in science errors in sense, both err, and being one-sided are proved false. But since, on the other hand, it is a quality of errors opposed to one another, to become identified and to pass, the one into the other, it is given to us to assist at a like spectacle in this case also, and to see the determinists change into arbitrarists and the believers in free will into determinists. The

first, in fact, passing from cause to cause, abandon
the concept of cause at the end of the chain, as
though (to use the expression of Schopenhauer),
they were dismissing the hired carriage, made
use of during the day for their own affairs, and
return to free will. The others, being unable to
justify freedom in the world of reality and of
experience, justify it in a transcendental way, as
the effect of a divine cause, which excludes free
will, and excludes it also when it concedes it ; for
by the very fact of conceding, it determines,
limits, and produces it.

But with this explanation of our thesis, and *General form of this antithesis: materialism and mysticism.*
of the two theses opposing it, we are transported
into the heart of one of the greatest problems
of Gnoseology, so great in fact as to appear to
contain in it the whole problem of philosophy.
In fact, that which is called determinism and
free will in the Philosophy of the practical is
the same antithesis that in Gnoseology is called
materialism and mysticism. And that which we
here oppose to the two one - sided theses, as
theory of that liberty which is also necessity,
is called in Gnoseology, *idealism.* The thesis
and antithesis are therefore to be found in all
the particular problems of philosophy, since they
concern the logical form in universal. This,

then, is the reason why the question of freedom
of willing has become so grave and complicated
as to appear insoluble. To obtain a solution,
it was necessary to construct a Logic of philosophy, and intrinsicalty necessary to renew the
whole system of philosophy. Herbart wisely
counselled never to discuss the freedom of the
will with the laity, in order not to be misunderstood.[1]

Had this advice been followed, we should
not have seen both determinism and free will
torn asunder by advocates in the law courts,
dragging in the one or the other to suit their
purposes, and thus insulting good sense, which
should alone rule in those places. The freedom
of the will is doubted and discussed among
philosophers, as the reality of the external world
is doubted and discussed, but this is not done
because it is wished to set in doubt the existence of the boots of this gentleman or of that
gentleman's overcoat. If a confirmation be
sought that the question of the freedom of
willing is, as was said, the universal gnoseological or metaphysical question, let it be
observed how the determinists and the advocates
of free will affirm or deny the freedom of willing,

---

[1] *Einleit. in die Phil.* § 128, trad. Vidossich, p. 169.

not only in that field, but in all fields. Indeed, whoever, for instance, should admit spiritual activity to knowledge and deny it to the will, would not, properly speaking, be a determinist, but an intellectualist or an æsthetician. That is to say, he would be a theoretician, who, in denying the freedom of the will, would simply mean to deny the existence of a practical activity side by side with the theoretic; for freedom is the very essence of every spiritual form, and with the denial of the freedom of that form is denied the form itself. Determinism, arbitrarism, libertarianism reflect, then, the universal gnoseological thesis of naturalism and mechanicism in the special practical field.

Determinism of the will, like materialism and *The materialistic sophisms of determinism.* mechanicism in general, consists in nothing but the transference to philosophical speculation of the form proper to the physical disciplines. By dint of classifying practical facts and presenting them as empirical concepts, and thus as merely related by cause and effect, they end by forgetting that those formulæ are not thoughts and that their content is not real reality; and causes or motives (abstractive transformation of the actual situation) are given as agents of the will, and thus the agent is destroyed for the cause, the form for the abstract material. Hence these timid phrases that on close inspection turn out to be tautologies or mistakes : " Freedom is an illusion ; what prevails is always the strongest motive." But if we ask what is the strongest motive, we are told (and no other reply is possible) it is *that which prevails*. This, translated into our language, amounts to saying that the actual situation is the actual situation, and conditions the will, which is what it is and can be no other than it is.—Virtue is a mere product, like vitriol. Certainly, vitriol is also in its way a creation, a manifestation of the spirit, as is virtue, and if it be permitted to falsify vitriol by changing it into something material and mechanical, nothing forbids doing the same for virtue. Virtue, too, can be produced just like vitriol, that is to say, by setting in motion the spontaneous forces of the spirit and of so-called nature, which itself is also spirit, and nothing forbids endowing educators with the title of chemists and apothecaries of virtue.

But metaphors are not arguments—Statistics prove the determinism of human actions, which always reappear in the same way and in the same quantity whenever certain actual circumstances appear.—But Statistics, if they collect

and simplify facts and construct views and tables
that are more or less useful, do not thus prove
anything ; for neither are the instances that they
give as equivalent, really so, nor the relation that
they declare between certain facts a real relation.
If we turn from artificial formulæ to the immediate
observation of the real, we find ourselves con-
fronted with nothing but individuated volitional
acts, resulting from necessity and liberty.—The
individual has a constant character, of which action
is the consequence : *operari sequitur esse.*—But
the constant character is nothing but the abstraction of the single acts done by the individual.
It is therefore natural that the actions should
appear to be referable to the character which is
derived from them ; but it is not correct to
say that there is equivalence, for abstraction is
not equivalent to concretion.—The individual,
even if he can be conceived as free in respect
to his external environment, would be always
subject to the law of his own nature.—But the
law of his own nature is not a contingent thing,
but the law itself of the Spirit, or, precisely,
freedom, and it is quite clear that freedom
is not free not to be free.—The social organism
has its natural laws, which govern the action of
the individual.—The social organism is also

an abstraction, which is turned into a being only by the false interpretation of a metaphor. In all these examples, and in the many others that could be brought forward, the error is always the same as has been said : the substitution of the naturalistic for the speculative construction, Physic for Metaphysic. And since physical or naturalistic construction has no material other than given historical facts, the doctrines above mentioned, when they are not false, are always tautological and lead to the affirmation that the volitional fact is a fact, or that in it is the moment of necessity.

The mysticism of arbitrarism. Arbitrarism, on the other hand, arises in the same way as mysticism, from distrust of thought ; being unable to dominate the fact that should be explained, recourse is had to the inconceivable, to the absurd, to miracle ; subjective and individual ignorance is hypostasized and of it is made a metaphysical reality. Arbitrarism, like mysticism, has its element of truth, in the negation of determinism, that is, in the recognition of the impotence of the naturalistic method and in the affirmation that the truth lies beyond that method, in the concept of creation and of freedom. But freedom separated from its logical and necessary moment becomes transformed into

will, just as in mysticism in general God is transformed into the mystery, ready to receive all
individual caprices into himself, and to confer
upon them an appearance of truth.

The concept of freedom (necessity-liberty), *The doctrine of necessity-*
which is at once scientific and not mechanical, *liberty, and idealism.*
and if it surpass the categories of Physic, does
not surpass those of Metaphysic, is opposed to
both these views. As idealist philosophy, it
tends in general to conciliate the ideal with
the actual, thought with complete reality, philosophy with the whole of experience. With the
concept of freedom is eliminated the inertia
of determinism, and the unstable springing about
of arbitrarism. The gross material conception
of the real disappears, because that which seems
to be matter is revealed as spirit, the fact as
creation, necessity as the product of liberty.
But miracle disappears with them. For if the
spirit be the eternal, omnipresent, continuous
miracle, unattainable by the physical method,—
a continual miracle, omnipresent and eternal,
is no longer a miracle, but the same simple
and ordinary reality, which each one of us con-
tributes to create and each one of us can and
does think.

Strict determinism and strict arbitrarism are

not, however, the sole adversaries of the concept of liberty-necessity, as rigorous materialism and mysticism are not the only adversaries of idealism. There exists another which must be called more dangerous (if misunderstanding be more dangerous than error). This doctrine, since it goes by the name of dualism, spiritualism, and neocriticism in general philosophy, could be called the doctrine *of double practical causality*, in the field of the practical problem. The supporters of this line of thought, despite many individual differences, are all agreed in positing two distinct series of facts : one which obeys mechanical causality, another which is initiative and creation, or (as they say) obeys causality through freedom. There are thus two series that inter-penetrate one another or alternate at every instant and are mutually blended, the one in the other. Hence there is something of each in the voli-tional act, something of the strongest motive and something of free choice. Such a solution has some external resemblance with that which we maintain, but is intrinsically most different. Our solution is *fusion* of liberty and necessity, while this is *juxtaposition*; our solution is *conciliation*, this *transaction*. Like every juxta-position and transaction it displeases both the

contending parties, and falls into the power,
now of the one, now of the other. Thus, if,
according to the theories of that tendency, it
be maintained that freedom exists, but that
there are also causes tending to diminish it,
or that there exist volitional acts, but that involuntary acts also exist, one does not understand
how a series of facts that has its own law in
itself (freedom, the will) can ever be subor-
dinated to facts that obey a different law
(diminution of freedom, involuntariness of acts).
If this happen sometimes or many times,
we must suspect that it happens always, and
that the surviving freedom is a mask of freedom,
illusion. Thus, if it be affirmed that side by
side with causality, with equivalence of causes
and effects, or with the possibility of foreseeing
the effect by means of the cause, there is
another causality, in which the effect is not
equivalent to the cause, and that not only
is it not to be foreseen, but is such that
only after it has happened does it allow its
cause to be discovered; then the doubt arises
that one of the two causalities does not exist,
because either the effect is equivalent to the
cause, and so it must always be, or it is not
equivalent to it, and so it will never be; or

it can be foreseen by means of the cause, and so it will always be, or it cannot be foreseen, and never will be foreseen. The strict determinists and arbitrarists have the loyalty of error, and they are rare, because energetic spirits are rare, but the doctrine of double causality is tinged with some of the rouge of truth, and thus seduces the many, and is proper to weak and irresolute spirits, as indeed are dualism, spiritualism, agnosticism, neocriticism, of which this doctrine forms a particular case. When the absurdity of determinism and of arbitrarism has been recognized (and their very presence is an autocriticism), it is necessary to satisfy with a new and single concept the claim that they represent, certainly not with *the sum of two errors*, and the new single concept is that of true freedom.

Its character of transaction and transition. The doctrine of double causality has had its historical importance, not because it is a *transaction*, but rather because it is a *transition*; that is, a gradual approximation to the true concept, with the introduction into the naturalistic concept of an element of ferment and dissolution : the concept of a causality by means of freedom, that is, of a causality that is so only in name. The concept of freedom cannot tolerate that of

causality at its side, and of the two series
posited, one of the two is not real in itself,
but simply a particular product of the other :
mechanical causality is not a fact, nor a conception, but an instrument created for its own
ends by spiritual freedom itself. And only in
this sense can it be admitted that freedom avails
itself of causality for its effectuation, and the
truth of the observation be realized, that the
classifying of the perceptions in series of cause
and effect becomes itself also a presupposition of
will and action. The historical knowledge as
to the actual situation that precedes the volition,
since it includes of necessity philosophical universals in itself, so it can also include empirical
universals, concepts, and pseudo-concepts : the
consciousness of the productivity of the spirit
and the mnemonic formulæ in which this productivity is fixed, and for which it certainly appears
to be mechanical, but only to him who forgets
that the formulæ themselves are mechanical.

FREEDOM AND ITS OPPOSITE.   GOOD AND EVIL

Freedom of action as reality of action. SINCE, then, the volitional act is freedom, the question as to whether in a given case an individual has or has not been free, is equivalent to this other question: *Has there really been volition* (action) in that case? This question can have and has (as any one who lends an ear to such discussions as are frequently heard can verify) but two meanings. The first is, whether the case under discussion be *action* or *event*, and, therefore, if it be or be not accurate to present it as an individual act. For example :—Was Jacobinism the crime or the glory of Voltaire and Rousseau? Was the defeat of Waterloo the fault of Marshal Grouchy? The second is, if it be really a question of *action*, what, *precisely*, has that action been? For example :—What were the respective parts of Voltaire and of Rousseau in the propaganda of the revolutionary spirit and of the Jacobin mode of thought? What did Marshal Grouchy really

know and will when, instead of listening to
Exelmans and to others of his generals and
marching whither the cannon was thundering, he
obeyed to the letter the order he had received
and attacked the Prussian army corps of
Thielman?

There is a third meaning that is to be excluded : *Inconceivability of the*
namely, as to whether at a given moment of time *absolute absence
of action.*
there has been any sort of action or, on the
contrary, a void and total absence of action.   For
the only case in which the individual does not
act is that in which he is dead or partially dead,
be the death physiological or spiritual, that of a
corpse or of a madman.   The glory of putting
poor madmen on a level with the guilty and the
delinquent is to be left to the thinkers of the " new
school of penal law."   In every other case, man
always acts, always wills, and is always responsible
and free, because life, so long as it lasts, is nothing
but a web of volitions and therefore of free acts.
He is also responsible for the acts that contribute
to put man in such conditions as amount to
madness more or less transitory, and so of
irresponsibility : such is the case of drunkenness
and of moral dangers imprudently sought, and so
on.   At no point of life does the *practically indifferent* exist.

O

Those actions, too, that appear to be neither willed nor free, because they have become habitual, mechanicized, instinctive, are willed and free, not indeed because (though this be true enough in itself) habitual acts were once acts of will, but because (as we have already had occasion to remark), although they have become facts almost external to the individual willing, yet it is always the will that permits them to act and can always arrest their action: they are therefore to be looked upon as conditions of fact that every new volition modifies, even when it accepts them. A machine is not the work of the arm that moves it, but of hundreds and thousands of other arms that were previously moved in order to construct it. But once constructed, that which sets in motion the machinery is always the work of one arm, an act of will, just as an act of will can stop its movement and finally cause its disaggregation and destruction.

Non-freedom as antithesis and contrariety. But excluding the absolute absence of freedom of action (and of existence in so far as it is action), and on the other hand the presence of something different from it called causality having been previously excluded from the idea of freedom, it remains nevertheless indubitable that in the very bosom of freedom, there is *non-freedom.* Every volition is at the same time nolition, as every affirmation is negation. Volition is love, nolition hate; and, as we know, every love is hate, and the more we love, the more we hate. Antigone was born to love intensely, and for that very reason, to hate profoundly. What can be that which we hate in love and abhor in volition? What can this internal enemy be, which does not consist either in the absence of volition or in the presence of an extraneous and indifferent element?—Since it is neither absent nor indifferent, it cannot be anything but the *opposite or contrary* of freedom, antifreedom, which constitutes the contradiction in its effective concretion.

Freedom is an indissoluble nexus of necessity and freedom : the force that tends to annul it is antifreedom, the scission of that nexus, the analysis of that synthesis. On the one hand it aims at making liberty fall into nothingness, by compelling it to the inertia of the fact, and on the other, to make a leap into the void, by impelling it to will, a sterile endeavour—two movements that are one-sided and absurd, and become identified through the considerations already established in relation to determinism and arbitrarism. Therefore the opposite of freedom is qualified indifferently, either

Nullity and arbitrariness of non-freedom.

as the *passive*, taken by itself, opposed to the active, the fact that resists the new creation, or as the *active*, taken by itself and abstract, opposed to the passive : will opposed to liberty. Anti-freedom is either the material fact or arbitrary choice, but the first is resolved into will, the second into material fact. Only by an act of will can the fact that should continue to develop be fixed as a fact and so appear as a material fact, and only by a persistence in that fact, which should be surpassed, can will give itself the appearance of a content. The undertaking is contradictory, and the solution, the absence of freedom, is a contradiction.

Good as freedom and reality, and evil as its opposite. Freedom and its opposite, freedom and its internal contradiction, freedom and will, are what is designated by the terms *good and evil*. With us these terms are given an altogether generic meaning, as they are taken as the representatives of all the other couples of opposites that are wont to be enunciated in the field of practical activity, as helpful and harmful, useful and useless, honest and dishonest, meritorious and blameworthy, pious and impious, lawful and sinful, and so on. All these formulæ either answer to the subdistinctions of the practical activity (which we shall study further on), or are the same distinction, variously formulated, with reference to psychological classes. But all are to be reduced to those of good and evil for the purposes of the philosophical study of the practical activity in general, without ulterior determinations of them as moral or utilitarian good, moral or utilitarian evil, or any other form there may be, and without regard to the various empirical material, with which they may be filled.

That practical good and evil are to be conceived as will and anti-will, and the good, therefore, as the reality and the bad as the irreality of the will, the good as something positive and the bad as something negative,—is the solution imposed by the impossibility of thinking the two others that differ from it: namely, that which considers the distinction between good and bad as inexistent (abstract monism of values), and that which considers the good as transcendent in respect of reality, which is always evil, unless the good deign to descend and modify it (abstract dualism of values). For the criticism of the abstract monistic view, it is necessary to distinguish between those doctrines that deny, not only the distinction between good and evil, but also all the analogous distinctions in every field of activity, including that of thought, and the doctrines that

Critique of abstract monism and of the dualism of values.

allow the distinction to subsist in other fields, but deny it in that of the practical. The first, which deny the distinction between true and false, are the suicide of Philosophy, the second, which deny it only between good and evil, are the suicide of the Philosophy of the practical : that is to say, both are founded upon errors that we have already criticized and surpassed, and upon which it would therefore be otiose to insist. As to the dualistic view (still common among right-thinking professors of philosophy, that is, among the lazy and the most lazy) it will be requisite to discuss this point seriously, when it has been demonstrated in what way Reality can place itself beneath the yoke of Value and of Goodness, which would be inferior to it by hypothesis, through the very fact that they were *unreal*: Reality living, these others dead ; Reality like "the four bedevilled" of Giusti bent upon *doing* so, they, like the "two hundred simpletons" of the same poet, bent upon *saying* no. For if Value and Goodness be real, they will be the true Reality ; and that which was first called by the name will be feigned reality, altogether identical with what we have indicated as the moment of contradiction and of will, arising in the very bosom of the practical activity.

An instance that is always formidable has

certainly been cited against the thesis of evil as *Objections to the reality of evil.*
something negative and unreal, and of good as it-
self the only positive and real: it has actually been
affirmed that this thesis offends against good sense.
What? Is evil unreal? Is it nothing? Unreality
and nothingness are then the knavish trick of some
wicked person who starts a calumny, which, being
received and believed, injures an honest man?
Unreality and nothing, the passion that drags the
gambler into economic ruin and moral abjection?
So the world is all good, all rose-coloured, all
sweet; and crimes, cowardice, foolishness, and
baseness are illusions, and there is no reason to
lament; so the feeling of life should be expressed
with a perpetual smile, like that upon the lips of
the wounded warriors in the marbles of Aegina?
—But let good sense and its advocates remain
tranquil. If evil be a nothing, that does not
mean that it is nothing; if the vanity that seems
to be a person, be vanity and not a person, that does
not mean that it has not really the appearance of
a person and should not be really combated and
dissipated. The wise, who having defined evil,
deny toothache, or like the stöical Posidonio
forget the gout that transfixes them, need
Giambattista Vico to remind them how no
philosophy is able to save them from anxiety on

behalf of "their wives in childbirth" and of "their sons who languish in disease"! The world is precisely that mixture of good and evil, which good sense says it is, and the sweet is always tempered with the *amari aliquid.* It cannot be adequately expressed either with lamentations only, or only with laughter. The thesis that we have enunciated wishes to abolish, not the consciousness of evil, but the false belief that this is something substantial, and thus prevent one evil from being increased by another, evil by error, *moral* trouble by *mental* confusion.

Evil within and without synthesis.

Evil is either felt as evil, and in this case it means that it is not realized, but that in its place is realized the good. The gambler of the example, at the moment he knows he is doing himself economic harm, does not play; his hand is held; and it is held, because to *know*, in the practical sense, equals to *will*; and to know the harm of gambling means to know it as harm, and so to dislike gambling. If he take to dice or cards again, this arises because that knowledge is obliterated in him, that is, because he changes his mind; and in this case play is not looked upon any longer as harmful; it is willed, and so at that instant again becomes the good for him, because it satisfies one of his wants. The

calumniator, if he understand the idea that is
passing through his mind, or rather the impulse
that has seized him, as calumny, is for that very
reason repugnant to it and does not pronounce
those evil words : in that case indeed he is not
a calumniator, but an honest man who resists a
temptation (and no other definition of an honest
man can be given). But if he pronounce them,
this means that the opposing repugnance was
not present or is no longer present : and therefore those words are no longer for him a wicked
act of calumny, but a simple satisfaction of a
desire to amuse himself, or to reject the evil that
has been done to him, and therefore a good.
In the same way, he who asserts what is false,
he who renders himself guilty of error, if he be
aware of himself as frivolous or a charlatan or
disloyal, would be silent : if he talk and write
and print false insinuations, this happens either
because the will for truth does not exist in him,
or is for the time being suppressed, and with it
the desire to seek it out and to diffuse it ; that
is to say, for that will has been substituted
the other of withdrawing from a painful labour,
or of obtaining easy praise and gain ; so, for one
good has been substituted another. As a rule,
it is admitted that we will the good and do

evil. " I do not do the good that I will, and I do the evil that I do not will " (οὐ γὰρ ὃ θέλω ποιῶ ἀγαθόν, ἀλλὰ ὃ οὐ θέλω κακὸν τοῦτο πράσσω), said St. Paul.[1] But it is a question of psychological confusion, owing to which a series of moments and alternatives is simplified into one single act, inexistent because contradictory.

Affirmative judgments of evil as negative judgments. Thus evil, when real, does not exist save in the good, which opposes and conquers it, and therefore does not exist as a positive fact. When on the contrary it exists as a positive fact, it is not evil, but good (and in its turn has for shadow an evil, with which it strives and conquers). The judgments that we give when we judge an action to be foolish or wicked, a statement false, a work of art ugly, are all metaphorical. In delivering them we do not mean to say that there is an *existence* called error, ugliness, foolishness, but only that there is a given existence and that another is wanting. He who has launched a calumny, dissipated his property, soiled a canvas, printed a worthless book, does not, strictly speaking, deserve negative denominations, because to judge means to place oneself in the conditions of the person judged, and in those conditions there was

[1] Rom. vii. 19.

neither evil nor ugliness nor error nor folly; otherwise the acts that are the objects of the judgment would not have been accomplished, and in so far as they are accomplished they deserve positive judgment. But what is meant by the negative form of those judgments is that such an act is this and not another, that it is utilitarian and not moral, a commercial and not a literary or scientific fact, and so on.

There is a very ancient saying to the effect *Confirmations* *of the* that every one seeks his own good and that no *doctrine.* one deliberately wills his own evil, and, therefore, that if the practically good man be the wise, then the bad man can but be the ignorant. Now if we remove from the thesis its intellectualist veneer, and translate wisdom and ignorance into practical terms, we see that wickedness is here looked upon as a limit, as a tendency toward the good, that has failed, not as the will for an evil. The dispute as to who sins the more, he who is conscious of the evil, or he who has no consciousness of it, is also illumined by the theory that we have here exposed, which declares that both parties to the dispute are right and wrong. For instance, he who is completely without moral consciousness, is morally innocent, whereas he who is more or less possessed of one, is also more or less of a sinner, for the law itself makes him so (τὴν ἁμαρτίαν οὐκ ἔγνων εἰ μὴ διὰ νόμου, also said St. Paul[1]).   But with this saying it is not desired to put the innocent above the sinner, but the contrary.   That declaration of ignorance is the gravest condemnation, for it is thus recognized that the individual in question is unable to sin, and therefore unable to do right, since the possibility of sinning is all one with that of doing right.   The poet inspires admiration, but he who does not know how to be anything but a poet, and is therefore unable to reason and to act, is deficient.   The shrewd man is praised, but he who is *only* shrewd cannot be praised.   The animal is a being, worthy of all esteem, but to call a man an animal, that is, to tell him that he is nothing but an animal, is to do him a great injury.   In other words, while we recognize as good all that a man effectively does, we do not intend to cancel the distinction between one form and another of human activity, and between one act and another, between the utilitarian and the moral man, between fanciful and logical production, between animal and man. Nor do we mean that those emphatic expressions of negative character that we continually utter

[1] Rom. vii. 7.

to one another and to ourselves, and by means
of which we urge ourselves and others to more
lofty modes of existence, are to be abandoned.

Here occurs an opportunity of tying a thread *The poles of feeling (pleasure and pain) and their identity with their practical opposites.*
that we had left loose when discussing the theory
of feeling, or rather the distinction of feeling
into the two poles of *pleasure and pain*, understood, not as a psychological distinction of greater
or less, or of *mixed states*, but as a philosophical
distinction of *pure states*, or of terms that are
truly opposed. When the vague and indeterminate term of " feeling " is directed toward
theoretical facts and is determined by theoretical
philosophy as æsthetic activity or speculative
thought, or in some other way, the terms of pleasure
and pain are, strictly speaking, not applicable to
it. The pure theoretic activity considered in
itself, cannot be polarized, as has been seen ; it
will always attain to the beautiful, always to the
true. Only in so far as the theoretic activity is
also practical activity, by the law of the unity of
the spirit, will the polarization of good and evil,
which in that case are called beautiful and ugly,
true and false, take place through it if not in it.
If the term " feeling " be on the contrary directed
to practical facts, and its synonymity with the
practical activity (of which feeling would be a

distinguishing characteristic) made clear by the Philosophy of the practical, it is clear that to it belongs immediately and no longer mediately that polarity of good and evil. Good and evil then become what theoreticians of feeling call *pleasure and pain.* These terms are identical with the preceding, as feeling is a fact identical with the practical activity, generically considered.

Doctrines concerning pleasure and happiness : critique. This theory of pain and pleasure, as the synonyms of the practical positive and negative, helps to put an end to a long series of questions arising in connection with such concepts. Above all, the dispute as to whether pleasure be positive or negative will appear to be unfounded, and, therefore, whether pain have a positive or a negative value, or, finally, whether both be negative : unfounded, since "pleasure" means "positive" and "pain" "negative." At the most, it may be admitted that pain has also a positivity, which is however nothing but the positivity of the negative, that is the real existence of the negative pole.—The theory that man always proposes to himself pleasure as an end is, on the contrary, not only not unfounded, but of such evident truth as not to require enunciation, much less efforts to prove it. If pleasure be nothing but activity, it is natural

that man should have no other end save
pleasure, that is, activity, life itself. The
correction that has been suggested by others,
to the effect that man wills, not indeed pleasure,
but activity, of which the outcome is pleasure,
has but slight exactitude, for the two terms
are not distinguishable, and the result is not
separable from the activity; the pleasure of
travelling is not separable from travelling. That
polemic has value at the most against empiricism,
which limits pleasure to an arbitrarily determined
group of pleasurable facts, that is to say, circum-
scribes activity to certain particular manifestations
of activity, collected in groups or classes, and
substituted for the universal concept. Finally,
by means of the identification of pleasure and
pain with good and evil in general which we have
given, all disputes as to the concept of *happiness*
disappear, as to whether it be or be not distinct
from that of the good action, practically coherent,
and if man propose to himself *happiness* as an
end. "Happiness" is equal to "pleasure," and
"pleasure" is equal to "activity." To will the
good (that is, to will well and energetically), and
to be happy, are the same. The objection
raised by some, that man does not will happiness,
but a certain happiness, that he does not will

pleasure, but a certain pleasure, not the good,
but a certain good, is valid ; but this only amounts
to distinguishing volitional man in the act, from
the theory of the will, constructed by the
philosopher. If Tizio wishes at this moment to
go to bed and Caio to take a moonlight walk,
bed and walk are the affairs of Tizio and of Caio ;
for the philosopher there is no Tizio, no Caio,
but man in universal ; there is neither bed nor
moon, but pleasure and the good.

Empirical con-
cepts relating
to good and
evil.
The practical activity, the will, which is
also strife between good and evil, can be
illuminated now from this side and now from
that by that indivisible unity, according to the
accidents of discourse and the varying situations
of life. In this way arises a series of concepts
which, in so far as they are unilateral, are
empirical, and only become again philosophical
in the thought of the unity of which they form
part. Thus, to make use of a comparison, space
in geometry can be analyzed and split up into
a first, second, and third dimension ; but as
spatiality, it is a *unicum*, which does not possess
either one or two or three dimensions ; and
when in measuring or constructing plans of
measurement, we proceed to think one of these
dimensions, we become aware that we cannot

think them, save all three together, or not as
three, but as one.   The empirical, practical
concepts that arise upon the antithetical and
dialectical nature of the will, have had much
importance, and it is fitting, therefore, that we
should mention and explain at least the principal
among them.

If the situations of life lead to the directing *Duty of being,*
ideal, in-
of the attention chiefly to the aspect of the will *hibitive, and*
imperative
striving against inaction and arbitrary choice, *power.*
it is posited in this strife, in this becoming, as
something that *is not* but *must be*, not as *real*,
but as *ideal.*   If the greatness of the ideal
that is to be and to fill the soul with joy, be set
in relief in this struggle, then the ideal appears
sweet and smiling, as a *joy-bringing and beatific*
vision.   If, on the other hand, the effort of its
becoming be set in relief, the ideal can be made
into a metaphor, as will opposed to will, as
legitimate against rebellious will ; and then it
assumes a sour, rough, and hard appearance, and
the names of *inhibitive or imperative power*, in
so far as it impedes the will, or promotes liberty.

There is no less opportunity and interest in *Evil, remorse,*
etc. ; good,
making clear that relation, from the point of *satisfaction,*
etc.
view of the negative term, or of evil.   A
series of descriptive concepts then appears, which

P

present the consciousness of evil, now as obstinate *blindness* (*cor induratum*), now as *disquiet* and *scruple*, which induce vigilance and circumspection, now as *humility*, which does not permit forgetting how easy it is to slip into evil. But it is worthy of note that the series of words and empirical concepts that serve to illuminate the *satisfaction* of the good, the *victory* won over oneself, *tranquillity* of conscience, is far less rich. Perhaps this arises precisely because there is less practical interest in celebrating the pleasure of victory than in the inculcation of the necessity for strife and the abhorrence of evil. Why draw attention to joy and to repose when man is already too much inclined to allow himself joy and repose; does not Life allow them to itself and cause other problems to follow on each solution, new perils to follow perils overpast, and the necessity for new struggles? It is therefore of importance to direct the greater sum of attention to those aspects from which the eye is most frequently turned aside. Finally, these various aspects can be placed in relation with the greater or less frequency with which each appears in individuals, thus arriving at the construction of the concepts of *virtue and vice*, and of the models of *the virtuous man, the honest man, the deliberate man, the clever man,* and their opposites, *the vicious, the dishonest, the unreflective, the incapable man,* and so on.

The same thing happens with these empirical practical concepts as with all the other empirical concepts, of which we have spoken in general. *Their incapacity for serving as practical principles.* They have been stiffened into philosophical concepts, for the hasty satisfaction of the philosophical need of man. Hence, among others, many of the disputes as to the principle of the Philosophy of the practical. Some indeed maintain that such a principle is to be found in *duty or the imperative; others in the idea or the ideal, others in the joy of good, others in the abhorrence of pain, others in virtue, others in enthusiasm,* and so on. Each of the above-mentioned theoreticians has the sharpest eyes for the discovery of the defects in the theories of others, but is short-sighted as regards his own. Those who maintain the ideal satirize the form of the categoric imperative as suggestive of police or *gendarmerie*; those of the imperative and of duty deride the quietist form and the insipid ecstasy proper to the contemplation of ideals; those of the avoidance of pain do not spare their sarcasms for the hunters of joy; those of joy call these plunged in sorrow hypocrites, who also obtain enjoyments for themselves, if in no other way, then secretly: *si non caste, caute.* The truth is that all are wrong as philosophers, because they all find the principle of the will, not in itself but in an empirical concept, which gives to it an abstract and mutilated appearance. And, on the other hand, all are right, because those aspects are all real, and in each one of them the others can be implicitly shown. The categoric imperative, for instance, contains in itself both the will, which, in so far as it commands itself, is the true will, the joy of being and the sorrow of not being what we wish to be, the ideal, and the necessity of self-realization, and so of entering into strife against irreality, thus becoming imperative, and so on.

Its char-acteristics. If none of the formulæ given above, owing to their empirical character, be able to indicate with precision the principle of the Philosophy of the practical, and all are more or less convenient *synecdoches*, for this reason none of those concepts are to be treated as rigorous concepts. If they be so treated, there is not one of them, however justified it may seem to be, that is not able to cause rebellions and has not done so. The type of the dutiful man has been reproached with being so much preoccupied with duty that he does not really perform it, because he forgets the impulse of the heart; of the type of the virtuous man it is said that he, as it were, ceases from being so by the very fact that virtue becomes in him a profession; of the type of the honest man, that there is nothing more base than the race of honest men; of the type of the *pious Aeneas*, that his piety is egoism; and in general of all these cases it has been recalled that a little vice is necessary for virtue, as alloy for metals. Repentance and remorse, too, although they be highly recommended as means of purification, have had their detractors; does it not suffice (they say) that an evil deed has been committed? Must the offence be aggravated by losing time over it, as though anything could be remedied with sorrowing and lamentation? But others have replied that, given human iniquity, it is better to exceed in the matter of remorse than to pass rapidly over it. Humility has been opposed with the *sume superbiam* as being more virile, and with the *laudum immensa cupido* as being more noble; the habit of self-tormenting with the *servite domino in laetitia*, as, on the other hand, the over-confident has been admonished with that other not less biblical dictum: *beatus*

homo qui semper est pavidus. These are objections
and replies that may all of them have value for
the empirical situations to which they refer;
but they have neither truth nor value in philosophy, for which they are all of them false,
because the distinctions from which they derive
are not philosophical. Remorse, for instance, has
a value, not in itself, but as a passage to activity,
without which such passage would not take place;
the virtuous habit has a value, not in itself, but
in so far as it is practised and constantly preserved; duty cannot differ from the aspiration
of the soul, and both cannot differ from the
volitional act; confidence is at the same time
trepidation, and humility must be one with the
pride of merit. To sum up, for the philosopher,
the dialectic of the will is all in the concept of
will, with its polarization of good and evil, which
is the actuality and concreteness of that concept.

III

THE VOLITIONAL ACT AND THE PASSIONS

IF the volitions followed one another, so to speak monadistically, each one shut up in itself, simple, impenetrable, indecomposible, it would be impossible to understand the moment that there is in them of arbitrary choice, of evil, of contradiction. But it is not so. The individual is solicited simultaneously by many or, more exactly, by infinite volitions, because the individual is at every moment a microcosm and in him is reflected the whole cosmos, and he reacts against the whole cosmos by willing in all directions. This infinity of volitions that is in every individual, can be proved by a very obvious fact : by what occurs in the contemplation of works of art, in which the same individual is able to reconstruct in himself the most various actions and psychological situations, and to feel himself in turn mild and sanguinary, austere and voluptuous, Achilles and Thersites. This

The multiplicity of volitions and the struggle for unity.

would not happen, had he not to some extent in himself the experience of all these various volitional attitudes. But even if we wish to restrict ourselves to those volitions that are the most closely connected with the historical situation, thus limited as well as may be (every historical situation is in reality a cosmic situation), restricting ourselves to what are called volitions of the moment, we have always, if not a chaos, certainly a multiplicity, or at the least a duality, of volitions. Were the individual to abandon himself to that chaos, to that multiplicity, to that duality, he would instantly be lacerated, broken in pieces, destroyed. But he does not abandon himself to it, for he is an individual, volitional and operating just because he renounces that feigned richness of the infinite and that pernicious richness of multiplicity or duality, limiting himself on each occasion to one single volition, which is the volition corresponding to the given situation.

Multiplicity and unity as bad and good. This volition is consequently the result of a struggle in which the individual drives back all the other infinite volitions, to attach himself to that one alone which the given situation must and does arouse in him. And when the given volition does not affirm itself fully in this struggle,

he falls a victim to multiplicity, in which is
found that arbitrary choice attached to a volition
which is not the one that should be willed,
which he feels he wills and that he does will
in a way. Hence the will becomes split up
in different directions and contradictory, action
not positive but negative, not truly action, but
rather passivity.

The multiplicity of volitions explains then
the moment of arbitrary choice, of evil, in the
practical activity. This could be defined as the
volition that conquers the volitions, as its contrary
arbitrary choice is *the contest of volitions with
volition.*

The volitions that are driven back on every *Excluded
volitions and*
occasion and excluded, to make way for the *the passions
or desires.*
volitional act, are variously denominated in
ordinary speech and by psychologists as *appetites,
tendencies, impulses, affections, wishes, velleities,
desires, aspirations, passions.* But, as is usual
with us, we do not intend to compose and defend
such classes in a naturalistic and psychological
sense, nor consequently to distinguish appetite
from desire, or affection from passion, with
boundaries that must of necessity be arbitrary
and undulating. What is of real importance is
only the distinction and the precise boundary, not

arbitrary but real, between the volition and volitions, or, as we can now say, the relation between
true and proper *volition* and *the passions or desires.*

*Passions and
desires as
possible
volitions.* Passions or desires are and are not volitions :
they are not volitions in respect to the volitional
synthesis, which, by excluding, annuls them as
such; they are on the other hand volitions, if
considered in themselves, for they are capable
of constituting the centre of new syntheses in
changed conditions. It has been said that we
cannot *will the impossible*, but that we can
perfectly well *desire it.* That is not exact,
because the impossible, the contradictory, cannot
even be the object of desire. No one wishes to
find himself at the same moment in two different
places, or to construct a triangle that should
be at the same time a square : and even if such
absurd wishes be manifested in words, the words
will be absurd, but the desires will either be
different from what is stated, or they will not
exist even as desires. In a certain aspect all
desires are desires of the impossible (and not
only some of them), if, that is to say, we consider
them as volitions that have not been realized and
which cannot be realized at that moment : but
from another point of view, they are all possible,
and can indeed be precisely defined as *possible*

volitions. This is proved by their becoming gradually actual as the actual situation changes. If (to choose a very simple illustration) an individual engaged in a certain work repel the desire for food and sleep with his volition and action, that desire is nothing at that point, as actual volition ; but it does not for that reason lose its intrinsic volitional character, for when the hour for the repast or for sleep has struck, it passes from possibility to actuality and becomes the will for food and sleep. The sophism previously criticized, by means of which a bad and unsuccessful act, that is to say one that is dominated by passion and caprice, is justified by proving that it has had a legitimate motive and answers to a good intention, appeals to this character of possibility, possessed by all desires, and artfully changes it into a character of actuality, thus substituting for the given the imagined situation.

The relation that we have defined between volition and passions or desires explains why the will has often seemed to be nothing but a conflict with the passions, and life itself a battle (*vivere militare est*), and at other times itself nothing but passions. The will is indeed homogeneous with the passions, and is opposed, not

Volition as conflict with the passions.

to the nature of the passions, which is its own nature, but to their multiplicity. For this reason, it has been said that only passion acts upon the passions : for the will is a passion among passions. Even the poet or the philosopher, who frees himself from the passions by objectifying them and making them material for æsthetic contemplation or for speculative research, succeeds in so doing, only because he is able to affirm the passion over the passions : the passion for poetry or for philosophy.

Critique of the freedom of choice. We must however beware of enunciating this relation in a false form, as happens with the theory called *freedom of choice*, where the will is conceived as the faculty that chooses one volition from among others and makes it its own. The will does not choose a volition (save metaphorically), but so to speak chooses the choice itself, or makes itself will among the desires which are not will. Nor should the possible actions that are excluded be looked upon as constituting a graduation in respect to the spirit, which should will a and not b, c, d, e, and so on, attributing to them, nevertheless, different values, which can be symbolized by the declining series of numbers, passing downward from the will which is 10, to 9, 8, 7, 6, and so on. In reality, the

volitions that are excluded (*b, c, d, e*) have no
actual value, for the very reason that they
are excluded. They may acquire it in other
situations different from the one analyzed, but it
is not possible to present the various situations
together in one, and far less to determine them
quantitatively and numerically, otherwise than in
a symbolical manner. The propositions that
present the will sometimes as the *strongest*
volition in respect to the passions or desires,
and sometimes as the *weakest* in respect to the
passions, which seem to be the strongest, that is,
according as we consider the active or the passive
moment of the will, its victory or defeat, are also
metaphorical and symbolical.

The relation established receives further light
from the generally admitted theory of the necessary
precedence of the *feelings* as condition for the
volitional act. The volitional act is preceded by
a jostling multiplicity of volitions, by a swarm of
passions and desires, which it dominates ; and
therefore it may seem that it follows, not the
volition, but something different from the volition,
to be called *feeling*. It is certainly different, but
only because it is the *plural* of that *singular*.
The nature of the passions and desires in respect
to the volitional act has not been clearly elucidated,

*Significance of
the so-called
precedence of
feeling over the
volitional act.*

and this is another of the reasons that have caused the customary category of "feeling" to appear and to be retained.

Polipathicism and apathicism. Finally and always through the established relation, the two opposed theories concerning the passions are excluded: that which makes the efficacious explanation of practical life to consist in giving free course to the passions, holding them all to be sacred as such: this theory could be called *polipathicism*; the other, which makes it consist of the eradication and destruction of all the passions, in order to give place to the exclusive domination of reason, of rational will, or of the will that really is will, and could therefore be called *apathicism*.

Polipathicism has the defect of not taking account among the passions of that which is passion *par excellence*, and which alone becomes actual, driving away the others: the will. Apathicism naturally possesses the opposite defect and takes account only of the will, and therefore not of that either, for the will becomes impotent when alone, just as in the other case it becomes a chaotic jumble of all the passions.

Erroneousness of both opposed theses. Such views as these are so openly unsustainable that they hardly appear at all in their strictness and purity, in the course of the history of philosophy, and then fugitively. But it is desirable to be attentive not to identify the theoretic formulæ given above with the programmes of certain groups, sects, associations, or individuals who have verbally proclaimed polipathicism and apathicism, whereas they have implied something very different, and could not have done otherwise. Complete polipathicism and complete apathicism could only be attained by the individual at the cost of disaggregation and annihilation. At the most, sects, groups, societies, and individuals have been able to conform to those formulæ as the simple expression of *tendencies*; or those formulæ are applicable to them by *hyperbole*, in the condemnation that it has been held desirable to inflict upon certain unhealthy tendencies. Certainly there are individuals whose passions are in such slight control as to suggest the absence of will; they run after every one of their desires, or leave their soul open to the onset of the passions that devastate it as the wind and the hail do the fields. Lorenzo the Magnificent (symbolizing with his wonted finesse a profoundly philosophical conflict) said to his son Piero, who was addicted to every pleasure and caprice : "And I never have any wish but you realize it for yourself." [1] The young rake whose adventures were sung by De Musset may afford an example of the same disaggregation, composed of the most violent kind of passions :

> Ce n'était pas Rolla qui gouvernait sa vie :
> C'étaient ses passions ; il les laissait aller,
> Comme un pâtre assoupi regarde l'eau couler. . . .

But even in these extreme and typical cases the will and the dominion of the passions are never altogether absent : otherwise it would be impossible to live, not only a lifetime, but a day, an hour, a minute. Thus too on the other hand, no individual, be he ever so apathetic and ascetic, ever frees himself altogether from the dominion of the passions and the desires. We read in the life of some saint or beatified personage, whose name escapes me, how he had attained to so great a degree of perfection that whatever food he put into his mouth, he tasted nothing but dry straw. Leaving to specialists the inquiry as to how a stomach of so slight a capacity for distinguishing one aliment from another could perform its function, and also as to the consequences for social productiveness of so strangely perfected an individual, it is certain that in order to nourish

---

[1] L. Domenichi, *Della scelta de motti, burle et facetie* (Firenze, 1566), p. 14.

himself and live, the saint in question must have
had the periodical appetite or desire of straw for
his food, if for nothing else. Apathy too is often
nothing but a most violent and tenacious,
though disordered, passion for ease. Activity
in any case reasserts itself with the dissolving of
apathy, a state nigh to inertia and to death, when
it dissolves *grata vice veris et Favoni*, that is, with
the appearance of the desires, of those "suave
impulses," those "heart-beats," that pain, and
that pleasure, which Giacomo Leopardi depicted
in his *Risorgimento*, overcome with astonishment,
as though face to face with the mystery of life.

The formulæ of polipathicism and of apathicism *Their*
historical and
have had other contingent and historical mean- *contingent*
meanings.
ings, but of a positive nature, which it is fitting
to examine, in order to prevent the usual
passage, so fruitful of errors, from philosophical to
empirical theses. The return to the world and
to nature, which is one of the characteristics of
the Renaissance and of the Reformation itself ;
the rights of the passions, which is one of the traits
of Romanticism in its initial period ; neo-paganism,
which has given to the Italy of our day its most
lofty poetry in the work of Giosue Carducci, were
each in their turn nothing but beneficial reactions
against the lazy monastic life of the Middle Ages,

against Protestant pedantry, against degenerate Romanticism, which despised the real world and dreamed of contradictory ideals. On the other hand, in different times and circumstances, Christian ascesis, Franciscan poverty, and Puritan strictness were beneficial reactions. So true is this, that we are wont to unite in our admiration heroes of abstinence and heroes of the passions, assertors of the spirit and assertors of the flesh, for all, in different ways, because in different historical situations, willed always the elevation of humanity. Every one of those historical manifestations can be and has been blamed and satirized, but only in its decadence, where it has exhausted its proper function, and is no longer truly itself, but its own mask. The friars of the stories of the sixteenth century are not the companions of St. Francis, as the indecent Italians of the late Renaissance are not the active merchants, philologists, and artists who promoted it, nor is there a greater lack of historical sense than the transference of the characteristics of the one to the other, as is the way of vulgar detractors and apologists. One and the same historical fact (as has been brilliantly said) always shows itself twice: the first time as *tragedy*, the second as *comedy*.

The cases that we have recorded, which have *The domina-tion of the passions and the will.* seemed to represent unbridled or exhausted passion, possess not a pathological but a physio-logical character, in so far as they really consist of a domination, a volitional synthesis, which conquers and contains divergent and ruinous passions. And with this we have answered the question as to whether or no the passions can be domin-ated, and whether man be slave or free. We can dominate them, and in that domination is life ; if we do not dominate them, we advance to meet death ; to dominate or not to dominate them are the very poles of the will, positive and negative, and we cannot think of the one as being abolished without thinking of the other as also abolished.

But the labour of dominating them is hard, as all life, " sweet life," is hard. The passions, driven back and restrained again and again by the will, yet rage within us, tumultuous, though conquered. We tear out the cumbersome plants, but not their roots and seeds. The man who considers himself hardened to the trials of life, still feels and suffers : the man who seems calm is yet always agitated within. As the labour that is called physical deposits poison at the base of the organism ; so does the labour called spiritual in the depths of the soul. Hence the bitterness in those men who have willed and laboured much ; hence their *cupio dissolvi*, their aspiration for that bourne where all is peace. The poet sublimely imagines old Luther, after his victories, in the midst of the people awakened by him to a new life :

> Yet with a backward look, he sighed :
> Call me, O God, to thee, for I am tired,
> Nor without malediction can I pray !

IV

VOLITIONAL HABITS AND THE INDIVIDUALITY

JUST because the passions are possible volitions *Passions and states of the* and therefore always have a definite content, it *soul.* is no slight error on the part of writers of treatises, to consider joy and sorrow, enthusiasm and depression, content and discontent, tranquillity and remorse, and other antithetical couples, as passions. These couples are empirical concepts constructed upon the dialectical distinction of freedom and anti-freedom, of good and evil; but the groups of the passions must on the contrary be empirical concepts formed upon the basis of the varying determination of the volitional activity, according to *objects*, that is to say, in its *particular* determinations. Thus we can talk of the passion for celebrity, for science, for art, for politics, for riches, for luxury, for women, for the country, for the city, for sport, for fishing, and so on, with infinite subdivisions and complications.

Passions understood as volitional habits. The distinction usually drawn between the affections, the impulses, the desires on the one hand and the passions on the other, is on the contrary justified, though it always has an empirical character; these being considered, not as the single and instantaneous desire or impulse that prompts to a single action, but as an inclination or habit of wishing and of willing in a certain direction. In this sense, passion would be a generic concept (always empirical), which could be divided (empirically) into the classes of the virtues and vices; for virtue is nothing but the passion or habit of rational actions, and vice the contrary.

Their importance. These passions and volitional habits are not rigidly fixed, for nothing in the field of facts is rigidly fixed. As the bed of the river regulates the course of the river and is at the same time continuously modified by it, so is it with the passions and volitional acts, which reality keeps forming and modifying, and in modifying, forms anew and in forming modifies. For this reason there is always something arbitrary in defining habits as though they corresponded to a distinct and limited reality; and for this reason the concepts of them are arbitrary and empirical. Habits are not categories, nor do they give rise

to distinct concepts; but they are the like in
the unlike, unlike, itself also, in itself, although
discernible in a certain way from other groups
of dissimilar facts. Their importance is great,
because they constitute, as it were, the bony
structure of the body of reality. In them *individuality* understood as an empirical concept,
has its foundation, for which, if it be not substance, neither is it a complex of casually
divergent states.

The nature of the passions as volitional habits *The control
of the passions*
to be both fixed and mobile, that is to say, only *in so far as
they are*
relatively fixed and relatively mobile, is the *volitional
habits.*
principle that aids the solution of several much-
debated and certainly important questions of the
Philosophy of the practical. And in the first
place, the passions being understood as habits, the
answer to the question as to whether or no they
can be controlled, and if the answer be in the
affirmative, then in what limits, receives a somewhat different meaning, which explains the interest
which that question has always aroused. Nothing,
in fact, removes our consciousness of freedom
and personality in so brutal a manner and
makes us feel our impotence and misery in so
depressing a way, as to find ourselves with our
good intention and action hardly begun, face to

face with the unchained forces of our passions
and of the habits that oppose it, which drown
with their deafening clamour the weak and timid
voice of the incipient action, vex it with their
arrogance, and drag it along paths well known
and abhorred. We fall then into mistrust and
baseness, believe ourselves lost for ever ;
freedom and will seem to be fables for the
adornment of sermons and the books of moralists.
The sage who recalls to man the absolute empire
that he possesses over his passions and exhorts
him never to be troubled and to repeat the twenty
or four-and-twenty letters of the alphabet, so
that the spirit may have time to recuperate its
strength, to resist and to conquer, seems to utter
the insipid babble of one who has never truly
loved and hated, and to measure the full and
overflowing souls of others on the model of his
own empty or almost empty soul. We laugh
freely at the "short legs" of ideals and good
intentions, and read again with satisfaction not
undiluted with bitterness, some little story like
Voltaire's *Memnon ou la sagesse humaine*, which
bears as motto the very appropriate epigraph :

Nous tromper dans nos entreprises,
C'est à quoi nous sommes sujets :
Le matin je fais des projets,
Et le long du jour des sottises ;

or at the most they conclude that there is no way to free oneself from a bad passion save with another one equally bad, from a vice with a vice, "as from a plank we pluck with nail a nail."

Nevertheless, he who torments himself and *Difficulty and reality of dominating them.* gets angry, or laughs and draws such conclusions as these, is not in the right. That is to say, he is right to laugh at ingenuous sages and at odious preachers and moralists, for their theories are certainly simplicist and false. But he is wrong in not understanding that his own theory is also simplicist and false, for it runs into the opposite extreme.—Habits and passions are habits and passions, because slowly formed : it is therefore a vain illusion to attempt to destroy them at a blow. Perhaps it is believed that the passions are tender flowerets or grasses that a child has attached to the surface of the soil ? They are a rank growth, strong oaks whose roots dive deep into the earth!—That is most true, but it is not for this reason impossible to modify and destroy them. They are indeed actually modified, for that very pain, that very disappointment, are a beginning of modification ; since we do not persist in what we abhor and follow, dragged along by force ; and little by little we end by freeing ourselves. The process of freeing ourselves from the passions, or from vicious habits, then, is effective, but slow, as the formation of those habits has been slow. We do not cure an illness with a sudden act of will, but nevertheless the will guides and directs the process of healing, and can open or close the entrance to the medicinal forces of nature. Now the passions or vicious habits are maladies that must follow their course, which, in order to be beneficial, must coincide with the cure. The sages who give receipts for freeing ourselves from them immediately are the Dulcamaras of moral maladies; but the existence of the Dulcamaras should not impel us to deny the existence of doctors, and above all of ourselves as doctors of ourselves. And we should certainly adopt a very bad and illusory method of cure, were we to accept the method so often recommended, of destroying passion with passion, or vice with vice, thus adding vice to vice, as those who treat the illnesses of the body with narcotics or with stimulants often add malady to malady.

Volitional habits and individuality. Habits, then, not less than single volitional acts, of which they were and are composed, can be and are continually conquered and modified, in so far as they are opposed to the new volitional syntheses. This confirms what has already been

said in criticizing the polipathetic view, which
ignores the volition for the volitions, as the
virtuous habit is ignored in favour of vicious habits.
But the theory of apathicism is also to be found
in this field, and it is needful to assert in
opposition to it, the great importance proper to
the volitional habits in giving concrete form to
virtue.   This second critical thesis is that which
affirms the value of *individuality or peculiarity*
in the practical field.

Every individual is furnished by mother *Negations of*
individuality
nature with certain definite habits, according to *for uniformity*
and their
the contingencies of reality among which he *critique.*
enters the world ; and he acquires yet others in
the course of life, owing to the actual conditions through which he passes and to the works
that he accomplishes.   Those habits which he
has from birth are called aptitudes, dispositions, natural tendencies : the others acquired.
The individual in his reality is, as has been
said, nothing but these groups of habits and
changes as they change.   Now is it rational and
possible (the two questions here form one) that
the individual in his willing and acting should rid
himself of such habits?   Is it possible to consider
them as things without value ?   Is it possible
to establish an antithesis between individu-

ality and rational action, as between good and
evil ?—The levellers who claim to impose the
same task upon all and wish to make of the
female a male, of the poet a reasoner, of the
man of science a warrior, of the saint a man
of business, and thus to give to every one a
part of the task of others ;—the dreamers of a
future society, in which all this shall have been
done, and the poet should attend to his poem,
after having played the philosopher for a couple
of hours, for another couple of hours the tailor,
and for yet another two the waiter at an inn ;—
all the pedants of abstract regularity, whom we
meet to our great annoyance in life ;—behold
the apathicists appear anew, for, as in the theory
of the volitional act, they advocated an abstract
action, conducted by the rational will alone in
the void of the passions ; so here, they advocate
an abstract rational habit, in the theory of
volitional habits, a model of human activity, to
which all individuals would be obliged to conform. Perhaps some such sensible observation
as this of Vauvenargues should suffice to confute
them : *Il ne faut pas beaucoup de réflexion pour
faire cuire un poulet ; et, cependant, nous voyons
des hommes qui sont toute leur vie mauvais
rôtisseurs : tant il est nécessaire dans tous les*

*métiers, d'y être appelé par un instinct particulier
et comme indépendant de la raison.* But since
it might be said that we wish to solve a grave
question with a joke, we will recall that the
volitional acts and the passions, volition and
the volitions, are of the same nature (though
the one is actual and the others only possible),
and that the nature of willing implies actual
definite situations, and that for this reason we
never will in universal but always in particular.
In the same way virtue, the virtuous habit of
the will, is not of a different nature to the
volitional habits in general, to the passions,
but is particular and individual as they are.
Those who make war upon individual habits
never succeed in substituting for them a universal
habit, which is inconceivable, but at the most
other habits, equally particular and individual.
The poet who will play the farmer, the tailor, and
the waiter, in the imagined society of the future,
will do all these things as a poet. This may
perhaps be an advantage, but may also perhaps
be the contrary, as future consumers of grain,
of garments, and of repasts will become aware.
For the rest, do we not even now see women
devoting themselves to the severe studies of
philology, of philosophy, and of mathematics?

But with the rarest exceptions, they remain
always women : their production, which is without originality, is not like that of man, done
with the complete dedication of the whole being to
the search for truth and of artistic perfection ;
and if in the midst of the most abstruse inquiry,
the image of themselves as wife or mother pass
through their minds, they desert, at the critical
moment, the philosophical categories, the formulæ
of flexions, the ruled or tangential spaces, and sigh
for their unborn sons and for the husband that
they have not found. Is this distortion of natural
habits useful? Generally speaking, it is not.
It is a doing and an undoing, a despisal of
the riches wisely accumulated and capitalized by
Reality in the course of its evolution.

*Temperament
and character.
Indifference of
temperament.*

Certainly the disposition natural or acquired
is not virtue, and the *temperament* (since temperament is nothing but the sum of habits and
aptitudes) is not *character*. But virtue and
character presuppose habits and passions, of
which they give the rational and volitional
synthesis : they are the form of that matter.
And as matter considered in the abstract is
neither good nor bad, so the habits and the
passions (as has been very well observed) are
not in themselves either virtues or vices : they

are facts. And it is necessary to take account of facts; otherwise, they revenge themselves. On the other hand, habits and passions certainly change; but not all of a sudden and capriciously, rather, little by little, and always on the basis of existing habits and passions.

The first duty of every individual who wishes to act effectively, consists, therefore, in seeking for himself, in exploring his own dispositions, in establishing what aptitudes have been deposited in him by the course of reality, both at the moment of his birth, and during the development of his own individual life: in knowing, that is to say, his own habits and passions, not in order to make of them a *tabula rasa*, but to use them. The search is not easy and the preparatory part of life, namely youth, is spent upon it. Few are the fortunate individuals who have at once a clear and certain knowledge of their own being and of their duty; the majority seek and find it after many wanderings; and if such wanderings sometimes (as is written in the dedication of the *Scienza nuova*) "seem misfortunes and are opportunities," at others they are but a fruitless moving to and fro; hence those that are undecided during the whole of their lives, the eternal youths, those who aspire

The discovery of the proper self.

to all or to many of the directions of human activity and are incapable in all. But when our own being unveils itself and we see our path clearly, then to disordered agitation succeeds the calm of sure and regular work, with its defeats and victories, its joys and sorrows, but with the constant vision of the Aim, that is, of the general direction to be followed. Vainly will he who is endowed and prepared for guiding mankind in political strife and has a clear and lively perception of human strength and weakness, of what can and of what cannot be done, and is furnished, so to speak, with practical sense (with the sense of complications and slight differences), will try (save in the rarest and most exceptional cases, and this reserve is to be understood in all that we are saying here) to acquire a place among those who cultivate the abstract and universal, operations demanding almost opposite aptitudes; vainly will he who was born to sing attempt to calculate ; vainly will he whose mind and soul were made to accentuate dissensions in their bitter strife bend himself to be a conciliator and a peacemaker. It is worse than superfluous, it is stupid to weep over one's choleric or phlegmatic temperament. There

have been choleric saints that have even used
the stick, and phlegmatic saints who have succeeded admirably in patient persuasion: the
mild Francis, "all seraphic in his ardour," and
the impetuous Dominic "whose blows fell on
the boughs of heresy." Reality is diversity and
has need of both, and each is praiseworthy if
he do that well to which he has been *called*.

This concept of the *vocation* has a mystical and *The idea of "vocation."*
religious origin and preserves that form; but it is
clear that by means of the previous considerations
we have divested it of that form and reduced
it to a scientific concept. The individual is
not a "monad" or a "real," he is not a "soul"
created by a God all in a moment and all of a
piece; the individual is the historical situation
of the universal spirit at every instant of time,
and, therefore, the sum of the habits due to
the historical situations. Those modes of conceiving and talking of one *and the same* individual
in two *different* situations, or of two *different*
individuals in the *same* situation, are to be
avoided, because individual and situation are
all one. But when the individual has been
thus defined, it remains none the less true
that each individual must direct his life according
to pre-existing habits and personal dispositions,

R

and thus we discover the true meaning of the
mythologies and religions that have been mentioned, and the struggles to find the suitable
employment can be expressed with the words
that religion has taught us when we were children :
the "vocation" and the special "mission" that
is allotted to us in life, until the last giving of
accounts and the words of dismissal and repose :
Nunc dimitte servum tuum, Domine! We are
the children of that Reality which generates us
and knows more than we, the Reality of which
religions have caught a glimpse and called it
God, father, and eternal wisdom.

Misunder-
standings as to
the rights of
individuality.
Evil
individuality.

The affirmation of the rights that belong
to individuality in the practical field has several
times assumed and still assumes (in our time,
more than in the past, owing to materialism
and naturalism) a form, no longer symbolical
and mystical, but wrong and irrational, that
it is desirable to remark upon here, always in
order to avoid possible equivoques. Indeed
many look upon the respect due to their own
beings as due to their caprice, that is to say,
to what is on the contrary the negation of
being : the right of the individual as the right
to commit follies, or to a disaggregate individuality. The declared necessity of temperament

for character is exchanged for admiration of temperament considered in itself, which, as such, is neither admirable nor blameworthy; but when separated from character becomes vice and folly. Hence the admiration that has even become a literary fashion, for the dissolute, for the violent, for homicides, for the criminals of the public prisons, illustrated by a few courageous and energetic souls among them, whereas they are as a rule weak, vile, and turbid.

Various theories are also erroneous, in which *False doctrines as to the connection of virtues and vices.* it has been sought to establish the relation between the passions and the will, temperament and character, passions and temperament being understood as vicious passions and evil temperament; that is, not in themselves, but in their antithesis to the rational will: hence the vain and paradoxical attempts to join together and harmonize virtue and vice. Thus it has been maintained that in certain vices are foreshadowed the virtues which will or can be developed from them; for instance, military valour in ferocity, industrial capacity in greed; whereas ferocity and greed are wilful acts and contradictions incapable of generating any virtue, as is seen in the customary cowardice of the ferocious and

the ineptitude of the greedy and covetous. Such
a connection of virtues and vices has on other
occasions been presented as a mixture or co-
temperament, and it has been affirmed that
the vices enter into the composition of the virtues,
as do poisons into the composition of medicines.
Finally, virtue and vice have been placed in
causal relation, and the causes of civil progress
have been found in human vices. But the vices,
as they are not the antecedents, so are they
neither the ingredients nor the causes of the
virtues. These are strength, those the lack of
strength. It is generally affirmed that in every
individual the virtues are accompanied by their
correlative vices, but if this possess some
approximate value as an empirical observation,
strictly speaking it has none, because men can
be conceived and are actually found, whose
virtue, far from yielding to excesses and to vices,
is eurythmic and temperate. But perhaps that
common saying aims at something else that it
fails of explaining well; namely, that every power
has its impotence and every individual his limit;
but this does not mean vice or defect; it is nothing
but the tautological affirmation that the part is
not the whole and the individual not the universal.

But if the individual do not exhaust the

universal, the universal lives in individuals; Reality in each of its particular manifestations. Therefore the affirmation of the right of individuality does not deny the right of universality; or it denies it only in that abstract form in which, to tell the truth, it is by itself denied. The individual is under the obligation to seek himself, but in order to do this he has also the obligation of cultivating himself as man in universal. A school that represented simply a cultivation of individual aptitudes, would be a training, not an education, a manufactory of utensils, not a nursery of spiritual and creative activities. The true specialism is universalism, and inversely, which means that if the universal do not act without specializing itself, yet specialization is not really specialization if it do not contain universality. If the two terms that are by nature indissoluble be divided, there remains only fruitless generalization or stupid particularization, and if our times have sinned in this latter respect, other times have sinned in the opposite. He is well-balanced who between these two forms of degeneration both knows and fills his own proper and individual mission so perfectly that he fulfils at the same time with it and through it the universal mission of man.

V

DEVELOPMENT AND PROGRESS

Multiplicity and unity: development. THE demonstration hitherto developed, that evil is negativity or contradiction, and that this contradiction takes place owing to the multiplicity of the desires in respect to the singleness of character of the volitional act, gives rise to the further question: Why should there be such a multiplicity, concurrent with the demand for unity, and thus be generated strife and contradiction? Here it would be fitting to observe that we must have filled our mouths very uselessly for a century with the word evolution, if such a question as this be renewed, or we remain bewildered and embarrassed before it. For the reason of that fact, which seems without a reason, is to be found precisely in the concept of "*evolution.*" This concept resumes most ancient views, and has been substituted in modern times for that of an immovable Reality, of a God who exists perfect and satisfied in himself, and creates a world for his own transitory pleasure ; or for a complex of beings, eternally the same, with variations that are only apparent.   The concept of evolution has entered so profoundly into the blood and bones of modern man that even those repeat it who would be incapable of analyzing and understanding it ; even the least acute of all, the positivist philosophers who like to call themselves " philosophers of evolution."

But before it acquired, as a vague and confused formula, so great a publicity as quite to amount to popularity, a philosopher of genius had analyzed and synthetized it, induced and deduced it in an unsurpassable manner, with the speculative formula of reality as *becoming* ; that is, as synthesis of being and not-being, being and not-being being thus unthinkable separately, and only thinkable in their living connection, which is becoming and *development* (evolution).   Reality is development, that is, infinite possibility that passes into infinite actuality and from the multiplicity of every instant takes refuge in the one, to break forth anew in the multiple and produce the new unity.   The inquiry into the dialectic of the volitional act enters in this way into the very heart of reality.   In order to deny multiplicity, contradiction, evil and not-being, it would be

Becoming as synthesis of being and not-being.

necessary to deny at the same time unity, coherence, good and being.

Nature as becoming. Its resolution in the spirit.

But if by the theory that has been recorded we have explained the necessity of evil for good, or the necessity of the not necessary for the necessary in the volitional act of man, the identification of the volitional act, which is man's, with reality which is of the universal whole, might seem to be too audacious. For (it will be said) the complex of other beings, that we are wont to separate from the complex of human beings and to oppose to it as nature, either is motionless and does not develop, or develops without any consciousness of good and evil, of pleasure and pain, of value and disvalue. Both theses have been maintained and nature has been represented, now as *without history, now as developing itself in an unconscious or mechanical manner.* But the contradictions and absurdities of both theses have been together perceived. "Motionless beings" is a phrase without meaning, to such a degree that even empirical science has everywhere pushed its way into history, and has talked of the evolution of animals and vegetables, of the chemical elements, and even of a history of light and heat. The other expression, "unconscious beings," is not less empty, because being and

activity are not otherwise conceivable save in
the way that we know our being, which is
consciousness; and although empirical science
certainly points to more and more rudimentary
and tenuous forms of consciousness in beings,
always differently individualized, yet it has never
been able to demonstrate the absolutely unconscious. If so-called nature be, it develops, and
if it develop, cannot do so without some consciousness. This deduction is not a matter of
conjecture, but a logical and irrefutable consequence. What is there, then, that persists in
men's souls, as an obstacle to the acceptance
of this consequence, in accordance with the profound belief of humanity in a community of all
beings with one another and with the Whole,
as manifested in philosophies and in religions, in
the speculations of the learned and in ingenuous
popular beliefs? A scholastic prejudice, an idol
of the intellect, the hypostasis of that concept of
"nature" that Logic has taught us is nothing but
the abstract, mechanicizing, classifying function of
the human spirit; a prejudice arising from the
substitution of the naturalistic method for reality,
by which a function is changed and materialized
into a group of beings. Those idealists were
also slaves of the error of a like hypostasis,

who, though they thought everything as an activity of the spirit, yet stopped when face to face with *Nature*, making of it an inferior grade of the Spirit, or, metaphorically, a spirit alienated from itself, an unconscious consciousness, a petrified thought, and creating for it a special philosophy (as though all the other did not suffice), entitled precisely, *Philosophy of nature.* But modern thought knows henceforth how man creates for his use that skeleton or *mannequin* of an immobile, external mechanical nature, and he is no longer permitted to fall back into equivoque and substitute this for entity or for a complex of entities. Nor should he find any difficulty in discovering everywhere activity, development, consciousness, with its antitheses of good and evil, of joy and sorrow. Certainly the stars do not smile, nor is the moon pale for sorrow : these are images of the poets. Certainly animals and trees do not reason like men ; this, when it is not poetry, is gross anthropomorphism. But nature, in her intimate self, longs for the good and abhors the evil, she is all wet with tears and all a-shiver for joy; strife and victory is everywhere and in every moment of universal life.

This conception of reality, which recognizes the

indissoluble link between good and evil, is itself *Optimism and pessimism: critique.* beyond good and evil, and consequently surpasses the visual angles of optimism and pessimism—of optimism that does not discover the evil in life and posits it as illusion, or only as a very small and contingent element, or hopes for a future life (on earth or in heaven) in which evil will be suppressed ; and of pessimism, that sees nothing but evil and makes of the world an infinite and eternal spasm of pain, that rends itself internally and generates nothing.   It confronts the first with the fact that evil is truly the original sin of reality, ineliminable so long as reality exists, and therefore absolutely ineliminable as a category : the second, with the other category the good, equally ineliminable, for without it evil could not be.   And it is easy to show how the optimist declares himself a pessimist, the pessimist an optimist, out of their own mouths.   The setting free from individuality and from will, which the pessimist proposes as a radical remedy, is the remedy that reality itself applies at every moment, for we free ourselves from the contradiction of individuality and of wilfulness by the affirmation of the rational will, with which the same pessimist cannot dispense, for the effectuation of his programme of ascesis or of suicide, which, according as it is understood, is either not a programme, or a programme altogether capricious and without universal value. In truth, there is no need to oppose a eulogy of Life with a eulogy of Death, since the eulogy of Life is also a eulogy of Death; for how could we live, if we did not die at every instant?

Dialectic optimism.

The dialectic conception of reality as development, that is, as a synthesis of being and not-being, can certainly be termed optimistic, but in a very different signification to that of abstract optimism. The synthesis is the thesis enriched with its antithesis, and the thesis is the good, being, not the bad or not-being. But who will wish seriously to oppose this logical consequence? Is it not a fact that men hope and live, although in the midst of their sorrows? Is it not a fact that the world is not ended and does not appear to have any intention of ending? And how would that be possible, if the moment of the good did not prevail, just because the positive prevails upon the negative and Life constantly triumphs over Death?

Concept of cosmic progress.

This continuous triumph of Life over Death constitutes *cosmic progress.* Progress, from the point of view whence we have hitherto regarded it, that of individualized activity, is identical

with activity; it is the unfolding of this upon
passivity. Every volitional act, like every
theoretical act, is therefore to be considered in
itself, that is, only in relation to the given situation from which it breaks forth. In every new
situation the individual begins his life all over
again. But from the cosmic point of view, at
which we now place ourselves, reality shows itself
as a continuous growing upon itself; nor is a
real regress ever conceivable, because evil being
that which is not, is irreal, and that which is is
always and only the good. The real is always
rational, and the rational is always real. Cosmic
progress, then, is itself also the object of affirmation, not problematic, but apodictic.

The difficulties that can be and are opposed *Objections and*
to this thesis all arise from the confusion of the *critique of*
them.
truly rational with that which is falsely so called,
between the true real and that which improperly
assumes this name, that is, between the real
and the unreal. Thus will be remembered the
instance of the end of the great Græco-Roman
civilization, without adequate parallel in universal
history, followed by the return of barbarism in
the Middle Ages; or the common example of
the shipwreck of noblest enterprises; or (to
remain in the field that more nearly interests

us) the philosophic decadence, owing to which, a mean positivism was able to follow the idealism of the beginning of the nineteenth century, which stands to the former as the eloquence of an Attic orator to the stuttering of an ignorant school-boy. Did the Middle Age, then, represent an advance upon that Rome, whose memory lingered in the fancy as an image of lost dignity during that same Middle Age? Was the victory of European reaction over the citizen civilization of the Revolution and of the Empire progress? and in Lombardy, the new Austrian domination following upon the Kingdom of Italy? or in the Neapolitan provinces the Bourbon restoration after the Republic of 1799 and the French Decanate? Was Comte an advance upon Kant, Herbert Spencer upon Hegel? But different points of view are confused under the same name in these questions, and, therefore, we do not succeed in immediately arranging those facts beneath the principle that has been established. It is therefore necessary to analyze. It will then be immediately seen that ancient civilization, in what it possessed of truly real, did not die, but was transmitted as thought, institutions, and even as acquired aptitudes; hence it kept re-appearing in the course of the centuries and still

keeps reappearing : it certainly died in what it
had of unreal, that is to say, in its contradictions,
for instance, in its incapacity to find political and
economic forms answering to the changed conditions of spirits. In like manner, the Middle
Age, which was evidently in part progress,
because it solved problems left unsolved by the
preceding civilization, posed others that it did
not solve and that were solved in the succeeding
centuries ; but if the posing of these new
problems, which, while destroying the old, failed
to substitute provisionally anything, was apparently
not progress, neither was it regress, but the beginning of new progress. The same is to be said of
precursors, conquered in their time, but conquerors
in history, of the restorations and reactions that
are so only in name, because they contain in
themselves that with which they contend, if for no
other reason, then for the very reason that they
contend : of heroes and initiators, who were conquered and martyrized, yet knew that they were
triumphing and did triumph in dying ; the cross
and the pyre will become symbols of victory : *in
hoc signo vinces*. And finally, if the positivism
of the second half of the nineteenth century seem
as a whole so greatly inferior to idealism, that
comes from its not being philosophy at all, but a

hybrid jumble of natural sciences and metaphysic, thus intensifying an error that already existed in germ in idealism, and fecundating the problem for a better solution. Many philosophers living to-day are inferior to Socrates, because they have not even risen to the knowledge of the concept; but those who in our day have attained to the level of Socrates, are superior to him, because besides his thought they contain in themselves something that Socrates had not; and those philosophers who are logically on a level with Protagoras, surpass him, just because they are the Protagorases of the twentieth century. There is therefore never real regression in history; but only contradictions that follow upon solutions given, and prepare new ones.

Individuals and History. The solutions, once attained, are acquired for ever; the problems that have once been solved, do not again occur, or, which is the same thing, they recur in a different way to those of the past. The web of History is composed of such labours, to which all individuals collaborate; but it is not the work and cannot be the purpose of any of them in particular, because each one is exclusively intent on his particular work, and only in *rem suam agere*, does he also do the business of the world. History is happening, which, as has been seen, is not to be judged practically, because it always transcends individuals, and to these and not to history is the practical judgment applicable. The judgment of History is in the very fact of its existence : its rationality is in its reality.

This historical web, which is and is not the work of individuals, constitutes, as has been said, the work of the universal Spirit, of which individuals are manifestations and instruments. In this way are implicitly excluded those views which attribute the course of things to Fate, to Fortune, or to Chance, that is, to mechanism or caprice, both of them insufficient and one-sided, like determinism and free will, each one invoking the other when it becomes aware of its own impotence.   The idea of mechanical origin, of an evolution that takes place by the addition of very minute elements, is now being abandoned, even for that fragment of history called *History of Nature* (the only true and possible Philosophy of Nature), in which is beginning to reappear the theory of successive crises and revolution, and the idea of freedom, whose creations are not to be measured or limited mathematically. But the supreme rationality that guides the course of history, should not, on the other hand, be conceived as the work of a transcendent Intelligence

Fate, Fortune, and Providence.

S

or Providence, as is the case in religious and semi-fanciful thought, which does not possess other value than that of a confused presentiment of the truth. If History be rationality, then a Providence certainly directs it ; but of such a kind as becomes actual in individuals, and acts, not on, but in them. This affirmation of Providence is not conjecture or faith, but evidence of reason. Who would feel in him the strength of life without such intimate persuasion ? Whence could he draw resignation in sorrow, encouragement to endure? Surely what the religious man says, with the words "Let us leave it in God's hands," is said also by the man of reason with those other words : "Courage, and forward"?

The infinity of progress and mystery. The Spirit, which is infinite possibility passing into infinite actuality, has drawn and draws at every moment the cosmos from chaos, has collected diffused life into the concentrated life of the organ, has achieved the passage from animal to human life, has created and creates modes of life ever more lofty. The work of the Spirit is not finished and never will be finished. Our yearning for something higher is not vain. The very yearning, the infinity of our desire, is proof of the infinity of that progress. The plant dreams of

the animal, the animal of man, man of superman ;
for this, too, is a reality, if it be reality that with
every historical movement man surpasses himself.
The time will come when the great deeds and
the great works now our memory and our boast
will be forgotten, as we have forgotten the
works and the deeds, no less great, of those
beings of supreme genius who created what
we call human life and seem to us now to have
been savages of the lowest grade, almost men-
monkeys. They will be forgotten, for the
documents of progress is in *forgetting*; that is,
in the fact being entirely absorbed into the new
fact, in which, and not in itself, it has value.
But we cannot know what the future states of
Reality will be, in their determined physiog-
nomy and succession, owing to the "dignity"
established in the Philosophy of the practical,
by which the knowledge of the action and of
the deed follows and does not precede the
action and the deed. *Mystery* is just *the infinity
of evolution*: were this not so, that concept
would not arise in the mind of man, nor would
it be possible to abuse it, as it has been abused
by being transported out of its place, that is to
say, into the consciousness of itself, which the
spiritual activity should have and has to the

fullest degree, that is, the consciousness of its eternal categories.

Illegitimate transportation of the concept of mystery from history to philosophy.

The neglect of the moment of mystery is the true reason of the error known as the *Philosophy of history*, which undertakes to portray the plan of Providence and to determine the formula of progress. In this attempt (when it does not affirm mere philosophemes, as has very often happened), it makes the vain effort to enclose the infinite in the finite and capriciously to decree concluded that evolution which the universal Spirit itself cannot conclude, for it would thus come to deny itself. In Logic that error has been gnoseologically defined as the pretension of treating the individual as though it were the universal, making the universal individual; here it is to be defined in other words as the pretension of treating the finite as though it were the infinite, of making the infinite finite.

Confirmation of the impossibility of a Philosophy of history.

But the unjustified transportation of the concept of mystery from history, where it indicates the future that the past prepares and does not know, into philosophy, causes to be posited as mysteries which give rise to probabilities and conjectures, problems that consist of philosophical terms, and should therefore be philosophically solved. But if the infinite progress and the infinite perfectibility

of man is to be affirmed, although we do not
know the concrete forms that progress and perfectibility will assume (not knowing them, because
now it imports not to *know*, but to *do* them), then
there is no meaning in positing as a mystery
the immortality of the individual soul, or the
existence of God; for these are not *facts* that
may or may not happen sooner or later, but
concepts that must be proved to be in themselves
thinkable and not contradictory, or to determine
in what form they are thinkable and not contradictory. Their thinkability will indeed be a
mystery, but of the kind that it is a duty to
make clear, because synonymous with obscurity
or mental confusion. What has so far been
demonstrated has been their unthinkability in the
traditional form. Nor is it true that they correspond to profound demands of the human soul.
Man does not seek a God external to himself and
almost a despot, who commands and benefits
him capriciously ; nor does he aspire to an immortality of insipid ease : but he seeks for that
God which he has in himself, and aspires to that
activity, which is both Life and Death.

TWO ELUCIDATIONS RELATING TO HISTORIC AND
ÆSTHETIC

The relation of desires and actions; and two problems of Historic and of Æsthetic. FROM the consideration of the practical activity in its dialectic, and in particular from the theory relating to desire and to action, shines forth, if we mistake not, the full light that has hitherto perhaps been invoked in vain upon certain capital points of Historic and Æsthetic, which, when treating of those disciplines, we were obliged either hardly to touch upon, or to develop in a manner altogether inadequate. The reason of this was that an adequate development, to be convincing, demanded as presupposition, a minute exposition as to the nature, the relations and the constitution of the practical activity, all of them things that could not be treated incidentally.

History and art. History or historical narrative is, as we know, very closely related to art, in contradistinction to the abstract sciences, since both art and history do not construct concepts of class, but represent concrete and individuated facts. History, however, is not art pure and simple, but is distinguished from it, because artistic representation is in it continually illuminated with the critical distinction between the real and the possible, what has happened and what has been imagined, the existing and the inexisting, with the consequent determinations connected with them, as to this or that particular mode of reality, event, and existence, that have taken place. In every historical narrative are always to be found, understood or implied, the affirmations that the narrative is real, that a different narrative would be imaginary, that the reality of the event in question properly belongs to this or that concept of politics, rights, war, diplomacy, economy, and so on. All this is quite absent from art, which is by nature ingenuous and free of critical discernment ; so much so, that hardly have its representations become objects of reflection, than they are dissolved as art, to reappear with a changed appearance (no longer youthful, but virile or senile), as history.

But if this distinction between art and history *The concept of* be precisely determined gnoseologically, when it *existentiality* *in history.* has been said that in history the predicate of

existentiality is added to mere representation
(and, therefore, all the other predicates connected with the case, referring to the various
forms of existence), and that therefore, the representative and artistic form of history contains
in itself rational and philosophical method as
precedent, yet there always remains the ulterior
philosophical problem : What is the origin of that
predicate of reality or existentiality on which all
the others lean ? We have already demonstrated
that it was altogether inadmissible to derive it
from a mysterious faculty called *Faith*, or to
consider it as the apprehension of something
extraneous to the spirit in universal, as *a datum
or position.* And we also stated that if the spirit
recognize its existence, yet it cannot attain to
the criterion elsewhere than from itself; which
criterion was nothing but the first reflection of
the spirit upon the practical activity itself, giving
rise to the duplication of reality that has happened
and reality only desired, or of reality and irreality,
of existing and inexisting.

*Its origin in
the Philosophy
of the practical:
action and the
existing,
desires and
the unexisting.*
All this now becomes a simple consequence
of the connection that has been made clear
between desire and action. The cognoscitive
spirit, when it apprehends and ideally remakes this
connection, has, in enunciating it, also enunciated

for the first time the couples of terms that we have already mentioned and that variously express the criterion of existence. To distinguish desires from actions is tantamount to distinguishing the unreal from the real, the existing from the unexisting, and to think the practical act is tantamount to thinking the concept of existence and of effectual reality. For the determination of the relation between desire and action, and only for that, the criterion of existence is not necessary, because that relation is itself that criterion. To say "this is a desire" means, "this does not exist"; to say "this is an action" means, "this exists." The desires are possibility; the resolutive and volitional act or action, is actuality. And it is also evident that existent and inexistent are not separable, as though the inexistent were heterogeneous to the existent; the inexistent exists in its way, as possibility is possible reality; the phantasm exists in the fancy and desire in the spirit that desires. Thus the posing of the one term is also the posing of the other, as correlative. What is repugnant and contradictory is the introduction of the one term into the other. This takes place, for instance, when in narrating the history, reality that has happened is mingled as one single thing with reality dreamed of or desired, and history is turned into *legend*.

History as distinction between actions and desires, and art as indistinction. It can be said that history always represents actions, and in this is implicit that it represents at the same time also desires, but only in so far as it distinguishes them from actions : history, therefore, is perception and memory of perception, and in it fancies and imaginations are also perceived as such and arranged in their place. And it would also be possible to say that art represents only desires, and is therefore all fancy and never perception, all possible reality and never effectual reality. But since to art is wanting the distinctive criterion between desires and actions, it in truth represents actions as desires and desires as actions, the real as possible, and the possible as real ; hence it would be more correct to say that art is on the near side of the possible and the real, it is pure of these distinctions, and is therefore pure imagination or *pure intuition*. Desires and actions are, we know, of the same stuff, and art assumes that stuff just as it is, careless of the new elaboration that it will receive in an ulterior grade of the spirit, which is indeed impossible without that first and merely fantastic elaboration. Likewise when art takes possession of historical material, it removes from it just the historical character, the critical elements, and by this very fact reduces it once more to mere intuition.

It must further be noted that the purely *The purely fantastic and the imaginary.* fantastic, which is the representation of a desire, must not be confounded with the mechanical combination of images, that can be made idly, for amusement, or for practical ends. This operation (analogous to that of the intellect upon the pure concepts and representations, when it arbitrarily combines them in the pseudo-concepts), is secondary and derivative ; and it presupposes the first, which provides it with the material that it cuts up and combines. Nothing is more extraneous and repugnant to poetry than this artificial *imagining*, precisely because it is external and repugnant to reality. Hence his would be a vain objection who should coldly and capriciously combine the most different images and ask for an explanation of the whole, with desire as the fundamental principle. Such combinations as these, since they do not belong to poetry, are void of real psychical content.

But if the relation between desire and action *Art as lyrical or representation of feelings.* be the ultimate reason for the distinction between art and history, and this distinction be the theoretical reflection of that real relation, the conception of art as representation of volitional facts, taken in their quite general and indeterminate nature, in which desire is as action and action as desire, reveals why art affirms itself as *representation of feeling*, and why a work of art does not seem to possess and does not possess value, save from its *lyrical* character and from the imprint of the artist's personality. The work of art that reasons or instructs as to things that have happened, and finds a substitute for intimate and lyrical connections in historical reasonings and connections, is justly and universally condemned as cold and ineffectual. We do not ask the artist for a philosophical system nor for a relation of facts (if all this is to be found in his work it is *per accidens*), but for a dream of his own, for nothing but the expression of a world desired or abhorred, or partly desired and partly abhorred. If he make us live again in this dream the rapture of joy or the incubus of terror, in solemnity or in humility, in tragedy or in laughter, that suffices. Facts and concepts, and the question as to the metaphysical constitution of reality and how it has been developed in time, are all things that we shall ask of others.

Identity of ingenuous reality and feeling. It may seem that in this way the field of art has been much restricted and the ingenuous

representation of the real excluded from it.   But
this ingenuous representation is just the representation of reality as dream.   For reality is
nothing (as we henceforth know) than becoming,
possibility that passes into actuality, desire that
becomes action, from which desire springs forth
again unsatiated.   The artist who represents it
ingenuously, produces the lyric for this very
reason.   For him there is no necessity to reach
it from without, as a new element: if he do
this, he is a bad artist, and will be blamed as
a hunter of emotions, emphatic, convulsive, weari-
somely sentimental, forcedly jocose, an introducer
of his own caprice into the coherence of the work,
a confounder of his empirical with his artistic personality, which exists in the empirical individual,
but is not equivalent to it.   The feeling that
the true artist portrays is that of things, *lacrymae
rerum* ; and by the identity of feeling and volition,
of volition and reality already demonstrated in the
Philosophy of the practical, things are themselves
that feeling.   The characteristic that Schelling
and Schopenhauer noted in music, of reproducing,
not indeed the ideas, but the ideal rhythm of the
universe, and of objectifying the will itself, belongs
equally to all the other forms of art, because it is
the essence itself of Art, or of pure intuition.

Artists and the will.

An obvious confirmation of this theory is also the empirical observation often made, that the men who lose themselves in desires are rather poets than men of action, dreamers rather than actors ; and in respect to this, that poets who seem to have the soul overflowing with energetic plans, magnanimous loves, and fierce hatreds are the most incapable in the field of action, and the worst of captains in practical struggles ; because those plans, those loves and hates, are not will, but desires, and desires already weakened as such, because they are no longer in process of volitional synthetization, but have become the objects of contemplation and of dream. He who reads the biographies of artists, or has dealings with artists in daily life, almost always has the impression that their gusts of passion are nothing but poetry *about to break forth*, as a green bud that opens and breaks the brown sheath. And if this process be painful, that is because every travail of birth is painful. One sees, indeed, how everything generally ends *par des chansons*. A fine poem and the sufferer is calm again.

Actions and myths.

This also explains why individual actions and practical collective movements are accompanied with hopes, beliefs, and *myths*. These have no logical or historical truth, but it is on the other hand impossible to criticize them, because they are not error, but fantastic projection of the state of soul of individuals and groups of individuals in action, and testify to the existence of desires ready to transform themselves into will and action. Utopias are poetry, they are not practical acts; but beneath that poetry there is always the reality of a desire that is a factor of future history. Hence it also happens that poets are thought of as *seers*, when the utopia of to-day becomes the reality of the morrow. The utopian and semipoetic Address of the Italian patriots to the Directory of June 18, 1799,[1] the not less utopian Proclamation of Rimini of 1815, the song of Manzoni, in which rang out the fateful verse,

> We shall not be free if we are not one,

will become, for the Italians of 1860, effective action and *historical event*.

Pure intuition, ingenuous representation of reality, representation of feeling, lyricism and personal intonation, are then all equivalent formulæ, all of them definitions of the æsthetic activity and of art. And it would be superfluous to repeat that art thus characterized remains

Art as the pure representation of becoming and the artistic form of thought.

[1] B. Croce, *Relazioni dei patrioti napoletani col Direttorio e col Consolato e l' idea dell' unità italiana*, Napoli, 1902, pp. 69-73.

the concrete form of the superior theoretical grades of the spirit. In fact, logical thought or concept is also volition, owing to the unity of the spirit, and the representation of such volition is the logos made flesh, the concept that incorporates itself in language, palpitating with the drama of its becoming. What word of man is there that is not personally and lyrically coloured, whether he communicate the truth of science or narrate the incidents of life? And how could we deny a place among the dramas that agitate human life and art portrays, to that drama of dramas, which is the drama of thought and of the historical comprehension of the real?

VII

HISTORICAL ANNOTATIONS

I. For the reasons stated in their place, a history *The problem of freedom.* of the concept of freedom would end by becoming almost a general history of philosophy. Denied in different ways in the mechanistic and deterministic conceptions (from the Stoics to Spinoza), and in the theological and arbitraristic (from Epicurus to St. Augustine and the mystics), that concept afterwards continually assumed a more and more conciliatory form; an indication that the question must be put in an altogether different way. This movement culminated in the Kantian theory, in which freedom, defended against the psychologists, is withdrawn from natural causality and affirmed *a priori*, as causality by means of freedom; but, at the same time, Kant did not succeed in fully justifying it, owing to his failure in the solution of the antitheses, the defect of the Kantian philosophy, which never really became a system. The

273   T

embarrassments and absurdities to which the
unsolved antithesis between liberty and causality
gives rise, are sufficiently exemplified in a proposition to be found in the *Critique of Practical
Reason* : "It would be possible to foresee what
man will do in the future, if we possessed all the
facts ; yet he would be perfectly free."[1] But
notwithstanding these contradictions and embarrassments, the energetic affirmation of the
principle of freedom by Kant (which had an
altogether special certitude in Kant, in respect to
the other two postulates of the practical reason,
God and immortality, from which in this respect
it was distinguished) helped to make prevalent
the conviction of the impossibility of eliminating
that concept or of escaping from it, and made of it
the field of battle, where the fortunes of philosophy
were decided. The problem of the freedom of
willing is really solved or near to a solution, in
those philosophies which do not fatigue themselves with it as a particular problem, but treat
of it as something to be understood of itself,
provided there be a non-mechanistic conception
of reality, such as would not need special
defence. This happens, not only with sentimentalists and mystics such as Jacobi and

[1] *Kr. d. prakt. Vern.* p. 119.

Schleiermacher, but also and above all in the Hegelian philosophy. Perhaps no philosopher has been less occupied with the problem of liberty than Hegel, just because he was always occupied with it. The will is free (he contents himself with saying); freedom is the fundamental determination of the will, as gravity is of matter; thus as gravity is matter itself, so is freedom the will. Hegel consequently saw true in the contest between arbitrarism and determinism, recognizing in determinism the merit of having given its value to the content, the datum, in opposition to the certainty of abstract auto-determination, so that freedom understood as free will is considered to be illusion. Free will is both determined and indetermined.[1] But how Hegel could conciliate this theory of freedom with the mechanistic concept of nature that persists in him is another question. His failure to attain to this conciliation was perhaps among the reasons that made his profound solution of the antithesis between determinism and indeterminism seem a vain playing with words.

After Hegel, a return was made to the Kantian doctrine, variously modified, in which is posited, now a double causality, now a com-

---

[1] *Phil. d. Rechtes*, §§ 4, 15.

position of diverging forces, now a double point of view, now two worlds, the one included in the other and dominated, the one by the principle of the conservation of energy, the other by that of increase. Such contradictory doctrines are to be found for example in Lotze and Wundt, to the latter of whom belongs the formula that the causal explanation is certainly to be applied to spiritual facts, but *a parte post*, not *a parte ante*.[1] The philosophy of Bergson represents in a certain way a return to the sound idealistic view, which declares that the dilemma of determinism and indeterminism is surpassed.[2]

The doctrine of evil.

II. The conception of the relation between bad and good, as reality opposed to reality, is mythological and religious (Parseeism, Manichæism, Jewish-Christian doctrine of the devil, etc.). But evil had already begun to reveal itself to the philosophical reflection of the ancients as the unreal, the not being; and this is explicitly affirmed in Neoplatonism. It was not, however, possible to understand this function of unreality, real in its way, without a general dialectical conception, which became very slowly mature. Without a dialectic conception, evil, conceived

---

[1] Lotze, *Grundzüge der Ethik* (Leipzig, 1884), pp. 26, 30-31 ; Wundt, *Ethik*[2] (Stuttgart, 1892), pp. 463-464.

[2] *Essai sur les données immédiates de la conscience* (Paris, 1898).

as unreality, becomes mere illusion, not so much
a moment of the real as an equivocation of
man philosophizing. This is clearly to be seen
in Spinoza, who opposes the full laws of reality
to the narrow laws of human nature, saying :
*Quidquid nobis in natura ridiculum, absurdum
aut malum videtur, id inde venit quod res tantum ex parte novimus, totiusque naturae ordinem
et cohaerentium maxima ex parte ignoramus,
et quod omnia ex usu nostrae rationis dirigi
volumus, cum tamen id, quod malum esse dictat,
non malum sit respectu ordinis et legum universae
naturae; sed tantum solius nostrae naturae legum
respectu.* For indeed, if evil, error and wickedness were something that had essence, God, who
is the cause of all that has essence (continues
Spinoza), would also be the cause of evil, of error,
and of wickedness. But this is not so, because
evil is nothing real. *Neronis matricidium* (he
observes) *quatenus aliquid positivum compre-
hendebat, scelus non erat : nam facinus externum
fecit, simulque intentionem ad trucidendam matrem
Orestes habuit, et tamen, saltem ita uti Nero, non
accusatur. Quodnam ergo Neronis scelus? Non
aliud quam quod hoc facinore ostendit se ingratum,
immisericordem ac inobedientem esse. Certum
autem est, nihil horum aliquid essentiae exprimere,*

et idcirco Deum eorum non fuisse causam, licet causa actus et intentionis Neronis fuerit.[1] But Spinoza was not able to determine in what sense Nero was really ungrateful, implacable, and disobedient, nor in what way such a judgment could be justified, owing to his idea of Substance, not as subject, spirit, activity, but as cause.

Kant did not succeed in understanding the nature of evil; for him good and evil were "the categories of freedom,"[2] and the view of Fichte who makes the radical evil to be *vis inertiae*, laziness (*Trägheit*), which is in nature and in man as nature,[3] represents progress in respect to the Kantian position. But only with the Hegelian dialectical view of evil, understood as negation, is evil at the same time given its right place; and its unreality, contradiction, which is no longer the product of illusion of thought, but of things themselves, in intimate contradiction with one another, if it be a blemish, is shown to be the blemish, not of human thought, but of reality.[4]

Decision and freedom.

III. Free will, too, is not considered as a

---

[1] *Tract. theol.-pol.* vi. c. 6; *Ethica*, p. iv. intr.; *Epist.* 36 (*Opera*, pp. 208, 378, 597).

[2] *Kr. d. pr. Vernf.* p. 79.

[3] *System der Sittenlehre*, in *Werke*, iv. pp. 198-205.

[4] See my study: *Cio che è vivo e ciò che è morto della filosofia di Hegel* (Bari, 1907).

quality and character of complete liberty, but as
its negation, will as contradiction, in the Hegelian
philosophy.   It was preceded in this respect, not
only by Kant, but also by Descartes.   Descartes
wrote of the decision of indifference : *Cette in-*
différence que je sens lorsque je ne suis point porté
vers un côté plutôt que vers un autre par le
poids d'aucune raison est le plus bas degré de ma
liberté, et fait plutôt paraître un défaut dans la
connaissance qu'une perfection dans la volonté : car
si je connaissais toujours clairement ce qui est vrai
et ce qui est bon, je ne serais jamais en peine de
délibérer quel jugement et quel choix je devrais
faire ; et ainsi je serais entièrement libre, sans
jamais être indifférent.[1]

Among the false formulae of the *freedom of*
choice can be mentioned that of Rosmini, who
calls it *bilateral* freedom, or that of performing or
not performing a given action.[2]   But since the
spirit cannot be reduced to complete passivity,
not to perform a given action is equivalent to
performing a different one ; and if this other
action that presents itself before us be also not
willed by us, then it will be another, and so
on.   Thus it is not a question of bilaterality, but

---

[1] *Medit.* iv.
[2] For example, *Compendio di Etica* (Roma, 1907), p. 56.

of multiplicity of tendencies : not of the choice between two volitions, but of the synthesis of many appetites in one, which is the will or freedom.

Conscience and responsibility   We may mention the disputes that have been preserved in the *Memorabilia* as to the greater responsibility of him who knows more (or wills more), as compared with him who knows less (or wills less), as to whether he that acts voluntarily be more unjust than he who acts involuntarily (ὁ ἑκὼν ἢ ὁ ἄκων). In this connection it is to be observed that he who voluntarily does not write or read well is certainly more grammatical than he who reads and writes ill through ignorance ; and therefore that he who commits injustice while knowing what is just, is more just than he who commits it because he does not know what is just ; and that he is better, who says what is false when he knows what is true, than he who says what is false, not knowing what is true. The dispute leads to the celebration of knowledge of self, or, as we should say, of knowing and possessing oneself.[1]

These thoughts are discussed anew in the *Hippias minor*, where the multiple difficulties are placed in relief and a conclusion reached that

[1] *Memor.* iv. c. 2, § 19 *sqq.*

does not even satisfy those who propose it.[1] It is henceforward clear that the question must be solved in the sense that he who is conscious of sinning is certainly a sinner, whereas he who is not conscious of so doing, does not sin at all ; but this being even incapable of sinning is in itself a sin, and places the man who is in such a condition yet a degree lower. In the polemic of Pascal with the Jesuits—who maintained that in order to sin it was necessary to be conscious of one's own infirmity and of the suitable remedy, the wish to be healed and to ask it of God—the Jesuits were theoretically on the side of reason. *Croira-t-on, sur votre parole* (wrote Pascal), *que ceux qui sont plongés dans l'avarice, dans l'impudicité, dans les blasphêmes, dans le duel, dans la vengeance, dans les vols, dans les sacrilèges, aient véritablement le désir d'embrasser la chasteté, l'humilité et les autres vertus chrétiennes?* Nevertheless, it is inevitably so, if those acts of theirs are to be judged to be vices (and if they really are so). Hegel places himself on the side of Pascal, who accepts and refers to the following argument and reduction to the absurd : *Ils seront tous damnés ces demi-pécheurs qui ont quelque amour pour la vertu. Mais pour ces francs-*

---

[1] *Hippias minor*, 375.

pêcheurs, sans mélange, pleins et achevés, l'enfer ne
les tient pas : ils ont trompé le diable à force de s'y
abandonner.[1]

A reduction to the absurd which is not such:
because the formula given as absurd expresses
at bottom a very simple truth, which Hegel too
stated in his own way, when he said that it was
necessary to prefer self-will, evil, the erring
Spirit, to the innocence of plants and animals, or
of Nature.[2]

The concept of duty.

IV. A classical example of the disputes as to
the principle of the Philosophy of the practical,
arising from the consideration of this principle
in its empirical formulations, can be furnished
from the polemic of Herbart against Kant on the
subject of *duty*. Herbart demonstrated that
duty is not an original but a derived concept,
and that it appears only when there is disagreement between the practical *ideas* and the *will*.[3]
But it would be possible to demonstrate with
the same method that the practical ideas are
derived concepts, because they do indeed presuppose the moral will, from the manifestations of
which they are constituted by means of abstrac-

---

[1] Pascal, *Provinc.* I, iv. ; Hegel, *Phil. d. Rechtes*, § 40.
[2] *Enc.* § 248.
[3] *Allg. prakt. Phil.* pp. 121-122 ; *Einl. i. d. Phil.* (trad. ital.), pp.
118 171, 224.

tion. Herbart was in the right against Kant, but he afterwards let the axe fall on his own feet. The hard formula of the imperative preferred by Kant had already been combated by Frederick Schiller, who accentuated the moment of pleasure, sympathy and enthusiasm in the good action.

As to the other concepts and to the disputes *Repentance* to which they gave rise, it will be opportune to *and remorse.* mention repentance and remorse. Spinoza does not see that it has value as a necessary negative moment, for he declared : *Poenitentia virtus non est, sive ex ratione non oritur; sed is qui facti poenitet bis miser, seu impotens est. Nam primo prava cupiditate, dein tristitia vinci se patitur*; and he concludes by assigning to it value for altogether empirical motives. Men rarely live (he says) *ex dictamine rationis*; and yet repentance and other similar affections do more good than harm, and if it be necessary to sin *in istam partem potius peccandum. Terret vulgus, nisi metuat.*[1] But it was Hegel who instituted a regular persecution of the concept of repentance and remorse. There are certain passages in his works that should be read in connection with this question, in order that we may clearly see how he had an eye to contingent and histori-

---

[1] *Ethic*, iv. prop. 54, p. 480.

cal events in his criticism. "In the Christian
world in general (he writes) there is in force
an ideal of the perfect man, who cannot exist as
multitude in a people; and if this ideal is found
realized in monks, quakers, and such-like pious
folk, it must be remarked that a mass of these
sad creatures does not constitute a people, just
as lice and parasitic plants cannot exist by themselves, but only on an organic body. In order
to constitute a people, it would be above all
desirable to destroy that lamblike gentleness of
theirs, that vanity which is occupied solely with
their own persons, the caring for them and
holding them dear, and has always before it the
image and consciousness of its own excellence.
For life in the universal and for the universal
demands, not such vile and listless gentleness,
but an energetic gentleness, not a thinking of
oneself and one's own sins, but of the universal and of what should be done for it. To him
who nourishes so false an ideal, men must always
appear to be affected with weakness and corruption, and that ideal to be so constituted that it
can never be translated into reality. They
attribute importance to trifles, to which no
reasonable person pays special attention, and
believe that such weaknesses and defects exist,

even when they are not remarked. Nor should
we admire their greatness of soul, but note rather
that their corruption lies precisely in standing
still and looking at that which they call weaknesses and errors, and in making out of nothing
something that exists. A man with such weaknesses and defects is immediately quit of them,
if he do not attach to them importance." The
observations that Hegel makes in his *Æsthetic*,
regarding the type of the Magdalen in Italian
art, are in this respect especially curious. "In
Italian painting the Magdalen appears, both
within and without, as the *beautiful sinner*; sin
in her is as seductive as conversion. But here
neither sin nor sanctity are to be taken too
seriously. She was pardoned, because she had
loved much; she sinned through love and beauty;
and the affecting element lies in this, that she has
scruples about her love, and beautiful and sensible as she is, sheds torrents of tears. But her
error is not that she has loved so much; her
beautiful and moving error is precisely that she
believes herself to be a sinner, whereas her
sensitive beauty gives the impression that she
could not have been otherwise than noble and
of lofty senses in her love." [1]

[1] *Gesch. d. Phil.* ii. 240-241 ; *Vorles. üb. Aesth.* ii. 162-163.

The doctrine of the passions. V. The relation between the passions or desires and the will has rather been studied at the moment of strife between the will and the passions, than for itself and within its two terms, although Aristotle had already begun an analysis as to the diversity of appetites or βούλησις in respect to the intention or προαίρεσις, observing that the intention relates only to what can be done, whereas the appetition relates also to things that are impossible.[1] The opposed schools of the Cynics and Cyrenaïcs, Stoïcs and Epicureans, and others such, were chiefly concerned with the antithesis of the passions and the rational will; but the formulæ of all these schools, if they have some empirical value as precepts of life more or less suitable for definite individuals, classes and times, possess none or very little for philosophy. Cynics and Cyrenaïcs, Stoïcs and Epicureans, they seem rather to be monks following this or that rule than philosophers. The question as to the mode of freeing oneself from the passions and of dominating them, which lingered till the treatises of Descartes and Spinoza, has also a chiefly empirical character. G. B. Vico took up a position opposed to the two opposed degenerations arising from those practical tendencies, that of

[1] *Eth. Nicom.* Bk. iii. cc. 2-3, 1111-1113.

"quenching the senses," and of "making a rule
of them." He despised both Stoïcs and Epicureans as "monastic or solitary philosophers,"
and maintained as "a philosopher politician,"
that it is needful "not to tear away his own
nature from man, nor to abandon him in his
corruption," but "to moderate the human passions
and to make of them human virtues."[1] Rarely
has the defence of the passions enjoyed an equally
limpid philosophical enunciation; as a rule, and
even in Hegel, it has been directed chiefly against
certain social tendencies, rather than against
philosophical doctrines.[2] The absolute abandon-
ment to the passions or their absolute destruction,
are theories that have not had true and proper
representatives.—The confusion between the
various meanings of the word "passion," understood now as appetition, or concrete and actual
passion, now as a state of the soul (joy and
sorrow), now as volitional habit, is to be found
in the various treatises that we have already
had occasion to record. It is natural that their
character of indifference when understood as
habits should have often been observed. Thus
for Descartes, *elles sont toutes bonnes de leur*

[1] *Scienza nuova seconda*, degn. 5.
[2] *Phän. d. Geistes*, pp. 484-486 ; *Encycl.* § 474 ; *Phil. d. Rechtes*,
§ 124 ; *Phil. d. Gesch.* pp. 39-41.

nature et nous n'avons rien à éviter que leurs mauvais usages ou leur excès.[1]

Virtues and Vices.

On the other hand, the erroneous form of the defence of the passions, consisting of making them the preparation or cause of the virtues, is already to be found in the English philosophers of the seventeenth and eighteenth centuries (More, Shaftesbury, etc.); and in the celebrated *Fable of the Bees* of Mandeville, it assumes the aspect of a paradoxical theory, in which the vices are looked upon as promoters and factors of progress, morality as inefficacious and harmful for this purpose. And La Rochefoucauld had written: "*Les vices entrent dans la composition des vertus comme les poisons dans la composition des remèdes.*"[2] All these are false or crude forms, in

The doctrine of individuality: Schleiermacher.

which is involved the doctrine of the right to individuality, and they have always constituted and still constitute its danger. This doctrine received its most energetic expression in the romantic and preromantic period, thanks above all to Schleiermacher, after it had been referred to in a rather vague way by Jacobi.[3]

"For some time" (writes Schleiermacher in the *Monologues*) "I too was satisfied that I had

---

[1] *Traité des passions*, iii. § 211.
[2] *Maximes*, n. 182 (Ed. Garnier, p. 43).
[3] *Woldemar*, pp. 112-113.

discovered Reason ; and venerating equality with
the *Unique Being* as that which is most lofty, I
believed that there was one single measure for
every case, that action should be in all of them
the same, and that each one is distinguished from
the other only in so far as it occupies a place of its
own in space.   I believed that humanity manifested
itself differently only in the variety of external
facts ; but that the internal man, the individual,
was not a being peculiarly (*eigenthümlich*) constructed, and that each was everywhere equal to
the other."   " But afterwards was revealed to me
that which instantly raised me to a high state of
exaltation : it became clear that every man must
represent humanity in his own way, in an altogether individual combination of its elements, in
order that it may manifest itself in every mode,
and that everything most different may issue from
its bosom and become effectual in the fulness
of time and space. . . . Owing to this thought,
I felt myself to be a work individually willed and
therefore elected by the Divinity and such that
it must enjoy a particular form and culture ; and
the free act to which this thought belongs has
collected and intimately joined together the
elements of human nature in a peculiar existence."
" While I now do whatever I do according to my

U

spirit and sense, my fancy places before me as very clear proof of the internal determination, a thousand other modes, in which it would be possible to act otherwise without offending the laws of humanity : I rethink myself in a thousand different forms, in order to discover with the greater certainty that which is especially mine."[1]

Romantic and very modern theories.

But this peculiarity (*Eigenthümlichkeit*), opportunely placed in relief by Schleiermacher, and a thought much loved by the Romantics (Herder, Jacobi, G. Humboldt, the Schlegels, etc.), is often seen to degenerate into individual caprice, even in those times, as may be observed in the sort of caricature which Frederick Schlegel made of the Fichtian I, become the individual I, and in the notorious *Lucinde*, to which the same Schleiermacher inconsiderately devoted a series of letters of comment and defence. The last offshoots of the Romantics were Max Stirner and Frederick Nietzsche : in the former the value of individuality becomes changed into an affirmation of spasmodic egotism ; in the second there is a continuous mixture of true and false, of good and of bad individuality, as is natural in a writer whose

[1] *Monologen*, in *Werke*, i. 366-368, 372.

Eigenthümlichkeit was rather that of a poet than of a thinker.

VI. We have discussed elsewhere Hegel's *The concept of development and progress.* concept of development, and his thought as synthesis of opposites, which essentially belongs to the Hegelian philosophy and has been superficially treated and adopted by other philosophical schools, and this is not the place either to retrace their history or to demonstrate into what errors Hegel fell through abusing the truth that he had discovered. Among the errors of that philosophy (as for that matter of all contemporary philosophies and of those that have followed one another down to our own day), is to be noted the persistence of the concept of Nature as a mode of reality opposed to the mode of the Spirit, whence came a dualism that was not effectually surpassed, save in appearance. The doctrine of development by opposites is to be understood as accepted and maintained here, with the correction of the concept of nature, and also the doctrine of the synthesis of opposites, free from the use or abuse of it by Hegel for distinct concepts (and worse still, for empirical concepts). As for the concept of Providence, which is neither Fate nor Fortune, nor the work of a transcendent God, this, in its modern form, goes back to the *Scienza nuova* of Vico and is not to be confounded with the personal religious beliefs that Vico held and kept distinct from his philosophical concept as to immanent Providence. The same concept reappears in the Hegelian philosophy under the form of the Idea, or of the *astuteness of Reason*, which avails itself of men as its instruments and managers of business.[1] Finally, the conception of cosmic progress was extraneous to the oriental world, to the Græco-Roman, and to the Christian worlds, prevailing in turn in the latter that of decadence from an original state of perfection and of circles or returns. In its modern form it takes its origin from thinkers free of these religious views, who merge in the philosophies of becoming and of evolution. But the concept of progress destroyed itself in many of these rationalistic philosophies, the "disappearance of evil" being posited as possible (Spencer), and a definite state of perfection conceived (though transferred from the past into the future), that is to say a Reality that should be Reality, indeed, perfect Reality having ceased to be development, that is to say, itself.

[1] See the study of Hegel mentioned,

THIRD SECTION

UNITY OF THE THEORETICAL AND THE PRACTICAL

THE study of the practical activity in its relations that we made in the first section has removed all doubt as to the thesis that the practical activity presupposes the theoretical, or that *know-ledge is the necessary precedent of volition and action.*[1] But the succeeding study of the practical activity in its dialectic having led to the result that the practical activity is reality itself in its immediacy, and that no other reality (or we may say *other nature*) is conceivable outside will-action, compels us also to affirm the opposite thesis, that the theoretic activity presupposes the practical, and that *the will is the necessary precedent of knowledge.*[2] And it is a precedent, not indeed in the sense admitted from the beginning, of the necessary implication of the will in every theoretical act, as will to know, by means of the unity of the Spirit[3] (for this will is

Double result: precedence of the theoretical over the prac-tical and of the practical over the theoretical.

---

[1] Section I.   [2] Section II.   [3] Section I. c. 3.

293

subsidiary and not constitutive; but if it become
constitutive it produces, as has been seen,
wilfulness and the theoretical error[1]), but
precisely in the sense of a constitutive will,
without which no knowledge would be thinkable.

Knowledge, indeed, is knowledge of something: it is the remaking of a fact, an ideal
recreation of a real creation. If there have
not previously been a desire, an aspiration, a
nostalgia, there cannot be poetry; if there have
not been an impulse or a heroic deed, the epic
cannot arise; if the sun do not illumine a
landscape, or a soul invoke a ray of sunlight
upon the countryside, the picture of a luminous
landscape cannot exist. And if there be not a
world of reality that generates a world of representations, Philosophy, which is the search for
the universal, is not conceivable, nor History,
the understanding of the individual.

*Error of those
who maintain
the exclusive
precedence of
either.*
The indubitability of this affirmation, which no
force of sophistry can destroy, renders fallacious
both the opposite theses, which have several
times been variously proposed and maintained:
the exclusive priority of the theoretic, and the
exclusive priority of the practical.

Those who maintain them enter into so

[1] Section I. c. 4.

desperate a contest with reality, that in order
to issue from it without too much dishonour,
they are finally compelled to call in the aid of
a third term, which is in turn either thought
that is not thought, or will that is not will,
or something grey that contains in itself thought
and will, without being either the one or the
other, nor the unity of that duality. On the
one hand is postulated a Logos, a thought *in se*
(one does not understand how this can ever think
and be thought), and it is made to adopt the
resolution (which one does not understand how
it can ever adopt) of coming forth *from itself* and
creating a nature, in order to be able to return
finally to itself, by means of this alienation,
and to be henceforth *per se*, that is to say, able
to think and to will. The defect of this artificial
construction, its mythological and religious origin,
can be said to have been already revealed, in
the comparison employed with reference to it
by the author who maintained it (Hegel), to the
effect that the Logos is God *before* the creation
of the world : a God, that is to say, altogether
unreal and absurd. On the other hand, the
excogitation of a *blind Will* (Schelling, Schopenhauer) completely tallies with this Thought that
does not think because it has not previously

willed, and that does not truly will because it has not previously thought, and all of a sudden fashions for itself the instrument of knowledge, to succeed in surpassing itself in this alienation from itself, by means of liberation from willing obtained in the contemplation of the ideas and in asceticism. Here, too, we must repeat that the one error passes over and converts itself into the other, and this inevitable conversion causes the other secondary and hybrid forms of theory to have but slight interest, those in which the priority has been conceived as that of fancy, or feeling, or the unconscious, or the indifferentiated, and the like, all of which represent vain efforts to suppress one of the two fundamental forms of the spirit, or to derive them from a third, which consciousness does not reveal.

Problem of the unity of this duality. This however does not mean that the demand to conceive the link of that duality, or the unity of the theoretical and the practical, manifested in all these erroneous attempts, is not legitimate. But in order to conceive this, it is necessary to insist above all upon the reality of this duality, of which is sought the connection and the unity.

Not the duality of opposites. This connection cannot be the relation or synthesis of opposites. The theoretical is not

the opposite of the practical, nor the practical
the opposite of the theoretical : the opposite
of the theoretical is error or the false, as
the opposite of the practical is the volitional
contradiction or evil. The theoretical, far
from being negative, is positive, not less than
the practical, and inversely. Neither form can
therefore be in any way debased to a simple
opposite. Opposition is intrinsic to the spirit
and is to be found in each one of its forms :
hence the general value of the spirit (activity
against passivity, rationality and reality against
irrationality and unreality, being against not-
being) and that of its special forms (beautiful
against ugly, true against false, useful against
useless, good against evil). But precisely for
this reason, it cannot constitute the character of
one form in respect to the other : neither that
of the true against the good, nor that of the
beautiful against the useful, and so on.

Nor can the connection be thought as are *Not duality*
of finite and
thought the subdivisions of the theoretic and *infinite.*
the practical forms, or according to the relations
of individual to universal, of finite to infinite,
the first of which terms conditions the second,
but is conditioned by it only in an implicit
manner. Of the two theoretical forms (and

we shall see further on that the forms of the
practical are also two), the æsthetic precedes
the logical and is autonomous : a song, a story,
a statue, do not express any concept ; but the
philosophy that gives the concept, is at the
same time fancy, expression, word : the prose
of the philosopher is his song. The æsthetic
form is the knowledge of the individual ; the
logical that of the universal, which is also
individual. But this relation that arises within
the theoretic, as within the practical form,
cannot be transported to the relation of the two
forms without logical incoherence : the subdivision, so to speak, is not the division. Thought
is not the finite in respect of willing, which is
the infinite ; nor is the will the finite in respect
of thought, which is the infinite. Thought and
will are both of them at once finite and infinite,
individual and universal. He who passes from
action to thought, does not limit his own being
by becoming finite ; nor does he limit it by
passing from thought to action ; or better, in
both cases he makes himself finite to attain to
the infinite ; poet to open to himself the way to
the thought of the eternally true ; man of action,
that he may dedicate his work to the eternal
good.

The two forms, theoretical and practical, both *Perfect analogy of the two* positive, both a connection of finite and infinite, *forms, theoretic and practical.* correspond in everything, as has already appeared from our exposition, in which the appeal to the one from the problems of the other has always aided a better penetration of the nature of such problems and the finding of their solution. Thus in both there is genius and creation (geniuses of art and of thought, and geniuses of action); in both, reproduction and judgment take place in the same way (æsthetic taste, practical taste; history of art and history of philosophy, history of actions); in both arise representative concepts and empirical rules. The analogy will be better illustrated by what is to follow, when will be demonstrated the corre- spondence between art and economic, logical thought and ethicity, historical discrimination and ethical discrimination, empirical concepts and laws of action, and so on.

If this analogy exclude the possibility of the two *Not a parallelism,* forms being *unequal*, it must not, on the other *but a circle.* hand, be perverted with the object of conceiving them *parallel*, as would perhaps be pleasing to the parallelists of spirit and nature, soul and body; this is an expedient that is certainly easy, but certainly not satisfying. They are not parallel, but are on the contrary bound, the one to the other, in such a way that the one proceeds from the other. From the æsthetic apprehension of reality, from philosophical reflection upon it, from historical reconstruction, which is its result, is obtained that knowledge of the actual situation, on which alone is formed and can be formed the volitional and practical synthesis, the new action. And this new action is in its turn the material of the new æsthetic figuration, of the new philosophical reflection, of the new historical reconstruction. In short, knowledge and will, theory and practice, are not two parallels, but two lines, such that the head of the one is joined to the tail of the other; or, if a geometric symbol also be desired, such that they constitute, not a parallelism, but a *circle*.

The circle of Reality: thought and being, subject and object. They constitute therefore the circle of reality and of life, which is duality-unity of thought and being, of subject and object, in such a way that to think the subject is the same as to think the subject of an object, and to think an object is the same as to think the object of a subject. In truth, it sometimes seems strange and almost impossible that such hard and difficult questions should have arisen as to the objectivity of knowledge, and as to whether thought attains to being, or whether there be a being beyond thought. Thought is such, precisely because it affirms being, and being is such, precisely because it is generated by a thought. It is only when we remember that in those questions were included others of a very difficult and intricate nature, concerning divine transcendency and the content of the concept of nature (gnoseological questions, which it is the glory of modern philosophy to have asked and solved) ;—it is only then that we understand how the relation of thought and being, of knowing and of willing, has also become obscure. Kant was forced to come to a stop before the mystery of reality, because he had not altogether conquered transcendency, nor altogether surpassed the false conception of nature as *ens*, given by the naturalists. It revealed itself to him, not as a circle, but as an assemblage of lines diverging or joining to infinity. Hegel made two of will and nature, owing to the insufficiency of his gnoseological theory relating to the natural sciences, and was led to posit a Philosophy of nature in opposition to a Philosophy of the spirit, thus permitting to exist a form of non-mediate dualism, after he had destroyed so many, or making it mediate in the artificial manner to which we have referred. The shadows of that gnoseology having been dispersed, the relation between theory and practice, subject and object, appears in full light ; and the answer becomes very simple to the question as to how, when everything is unconvertible relation of condition and conditioned, thought and being are reciprocally condition and conditioned, and as to how the vicious circle is avoided. The criticism of vicious circles includes in itself and affirms the idea of a circularity that is not vicious ; thought and being are not a succession of two finites, but an absolute relation, that is, the Absolute itself. To express ourselves mythologically, if the creation of the world be the passage from chaos to cosmos, from not-being to being, this passage does not begin either with the theoretic or with the practical, with the subject, or with the object, but with the Absolute, which is the absolute relation of the two terms. *In the beginning was neither the Word nor the Act; but the Word of the Act and the Act of the Word.*

Critique of the theories as to the primacy of theoretical or of practical reason. It is well to state again that in consequence of the relation and correlation established, all the questions as to the primacy of thought or will, of the contemplative or active life, and speaking more empirically, of the thinker or the man of action, disappear. To pose such problems is as though one were to ask which of the two semicircles of a circle has precedence. Similar questions, always insoluble or badly solved, have their origin in internal obscurity as to the fundamental correlation. When man has attained to the summit of knowledge (a summit that is certainly not Art, nor, strictly speaking, Philosophy, but History, the knowledge of the concrete real, that is, the actuality of philosophy), when he has completely penetratéd the actual situation, can he perhaps stop at this point and say *hic manebimus optime*? Can he arrest life which is raging and demanding to be continued? And if he succeed in suspending it for an instant in thought, why has he suspended, if not to continue it? Knowledge is not an end, but an instrument of life: knowledge that did not serve life would be superfluous and harmful.—On the other hand, when a man has willed and has thrown himself into action, when he has produced another piece of life, can he blindly continue to produce life for ever? Would not blindness impede the production itself? Therefore he must rise from life to knowing, if he wish to look in the face the product that he has lived, and surpass it with thought, for which life is now means and instrument. Knowledge serves life and life serves knowledge; the contemplative life, if it do not wish to become insipid ease, must lead to activity, and that activity, if it do not wish to become an irrational and sterile tumult, must lead to contemplation. Reality, in specifying aptitudes, has formed men of thought and men of action, or of prevailing thought or prevailing action, these not superior to those, for they are collaborators.—Thus the discussions as to whether human progress be moral or intellectual, or whether the propelling force be the practical and economic activity, or philosophy, or religion (Buckle, Kidd, etc.), are shown to be vain.

New pragmatism: life conditioning Philosophy.

It is rather to be considered that from this bond between theory and practice is obtained a pragmatism of a new sort, of which the pragmatists have never thought, or at least have not been able to distinguish from the others and to give it value. If Life condition Thought, we have in this the apodictic demonstration of the always historically conditioned form of every thought; not only of Art, which is always the art of a time, of a soul, of a moment; but also of Philosophy which can solve only those problems presented by Life. Every philosophy reflects and cannot but reflect the preoccupations,

as they are called, of a definite historical moment;
and this, not in the quality of its *solutions* (in
which case it would be and is indeed bad
philosophy), but in the quality of its *problems.*
Thus it is at once contingent and eternal, mortal
and immortal, extratemporal and living only in
time and history.

Finally, with the establishment of the duality- *Deductive con-*
firmation of
unity of the theoretical and the practical, we have *the two forms*
and deductive
demonstrated that which at the beginning of *exclusion of the*
third (feeling).
the exposition had only been asserted and presupposed: namely, why a *practical* form of the
spirit must be placed beside the theoretical,[1] and
why there is no *third* form beyond these, whether
it be called *feeling* or by any other name.[2] The
theoretical form postulates the practical, because
the subject postulates the object; but the spirit
does not postulate a third form intermediate
between the two, or unity of the two, because it
is itself precisely mediator and unity of itself,
subject-object.

[1] Section I. c. I.   [2] Section I. c. 2.

SECOND PART

THE PRACTICAL ACTIVITY IN ITS SPECIAL FORMS

FIRST SECTION

THE TWO PRACTICAL FORMS: ECONOMIC AND ETHIC

I

DISTINCTION OF THE TWO FORMS IN THE PRACTICAL CONSCIOUSNESS

ALL that has been developed in the preceding *The utilitarian or economic* book concerns the practical activity *in general*: *form, and the* *moral or* therefore no account has been taken of the *ethical form.* special distinctions of the practical forms, as though there were none, or they have only been alluded to as something problematical; and when exemplifications have been given, recourse has been had indifferently to one or to the other of the forms commonly admitted, whether or no they are to be held philosophically distinguishable. Now, on the contrary, we affirm in an explicit manner that the spirit, which we have seen distinguished as theoretical and practical, is sub-distinguished as practical spirit, into two forms, of which the first may be called utilitarian or *economic*, the second moral or *ethical*.

Insufficiency of the descriptive and psychological distinction. In affirming this sub-distinction, we are obliged to renounce (as we have already done for the practical in respect to the theoretical) a demonstration by the psychological method, which has already shown itself to be vicious. If indeed it were applicable in this field, we should doubtless be able to strike the intellect and persuade the soul for a moment, by pointing to the spectacle of life as a demonstration of the two forms, economic and ethic, showing on the one hand, farmers, commercial men, speculators, conquerors of men and of territories, wielders of the word or of the sword as instrument of dominion ; and, on the other hand, educators, benefactors, disinterested and self-sacrificing men, martyrs and heroes ; on the one hand, economic institutions (manufactories, mines, exchanges, exploration companies), and on the other moral institutions (educators and schools, charitable societies, orders of Sisters of Charity, or red, white, or blue Cross Companies, and so on). What can be better proof of the reality of the bipartition enunciated ? Cannot we touch it, as with the hand ? However (as already in the case of the distinction between the theoretical and the practical), what is touched with the hand is not on that account seized by the intellect, and indeed in a little while it also escapes the hand which had thought to be its master. For when we better observe the individuals who seemed to be merely economic, they seem to be also moral, and inversely ;—moral institutions are also economic, and economic moral. The benefactor calculates and wishes to attain his object with the same *cupiditas* as the peasant, all intent upon gain ; and the peasant in his turn is ennobled in his chase after lucre by the dignity of labour and by the moral impulses that sustain it ;—all charitable institutions are economic undertakings, and economic undertakings are subject to moral laws, so that in drawing up accounts there is no knowing where is that material distinction between the economic and the ethical activities. The truth is that here too it is not possible to start from contingent facts and from their classes with empirical limitations, to attain to philosophical distinctions, but that it is necessary to start from these, in order to interpret contingent facts, and finally to understand also the mode of formation of empirical classes. For this reason the psychological method revolves in a circle that is effectively vicious.

Deduction and the necessity of integrating it with induction.

Neither is it possible to proceed with the method that we shall call deductive solely ; that is, we see the necessity of the two sub-forms of the practical activity, which, being the object of the subject and therefore in every way analogous to the activity of the subject, that is, to the theoretical, must have a duplication of forms answering to the duplication of the theoretical activity into æsthetic and logical, and cannot posit the universal practical without positing the individual that shall be its vehicle. This deduction, although in every way correct and rigorous, cannot be convincing, save when it is also demonstrated that it responds to fact as revealed by observation, that is, when deduction is also induction, as the speculative method demands.

The two forms as a fact of consciousness.

Leaving, therefore, on this occasion also, the deductive proof to the complete development of the theory, we shall begin by appealing to observation of self, in order that every one may verify in himself the existence of the two different forms of volitional acts, termed by us economic and ethic. The economic activity is that which wills and effects only what corresponds to the conditions of fact in which a man finds himself; the ethical activity is that which, although it correspond to these conditions, also refers to something that transcends them.   To the first correspond what are called individual ends, to the second universal ends; the one gives rise to the judgment concerning the greater or less coherence of the action taken in itself, the other to that concerning its greater or less coherence in respect to the universal end, which transcends the individual.

If we wish to recognize only the moral form of *The economic form.* activity, we soon perceive that it draws with it the other, from which it is distinct; for our action, although universal in its meaning, cannot but be something concrete and individually determined.   What is put in practice is not morality in universal, but always a determinate moral volition : as Hegel remarked in a different connection, we do not eat fruit in general, but cherries, pears, plums, or, these cherries, these pears, these plums; we hasten to comfort in this or that way an individual, made in this or that way, who finds himself in this or that state of misfortune; we do justice at this or that point of time and space to individual beings on a definite matter.   If a good action be not solely our individual pleasure, it must become so : otherwise, how could we carry it out?   Thus, by closer examination, we realize that our action always obeys a rational law, even when its moral law is suppressed, so that, when every inclination that transcends the individual has been set aside, we do not on that account remain the prey of caprice. We shall desire only our own will, we shall follow only our own individual inclination; but, even so, it is necessary to will this will and this inclination coherently, not to undulate between two or more volitions at the same time. And if we succeed in really obtaining our desire, if, while the moral conscience is for a moment suspended within us, we abandon ourselves to the execution of a project of vengeance and attain to it in spite of many obstacles, thus executing a masterpiece of ability, a practical masterpiece; even when, in this case, *populus non plaudit*, we for our part certainly *nos nobis plaudimus*, and feel most satisfied, at least so long as lasts the suspension of the moral consciousness; for we have done what we willed to do, we have tasted, though but for a little while, the pleasure of the gods. Whereas if, although we follow our desire, we do something different from it, or mingle several mutually exclusive desires with one, and having decided not to drink wine, for example, in order to obey the advice of the doctor and to remain in good health, we yet yield to

the wish to drink it, that pleasure is, so to say,
poisoned by preoccupation, the taste is at the
same time distaste, unless we succeed in forgetting
for some moments the advice of the doctor, or
think that very possibly he does not know what
he is saying. We continually apply the same
criterion to the incidents of life ; actions and
individuals, of whom we cannot morally approve,
drag from us sometimes cries of admiration for
the ability with which they have conducted themselves, for the firmness that they display, worthy
(as is said) of a better cause. The Epicurean
Farinata, who raised himself erect on his red-hot
bed, or the impious Capaneus who cursed Jove
beneath the rain of punishing fire, obtain from us
that esteem which we refuse to those sad souls
who lived without infamy and without praise.
Art has celebrated in tragedies and poems the
strong characters of great criminals, but it has
turned to ridicule in comedies little criminals,
the violent who show themselves timid, the
astute who let themselves be cheated.

As we cannot fail to recognize this form of *The ethical form.*
the practical activity, quite individual, hedonistic,
utilitarian, and economic, and the importance that
it possesses, joined to or separated from morality,
as the case may be, and the special practical

judgments that have their origin in it (the judgment of convenience, whether it be called utilitarian or economic), so it would be impossible not to recognize the moral form. Yes, the volitional act satisfies us as individuals occupying a definite point of time and space, but if it fail to satisfy us at the same time as beings transcending time and space, our satisfaction will be ephemeral and will rapidly be changed into dissatisfaction. To one desire succeeds another, and to this another, and so on to infinity ; but the one is different from the other, and the new either condemns the old or is by it condemned. If we succeed in arranging our pleasures in series and classes, and in subordinating and connecting them, certainly there will be some gain ; but the gain will not have been a true one on this occasion either. We shall at the most be able to guide our life according to some plan, and for a certain time that has not the exactitude of the moment ; instead of the instantaneous will to which succeeds a different will, we shall have general ends for which we shall work. We shall propose, for instance, to do certain work and to abstain from doing certain other work, in order to marry a loved one, to win a seat in Parliament, or to obtain literary fame. But those ends are also merely contingent (they are general, not universal), and consequently cannot assuage our thirst. When we all have attained to them, we shall experience *le déboire* that *la cueillaison d'un rêve au cœur qui l'a cueilli* always leaves behind. The company of the fair beloved will weary, the political ambition realized will leave the soul empty, literary fame will seem the shadow of vanity. Perhaps too, we shall change our side, like the sick man who cannot rest on his bed of feathers, and begin to follow other ends ; the lover deluded with matrimony will turn to other loves ; the ambitious man, weary of political life, will think of new ambitions, or of that of not having any, and of retiring to so-called domestic peace ; the seeker for literary fame will long for ease, silence, and forgetting. But in vain : dissatisfaction persists. And it will always persist, and pallid Care will always sit behind us, on the croup of our horse, if we are not able to tear from the contingent its character of contingent, breaking its spell, and bringing ourselves to a full stop in that *progressus ad infinitum* from thing to thing, from pleasure to pleasure, to which it impels us, if we be not able to place the eternal in the contingent, the universal in the individual, duty in desire. Then only do we acquire that internal peace, which is not in the future, but in the present, because eternity is in the moment, for him who knows how to place it there. Our actions will always be new, because reality always places new problems before us, but if we accomplish them with lofty souls, and with purity of heart, seeking in them that which surpasses them, we shall on every occasion possess the Whole. Such is the character of the moral action, which satisfies us, not as individuals, but as men, and as individuals only in so far as we are men; and in so far as we are men, only by means of individual satisfaction.

Impossibility of eliminating it. Those men in whom the moral consciousness is wanting, or is confused and intermittent, make us fearful—fearful for ourselves, obliged to be on our guard against them and to ward off their snares and injuries, and fearful for them, for if they have not already fallen the prey to the most terrible torments, they certainly will do so. They are like people dancing unconsciously upon ground that has been mined; the conscious spectator trembles for them, they do not; but if by chance they escape the danger, they will be retrospectively horrified when they look back. The inebriation evaporates and the clear outlines of reality reappear, but that which restores form to those outlines is the eternal, not the contingent, morality, not desire. We see this take place in an intense form in what are called *conversions*, followed by the intention of leaving the world and its false joys and retiring to a cloister; or, without metaphor, of becoming regenerated, of beginning a new life with new ideal presuppositions. But intensive conversions are catastrophes which occur, like popular revolutions, when continuous evolution is impeded. The wise man is converted and renewed at every moment, without the solemnity of a conversion, and with the *memorare novissima* he retains in the contingent, his contact with the eternal. He knows that he must love things and creatures one by one, each in its individuality, for he who does not love thus is neither good nor bad, not even being a man. He will wish for literary fame, political power, matrimony, according to his aptitudes and to the conditions in which he finds himself; but he will wish for all these things without wishing for them; he will wish for them, not for themselves, but for that which they contain of universal and constant; he will love them in God, ready to abandon them immediately their ideal content shall have left them; he will seriously desire them with all ardour for themselves, but only when their self is also "his other self." No thing, no creature possesses unconditioned value, which belongs only to that which is neither thing nor creature. The value of our individual life is conditioned for each of us, and we must guarantee and defend it as vehicle of the universal, and we must be ready to throw it away, as a useless and pernicious thing, when it does not serve this end, or rebels. But the value of every being dear to us is not less conditioned, and Jesus said with reason, when preparing himself for his divine mission, that he had come to separate men from their wives, their sons, their friends, and from their native land. That separation in union, that union in separation, is the moral activity, individual and universal.

Confirmed by facts.

Thus it happens that art, which has celebrated strong characters, able men and affairs well conducted, has also celebrated, and with greater liveliness, those strong men who have placed their strength at the service of that other strength which surpasses them and makes them eternal. For this reason, no embittered soul, no sceptic and pessimist remains long firm in his negation of all moral light; such negations are indeed as a rule true *amantium irae*. The

singer of the lesser Brutus who had thus fero-
ciously imprecated :

Foolish Virtue, hollow mists and fields
      Of restless ghosts
Are thy schools, and Repentance turns her back upon
    thee, . . .

is the same who, on witnessing a slight act of
generosity, exclaims with emotion :

Fair Virtue, when my spirit becomes aware of thee,
It exults, as at a joyous event. . . .

The coldest and most self-contained philosophers,
when they speak of it, find themselves sometimes
impelled to adopt a poetic tone, and Aristotle
will say of Justice that it is "a more wonderful
thing than Hesperus or the Morning Star,"[1] and
Emmanuel Kant will compose an apostrophe to
Duty, and will write at the end of the *Critique
of Practical Reason*: "Two things fill the soul
with ever new and ever increasing veneration
and admiration the more often and the longer
reflection is occupied with them: *the starry
heaven* above me, and *the moral law* within me."
And even the great mass of rhetoric that has for
its object virtue or the moral law is a homage
rendered to this supreme force of life, reality of
reality.

---

[1] *Eth. Nicom.* l. v. c. 1, 1129 b.

The impossibility of suppressing the economic or the moral form of the activity in our practical consciousness, the continual appeal that the one makes to the other, the revolving of our practical judgment about the two aspects, both of them necessary, of the useful and the honest, energy and goodness, pleasure and duty, explain why the Psychology and the Description of practical life have constituted the two kinds of types and classes, of economic and of moral men, of economic and of moral institutions. Such rough and approximate distinctions have however at bottom, in this as in other cases, an intimate and rigorous distinction, which every one will find evident in himself, if he look inward upon himself and fix his gaze persistently on the universal forms of the spirit that acts within him.

II

CRITIQUE OF THE NEGATIONS OF THE ETHICAL FORM

THE distinction of the two forms, well known *Exclusion of materialistic and of intellectualistic criticisms.* to the inner consciousness, will appear more clearly when we examine the reasons for which the one or the other of them has been denied. We say the one or the other, because we have now freed ourselves from the obligation of refuting the theses that have their origin in presuppositions, both materialistic and intellectualistic, and therefore deny the moral and economic activities, either because they do not admit the concept of spiritual activity itself, or because they do not admit the more special conception of practical activity. The greater number of those who deny morality are nothing but mechanicists, empiricists, materialists, and positivists, to whose brains not only do economy and morality appear inconceivable, but also art and science and, in short, every spiritual value. They ask: Where is this moral principle of which you discourse?

Point it out to us with your finger. But they also ask : Where are the categories or the pure concept? Where is the æsthetic synthesis and the pure intuition? Where is the *a priori* of perception and of history? Where are all these fine things you talk of as though they existed, and that we neither see nor touch?—And for our part, we can henceforth let them say what they will, only praying in our hearts that God may illuminate them and make them discover (at least when they are near to death and the dense veil of their bodies has become more thin) that if the universals were *things* that it was possible to perceive as we do individual things, they would not be universals.

The two possible negations. When the double assumption of a spiritual activity and of a practical form of it has been admitted, it is not possible to do otherwise than either to deny the economic for the moral form, or the moral for the economic. What might seem to be a third possibility, that of denying the two forms, is reducible to the first, because, when the distinction of the terms has been suppressed, there remains nothing but the practical activity considered in general, which coincides with the individual and economic activity. We shall begin then with the examination of the negation of morality for economy, which is the thesis of *utilitarianism*. Those same materialists have recourse to utilitarianism when they wish to present some sort of a Philosophy of the practical, but with what little right they avail themselves of such aid, is clear from what has already been said : the useful is always value and teleology, and materialism, in all its sub-forms and varieties, is incapable of positing the smallest concept of value and finality.

Utilitarianism affirms that no other volition exists save that which answers to the merely individual determination, or, as it is also expressed, to the pleasure of the individual, understanding by pleasure, not the generic pleasure that also accompanies moral satisfaction in the individual, but that which is exclusively individual. Actions, therefore, as it says, are what concern it, not their motives, that is, the motive of the individuality of the act abstractly conceived, not that of the spirit become concrete in it ; thus, not killing for fear of punishment and not killing because repugnant to one's own conscience, become the same thing. They are the consequences of different conditions, but in both cases of the same motive, which is personal convenience. And as there does not exist a pleasure

The thesis of utilitarianism against the existence of moral acts.

that cannot be and is not substituted for a different pleasure, so there is not an action, however moral it be called, that cannot be interrupted and changed, when different conditions present themselves. Every action, every man has his price : it is all a matter of discovering what that price is. He who seems to place the glory of his country above all other aspirations, although he cannot, for example, be corrupted by money, by vanity, or by pleasure, will yet always have in him some weak point that a more expert corrupter will discover or be able to discover ; and when the discovery has been made and the suitable transaction proposed, the glory of his country will be abandoned, because it has been well compensated for by something else. This way of looking upon human actions has appeared to be concrete, exact, rational ; and the utilitarian theory, if it have often been called *hedonistic*, and sometimes even *æsthetic* (understanding by æsthetic, individual pleasure), is also wont to be decorated with the name of ethical or practical *rationalism, rational morality.*

Difficulties arising from the presence of these. All would go very well, and the practical activity would in this way be entirely explained and unified, if we did not at every moment of life run against the distinction between mere pleasure and duty, between the useful and the honest action, and if there did not arise in our conscience an invincible distinction between the things that have a price and those that have none, and if an abyss did not differentiate among apparently similar actions that which has a merely utilitarian from that which has a moral motive. The utilitarians even (who, although bad philosophers, are men, and as such carry at the bottom of their souls a far better philosophy than they profess in books and in the schools) are not able to suppress that distinction in themselves and to deny all recognition to the power of morality, to which, as men, they submit at every moment. How then are they to behave? How are they to explain the genesis of that distinction which, by the premises that they have posited, cannot be other than illusion? What is there that gives effective existence to the fallacious category of morality, side by side with the veracious one of utility?

There have been several attempts to solve that hard resisting term of morality. The first, which was logically bound to present itself, was that of considering facts called moral as nothing but empirical groups of utilitarian facts, and of explaining the false category as an hypostasis

Attempt to explain them as quantitative distinctions.

of those empirical groups, arbitrarily reduced to
a rigorous and philosophical concept. Banking,
usury, commerce, industry, agriculture, and labour
are empirically distinguished, yet are all economic facts. Courage, prudence, temperance,
chastity, justice, modesty are empirically distinguished, yet are all moral facts. Why not
unite the two series, and recognize the unity
and continuity of nature by the insertion among
them of other types and terms? Morality
is also utility, but the utility of the *greater
number*; interest is interest, but *well understood*;
pleasure is pleasure, but pleasure of *greater
duration and quantity*, preferred to another less
intense, or more fugitive; egoism, egoism of family,
of race, of human race, egoism of *species*, altruism;
eudemonism, but *social* eudemonism, enjoyment,
but enjoyment of *sympathy*, utility, but utility of
conforming, not to one's own individual judgment,
but to that of *public opinion*. Thus are moral facts
included in utilitarian, in the same way as the
number a hundred thousand is not less a number
than two or three and the others inferior to it,
because it is composed of three and of two and
of other numbers less than itself. Cæsar Borgia
murders his brother and thus gets rid of a rival
both in love and in politics, that is, he seeks

his advantage ; but Giordano Bruno also seeks his own advantage, and nothing else, when he allows himself to be burned in order to assert his philosophy, because, for one constituted as he, with that demoniacal fury of his for philosophical truth, the pyre must have seemed a very miserable and negligible thing, just as his brother's blood seemed to Cæsar Borgia. Call the one of these actions utility of a complexity of ten and the other utility of a complexity of a hundred, or give to the complexity a hundred the name of morality, of well-understood self-interest, of sympathy, of altruism, and so on, and to the complexity of ten that of utility, of individual interest, of egoism : the two actions will not thus have been declared of a different nature.

But the fact is that they have already been *Critique.* declared of a *different nature* by the utilitarians themselves. No one, indeed, will have been deceived with the ingenious phraseology excogitated : *well-understood* interest is no longer mere self-interest ; the egoism of *species* is not egoism, *durable* pleasure is not mere pleasure. The difference between the one term and the other is not quantitative, and even where a *greater* quantity is talked of, a *greater* duration, a *greater* number, arithmetical definitions are not posited, but symbols pointing to qualitative differences. There is a difference, not of complexity but of nature, between the action of Cæsar Borgia and that of Giordano Bruno; there is no common measure between baseness and moral elevation as there is between undulating plains and mountains. The two series, of empirical utilitarian concepts and of empirical moral concepts, are not only irreducible to a single series, but remain obstinately distinct and irreducible. All that can be done, and has been done, is to unify them verbally; and in this the utilitarians have shown themselves as bold as it was possible to be in so miserable an enterprise. But the identity or similarity of words does not suffice to cancel the profound distinctions of things.

Attempt to explain them as facts either extraneous to the practical or irrational and stupid.

There would have been an immediate passage from the consciousness of the puerility of such identifications to the recognition of a distinct ethical form, if purpose and prejudice had not made resistance, prompting, on the contrary, the search for new expedients for setting themselves free in theory from the tedious and recurring phantom of morality. On this occasion also these expedients must have been just two: that is, to declare morality or concept *extraneous* to the practical, or

intrinsic to it indeed, but *contrary*. The first was
attempted, but feebly, when morality was spoken
of as the fantasticality of poets, as the dream or
rosy illusion caressed in life. No attention was
paid to the fact that what the poet imagines
cannot be contradictory and absurd, but must
indeed be founded in the reality of life and in the
nature of things; and that morality is not the
æsthetic form in which it is reproduced and
represented, but practical form or action. But
the unmaintainability of this attempt was too
evident for its success. The other expedient,
on the contrary, has always had and still has
great success. This turns morality into a practical contradictory concept, that is, into something certainly practical, but without motive,
incoherent, and in contradiction to the healthy
development of the practical. It is true that it
is usually enunciated in very different words from
those used by us. They speak as follows : What
is called a good and virtuous action is nothing
but the product of the association between certain
acts that are for us the means to a pleasure, and
that pleasure itself; so that gradually, even where
the primitive pleasure is absent, those acts are
sought and repeated for themselves, as though
in themselves pleasurable. The savage fought

against the enemies who assailed his tribe, that he might not be made a slave or sacrificed to the idol of another tribe, that is to say, in order to defend his personal liberty or his life; but later on, man, forgetting that the tribe or the city or the State were simple means for protecting life and goods, defends them for themselves and allows himself to be despoiled and slain for his country. In the same way (to employ the classical example), money is first sought as a means to enjoyment, and to form a supply for procuring a life more comfortable and secure; but by degrees he who amasses money turns in his soul the means into the end, and becomes avaricious, that is, he finds delight in the mere possession of money, and sacrifices for that all his other joys, even an easy life, food, house and sleep, which he originally intended that money should obtain for him. Morality arises entirely from a similar process of association between means and end, and the case of the miser explains by analogy every act of virtue that cannot be directly reduced to simple pleasure and individual utility.

Associationism and evolutionism. Critique. Now the association here discussed is neither that of logic nor of æsthetic, nor valid association, synthesis, but irrational and fallacious association. It is only possible to exchange means for end as the result of a bad association of ideas: therefore that association is folly and stupidity, as the miser adduced as an example is stupid and foolish, being called " miser " precisely for this reason, with the intention of blaming him (for this word does not mean " economic " or " provident "). And behold! morality should be defined as that which is practically irrational, foolish, stupid, the product of illusion and confusion, or the *contrary* of the practical activity, which is clear-sightedness, rationality, wisdom. Thus defined, it is at the same time annulled. Indeed, irrationality is that which is condemned to be perpetually subjected to the rational; and what is called the moral man, if he were nothing but a false associator of ideas, would be constantly confuted by the man of good sense, by the utilitarian, who would prevent him from committing the stupidity of sacrificing himself for his children, for his country, or for knowledge; or, were he to persist, would cover him with contempt and ridicule. The fear that to discover its origin would be tantamount to abolishing morality would therefore be perfectly justified in this new sense also; or better, it would not be a question of a fear, but of a fact: morality would be in a state of progressive annulment, as the effect of increasing instruction, both in the individual and in society. It has been replied that neither this fear nor this fact arises, because that false association is *indissoluble*, being a product of *heredity*, or, to speak of it in proper terms, it is hereditary stupidity (evolution-istic utilitarianism). But whether inherited or acquired, it is so dissoluble as to be dissolved in the theory proposed : *lux facta est*, and no one succeeds in obscuring it any longer. If, not-withstanding that pretended light, morality be not dissipated, if recourse be had to the miserable subterfuge of insuperable heredity (which is surpassed at the very moment in which its origin is made clear), this means to say that, for the moralist himself, morality is not the irrational, but something very rational. He does not suc-ceed in identifying it with the merely individu-ally useful, but neither can he reject it as the pure and simple negative of this. And since he does not wish to abandon the utilitaristic hypothesis, there is no other path open to him but that of recourse to *mystery*.

A desperate attempt : theological utilitarianism and mystery. This is precisely what happens in the last form of utilitarianism, which has seemed to be capricious and extravagant, but is on the contrary profoundly auto - critical, since it reveals the ultimate essence and defect of the doctrine : what is known as *theological utilitarianism.* Human actions are always inspired by what is merely useful to the individual, and if a number of these seems to diverge from this criterion, this happens because account is not taken of an actual fact, by means of which even the actions which seem to be divergent are reduced to the common measure. This given fact is the life beyond this world, in which God rewards or punishes him who has obeyed or disobeyed his will, in the life of this world. He who in this life seems to resist the impulse of his personal advantage and performs sacrifices of every sort, even to that of his own life, follows equally with the others his personal advantage ; and believing in God, in the immortality of the soul, and in the reward and the punishment that await him, he regulates his action according to these actual facts. *Intuition-istic* Ethic, which places a moral duty at the side of individual pleasure, but indeducible from it, is in reality deduced from individual pleasure, and is likewise turned into *rational* or utilitarian Ethic by means of the transcendental datum. In this way the solution makes shipwreck in mystery ; since God, immortality, the other life, the divine command, punishments and rewards, cannot be defined and justified by means of thought and concept. When utilitarianism becomes theological, it abandons the philosophical field, confessing by so doing its philosophical defeat. And to philosophical consideration the distinction between the individually useful and that which is also superindividual shines out ever more clearly after the many vain attacks of utilitarianism, the affirmation of the moral form, as united and distinct from the utilitarian ; the *autonomy* of Ethic against every form of *utilitarianism* and every *heteronomous Ethic*.

III

CRITIQUE OF THE NEGATIONS OF THE ECONOMIC FORM

IF in the course of philosophical history, the theory of utility has sought to cause the disappearance of the other practical term, which is morality, by swallowing it up, we are not to believe that morality has been for its part more modest and discreet and has not in its turn attempted to devour its companion. One exaggeration has been met with another; to utilitarianism has been opposed that error which may be called *moral abstracticism*, by means of which is refused to the concept of utility the place that belongs to it in the organism of the spirit.

The thesis of moral abstracticism against the concept of the useful.

Such a refusal (analogous to our analysis of the utilitarian theory) cannot take place, save in three ways: that is, in so far as value is denied to the useful, either as *practical* concept, or as *positive* concept, or as *philosophical* concept.

Here too we naturally do not take count of the theses of the materialists or of the intellectualists, which (especially those of the former) have raged in the field of Economy not less than in that of Ethic, giving rise to insane attempts to explain the useful on mechanical principles, or with the contingencies of historical evolution.

The useful as the means or as theoretical fact.

The useful (it has been said) is nothing but the *means* to obtain a certain end. For example, if I take a walk every day with a view to keeping myself in good health, the daily walk is the suitable means and is therefore useful; if, on the contrary, I find that it makes me ill, this means that it is not the suitable means and it would be, and I should declare it to be, useless or harmful. Now by the demonstration given above, it is known that means and end are indistinguishable in the *practical*, for what is called means is nothing but the actual situation (and the knowledge of it), from which arises the practical act, and to which that act corresponds. Thus it is most possible to separate the means from the end; but in so doing, the consideration of the practical act is abandoned, and we pass to that of its theoretical antecedent; and if the mere theoretical antecedent be called "useful" or "practical" in ordinary speech (remembering the practical act, to which it has been or it is presumed that it may be united) then a metaphor is employed, against which there is nothing to be said. Those, then, who define the useful as the means should once for all realize that with such a definition they remove that concept from the circle of the Philosophy of the practical and transport it into Logic, where the relation of means and end is the very same as that of cause and effect, and it again becomes part of the theory of empirical concepts, in which cause and effect are wont to be posited as terms separately conceivable. This has been more or less consciously recognized, when the useful has been defined as the *technical*, for we know that the technical is nothing but knowledge thus made into a metaphor, owing to the relation that it has or is presumed to be capable of having, with an action that has been done or is about to be done.

The theoretical character of the technical has, on the contrary, been obscured, when technical knowledge has received the name of *hypothetical imperatives*, distinct and ranged beside the *categorical*. The imperative is will, and is therefore always both categoric and imperative : *a* is willed (categorically), but *a* would not be

Technical and hypothetical imperatives.

willed if the condition of fact and situation *b* did not exist (hypothetically). The merely hypothetical imperative is the knowledge that remains when abstraction is made of the practical act or of the will; and is no longer an imperative, but a theoretic affirmation. Where effective will is not, imperatives cannot be talked of.

Critique: the useful is a practical fact. Having made clear that the definition of the useful as *means* implies the negation of the useful as a practical fact and its reduction to a theoretical category already known, we must exclude the possibility of such a reduction, for in the useful, the practical character, the effectivity of the will, is ineliminable. "It is useful for me to take a walk" means, "It pleases me to take a walk," "I will to do it." It is a question, not of contemplation or of reasoning, but of volitional movement. The knowledge that precedes the utilitarian act is one thing, the act itself is another. The old man has the same knowledge as the young man, he has indeed much more (*si jeunesse savait, si vieillesse pouvait !*), but he does not will what the young man wills : he knows that by traversing so many kilometers he will arrive at a certain definite point; but it is not useful for him to go there, because it is not useful for him to traverse those kilometers, or to submit to that exertion at the risk of an illness.   The utilitarian will is expressed, not in merely hypothetical imperatives, but in those categoric imperatives that are at the same time hypothetical.   The general formula is " will ! " or " will that you will ! " or " be coherent in your willing ! " as the individuated forms are those that we are continually repeating to ourselves, " now, to bed ! " " now, up you get ! " and the like ; which, when developed, mean : "go to bed " (if you wish to rest yourself), "get up " (if you wish to work), and so on.   The distinction between the cognoscitive and the volitional theses is here evident.

Since then, owing to the unalterably practical character of the utilitarian fact, it was not possible to insist upon its reduction to the technical, and since, on the other hand, it was not desired to recognize it as a practical category side by side with the practical category of morality, they have tried to think of it as something certainly practical, but at the same time of little value, to beware of it, to combat it, to free ourselves from it.   "Useful" has in this way become synonymous with wilfulness, with individual caprice, with will more or less perverted, and (looking upon

The useful as the egoistic or immoral.

immorality as the individual I, shut up in itself and rebelling against the universal) with *egoism*. This theory is supported by certain common modes of speech, in which the moral man is opposed to the man intent upon what is useful to him as an individual, the ethical to the economic life. But it is a question of phrases, true, perhaps, in a certain sense, but inexact when understood or interpreted as affirmations of a contest between morality and utility.

Critique: the useful is amoral. We discover at once that the contest is inexistent, by merely thinking of the case already mentioned, of the man in whom the moral conscience is not developed or has been suppressed, or of the case-limit called *innocence*. What is done in innocence responds, no doubt, to individual pleasure, and so to what is useful for the individual, as he feels it in the given circumstances: were this not so, what is done would not be done. But innocence is not immoral on this account. It will be *amoral*, because it is merely individual volition deprived of the light of the eternal; it will never be *immoral*. Thus (to make use of the comparison and analogy of the theoretic activity) the images that the poet creates will be without philosophy, but will not for this reason be antiphilosophical. Because, were that so, they would have to be partially philosophical, that is to say, to enter into strife with philosophy; but there is no such strife, and, therefore, those images, although philosophically not true, are none the less not philosophically false. Yet they are theoretical acts, in the same way that philosophy is a theoretical act. The philosophical innocence of the poet does not change his intuitive knowledge into bad philosophical knowledge, into a negative of philosophy.—Further, the useful not only is not the negative of morality, but, as we know, is also a fact that unites itself very well with morality, as the word is joined to the thought, making it concrete and palpable, so much so that thought without words is impossible. What honourable man would tolerate being judged disuseful? What moral action would be truly moral, were it not at the same time useful? The good action is good, because it is not bad, that is, it absolutely excludes the bad at the point in which it becomes effective; but certainly it is not so, because disuseful; indeed, in being good, it is also useful, because it absolutely comprehends the useful in itself at the point in which it becomes effective. The union of morality with utility suffices to eliminate the concept of the useful as a negative. Certainly negative and positive do unite to give rise to becoming and to development; but their union is that of strife, not of concord.

The useful as ethical minimum. The third way of eliminating the concept of the useful from Philosophy, or from the Philosophy of the practical, is that which makes of it a concept of ethical description, or an empirical and psychological concept designating certain groups of very minute ethical facts, the rudimentary ethical consciousness. Hence the illusion of the existence of volitional acts indifferent in respect to morality. These acts are really indifferentiated for the mind that is examining them, which sometimes does not take the trouble to do so minutely, save when such an examination is seriously undertaken, and then they are always differentiated into good or bad. Thus it is generally said that eating and sleeping, playing at cards or at billiards, are things that appertain, not to morality, but to individual utility, and that each one may conduct himself as he wills in respect to them, whereas individual choice is excluded when it is necessary to fulfil one's own obligations of social work or of respecting the life of one's neighbour. But if we observe attentively, we see that also in eating or in sleeping, in playing cards or billiards, one acts morally or immorally, since, for example, it is immoral to ruin one's health with eating too much, or with sleeping too little, or to corrupt soul and intellect with card-playing and dawdling in billiard-rooms, when one can do something better.

But the useful is none of all these things ; it is not the complex of ethical micro-organisms, in which we discover with the microscope the same facts of life and of death that we observe with the naked eye in macro-organisms. No microscope will ever discern in it the oppositions of moral good and evil, because these oppositions are not really there ; there are only those of utilitarian or economic good and evil. For the useful is not the moral minimum, but the *premoral*. In this case it is a question, not of approximative, but of rigorous difference ; not psychological, but philosophical.

Critique : the useful is premoral.

Finally, it is necessary to consider the attempt to present the utilitarian conscience as a moral conscience, *different and inferior* to another moral conscience placed over it, not as a new mode of eliminating the concept of the useful, by absorbing it in that of morality, but as a confession of the autonomy of that moment of the spirit. It would be moral, because there is no contradiction to be found in it that can cause it to be judged immoral, and if it be so judged, this happens

A desperate attempt : the useful as inferior practical conscience. Confirmation of the autonomy of the useful.

because it is looked at from the point of view of
the superior conscience, or because the superior
conscience is erroneously transported into the
inferior. But this has importance precisely
because it is not moral, and because the value
that it is admitted to possess, far from being
morality, is spirituality; that is to say, it constitutes a peculiar spiritual value, different from
morality. " Better a will of some sort than no
will at all " is a common saying which means that
prior to morality, there is another and more
elementary spiritual demand. The distinction of
the two consciences, then, is philosophical, not
one of more or less, a distinction of degrees, but
not of empirical degrees, which coincides with our
conclusion. Thus, to return to the usual comparison, the poetical figuration is true, and can only
be judged false by him who looks upon it from a
philosophical point of view, or himself falsifies
it by turning it into a bad philosopheme. But
the truth of that figuration is not philosophical, and
remains purely and simply poetical truth. It
will be said that morality is implied in utilitarian
volition, because, when the individually useful is
posited, the universal, which will dominate and
correct it, is promoted, in the same way as it
has been said that philosophy is implied in the

æsthetic intuition, since by positing the individual imagination is posited the claim of the universal, which surpasses and renders it untrue. But since the æsthetic conscience is distinguished from the philosophical, precisely because that which in the latter is *explicit* is only *implicit* in the former, so, in like manner, the utilitarian conscience is distinguished from the moral conscience, because that morality which becomes explicit and effective in the second, is only implicit or actually inexistent in the first. The difference between *implicit* and *explicit* is another way of enunciating the distinction between the two consciousnesses or practical forms, the autonomy of both being thus recognized.

IV

RELATION BETWEEN THE ECONOMIC AND ETHICAL FORMS

Economic and ethic as the double degree of the practical. THE respective distinction and autonomy of the two forms, economic and ethic, as we have hitherto been expounding it, and as results from the words "inferior" and "superior" just now used, is that of two degrees, at once distinct and united, such that the first can stand without the second, but the second cannot stand without the first. The moment of distinction lies in that possibility of existence independent of the first; the moment of unity is in the impossibility of independent existence of the second. If the first were wanting, there would be identity; if the second, there would be abstract distinction or separation. For this reason we have insisted upon showing that there are actions without morality, yet which are perfectly economical, whereas moral actions that are not also perfectly useful or economical do not exist. Morality

348

lives in concrete, in utility, the universal in the individual, the eternal in the contingent. Hence our reason for reducing the theses that denied the distinction between the two practical forms to an exclusive affirmation of the economic form, this latter being as it were the general form, which of itself involves both itself and the other.

Even when both the practical forms, economic and ethic, utility and morality, are admitted, the gravest errors arise from failing to understand the connection of unity-distinction that exists between them, conceiving them as juxtaposed or parallel, and the respective concepts as coordinated. *Errors arising from conceiving them as co-ordinated.*

In truth, if utility and morality were coordinate concepts, each included as species beneath the general concept of practical activity, the first consequence that could be drawn from this (and it has been drawn) is that morality is conceivable without utility. This has given rise to the absurd concept of *disinterested* actions, that is, of those moral actions that should hold themselves aloof from any sort of impure contact with utility. But disinterested actions would be foolish actions, that is to say, wilful acts, caprices, non-actions. Every action is and must be interested ; indeed, *Disinterested actions. Critique.*

the more profoundly it is interested, so much the better. What interest is stronger and more personal than that which impels the man of science to the search for truth, which is his life? Morality requires that the individual should, in every case, make his individual interest that of the universal; and it reproves those who engage themselves in an insoluble contradiction between the individual interest of the universal and that which is merely individual. But it cannot claim to suppress the interest, that is, itself, in the same way that the volitional act dominates the passions, but cannot eradicate them without eradicating itself. Hence, as the volitional act triumphs over the passions as the *supreme passion*, so morality triumphs over interests as the *supreme interest*.

Vain polemic conducted with such an assumption against utilitarianism. The polemic of autonomous Ethic against the heteronomous Ethic of utilitarianism has had a false and fruitless beginning, owing to this fiction of disinterested actions. In the belief of conquering and more than conquering, it has been attempted to show that man accomplishes some actions without any personal interest, whereas on the contrary an easy victory has in this way been prepared for the adversary. Utilitarianism, in fact, has always been able triumphantly to make

the counter-demonstration that there is no
action, be it as lofty as you will, that does not
answer to a personal end. It is evident that
the hero has his personal interest in the *pro
patria mori*, just as the saint, who wishes to
direct his soul toward humility, finds his own
account in allowing himself to be abused, beaten
and splashed with mud ("in this is perfect joy,"
said Francesco of Assisi to Frate Leone).
Correct polemic should not enter upon the
useless task of denying this evidence; it should
on the contrary admit, as was admitted above,
that there is no action which does not answer
to an individual desire, since it is the individual
that performs it, and the universal is always
obliged to avail itself of individuals. But when
this point has been conceded and admitted, it
will prove, as was proved above, that the useful
action can either remain merely personal or
progress to the action that is universal-personal,
ethical-useful. And the ethical-useful action
itself is precisely the new spiritual category
that the utilitarian does not see.

A second erroneous but unavoidable consequence of the conception of useful and moral
as coordinated concepts is that while, according
to that theory, there can be ethical actions

*Actions
morally
indifferent,
obligatory,
supererogatory,
etc. Critique.*

economically disinterested or indifferent, so there can be actions that are useful and *morally indifferent.* The indifferent would not be those that are merely economic, and, therefore, neither moral nor immoral, which we have recognized as the necessary precedent of moral actions, reappearing always when a return is made to the state of innocence, or as soon as the moral conscience is abolished or suspended. They would on the contrary be economic actions that should persist as such, that is, as ingenuous and amoral, when the moral consciousness is already kindled, and consequently in the very circle of such a conscientiousness. They are altogether inadmissible when thus conceived, and to have admitted them is equivalent to annulling morality, as the recognition of the right of subjects to rebel at their pleasure would be to annul sovereignty, or a burlesque contract containing the clause that each party should be free not to observe the other clauses agreed upon, at his pleasure. Indifferent actions do not exist, either for economy or for morality, and those to which such a character is generally attributed are, as we know, indifferentiated, not indifferent, and always differentiable when more closely examined. Only he who places the useful and the moral, side

by side with one another, separate and impenetrable, is of necessity led to conceive of useful
actions morally indifferent, and as such *licit or
permissible*. Hence it also happens that moral
actions also seem to be *obligatory* compared with
the first; and that, in order to obtain equilibrium
at the other extremity, ultramoral or more than
moral actions, called *meritorious or supererogatory*,
are placed side by side with obligatory actions that
hold the mean. But morality does not grant
leave *not to do*, nor prizes for *doing more than
was required*: it simply imposes *doing*, doing
always what is morally good, always realizing
the universal, in ordinary as in extraordinary
life, on the occasions that occur every day, every
hour, every minute, as in those that occur every
year, every ten years, every century. Nothing
is indifferent to economy in its sphere and
nothing to morality in its sphere: in it,
economic actions with their premoral character
do not persist, but only moral actions subsist.
Economicity is certainly the concrete form of
morality; but it is never an element that
possesses a value of its own in the moral life.

A comparison with the theoretic activity will *Comparison
with the re-*
serve to make clearer this criticism of the *licit* *lation of art
and philosophy.*
or morally indifferent. Artistic intuitions or

2 A

expressions are neither true nor false philosophically, so much so that Philosophy, if it
wish to exist, must also become concrete itself,
as living speech, æsthetic form, intuition-expression, and place itself as an intuition among
intuitions, though it be an intuition *portans
mysteria*, that is, enclosing in itself the universal.
But the appearance of philosophy reacts upon
the pure intuitions, or upon the poetic representation of the world, in which existent and inexistent
were indistinct ; and the world of intuition trans-
forms itself into the world of perceptions, in
which those that once were poetic intuitions,
are now all of them critical or reflective images
penetrated by the concepts, divided into images
of existence and images of possibility. In
the world of perception or of history, no poetical
element can subsist as such ; what was a
bewitching truth in the field of art, were it
introduced into history, would give rise to dis-
harmony and become changed into a repugnant
lie, as we see is actually the case in history
mingled with inventions and fables. History too
assumes artistic form ; but it cannot tolerate in
its bosom art as an element standing alone.
Utilitarian or economic volitions and the moral-
economic volitions (universal and historical per-

ceptions or representations of the practical) proceed in a manner perfectly analogous (intuitions
of the practical).   Moral indifference belongs to
the first, when they are on this side of the moral
conscience, but within this conscience they lose
the right to innocence, as in history the pure intuitions, when they have become perceptions, lose
the privilege that they possessed as pure intuitions.
The ethical discrimination of the economic volitions, which takes place through the moral
conscience, is then in full correspondence with
the historical discrimination of the æsthetic intuitions, which takes place through the logical
conscience.

We owe to the false conception by coordination, *Other erroneous*
conceptions of
not only the two monstrous little concepts of *modes of action.*
disinterested actions and of those that are morally
indifferent, licit, or permissive, but others also,
which have been deduced by means of a somewhat different casuistic from the same general
hypothesis.   Indeed, in the preceding case, useful
and moral, posited as apart and parallel, were
maintained one extraneous to the other and at
peace between themselves.   But nothing forbade
that warlike plans should be attributed to those
two entities, just as when two coordinate animal
species are posited, we may suppose, either that

the individuals of each one mind their own affairs and allow the individuals of the other species to live and to prosper in peace, or that the one takes to persecuting the other, sometimes injuring or destroying it and sometimes being by it injured or destroyed. Thus were and are obtained concepts of *moral anti-economic* actions and of *anti-economic moral* actions, of *immoral economic* actions, and of *economic immoral* actions, four concepts which are all four to be rejected. Moral action can never be accomplished at a loss: morality is for the moral man the supreme advantage in the situation in which he finds himself, and it would be erroneous to measure it by comparison with what an individual without morality would do in the same situation, for, as we know, individual and situation are all one, in such a way that a like comparison is impossible. In a similar manner, an anti-economic action can never be moral; at the most it will not even be amoral, or will not even posit the primary and generic condition of morality, that is, it will not be action, but inert contemplation. An immoral action can never be economic, because immorality implies internal disagreement and strife between one volition directed to the universal and another directed to the merely individual, hence the result will be practical inconclusion and infecundity, dissatisfaction and remorse ; that is to say, just the opposite of utility and economicity. In like manner, an economic action can never be immoral : at the most (when it is merely an economic action), it will be amoral.

The bond of unity and distinction that exists between the concepts of the useful and the moral and the consequent negation of the formula of coordination, help to solve in a definite way the intricate questions relating to *pleasure and morality, happiness and virtue.*

Pleasure and the economic activity, happiness, and virtue.

First of all, we can here give yet another meaning to the indeterminate category of *feeling* with its poles of pleasure and pain, for it is clear that when feeling was distinguished from moral activity and set at variance with it, we had in view nothing but the pure economic activity. And in truth, of all the tendencies included in that concept as sketched out, this of economicity seems on the whole to prevail over the others, so much so that we shall henceforth be disposed to give to the word " feeling " the name of economic activity. Thus it was reasonably maintained, with implied reference to this meaning, that pleasure and pain are *proper* to feeling and *extraneous* to the

Pleasure, pain and feeling.

other spiritual forms, and that they only act in the others as *concomitants*. For if the theoretical forms give rise to the dialectic of true and false, in so far as the practical spirit can be introduced into them, it is clear that pleasure and pain come to those forms from the practical spirit, with which the theoretic spirit is always in unity. In the practical spirit too, the moral activity divides into pleasure and pain, in so far as it has concrete or economic form; and therefore in so far as it is economic, not in so far as it is moral. Pleasure and pain belong to feeling alone, because they belong to the economic activity alone, which is the practical in its general form, involving of itself all the other forms, practical and theoretic.

Coincidence of duty with pleasure.

When this has been established, pleasure or economic feeling or economic activity as positive cannot be at strife with duty or with the moral activity in its positivity, for the two terms coincide. The divergence existed only when they were conceived, not in unity and distinction, but in coordination. When we speak of a good action accompanied with pain, we make an inexact statement, or better, we make use of a mode of expression that must be understood, not literally, but in its spirit. The good action, as such, always brings with it satisfaction and pleasure, and the pain said to accompany it, either shows that the action is not yet altogether good, because it has not been willed with complete internal accord, or that a new practical problem, still unsolved and therefore painful, lies beyond the pleasurable moral action.

The other false idea, of *rigoristic or ascetic* Ethic, which makes war upon pleasure as such, derives from the plan of coordination, through the already mentioned casuistic of the conflict between the coordinated terms. Indeed, if it be legitimate to combat this or that pleasure, which enters into a contest with the moral act, it is not possible to abolish the category of pleasure, for the reason already given, that in this way the category itself of morality, which has its reality and concreteness in pleasure (in economicity), would be abolished: the concrete and real moral act is also pleasurable. The attempt to abolish pleasure is as insane as would be the wish to speak without words or any other form of expression, preserving thought pure of such sensual contacts, that is to say, producing an inexpressed and inexpressible thought. This last attempt has been made by *mysticism*, which either does not give thoughts at all, or, contradicting itself, gives them expressed and logical,

Critique of rigorism or asceticism.

like those of all other doctrines. Asceticism provides a complete counterpart to this in the practical field, for it might be called *mysticism of the practical* in the same way as the name of *asceticism of the theoretical* would not be unsuitable to mysticism.

Relation of happiness and virtue.

What has been said of the relation between pleasure and morality, is to be repeated of the other between happiness and virtue, a relation that is identical with the preceding, from which it differs only because expressed by means of empirical concepts of class. Happiness is not virtue, as pleasure is not morality, because there exist the pleasure of the innocent or of the mentally deficient, and the happiness of the child or the brute, who are without moral conscience. But virtue is always happiness, as morality is always pleasure. It will be said that a virtuous man may be unhappy, because he suffers atrocious physical pain or is in financial difficulties, and, therefore, that virtue and happiness do not coincide. But this is a vulgar sophism, because the virtuous man, who should be also happy, must be truly and altogether virtuous; that is to say, he must cure and conquer the ills of the body and of fortune with his energy, if he can, or, if it be impossible to conquer them, he must resign himself and take them into account and develop his own activity within the limits that they lay down. Every individual, not only the unfortunate individual of the example, has his limits; and everyone can transform his limits into pains by being dissatisfied with them, just as every one can, with resignation, transform his pains into limits and conditions of activity. It will be said that sometimes the evils that assail the virtuous man are not only incurable, but so intolerable as to render all resignation impossible. But he who does not effectively and absolutely resign himself, that is, does not accommodate himself to life, dies; and the occurrence of the death of the individual is neither happiness nor unhappiness: it is a fact or event.

Finally, the theory that *subordinates* pleasure or happiness, utility or economy, to duty, to virtue, to moral activity, is to be rejected. The subordination of the one term to the other is not possible on this side of morality, because only one of the two terms is present; and in like manner it is impossible in the moral circle, because, though the terms are certainly two, they are two in one, not one above and the other below; that is to say, they are distinct terms that become unified. Morality has complete empire

Critique of the subordination of pleasure to morality.

over life, and there is not an act of life, be it as small as you will, that morality does not or ought not to regulate. But morality has no *absolute empire over the forms or categories of the spirit*, and as it cannot destroy or modify itself, so it cannot destroy or modify the other spiritual forms, which are its necessary support and presupposition.

No empire of morality over the forms of the spirit.

Hence is apparent the remarkable fatuity of those who pretend to regulate morally the *function* of art, of science, or of economy and profess *moralistic* theories of art and philosophy and a *moralized* economic science. The poet, the man of science, the business man, must be as honest as others, but it is not given to them to tear in pieces the nature of poetry, of science and of industry, in the madness of honesty. Indeed, were this done or attempted, and the poet were to introduce extraneous elements into his work of art, through his failure to understand morality, or the philosopher to veil or alter the purity of truth, or the man of business foolishly to bring his own business to ruin, then and only then, would they be dishonest. To substitute the *single acts* of life that appertain to morality, for *the universal forms of the spirit*, and to predicate of these what should be predicated only of those, is so evident an absurdity that it could not be committed by anyone accustomed to philosophical distinctions. But what nonsense is so evident that idle babblers and elegant men of letters do not know how to cover with their ratiocinative and æsthetic flowers and to present to society or to the academic world as truth, or at least as a theory worthy of reflection and discussion?

Such, then, are the two forms of the practical *Inexistence of other practical* activity, and such their relation; and as it is *forms and impossibility of* not possible to reduce them to one alone, so it *subdivision of the two established.* is not possible to multiply them beyond the two, which altogether exhaust the nexus of finite and infinite. Hence, too, we perceive that the economic and also the ethic-economic activity do not each of them give rise to new subdivisions, because other terms of subdivision are not conceivable beyond the duality of finite and infinite. As there are no philosophical and ethical classes, nor categories of expression (rhetoric), nor categories of concepts (formalistic logic), so there are no economic categories and ethical categories beyond those that constitute utility (volition of the individual) and morality (volition of the universal).

V

THE PHILOSOPHY OF ECONOMY AND THE SO-CALLED SCIENCE OF ECONOMY

Problem of the relations between Philosophy and Science of Economy.

INTERNAL observation, confirming at all points rational necessity, has rendered clear the existence of a special form of practical activity, the utilitarian or economic, and of a correlative Economic or Philosophy of economy. But however irrefutable may seem the demonstration that we have given, yet it will never be altogether satisfactory, while a very important point is left obscure : the relation between our *Philosophy of economy* and the *Science of economy*.

This is a system of doctrine that takes various names and forms, and is presented in turn as political, national, pure, or mathematical Economy; it is a system of doctrines which, although not without precedents in antiquity, has been gradually formed, especially in recent centuries, and is now in fullest flower. A saying of Hegel is often recorded, not without satisfaction, for

364

even in his time he praised Economy as "a science that does much honour to thought, because it extracts the laws from a mass of accidentality."[1]

Has it the same object as our Philosophy of economy? If the reply be in the affirmative, how does it ever arrive at concepts altogether different? Or is it an empirical science, and if so, from what source does it derive the rigour and absoluteness by which it is removed from all empiricism and formulates truths of universal character? Two strict sciences with the same object are inconceivable; and yet as it seems, there must here be precisely two: hence the perplexity and disorientation that the affirmation of a Philosophy of economy must and does produce.

If the economic actions of man be considered, in their uncontaminated and undiminished reality, with an eye free from all prejudice, it is never possible to establish even a *single one* of the concepts and laws of economic science. Every individual is different at every moment of his life : he wills always in a new and different way, not comparable with the other modes of his or of others' willing. If A spent seven soldi to buy a loaf of bread yesterday, and to-day he spend the same amount

Unreality of the laws and concepts of economic science.

[1] *Philos. d. Rechtes*, § 189. *Zus.*

in making the same purchase, the seven soldi of to-day are not for this reason those of yesterday, nor is the bread the same as that of yesterday, nor the want that A satisfies to-day the same as that of yesterday, nor is the effort that his action costs him identical with that of yesterday. If the individual B also spend seven soldi for a loaf of bread, the action of B is different from that of A, as that of the A of to-day was different from that of yesterday. If we lead the economist on to this ground of reality (or rather to the side of this Heraclitean river, in which it is not possible to dip the same hands twice in the same water), he will feel himself impotent, for he will not find any point of support for the edification of any of his theories.—The value of a piece of goods (says a theorem of Economy) depends upon the quantity of it and of all the other goods that are upon the market.—But what does "goods" mean? Bread, for example, or wine? In reality, abstract bread and wine do not exist, but a given piece of bread, a given glass of wine, with a given individual who will give a treasure or nothing in order to eat the one or to drink the other, according to the conditions in which he finds himself.—Any sort of enjoyment, when protracted, decreases and finally becomes extinguished.—That is the law of Gossen, one of the foundation - stones of economic theory. But what are these enjoyments that are protracted, decrease, and end by becoming extinguished? In reality there exist only actions, which assume different positions at every moment, owing to the continual changing of surrounding reality, in which the volitional individual operates. The difference is qualitative, not quantitative : if the individual A eat the bread that he has bought for seven soldi, when swallowing the second or the tenth or the last mouthful, he has a pleasure, not inferior to that which he had when swallowing the first, but different : the last was not less necessary for him, in its way, than the first ; otherwise he would have remained unsatisfied in his normal want, in his habit, or in his caprice.—The economic man seeks the maximum of satisfaction with the least effort.— That is the very principle of Economy, but neither does this principle correspond with reality, most simple and general though it be. The individual A disputes for an hour, in order to save two soldi in the purchase of an object, for which he has been asked ten lire, thus attaining the maximum satisfaction for himself with the least means that is naturally at his disposal on that occasion. The individual B, making boast of his magnificence, lights his cigarette with a banknote of a hundred lire, thus likewise attaining for himself the greatest satisfaction to which he aspired, with the least means that he possessed, namely, by burning that paper money. But if this be so, we have here a question, not of greatest and least, but of individual ends and of relative means adopted, or (owing to the unity of means and ends already noted), of actions individually different.

Economic Science founded upon empirical concepts, but not empirical or descriptive. Certainly, it is quite possible to abstract in a greater or less measure from the infinite variety of actions and to construct a series of types or concepts of classes and of empirical laws, thus rendering uniform the formless, within certain limits. Thus is obtained the concept of bread and of the consumption of bread, and of the various portions of bread and of other objects, for which a portion of bread can be exchanged, and so on. In this way are full philosophico-historical reality and the method of logical necessity and of realistic observation of facts abandoned for a feigned reality and for a method of arbitrary choice, which, as we know, has its good reasons for existing in the human spirit, and does great service by the swift recall and easy control of the requisite knowledge. And if Economy consisted

in the establishment of a series of laws and
examples in the above sense (or when understood in this way), it would join the number of
the descriptive disciplines ; and in that case there
would be no necessity for us to speak of it
further, for it would suffice to refer back to
what has already been said of the relations of
the Philosophy of the practical with practical
Description, classes, rules, and casuistic. But
economic Science is not descriptive, and is not
developed according to the following formula :
goods are divided into the classes a, b, c, d, e, etc.,
and the class a is exchanged with the class b in
the proportion of 1 to 3, the class b with the
class c in the proportion of 1 to 5, etc. In
such a formula is always understood the *up and
down*, the *for the most part*, and *the very nearly* :
the classes *with their ups and downs* are as
stated ; the exchanges take place *for the most
part* in the proportions stated ; if things are
to-day *very nearly* thus, to-morrow they will be
so *very nearly*, in a different way.

On the contrary, the propositions of the
Science of Economy are rigorous and necessary.
" Granted that soils of different degrees of fertility
are cultivated, their possessors will all obtain,
besides the absolute rent, a differential rent, with

*Absoluteness
of its laws.*

the exception of the possessor of the least fertile soil" (Ricardo's law). "Bad money drives out good" (Gresham's law). Now, it is not conceivable in any case that soils of different fertility, all of them cultivated, should not give a differential rent. It will be said that the State can confiscate the differential rent, or that the possessor, owing to his bad cultivation or to his bad administration, may lose it; but the proposition does not remain less sound on this account. Nor is it possible that, when an unchangeable paper money is in circulation, gold coins should also circulate indifferently and on a par with it, when the total of the money in circulation lowers the value of the monetary unit beneath the metallic value of the better money. A madman who might be in possession of a hoard of gold pieces at the time of the circulation of the declining paper money (which causes poverty) would perhaps give it in exchange for the inferior money; but the wise man will keep it in his safe. The economic proposition expresses the rational necessity, not the madness, which is irrational. Those propositions, like all the others of economic science, are therefore certainly not descriptions, but *theorems*.

The denomination " theorems " makes us think

at once of the mathematical disciplines, among *Their mathe-matical nature.* which alone can economic Science find a place. The propositions of that science being excluded from philosophical, historical, or naturalistic science, there remains nothing that they can be, save *mathematical.* Yes, they are mathematical, but not pure mathematics, for in that case they would be nothing but arithmetic, algebra, or the calculus, that is, they would belong to the kind of mathematical disciplines called *applied,* because they introduce into the paradigms of the calculus certain data taken from reality, that is to say, taken from without the purely numerical conception. Economic Science, then, is a mathematic applied to the concept of human action and to its sub-species. It does not inquire what human action is; but having posited certain concepts of action, it creates formulæ for the prompt recognition of the necessary connections.

It is not surprising that such propositions *Its principles; their character* examined in their truth appear in one respect *of arbitrary postulates and* arbitrary and in another tautological. But it *definitions. Their utility.* is not thus that they are examined, and it is not thus that propositions of mathematics are ever examined, for their value lies solely in the service that they render. Certainly Ricardo's law relating to land of varying fertility is nothing but the definition of lands of various fertility, in the same way that Gresham's law relating to bad money is nothing but the definition of bad money. The same may be said of any other economic law, as, for example, that every protective tariff is destruction of riches, or that a demand for commodities is not a demand for labour, since these, like the preceding, are simply definitions of the protective tariff, of the demand for commodities, and of the demand for labour. And it could be proved of all of them that they are arbitrary, because the concepts of land, tariffs, commodities, money, and so on, are arbitrary, and because they become necessary only when that arbitrariness has been admitted as a postulate. But the same demonstration can be given of any theorem in Geometry; since it is not less arbitrary and tautological, that the measure of a quadrilateral should be equal to the base multiplied by the height, or that the sum of the squares of a cathetic should be equal to the square of the hypotenuse. This does not prevent Geometry from being Geometry, or negate the fact that without it we should not have been able to build the house in which we dwell, nor to measure this star upon which we live, nor the others that revolve around it or around which we revolve.

Thus, it would be impossible to find one's way in empirical reality without these economic formulæ, and that would happen which happened when economic science was still in its infancy; namely, that by its means measures of government were adopted, which were admirably suited to produce in the highest degree those evils which it was thought could be avoided by its help, a misfortune of which the Spanish government in Lombardy or in the Province of Naples in the seventeenth century, with its *cries* and its *pragmatics* in economic and financial matters, has left most excellent examples. Or what happens now, when ignorance, or deceitful interest, which profits by ignorance, proposes or causes to be adopted ruinous measures under the appearance of *publica salus*, arguing that they are good, or that they are good for different reasons than those for which they could be maintained. Such, for instance, would be the proposal for fresh expenditure on public works that are useless or of little use during a period of economic depression in a country, and instead of relieving, increase the general depression; or the increase of protective tariffs, when industrial progress is slow, which ought to encourage industry, but on the contrary produce an industry that is unstable and artificial, in place of one that is spontaneous and durable.

Comparison of Economic with Mechanics, and reason for its exclusion from ethical, æsthetic and logical facts.
The special form of application of mathematics, which we find in economic Science, has been compared on several occasions with that which takes place in Mechanics. "The economic man" of the first has seemed to be altogether like the "material point" of the second, and Economy has been called "a sort of Mechanics," or simply "Mechanics." All this is very natural, for Mechanics are nothing but the complex of formulæ of calculation constructed on reality, which is Spirit and Becoming in Metaphysic, and may be abstracted and falsified in Science, so as to assume the aspect of Force or a system of forces, for the convenience of calculation. Economy does the same thing, when it cuts off from the volitional acts certain groups, which it simplifies and makes rigid with the definition of the "economic man," the laws of "least means," and the like. And owing precisely to this mechanicizing process of economic Science, it is ingenuous to ask oneself why ethical, logical, or æsthetic facts are not included in Economy, and in what way they can be included. Economic science is the sum of abstractive operations effected upon the concept of Will

or Action, which is thus *quantified*. Now since moral facts are also will and action, and since economic Science is not occupied with qualitative distinctions, not even with the quality itself of that economic fact which it employs as its material, it is clear that Science cannot lay any stress upon moral distinguished from economic facts, nor can it receive them in a special class, because its assumption is the indistinction of the two orders of facts, and they are included in that indistinction. As to æsthetic or scientific facts, these, taken by themselves, are not facts, but representations and thoughts of facts, and as such escape economic calculation : considered in the unity of the spirit, they are certainly facts, that is to say, volitional products, but as such are already found included with these in the indistinction of economic Science.

As a mathematical discipline, economic Science is ultimately *quantitative*, and it remains so, even when it makes use of the smallest possible number of numerical and algebraical signs (even when it is not *mathematical Economy* in the strict sense of the word). The attempts, both of philosophism and historicism, which claim to deny Economy, by criticizing its abstractness and its arbitrariness, and to make it philosophical

Errors of philosophism and historicism in Economy.

(or as they say *psychological*) and historical are
therefore to be reproved. If Economy do
not give the universal truth of Philosophy, nor
the particular truth of History, Philosophy and
History are in their turn incapable of making
the smallest calculation: if Economy have not
eyes for the true, Philosophy and History have
not arms to break and to dominate the waves
of fact, which would oppress man with their
importunity and finally prevent him from seeing.
Hence the absurdity of *philosophism* and *historicism*; hence too, the sound tendency of Economy
to constitute itself *pure* Economy, free of *practical*
questions, which are also, it is clear, historical,
not abstract and scientific questions.

*The two
degenerations:
extreme ab-
stracticism and
empiristical
disaggregation.*
But economy has in itself other enemies
besides these that are external, in so far as it
is certainly a mathematical discipline, but an
applied mathematic, that is to say, one that
assumes empirical data. These empirical data
can be infinitely multiplied, and hence result
infinite economic propositions, each distinct from
the other; and on the other hand, they can be
regrouped, simplified and unified, so as finally to
return to the indistinct *x*. If the first tendency
prevail, we have what is called economic empiricism, a cumbrous mass of disaggregated

propositions; if the second, a very general formula, which sometimes does not even preserve the smallest vestige of that concept of human action from which it started, and becomes altogether confounded with the formulæ of arithmetic, of algebra and of the calculus. Sound economic Science must be at once abstract and empirical, in accordance with its nature, connecting and unifying disaggregate propositions; but it must not allow distinction to be lost in unity, for the one is as necessary as the other. Those who are unacquainted with the generalities of Economic Science, and those acquainted only with its details, are alike incapable, though for different reasons, of calculating the economic consequences of a fact. The first see all the facts as one single fact, the second, all the facts as different, without any arrangement by similarities and hierarchies. The question as to the relative proportion of generalities and particulars to be given in treatises, is one that has been much discussed, but since this has only a didascalic and pedagogic importance, it is only possible to answer it, case for case, according to the nature of the various scholastic institutions that are held in view. To maintain that Economy must stop short at this or that degree of abstraction, and for example be limited to what are called external goods or riches, excluding services; or to capital, as a concept distinct from land and human labour, without striving to unify these three concepts, is altogether capricious. Every unification, like every specification, can be useful, and haters of abstracticism are also abstracticists, but only half so.

Glance at the History of the various tendencies of Economy.
All those acquainted with economic studies will have recognized in the concepts that we have explained, the *logical motives* of the history of Economy, the divisions, the polemics, the defeats and the victories of this or that school and the progress of that branch of studies. The quantitative character of economic science already appears in its classics; in the inquiries of Aristotle as to prices and value (*Politic* and *Nichomachean Ethic*); and this is apparent also in the rare mentions by Mediæval and Renaissance writers. Economists have always been mathematicians, even when they have not spoken of mathematical Economy. Our writers of the nineteenth century, Galiani, Genovesi and Verri, were mathematicians in their methods; Francesco Ferrara, the greatest Italian economist of the nineteenth century, was a mathematician. The economic principle, which is all one with the

excogitation of the economic man, was formulated
by the head of the physiocratic school, Quesnay ;
and if the title of *political Economy*, first given to
the discipline by Montchrétien in 1615, prevailed,
that of *social Arithmetic* also sometimes made
its appearance. Its progress has consisted, not
only in the discovery of new economic theorems,
but also in the connection and unification of
those that had previously been posited in
isolation, of material and immaterial goods, of
the cost of production and of rarity, of gross
and net produce, of agricultural rents and of all
the others that are not agricultural, of the production, distribution and circulation of riches,
of economic and financial laws, of social and
isolated economy, of the value of utility and of
the value of exchange. It has even been
possible to unite with the body of admitted
economic doctrines those of Marx, which seemed
revolutionary, for these are only definitions of a
particular casuistry founded upon the comparison
of different types of economic constitution.

But to conquer empiricism was not enough ;
economic Science was menaced in its existence
by the so-called *historical School*, which refused
to recognize abstract definitions and set up
against them the infinite variety of historical

facts; hence the strife with historicism conducted by Menger and the Austrian school. A consequence of the struggle against the political degeneration of economic science was the constitution of Economy as a *pure* science (Cairnes). This was all the more necessary, inasmuch as by confounding the abstract with the concrete, and in the concrete itself, Economy with Ethic, there was a desire manifested upon several occasions among German economists (ethical school), and among Catholics of all countries, for an economic Science that should have as its base Ethic. The conception of Economy as a science deduced from the *egoistic* hypothesis, has been the extreme form of the reaction against ethicism (for example in the treatise of Pantaleoni). The dangers arising from philosophism have been less, because recent times, in which that discipline has most flourished, have not sinned through excessive philosophy.

Of late, owing to the works of Jevons and of other Englishmen, of Gossen, of the Italians of the school of Ferrara, and of the Austrians, Economy has become at once more and more complicated and more simple, owing to the applications, extensions, and reductions that it has effected. But if with its progress it be able to become ever more exact and perspicuous, yet it will never for that reason become *organic* ; its character of a quantitative discipline, of an applied mathematic, in which the atomism of the postulates and of the definitions is insuperable, does not allow of such metamorphoses.

In this connection and as the seal upon what we have just been saying, it is fitting to observe that the phrase of Hegel referred to above can only have been interpreted as expressing admiration for the degree of truth attained by Economy, owing to the ignorance of Hegelian philosophy that has become usual ; as though Hegel meant that Economic science did much honour to the *thought*, that is, to the speculative reason. Hegel wished to say, on the contrary, that Economy does much honour to the intellect, that is, to the intellect alone, to that *abstractive* and arbitrary *intellect* which he hunted down in all his philosophy : that it is not indeed true and philosophical science, but a simple descriptive or quantitative discipline treated with much elegance. This praise also contained the demand for a delimitation, which, however, he did not expressly enunciate, develop and execute.

Signification of the judgment of Hegel upon the Science of Economy.

VI

CRITIQUE OF THE CONFUSIONS BETWEEN ECONOMIC
SCIENCE AND PHILOSOPHY OF ECONOMY

Adoption of
the method and
of definition of
Economy by
Philosophy.

THERE is no disagreement, then, between the
Philosophy of Economy described by us and
economic Science or Calculus, of which we have
just defined the nature, since there cannot be
any between two altogether heterogeneous
forms, the one moving within the categories
of truth, the other outside them, with objects of
a practical order. This reciprocal tolerance can
be disturbed only by Philosophy, when it compels
itself, either to invade the field of economic
Science, or to receive within itself, to a greater
or less extent, the method and the formulæ
proper to the latter. We have already referred
to the first, when we noted the inadmissibility
of the economic attempts of philosophism and
historicism, and we will say no more on the
subject. But it is opportune to draw attention
to the fact that we must distinguish among

these attempts those that we are accustomed to
meet with in many treatises on economy, pure or
political, and in the Science of finance (especially
in the prologues), which labour to discover what
economic action may be, and in what way it
differs from morality, what are pleasure and pain,
utility and value; whether the State be rational
will that levies a portion of the riches of the
citizens for the ends of civilization, or a simple
fact resulting from general economic laws and the
like. In all these efforts of the writers of treatises,
we have an example of the gradual passage from
empiria to philosophy, which is to be observed in
all the other fields of knowledge, and if it be only
possible to say in general that the Philosophy of
Economy is derived from economic Science, it is
certain, on the other hand, that it finds no small
incentive in the philosophical doubts and discussions which economic Science supports. On
the other hand, the claim to resolve philosophically and historically the economic Science or
Calculus is, as we have seen, altogether sterile,
or contradicts itself in development.

From the second of the cases stated above, *Errors that*
that is to say, from the mixture of economic with *derive from it.*
philosophic methods, arises a series of errors
that are very common and very grave, and of

which it is opportune to take some notice here.

These errors can be divided into three groups, according as they consist of (*a*) considering economic Science or Calculus as a method exclusive of every other, and alone capable of bestowing upon man all the truth that can ever be attained in the field of human actions; (*b*) in attributing the value of universal thought to the empirical thoughts upon which economic calculation is based; (*c*) in changing into reality the fictions excogitated for the establishment of the Calculus.

1st, Negation of philosophy for economy. Of the three groups, the first, which represents the most extended and radical form of the error, is, as usual, the least harmful, for the reason previously given, that the precise and loyal positions are those that are the most completely surpassed. Several cultivators of economic Science, among the most strict and mathematical, enter upon this desperate struggle against philosophy, which they ridicule as empty chatter and do not merely wish to subdue but altogether to destroy, substituting for it the methods of empirical observation and of mathematical construction, thus favouring a particular empirical and mathematical philosophy of their own, however much they may protest to the contrary. That the pretension is unsustainable, is to be seen, both from the contradictions in which they become entangled and from the very fury that animates them, which is, at bottom, vexation at not being able to free themselves from the contradictions in which they have become involved. For our part, we should like to say to those excellent economists, alike pure and mathematical, did this not appear to be pouring oil upon the flames :—Spare yourselves the trouble of philosophizing. Calculate, and do not think !

The other group is represented by a particular case of the empiristical error that we have already several times criticized, and many propositions of the kind that one hears in ordinary conversation, against which simple good sense has often rebelled, are to be reduced to it. Thus the empirical consideration of certain human actions as constituting richness and happiness, causes those individuals and peoples who possess property of that sort to be called rich and happy ; but to this is opposed, with evident truth, that every one is happy in his own way and that external conditions are not proof of internal satisfaction, which is alone real and effective.

2nd, Universal value attributed to empirical concepts. Example : protection and free trade.

2 C

The great dispute on free trade is also to be reduced to the same misunderstanding, for when we undertake to demonstrate that wealth is destroyed by protection, the demonstration is efficacious only if the wealth, said to be destroyed, is precisely that of which it was desired to assure the increase by protection; but nothing has been proved if it be a different quality of wealth that it may be desirable to acquire, even with the loss and the destruction of the other. For example, a people may find it advantageous from a political and military point of view to maintain in its territories the cultivation of grain or the construction of ships, even if that were to cost more than to provide itself with grain and ships from abroad; in this case, we should, strictly speaking, talk, not of the destruction of wealth, but rather of the acquisition of wealth (presumed national security), paid for with dear grain and dear naval construction. When the empirical ideas of free trade were raised to the dignity of *laws of nature* (reason), there was a rebellion against the economists, by which it was made clear that those laws of nature were laws, not absolute, but empirical, that is to say, historical and contingent facts, and that the economists who propounded them as absolute, were not at all men of science, but politicians, and represented (if not seriously, at least by unconscious suggestion, or, if it be preferred, by mere chance) the interests of certain definite classes or of certain definite peoples. And the rebellion was right, although it afterwards degenerated into the inconclusiveness of historicism, and absolutely denied to those false practical applications the formulæ and laws of Economy, which are *natural* in quite another sense, as nominal and therefore irrefutable definitions. Abstract principles, which are always inadequate to grasp the richness of reality, supply with a simple instrument him who passes from them to historical and sociological observation, which requires altogether different methods. Hence, for instance, the meaning of the school of Le Play, which in studying concrete economic conditions took note of religion, of family and political feelings, and of all the other things connected with the first; hence the admitted necessity of completing the analytic method (as it is called) with the synthetic, or (as it would be preferable to say) of neglecting abstractions when dealing with the problems of life and of directly intuiting life itself.

But what is particular to a philosophy that

3rd, Trans-formation of the functions of the calculus into reality. enters into hybrid wedlock with economic Science, is the transformation of those quantitative principles, of which we have seen the artificial origin, into effective reality. As a result, when this origin has not been observed, or has been forgotten, we may chance to hear the theories of Gossen on the decline of pleasures, as though they were " fundamental laws of human sensibility "; or that some *homo economicus* has appeared, constructor of diagrams and calculator of degrees of utility and of curves of satisfaction, as though these were real things. Some false conceptions derive from economic principles transported into the philosophy of the practical, which we have already had occasion to refute, such as that of a *scale of values*, which the volitional man is supposed to have before him whenever he deliberates, and that other of the embarrassment he experiences in choosing between *two equal goods*; and finally the belief that man *wills things*, whereas what he wills in reality is not things but actions.

The comparisons, metaphors and symbols, taken from Economy and used in ordinary conversation, lead to the false belief that mathematical constructions and those of the economic calculus are the real processes of the psyche or of the Spirit.

The quantification of volitional acts, taken *The pretended calculus of pleasures and pains, and the doctrines of optimism and pessimism.* as a real fact and introduced into philosophy, has given origin to the idea of a *calculus of pleasures and pains and of a balance of life*, to be established with the pleasures on the profit side of the account and the sorrows on the side of loss.   And there have even been ravings about a double mensuration of pleasures, to be based upon their *intensity* and *duration*.   But the real man, at the moment he enjoys, has before him only his own enjoyment, and at the moment that he suffers, only his own sorrow: the past is past and life is not to be described like the profit and loss account of a business.   The true economic man says to himself what Fra Jacopone sang in one of his lauds:

> So much is mine
> As enjoyed and bestowed for the love divine!

The sophisms that assume consistency owing to this false conception, are most strange.   Let the little dialogue of Leopardi with the seller of almanacs suffice for all.   No one would wish to live his life again, not because the sorrows always exceed the pleasures, as that dialogue suggests, but rather because man is not, as he believes, a consumer of pleasures.   He is a creator of life, and for this reason the idea of doing again what has already been done, of retreading the same path, of reliving the already past, is repugnant to him, even were it all made up of pleasures as suggested, because he aspires only and always to the future. *Optimism and pessimism*, being each of them respectively unable altogether to deny pleasure and pain, are obliged to have recourse to these calculations and balances, in order to defend their preconceived conclusions : but in so doing they fall from Scylla into Charybdis and each reveals its own sophistical nature.

Indeed, a philosophy that calculates is a philosophy that toys or dotes, and if we have certainly advised the economists and mathematicians to calculate and not to think, we must, on the contrary, cry to the philosopher :—Think, and do not calculate! *Qui incipit numerare, incipit errare !*

VII

HISTORICAL ANNOTATIONS

THE concepts of the useful and of the moral and the various attempts either to absorb the one in the other or to distinguish them, while recognizing their relations, are the problem on which has laboured the Philosophy of the practical as Ethic and Economic. Has this problem ever been fully solved? It will be permissible to doubt it, when we observe that a philosophical concept of the useful has been wanting until our own days; and that in consequence one of morality must also, strictly speaking, have been wanting, for it could not have been understood in its fulness and purity, owing to the obscure position of the term with which it is united.

I. The utilitarian character of Greek Ethic *Greek Ethic and its ingenuousness.* has been affirmed on several occasions; but one experiences a certain repugnance in applying so precise a term to the documents of ancient thought that remain to us. Socrates, it is true, posited the useful as the supreme concept of morality, and identified the good life with eudaemonia; but for him that useful was nevertheless distinct from the merely pleasing, since it consisted in what is useful to man as man, and his eudaemonia bore much resemblance to the tranquil conscience of him who fulfils his proper duties. Plato (for example, in the *Protagoras*) expounds the doctrine that good things are nothing but pleasant things, and bad things painful; but this doctrine is enunciated in order to place in relief the thesis that man does not do wrong, save through ignorance, and because the bad seems to him to be the good; without saying that in other dialogues the distinction between pleasure and the good is recognized. Nor can the most systematic of the ancient philosophers, Aristotle, be called without reserve a hedonist, a eudaemonist, or a utilitarian, on the strength of his doctrine of happiness. Happiness is the supreme good, it is an end for itself; but virtue is already included for Aristotle in happiness, virtue which is found there, not as an adjunct, but intrinsic, for which exterior goods are indeed necessary, but only as instruments. The virtuous man must be a lover of himself (φίλαυτος), that is to say, just, temperate, liberal of his possessions, ready to yield honours and offices to his friends; lover of himself, then, in the lofty signification of the word (lover, not of the empirical, but of the metempirical ego), as opposed to the wicked man, who is his own enemy. Even Epicurus could not be included among the hedonists, since for him pleasure is not an end, but a means for *calm*, which is the true good, and calm is tranquillity of the spirit, which only the virtuous man can enjoy.

It is therefore more exact to consider Greek Ethic in its general character, not as eudaemonistic and utilitarian, but here also, in relation to the new problem that we now have before us (in the same way as was done above, in respect to practical intellectualism), as *ingenuous*; for in truth that problem did not constitute the centre of inquiries and discussions, as they present themselves in our times, nor were the different schools divided upon it. They were distinguished from one another (as has been already noted in respect to the doctrine of the passions), rather by the different rules of life respectively laid down by each as preferable. The antitheses of the Cynics and Cyrenaics, of the Epicureans and the Stoics, have but a superficial resemblance to those of the ethical rigorists or abstractionists, hedonists or utilitarians, which have appeared as the result of the antithesis between pleasure and pain explicitly stated in modern times. It would be difficult to point out ethical rigorists and utilitarians among thinkers truly and properly so called. In order to discover the utilitaristic attitude at that period of history, it would be necessary to have recourse to some rhetorician, such as Carneades, ready to maintain indifferently the most opposed paradoxes, or to Callicles and Thrasymachus, so magnificently portrayed in the Platonic dialogues. These were rather men of the world than philosophers, giving the immediate and violent impression of the struggle for life, and for this reason they were at conflict with Socrates, the philosopher, whom they sometimes treated as a clown and utterer of paradoxes, sometimes pitied as a child, a " suckling " child, and objected to him that philosophers do not understand one iota about politics (as often has been and often will be objected by politicians, not altogether without reason). If it be wished, all the same, to find a reference to later utilitarianism among the sophists, the hedonists and the Epicureans, or among the Stoics, with their conception of life as a war against the passions, something of future rigorism and asceticism, or in certain discussions among the Platonic dialogues as to the relation between pleasure and pain, a first trace of the discussions upon the same argument that have become most complicated in modern times, by all means let this be done, provided it be never forgotten that it is an affair of glimmers, rather than of vivid light, of antitheses hardly accentuated, not of those that are well defined and stand out clearly.

II. The precise and it may be said violent *Importance of Christianity for Ethic.* affirmation of the antithesis, was the work of Christianity, which, conceiving pleasure and duty, nature and morality to be heterogeneous elements, did great service, both to the progress of civilization in general and in particular to Ethic. It is necessary to insist upon this, for the modern world was bound afterwards to react against this antithesis, and necessarily to assume an Antichristian, even a pagan attitude, and modern art and poetry are often inspired with an abhorrence of the tenebrous Middle Ages and of sad Christianity, and give a sigh of regret for Greece as for a lost Paradise, or a shout of jubilation as for a Paradise regained. But reactions are reactions and poetry is poetry : humanity never retraces its footsteps, though it is often wont to adorn the future with memories of the past. The Greece of our hearts is a new Greece, profoundly modified by Christianity; the Greece of Goethe and of Hegel is no longer the Greece of Sophocles and of Aristotle, but a Greece far richer and more intense. Thought, like life, never turns back, and if it be necessary eventually to attain to a theoretic conciliation between pleasure and duty, between the useful and morality, such a conciliation will be very different from that of still ingenuous Greek Ethic.

The three resulting directions: utilitarianism, rigorism, and psychologism.

The spectacle afforded by modern Ethic, from the Renaissance to the beginning of the nineteenth century, and also (with few exceptions) in the later periods is still altogether dominated by that antithesis, and therefore two currents are to be discerned in it: one that attaches itself to the first term of the antithesis, the useful, and denies the second, or resolves it in the first, the other, which denies the useful and retains moral duty as the exclusive form of the practical activity. This latter is *rigoristic* Ethic, child of Christianity and of ascetic oriental sources, which flowed into it together by direct filiation; the other is *utilitarianism*, child also, though illegitimate, of the distinction or rending asunder of the ancient unity of duty and pleasure, virtue and happiness, effected by Christianity. The antithesis sometimes seems to be solved and a Philosophy

of the practical appears, which, without clinging
exclusively to one term or the other, receives
both into itself. But this philosophy, when it
does not reveal itself at bottom (which generally
happens), as masked utilitarianism, or (a less
frequent case) rigorism attenuated in expression, has the defect of being, not philosophy,
but an empirical description of the so - called
principles of the practical, placed one beside the
other, without a profound definition or deduction
of either. This third direction may be called
intuitionism or *psychologism*.

Utilitarianism is principally represented by
English thought, to which belongs Hobbes, the
greatest of all utilitarians, who proclaimed, *in
statu naturae* (that is to say, in genuine reality)
mensuram juris esse utilitatem.[1] Similar doctrines
are to be found in Spinoza, who has also been
looked upon and criticized as a pure utilitarian.
But the matter is rather more complicated as
regards Spinoza. Of him it should rather be
said that he would have been the most resolute
of ethical rigorists, had he ever been able to
construct an Ethic. His determinism was an
insuperable obstacle to this, for it does not admit
distinctions of values, but considers the good,

Hobbes, Spinoza.

---

[1] *De cive*, c. i. § 10.

like being, in its abstractness, and therefore, the being of each one as *suum essere conservare*; hence the appearance of utilitarianism, assumed by the Ethic of Spinoza.

English Ethic.   From Hobbes descend Locke, Hartley, Hume, Adam Smith, Warburton, Paley, and others such; they are all less courageous and less coherent philosophers than he. Indeed, if Hobbes himself could not but be incoherent and could not avoid causing a desire for and therefore a state of peace to arise from a state of nature or of war, whence is discovered to the mind a source of the practical, altogether different from that of the useful alone, which was presupposed; with the mean and sophistical efforts of his successors, the incoherence becomes altogether irritating. The aid sought from associationism is among these efforts, and the excogitation of the example of the miser (found for the first time in 1731, in a discourse of the Rev. John Gay),[1] and also the admission of the principle of sympathy beside that of egoism, a principle which with a cast of the dice is made to disappear again, and to become absorbed in egoism itself. The inanity of utilitarianism, which has already in Hobbes a

[1] E. Albee, *A History of English Utilitarianism*, London, 1902, pp. 26-27.

tendency to disavow itself, by recognizing as true
laws not those of nature, but those revealed by
God (*in Scripturis sacris latae*),[1] and in Locke retained the divine side by side with the civil laws
and those of public opinion,[2] became evident in
the theological utilitarianism of Warburton and
of Paley. As for intuitionists and psychologists, such as Shaftesbury, Hutcheson, Butler,
these either left an unsolved dualism (as was
above all the case with the last), or, although possessing the most lively consciousness of moral
force, they yet strove to deduce it in some way
from the egoistical and utilitarian principle. The
French materialists of the eighteenth century,
such as Helvétius and D'Holbach, though less
subtle, are more consequent.

Rigoristic Ethic displayed its strength against *Idealistic Philosophy.*
anti-ethical utilitarianism and anti-philosophical
psychologism, not only in traditional scholastic,
but also in the explicit polemic undertaken by
Cudworth, Cumberland, Clarke and Price, against
Hobbes, Locke, and the other utilitarians who
followed them. The makers of great systems,
too, attached themselves to ethical rigorism,
Descartes (and in a certain sense Spinoza),

---

[1] *De cive*, c. iii. § 33.
[2] *Essay on Human Understanding*, Book II. c. 28, § 7 *sqq.*

Malebranche, Leibnitz, and the philosophy of
the school of Leibnitz, as the moral consciousness
declared itself in its true nature in Jean Jacques
Rousseau against the French materialists. But
rigorism also ended by contradicting itself in the
same way as utilitarianism, owing to its one-sided-
ness, when it recognized a principle that was not
merely utilitarian or that lost itself in mystery,
either by reasoning with the utilitarian principle
in the course of its development, or by receiving
utilitarianism into itself, without any mediation, in
the form of the morally indifferent. This is an old
evil, which had already appeared in the ἀδιάφορα
of Stoicism, and in all those exceptions to the
rigorous moral law, which ascetic Christianity
had been obliged to allow, in order to exist
side by side with the worldly life.

Kant and his affirmation of the ethical principle.

III. The strength and the weakness of
rigorism are to be clearly seen in the greatest
ethical system to which it led: the moral
doctrine of Emmanuel Kant. It was time that
the principle of Christian Ethic should be re-
affirmed, duty as clearly distinguished from
pleasure, giving to it that relief which it had
been without in the systems of Descartes and of
Leibnitz, after the materialistic and utilitarian
orgy that had lasted for more than a century,

and after the equivocal attempts at an approach and fusion of the useful and the moral. Kant did not indeed in this respect oppose Wolffian Leibnitzianism; and although the ethical concept of *perfectio* seemed to him to be empty and indeterminate, yet he was never able to prove that it was a eudaemonistic and utilitarian concept.[1] But that concept certainly had not the energy of duty and of the Kantian categoric imperative, which are true declarations of war against every heteronomous morality. This is the merit of Kant, after whom no serious philosopher can be anything but a Kantian in Ethic, as, after Christianity, to no one, not a wind-bag or an extravagant, is it given to be anything but a Christian. Moral action has no other motive than morality itself: to promote one's own happiness (said Kant) can never be *immediately* duty, and even less the principle of all duties.

But the mistake of Kant lies in not having well analyzed the concepts of pleasure, of happiness and of the useful, and in having thought that he could free himself from them, by placing them among another set of principles, which he called *hypothetical* imperatives and opposed to the *categoric*. We know that the imperative

Self-contradictions of Kant concerning the concept of the useful, of prudence, of happiness, etc.

[1] *Grundl. d. Metaphys. d. Sitten*, p. 70.

2 D

of those concepts is not less categoric than that of morality : it is a true imperative, not to be confounded with the knowledge of experience, metaphorically called imperative, because it assumes the appearance of a technique dealing with the practical. Kant was to some extent aware of this, for he subdistinguishes the hypothetical imperatives into *problematical* and *assertorial.* The first of these are technical and give rise to maxims of *cleverness (Geschicklichkeit)*; the second are *pragmatic* and consist of maxims of *prudence.* Observe the difficulties in which he becomes involved, through not wishing to recognize the autonomous character of these imperatives compared with the moral imperatives, that is to say, the categoricity of both. The imperatives of prudence and of happiness are concerned (he says) " with an end which can be assumed as real among all rational beings (in so far as the imperatives can be applied to them in their quality of dependent beings) ; and, therefore, an intention, which not only they *may* possess, but which it is assumed with certainty that they *do* possess, according to a necessity of nature, which is the intention of happiness." We should therefore conclude that they are concerned with an end not less serious than

that of morality. But Kant perceives the poison
in the argument and strives to turn them again
into imperatives concerning means: "ability"
(he continues) "in the choice of the means of
one's own well-being, may be called *prudence*;
therefore the imperative relating to the choice
of the means for one's own happiness, namely
the precept of prudence, is always hypothetical;
the action is ordered, not absolutely, but only
as means for another purpose." It is clear
that to be able to call that knowledge or ability
"prudence" is not sufficient to change the
imperative of happiness into mere ability and
knowledge. Kant perceives this also: "If it were
easy to give a definite concept of happiness,
the imperatives of prudence would altogether
coincide with those of ability and would also
be analytic. For it would be said in the one
case as in the other, that he who wishes the
end also wishes (necessarily, in conformity with
reason) the only means for the purpose within
his power. The concept of happiness is un-
fortunately so indeterminate, that although every
one wishes to attain to it, he is nevertheless
unable ever to say definitely and in accordance
with himself exactly what he desires and wishes.
The reason is that the elements which belong

to the concept of happiness are all empirical and must therefore all be taken from experience; and that for the idea of happiness is also required an absolute whole, a maximum of well-being in my present state and in every future state." In what shall happiness be placed? In riches? In knowledge? In long life? In good health? None of these things is without dangers. In short, it is impossible to determine with full certainty, according to any principle whatever, what would make man truly happy; therefore it is not possible to act according to a definite principle, but only according to empirical concepts; and the imperatives of prudence, strictly speaking, command nothing.—As we see, the only effective argument of Kant against the admission of the categoric imperatives of well-being, of utility, of happiness, is that he does not know exactly what they are. This did not authorize him to exclude those imperatives and reduce them to pseudo-imperatives, to hypothetic imperatives, or to empirical rules. In other passages of his works, Kant tends to the other solution of excluding the maxims of prudence from the pure practical reason, because they are maxims of self-love (*Selbstliebe*), or of the practical reason empirically or *pathologically* conditioned, since for him every pleasure that precedes the moral law and is independent of it, is pathological, that is to say, it belongs to the senses, to the inferior appetitive faculty, not to that which is superior and to reason. Kant often returns to this point and always experiences the same embarrassments and contradictions, as is proved by the variety of the arguments to which he has recourse.[1]

But the unrecognized autonomy of the useful, *Errors derived from it in his* of happiness, of well-being, generally revenges *Ethic.* itself; because, surreptitiously introduced, it causes itself to be unduly recognized afterwards. Thus it comes about that Kant creates, on the one hand, the monster of disinterested actions, and on the other, does not altogether exclude the concept of actions morally indifferent or permissible.[2] Thus, too, it happens that owing to the discord that he preserves between virtue and happiness, thinking vain the pretence of the Stoics and Epicureans to reconcile them in this life, he is led to postulate the existence of God and of the immortality of the soul, and to make of virtue a means of rendering oneself worthy of happiness in another life. " The cold duty of

[1] *Grundl.* p. 36 *sq.* ; *Kr. d. prakt. Vernft.* pp. 15, 21-28, 43, 145 ; cf. *Metaph. d. Sitt.* pp. 208-209.
[2] *Metaph. d. Sitt.* pp. 22, 23, 246.

Kant" (wrote Hegel) "is the last undigested morsel given by revelation to reason, and it weighs upon its stomach."[1] Consequently, the Ethic of Kant, although so different in tendencies and inspiration, yet joined hands with theological utilitarianism, ending at length by also declaring that moral obligation is inconceivable, without the idea of a God, who rewards and punishes in another life, and by declaring that God and the immortality of the soul cannot be otherwise affirmed than by means of moral exigencies. Moral rigorism, like utilitarianism, makes shipwreck in mystery.

Occasions for a philosophy of economy.   IV. Occasions and opportunities for a philosophical concept of the useful were not, to tell the truth, wanting to the thought anterior to Kant; but Kant let them all slip. Without attributing too much suggestive power to certain classes of virtues, such as *fortitude* or *prudence* (virtues that are generically economic, not exclusively moral), which had passed from the Greek into the Christian Ethic, nor to certain acute aphorisms of psychologists and moralists (for instance: *Il y a des héros en mal comme en bien;—Ce n'est pas assez d'avoir des grandes qualités, il en faut avoir l'économie;—La souve-*

[1] *Gesch. d. Phil.* iii. p. 535.

raine habilité consiste à bien connaître le prix des choses, etc.[1]), a first opportunity was certainly afforded by that inferior faculty of appetition, which the Wolffian philosophy had inherited from the Platonic, Aristotelian, and scholastic tradition.[2]

That faculty was parallel with the inferior faculty of knowledge, which that same philosophy had with Baumgarten attempted to develop into an independent science, *Aesthetica*, a development that should have led to the thought of an analogous transformation of the corresponding practical faculty, which might have become an *Oeconomica* or *Ethica inferior*, as from Æsthetic had been made a *Gnoseologia inferior.* But Kant also rejected Æsthetic, as science of a special theoretic form, science of intuition or fancy, conceiving instead, on the one hand a transcendental Æsthetic or doctrine of space and time, and on the other, a Critique of judgment, or doctrine of finality and morality, symbolized in nature;[3] thus he fell into other difficulties, when he wished to establish an analogy between the other forms of the practical reason and that of the theoretical.[4] Although he preserved the division of the faculty

---

[1] La Rochefoucauld, *Maximes* (ed. Garnier), nn. 159, 185, 224.
[2] Wolf, *Psych. emp.*, Frankfort and Leipzig, 1738, §§ 584, 880.
[3] Croce, *Estetica*, pp. 324-328.
[4] *Kr. d. prakt. Vern.* pp. 79, 108.

of appetition into inferior and superior (*untere und obere Begehrungsvermögen*), he failed to realize, as we have seen, the true philosophical concept of the *inferior*.

The problem of politics and Machiavellism. A second opportunity was presented by the series of treatises, which, from Machiavelli onward, had come to conceive of politics as a fact independent of morality, elaborating in particular those precepts and maxims of the "reason of state," of which we have already had occasion to expose the empirical character. But however empirical they were, those mental products gave rise to the problem of the relations between morals and politics, that is to say, as to whether the two terms could be considered as immediately identifiable. The thought of Machiavelli, in particular, constituted an enigma that all attempted to interpret in the most different ways, most by vituperating, some by defending it with strange reasons (Spinoza was among the defenders [1]), though they never succeeded in freeing themselves from its difficulties, for to that end would have been necessary the understanding of the spiritual value of the utilitarian will, even if amoral. It was only when this difficult concept was to some extent caught sight of (by De

---

[1] *Tract. theol.* c. iv. § 7.

Sanctis) that Machiavelli appeared at once justified and criticized; but while that concept remained obscure, the point of view of Machiavelli was never attained and the work was condemned for reasons of a moralistic character (Villari).[1] Kant, too, in his work on *Perpetual Peace*, treated the problem of the relations between morality and politics, affirming that no disagreement is possible between them, unless by politics is meant a *doctrine* of prudence, that is, "a theory of maxims for the selection of the means best adapted for the objects of individual advantage; that is, when the existence of morality is not altogether denied."[2] Here too, he was right, when he claimed that concrete political actions should be submitted to morality; but, on the other hand, he did not perceive that submission and identity presuppose a previous independence and distinction.

Finally, a third opportunity was offered, in the *The doctrine of the passions.* rehabilitation of the passions, begun by the philosophers of the seventeenth century and expressed, as has been said, in a notable manner by Vico. Now if the passions in general be

[1] Cf. Croce, in De Sanctis, *Scritti vari* (Napoli, 1898), i. pp. xiv-xvi, pref.

[2] *Zum ewigen Friede*, in *Werke* (ed. Rosenkranz-Schubert), vol. vii. pt. i. p. 370.

the volitional activity itself, considered in its dialectic, they are also the soul turned to the particular, the useful in respect to the universal, which is sought by morality. This is to be seen especially in Vico and better still in Hegel, very similar to Vico in this respect; he admirably developed this moment of *particularity*, which is passion, necessary for the concreteness of the universal. As the passions for Vico are human nature itself, which morality directs but does not destroy, and are neither good nor bad in themselves, and *utilitates ex se neque turpes neque honestae, sed earum inaequalitas est turpitudo, aequalitas autem honestas*,[1]—so, for Hegel, "passion is neither good nor bad in its formal character and only expresses the fact that a subject has placed all the living interest of his spirit, of his talent, of his character, of his enjoyment, in a single content. Nothing great can or has been accomplished without passion. Only a morality that is dead and too often hypocritical can inveigh against the form of passion as such. . . . Ethicity concerns the content, which, as such, is universal, something inactive, and has its active element in the subject: the fact that the content is immanent in it constitutes interest,

[1] *De uno univ. juris principio*, § 46.

and in so far as it dominates all the efficient sub-jectivity, passion."[1]

The same Hegel once observed: "As for *Hegel and the* what concerns utility, morality must not play the *concept of the useful.* disdainful towards it, for every good action is actually useful, that is to say, possesses reality and produces something good. A good action that were not useful would not be an action, would not possess reality. The inutility of the good in itself, as its unreality, is its abstractness. Not only is it possible to be conscious of utility, but we ought to be conscious of it, since it is true that it is useful to know the good: utility does not mean anything but that we are conscious of our own action. If this be blameworthy, it will also be blameworthy to know the goodness of one's own action."[2]

Hegel thus discovered the function of the use-ful when rehabilitating the passions, though in a fugitive manner. But Kant had not attributed importance to the problem of the passions in Ethic, and had not therefore been in a position to avail himself of the suggestion contained in the doctrine of the passions.

Fichte, in re-elaborating the Kantian philo-

---

[1] *Encykl.* § 474, and cf. other passages: *Phän. d. Geistes*, pp. 484-486; *Encykl.* § 474; *Phil. d. Rechtes*, § 124; *Phil. d. Gesch.* pp. 39-41.

[2] *Gesch. d. Phil.* ii. pp. 405-6.

*Fichte and
the elaboration
of the Kantian
Ethic.*

sophy, showed the relation between pleasure and duty in a manner that came very near to the truth. He gave precedence to what he called the *empirical* over the moral man, the former corresponding entirely to the merely utilitarian or economic. What, asks Fichte, will be his maxim of action at this stage? " As there is no other impulse in his consciousness save the natural, and as this is directed only toward enjoyment and has pleasure for its motive, that maxim cannot but be to choose what promises the maximum of pleasure in intensity and extension; that is, the maxim of his own happiness. This may likewise be sought in the pleasure of others by means of the sympathetic impulses; but the ultimate scope of his action always remains the satisfaction of those impulses and pleasures which arise from it, and therefore, his own happiness. Man at this stage is an intelligent animal." " But," he continues, " it is a fault to remain here, and man must raise himself to a stage at which he enjoys an altogether different liberty; he must be free, not only *formaliter*, but also *materialiter*, that is, he must attain to the moral stage." [1] That first stage, then, is formal freedom, and is no longer con-

[1] *System der Sittenlehre*, p. 180 *sq.* ; cf. p. 15.

sidered a pathological condition of the spirit, or as that merely technical knowledge of which Kant speaks. This would constitute no small progress, if Fichte had been conscious of all the richness of the concept of which he had caught a glimpse, and had made it fructify. But it seems that he was not aware of this, and certainly he took no advantage of it whatever.

V. The inventive genius of modern Ethic is *The problem of the useful and of morality in the thinkers of the nineteenth century.* exhausted with these thinkers. Their successors have reproduced the old situations, one after the other. Some, while accepting the Kantian morality, wished to temper and correct its exaggerations, which was not possible, save by a more profound speculative vision of the relation between pleasure and good, the useful and the moral; whereas they believed that they could attain to it by *also* taking account of pleasure and of happiness, and by conceiving a doctrine of happiness or eudaemonology side by side with Ethic, but subordinate to it (in Italy: Galluppi and Rosmini). Schiller had already recognized in Kant's time the unilaterality of Kant, and had made it the object of criticism and of epigram, which, however, does not mean that he had truly and properly corrected its errors. Others occupied themselves in various ways with the

enumeration and juxtaposition of the principles:
thus, for instance, Schopenhauer makes compassion arise beside egoism, which then divides
into benevolence and justice; and Herbart,
although he excludes the useful, because, according to him, "it refers to a point external to itself,"[1]
enumerates five practical ideas that are not all
truly moral. The affinity both of Herbart and of
Schopenhauer, with Shaftesbury, Hutcheson and
English and Scottish psychologism, is clear.
The study of the practical ideas of Herbart is not
without interest as an unconscious affirmation of
the necessity of the economic principle. The
first of these, indeed, *internal freedom*, consists in
being able to achieve with our own strength the
model that we propose to ourselves, and is
liberty, but not yet moral liberty. "To be able
to decide *according to motives*" (says Herbart on
one occasion) "is already a sign of psychical
health : to decide *according to the best motives* is
the condition of morality."[2] The second of the
practical ideas, that of *perfection*, is concerned
precisely with the strength of the will, taken in
itself, and resembles a combination of the Hellenic
virtues of fortitude and temperance. Here will-

---

[1] *Einleitung*, § 82 (Italian transl. p. 102).
[2] *Op. cit.* § 128 (It. tr. p. 172).

ing is considered in itself, independently of its
objects, and in this consideration there is no
other difference, save their strength, between the
various willings : the greater this is, the more it
is admired ; weakness displeases and strength
pleases the practical judgment, and this even
when it is unjust, iniquitous and wicked, and
notwithstanding such vices.[1] Lotze, following
Herbart, determines as requisites of actions, that
they must be possible, energetic, conscientious
on the one hand, and on the other, consequent,
habitual, individual, stating that these two series
of predicates apply equally to moral and immoral
actions.[2]—He does not think it worth while to
take count of the English utilitarians and post-
Kantian intuitionists, or of their French, Italian,
and German imitators ; because, just as the
appearance of a Hobbes, of a Hume, or of a
Shaftesbury, is important in their time, so the
appearance of a Bentham or of a Spencer out of
their time is insignificant, for these latter amuse
themselves with the useful, with association and
evolution (which according to them should become
the socially useful), and with the double principle
of egoism and of altruism. Stuart Mill alone

---

[1] *Allg. prakt. Phil.* p. 35.
[2] *Grundzüge der Ethik*, §§ 12, 14.

can afford some interest, when he says (with that mental inconclusiveness which has seemed to many to be acuteness and equilibrium) that moral pleasures differ from the sensual, not only in degree, but also in genus and in quality (*in kind*); and that justice is a class of socially useful actions that arouses feelings themselves also different, not only in degree, but also in genus and in quality (*in kind*), from those caused by useful actions. In short, the philosophy of the nineteenth century has not only been unable to progress, but has not even been able to maintain itself on a level with the practical doctrines of Fichte and of Hegel, in which a glimpse was caught of the relation of first and second practical degree, and there was a tendency to reconcile passion and ethicity.

Extrinsic union of Ethic and of economic Science, from antiquity to the nineteenth century.

VI. Certainly economic science, owing to its empirico-quantitative character, already noted, was not made to fill the void and to furnish a more positive and exact concept of the useful. The contact between Economy and Philosophy remained for a time extrinsic, since economic Science appeared in treatises upon the Philosophy of the practical, together with the other juridical and historical matter, which it was customary to include with it. The precedent for such a union could be found even in Aristotle's *Nichomachean Ethic*, which supplies certain notions as to the concept of price and value. Considerations on the same argument abound in the Scholastics, especially in St. Thomas, whose *Oeconomica* always forms part of his Ethic, as the doctrine for the government of the family. Finally, there is an ample discussion of the subject in the treatises of the seventeenth and eighteenth centuries, which took the name of *natural Rights.* It happened that the English moralists of the eighteenth century were also led to occupy themselves with Economy and the economists with Ethic, owing to the juxtaposition of the two concepts for didascalic reasons and for University convenience. Thus Hutcheson developed Economy, in his *Short Introduction to Moral Philosophy* (1747); and the *Essays* of Hume are occupied with moral and economic questions; and Adam Smith is the author, not only of *The Wealth of Nations*, but also of *The Theory of the Moral Feelings*, almost two parts of a Philosophy of the practical. The importance of economic studies had become so palpable at that time, that toward the end of the century, Buhle was led to include them in the history of philosophy (and we believe that

2 E

he was the first). He exposes at length in his work the ideas of Hume, of Smith, of Stewart, attributing it as a merit to the English writers to have reduced that material to philosophy by a method of treatment without example (he said) in previous centuries.[1] Finally, Hegel dedicated certain important paragraphs of his *Philosophy of Law*, in the section dealing with civil society,[2] to the "system of wants," or Economy. The cult of Economy has rather increased than diminished in the nineteenth century and the much-discussed social problem (especially capitalism and socialism) has not been without a certain influence upon treatises of Ethic, where, if we rarely find statements that are strictly economic, there is always plenty of chatter about property and production and the relations between the working and capitalistic class.

Philosophical questions arising from a more intimate contact between the two.

But a more intimate bond could not take place, save when attempts to understand the material of science and to place it in the system of the spirit were united with economic Science, properly so called. For since that science is occupied with human actions and appears to

[1] *Gesch. d. neueren Philos.* (1796–1804), sect. iv. cap. 18 (Fr. tr., Paris, 1816, v. 432-753).
[2] *Phil. d. Rechts*, § 189 *sqq.*

give advice as to conduct, in what relation
can it possibly stand to Ethic, which is also
occupied with actions and also gives advice?
—Such a question was in a certain way already
implied in the mediæval idea of a *justum pretium*,
to be placed beside the effective price, which is
realized according to the knowledge and convenience of each ; it forms the kernel of the
debate between the *subjective and the objective*
concept of value, that is, between the purely
economic consideration and another resulting
from moral exigencies, between the value that
is, and that which in a certain way should be.
It began to wax ardent, with the accusation,
of being theoreticians of egoism, hurled at the
great English economists, Smith and Ricardo ;
this accusation, taken up and modified by others,
became accepted as the true and proper designa-
tion of the function of Economy, which should
accordingly be that of studying human actions
in their exclusively abstract, egoistic aspect. But,
since abstraction is not full reality, the false task
assigned to Economy called for the aid of the
doctors. Such were the French economists, seized
with the mania of teaching generosity to the
cold Britons (Blanqui, etc.) ; such too were the
Germans, who wished to induce Economy to

mend its ways and to become conscious of its lofty duties towards the human race (Knies); such, finally, were the Christians and Catholics, who thought to purify or to exorcise that worldly and diabolical science by mingling with it ethical and economical considerations. It was rarely suspected that economic facts, as such, are neither egoistic nor altruistic, neither moral nor immoral; and when it was desired to philosophize the subject, some one got out of the difficulty by enumerating five groups of human actions, four egoistic and only one moral: the search for the satisfaction of one's own conscience, with the fear of blame attached (Wagner). The problem, especially in Austria, passed from the hands of the mathematicians into those of the psychologists. These have undertaken to seek out the resemblance and the difference between economic and ethical values. But on the psychological ground (as we have already remarked when discussing intuitionistic solutions), far from solving the antithesis, philosophy is dissolved. The mathematicians on the other hand, that is to say the economists, who employ the quantitative method, fascinated with the evidence of this procedure and failing to realize that it is empty evidence, instead of limiting themselves to the construction of their most useful formulæ, increase the confusion by beginning to philosophize in the strangest manner; as is to be observed in the case of Pareto, one of the most acute and learned of contemporary economists. In one of his recent writings he exposes the method of economic science with a string of propositions such as these: "*Il faut faire une opération de séparation. . . . Cette première opération accomplie, . . . il est nécessaire de substituer par abstraction, des conceptions simples, au moins relativement, aux objets réels extrêmement complexes. . . . Mais la science n'est réellement liée à une abstraction plutôt qu'à une autre. . . . Pour peu qu'on y trouve un avantage. . . . Cela ne suffit pas encore: il faut continuer à séparer et à abstraire. . . .*"

And after having thus advised us to treat facts without pity, mutilating them, grinding them down, substituting for them names or abstractions, Pareto continues undisturbed, as though all this were nothing: these theories, "*telles, au moins que nous les concevons, se séparant des anciens en ce qu'elles s'attachent aux faits et non aux mots*"![1]

If such be the facts, what will be the words?

VII. It is all the more necessary to under-

---

[1] "L'Économie et la sociologie au point de vue scientifique" in *Rivista de Scienza*, i. (1907) 293, 312.

The theories of the hedonistic calculus : from Maupertuis to Hartmann. stand the diversity between economic Science and the Philosophy of economy, between the quantitative and the qualitative processes, owing to the fact that since economic studies first flourished, in the eighteenth century, absurd ideas were introduced into the books of philosophers, as to the calculus of pleasures and the balance of life. Maupertuis' book, *Essai de philosophie morale* (1749), had a great influence in this direction. Here, a balance is presented, showing a deficit on the side of pleasures; and, following this lead, many Italian philosopher-economists of the same period occupied themselves with such calculations and balances (Ortes, Verri, Briganti, etc.), arriving at results, now optimistic, now pessimistic.[1] Galluppi, too, accepted the method as a good one,[2] and it is no marvel that the poet Leopardi made it his, steeped as he was in the sensualistic philosophy of the preceding century. But not only are the trivial optimistic sophisms of the utilitarians founded upon it, but likewise many of the pessimistic arguments of Schopenhauer and especially of Hartmann, the latter quite unconscious (being in other respects closely connected with the German idealist tradition)

[1] See M. Losacco, *Le dottrine edonistiche italiane del secolo XVIII* (Napoli, 1902).

[2] Galluppi, *Elementi di filosofia* (Napoli, 1846), ii. 265-266, 406 *sqq.*

that he was accepting an element of an altogether anti-idealistic, that is, of a mechanistic origin.

For all these reasons, it is important to oppose the concept of the useful (which is not indeed a concept, but an abstraction), given by economic Science, with its philosophic concept. This we have attempted to do in the preceding theory of Economy, as at once distinct from and united with Ethic. In that theory, we have especially striven to collect stray threads of aphorisms and observations of good sense as to the value of the will, even when amoral; as to the doctrines of happiness and of pleasure, of the inferior appetitive faculty, of others dealing with politics and the arts of prudence, of the new conception of the passions, considered as the spirit in its individuality;—we have striven to attach to these that which is as it were the philosophical result drawn from economic Science, that is to say, the idea of a form of value that would be neither the intellectual, the æsthetic, nor the ethical, and cannot by any means be resolved into an ethical anti-value or egoism;—and finally, we have attempted to unite all these threads into one, in order to form the bond that ethical rigorism has hitherto been unable to place between itself and reality,

between the universal and the practical individual,
at the same time justifying utilitarian activity
in its autonomy.   We believe that this historical
sketch will have contributed to make clear the
necessity of our attempt.

SECOND SECTION

THE ETHICAL PRINCIPLE

I

CRITIQUE OF MATERIAL AND OF FORMALISTIC ETHIC

IT is a much-disputed question whether the *Various* *meanings of* Principle of Ethic should be conceived as *formal* *"formal" and* *" material."* or *material.* The question, already difficult in itself, has become yet more difficult, so as almost to cause despair of its solution, owing to the fact that those terms, "formal" and "material," are understood (as often happens in philosophy) in a double sense. Hence, those who win assent to their thesis as to the formality of the ethical principle are afterwards wont to avail themselves of this assent, in order stealthily to introduce another thesis, which, although it be also beneath the banner of the "formal," yet has nothing to do with the first and is as false as that is true. And since those who maintain the material principle do the same thing, both alike come to expose their flanks to one another's blows. In the process of unravelling this tangled skein, we shall begin by giving to those two words the meaning that they usually bear in philosophical terminology, meaning by "formal" the universal and by "material" the contingent. And in this signification we affirm, above all, that the principle of Ethic is *formal* and certainly not *material*.

The ethical principle as formal (universal) and not material (contingent).

Were it material, it would express itself by means of propositions indicating a single volition or a group of single volitions as the true and proper essence of the moral volition; and the moral activity would consist of a determinate action or of a determinate group of actions. But the moral act is always that which surpasses the single or the groups of singles: to will and to effect the single and the series of singles as such, does not appertain to the ethical, but to the merely economic form. He who loves things for things' sake (be they such, and as many as you will, of this or that kind, one, many, infinite) does not yet love the universal, which is everywhere, and is not exhausted in any particular thing, nor in any number of things, however immense.

If we posit a material principle for Ethic,

we relapse as a consequence into *utilitarianism*, from which we thought we had escaped ; because, after having asserted the universal, it is now determined, either as a single or (which amounts to the same thing) as a feigned universal, a simply general concept of group or series. This vicissitude, however, presents itself in every sphere of philosophy : when the universal and formal principle of that sphere is materialized, we return to the sphere immediately below it. For example, an Æsthetic that posits as its principle certain single forms of art, thus substituting matter for form, relapses from art to life lived, which is the condition that precedes art and upon which art raises itself in order to intuite and to dominate life. Material Ethic has therefore been with reason discredited as heteronomous and utilitarian. Not indeed that it is so directly and admits itself so to be : on the contrary, it professes to be anti-utilitarian and does nothing directly, save to point to a given object as the true content of morality. But that object, being single, implies a merely utilitarian volition; and material Ethic is utilitarian, because, whatever it may do or say, it is logically reducible to utilitarianism.

Reduction of material to utilitarian Ethic.

The rejection of all material character from

Rejection of material principles.

the ethical principle is of the greatest importance, for it frees Ethic from a long series of concepts, each one of which has been proposed in turn as the true ethical principle, and several still find many supporters, both in ordinary thought and in treatises called scientific. For us, those concepts should not be examined comparatively, so as to arrive at preferring the one to the other, or a new one of the same type to all the concepts previously enunciated; but they are all false, for one and the same reason, as any other that may in future be excogitated will be false, if it contain in it anything material.

Benevolence, love, altruism, etc.; and critique of them.

A first group of such material principles is found in relation to the general concept of an action, directed toward the welfare of individuals, other than the individual acting. Morality (they say) is *sacrifice of self, benevolence, love, altruism, compassion, humanitarianism*, or simply *naturalism* of the Franciscan sort, which commands us to respect, protect, and love the animals also, since they too are God's creatures (brother Wolf, sister Fox). Such formulæ, especially those of *benevolence and altruism*, have been and continue to be successful; and hardly a doubt is harboured but that they determine in the most complete and satisfactory manner the proper principle of morality.

But in truth *others*, as individuals, have no rights that I too do not possess as an individual: I am another for the other, and he is an I for himself; and if each one provided for the good of others, neglecting and trampling upon his own good, the result would be perfectly identical to what would happen, were each one to provide for himself without concern for others. Morality demands the sacrifice of me for the universal end, but of me only in my merely individual ends; and, therefore, in this case, of me as of others. It has no particular animosity against me, so as to wish to sacrifice me at all costs to others. We must be severe, not only with ourselves, but with others also; exigent, not only with ourselves, but with others also; and so, on the contrary, benevolent not only toward others, but also toward ourselves; compassionate, not only toward others, but also towards this instrument of labour that we carry about with us and of which we sometimes demand too much; that is, our empirical individuality. Reality is neither democratic nor aristocratic, but both together; it abhors the privilege of some over others as much as that equality, according to which each one must have the same value as the other at every moment. All are in turn

masters and servants; worthy of respect as
bearers and representatives of good, worthy of
punishment and reprehension as clouding and
impeding the good. Morality never considers
individuals in themselves, but always in their
relation to the universal; and in this respect
there is no one who does not deserve to be saved
or to be suppressed; there is no animal or
other being of any kind that should not now be
favoured in its existence, now annihilated. No
individual is treated as an *end*, but all as *means*
for universal morality; and they only obtain the
dignity of ends, in so far as they are means for
universal morality. The rights of animals have
been written for and against; but in truth, a lamb
has now the duty of being slaughtered, now the
right of being left in peace, according to circumstances; in the same way that a man has now
the right to go for a walk with his friends and
to sing serenades beneath the windows of fair
ladies, now the duty of putting on a uniform and
of betaking himself beneath the walls of a citadel,
where he will be blown in pieces by the enemy's
grape-shot. Altruism is as insipid as egoism,
and is reducible at bottom to egoism; in much
the same way as sensual love, which has justly
been called "egoism for two." Indeed, why

should we be ready to sacrifice ourselves for others, and to promote their desire in every case and in spite of everything ? For what reason, save for the blind and irrational attachment to them which makes a man throw away his life or descend to abjection for a wicked woman furiously loved, suffer every shame and torment for an unworthy son, or yield to the impulses of sympathy inspired by an individual? This blind and irrational attachment to others is at bottom attachment to ourselves, to our nerves, to our fancies, to our convenience, to our habits. It is utility, not morality ; for morality wills us to be ready to separate ourselves from others as from ourselves, when the occasion arises, to leave wives and sons and brothers, and follow duty which transcends them all. " Thou only, O ideal, art true, . . ." or rather, by means of the ideal and of the universal, all things are true ; without the ideal, there is not one of them that does not become false, as there is not an organism that does not become vile clay, when abandoned by life.

There is another group of material principles *Social organism, State, interest of the race, etc.* which seems to surpass individuals, because it makes morality to consist of promoting either *Critique of them.* so-called *laws of nature* or so-called *institutions.* Of such kind are those that place morality in the

service of the *social organism and of the State,
or of the interest of the Species and of Life* (this
being understood as animal life or very near to
animality). But if it seem that contingent facts are
thus escaped, that is not really so. For none of these
concepts expresses the universality of the real, but
this or that group of its particular manifestations :
the life called social or political, this or that
animal species, this or that vital manifestation.
And none of these facts can be ethically willed
without exceptions. The moral man sacrifices
the State to the Church, or the Church to the
State, atrophies certain organs and suppresses
certain vital functions for universal ends, or for
the ends of what is called civilization ; he defends,
preserves and increases certain aptitudes of
the human race, but lets others disappear or
modifies them, always adapting the interest of
the species to that of the ideal. Were he to do
otherwise, he would again be substituting utility
for morality, his immediate affection for certain
things or for certain single and individual facts,
to the affection for them that should always
be *mediated*, that is to say, mediated by the
universal.

*Material re-
ligious prin-
ciples. Critique
of them.* A third group of material principles, called
religious, which make morality to consist of

conforming to the will of God and of the gods, is not intrinsically different from these. Where the idea of the transcendental and of religious mystery is introduced, there is darkness; and anything can be put into darkness. In the first place, nothing but darkness itself can be put there, and in this case the religious solution is agnosticism, confession of ignorance, such as we have hitherto treated, in criticizing theological utilitarianism or abstract ethical rigorism, which, by means of its insoluble contradictions, also leads to the idea of God and of mystery. But one's own will, caprice and individual interests can also be put there; and then religion becomes attachment to a being or to an order of beings, which, though they be imaginary, are not for that reason less individual; attachment to them is love or fear, sympathy or fear of the evil they can do, and tendency to avoid it by propitiation with prayers, adulation, gifts, services, worship. Religious principles, then, understood as material principles, also become converted, as all know, and we may add, know all too well, into utilitarian principles; because, through intently fixing the gaze upon this aspect of religion, they have forgotten to look at others more important and certainly more noble.

Formal principle as affirmation of a merely logical exigency.

The ethical principle is not adequately expressed, either by the *altruistic* concept, or by that of *natural formations* and of *institutions*, or by that of the *gods*; because all of these are general concepts, or sometimes merely individual representations; they are certainly not universal concepts. And by the necessity of the universal and the insufficiency of the merely general and individual, the ethical principle must be *formal* and not *material.* However (and here we enter into the new meaning of this word and into the new debate announced), the formal ethical principle has likewise been understood as not susceptible of extension beyond the enunciation of the character of universality, which the principle itself should possess. Its formula has seemed to be nothing but that of a *universal law*, to which all men can conform in complete harmony among themselves; of *respect towards all beings*, in the degree that appertains to each, of that which satisfies *the exigencies of reason and of conscience*, and so on. Now the formality claimed by this and similar formulæ has nothing to do with the formality first claimed; and since in the preceding debate we took the side of those who maintain formal as against material Ethic, so

here we must defend material against formal
Ethic; or better, an Ethic that is not material
against an Ethic that is not formal, save in the
pretentions of those who thus baptize it.

What does the formality of Ethic mean in *Critique of a*
formal ethic in
the new sense? Nothing but this : that it is *this sense :*
tautologism.
not necessary to inquire *what is the ethical*
principle, but that we must be satisfied with
saying that *whatever it be, it must be universal.*
But that it must be universal is a proposition
which belongs, not to Ethic, but to Logic ; the
principles of all philosophical sciences must
possess the character of universality, the logical
as the æsthetic, the principle of Ethic as that
of Economic, the moral categoric imperative as
the utilitarian categoric. Thus the thesis of
formality in the new meaning is reduced to
placing at the head of Ethic, not the ethical
principle, *but the logical exigency of the ethical*
principle, in the same way that a similar
claim in Æsthetic would result in placing
at the head of that science, not the formal
æsthetic principle, as for example, Intuition-
expression, but a formal æsthetic principle,
the claim for a law, so made that no form
of beauty could ever be excluded from it.
Instead of constructing the science, the affirma-

tion of logical necessity, which that construction must obey, is infinitely repeated; but the thesis of formality in the new sense would be better called the thesis of *tautologism.*

Besides the formulæ to which we have referred, namely those of the *categoric imperative, of the universal law, of the respect for being, of the rational and of conscience,* the formulæ of the *chief good, of duty* (*or of law*), *of the ideal, of true pleasure, of constant pleasure, of spiritual pleasure, of personal dignity, of self-esteem, of the just mean, of harmony, of proportion, of justice, of perfection, of following nature,* and so on, also belong to the tautological principles of Ethic; they are all tautologies, because they do not determine to what object those logical claims are applicable. To ask what is the form of will that produces a *constant, spiritual and true* pleasure, which makes *perfect, gives self-esteem, satisfies our conscience, strikes the just mean,* answers to what *ought* to be done, attains to *the supreme good,* and so on, is tantamount to asking, *What is the ethical form?* This is precisely what must be answered, if we do not wish to fall into tautology, and the reply cannot be the question itself.

And it is convenient to note here that many

of the formulæ that we have criticized as belonging to material Ethic, have also been frequently
employed as tautological formulæ, that is to say,
as symbols and metaphors of the ethical truth
to be determined.   The *others*, of which altruism
speaks, are at bottom not others as physically
distinct from us, but others in an ideal sense,
that is, as duty surpassing the empirical ego ;
God, of which religious Ethic speaks, is that indeterminate concept, that logical exigency, which
is also called the *categoric imperative* ; *the State
or Life* that one pledges oneself to serve is
not this or that State, this or that particular
form of life, but the symbol of the ideal ;   the
nature to be followed is that nature, or ethical
principle within us, which the speculative reason
must determine.   Thus do material principles
often progress, ceasing to be such, in order to
become tautological, that is, abandoning the
possession of undue determination, owing to the
consciousness of a want, of a lacuna to be filled.

Tautological meaning of certain formulæ, material in appearance.

The evil is that tautologism inevitably returns
to that undue possession, because, imagining
that it has established that ethical principle
which it has not established at all, and that it has
finally constructed Ethic, of which it has not
even laid the foundations, it sets to work to

Conversion of tautological Ethic into material and utilitarian Ethic.

explain moral and concrete facts by means of that empty form. The consequence of this is that utilitarian motives, as usual, fill the empty space. Why should we not violate a deposit that has been entrusted to us? Perhaps because (as they say) the moral law is a universal law? That does not suffice. Respect for the deposit cannot be deduced from this principle, for a universal law is equally thinkable, according to which is deduced in certain cases a respect for the deposit and in certain other cases the contrary. This then is the fact: that to restore a deposit confided to us may sometimes happen to be a bad action, as, for instance, to restore the weapon entrusted to us, when he who claims it intends to commit suicide or to assassinate. Thus it happens that not knowing how to put an end to the controversy in virtue of the true ethical principle, and wishing nevertheless in some way to use that empty formula, it comes to be filled with the only principle possessed, namely the utilitarian; and the reason given for respecting the deposit is said to be the desirability of respecting for engagements, for the ends of the individual, failing which (it will be said) no business would thenceforth be effected and the world of affairs would languish.

Formal Ethic, in the new sense, or as it would be better called, tautological Ethic, might be called *formalistic*, owing to its thus falling back into material, heteronomous and utilitarian Ethic, since *formalism* here (as in Æsthetic and Logic) is the caricature of formality, and almost a sort of materiality. In maintaining *formal* Ethic we do not wish that it should be *formalistic*; that is, that it should be again covertly material. And we wish that formal Ethic should also be material, always understanding by this that it must give, not the mere logical condition of the ethical principle, but *this ethical principle itself* in its concreteness, determining what moral volition is in its reality.

In what sense Ethic should be formal and in what other sense material.

THE ETHICAL FORM AS ACTUATION OF THE SPIRIT IN UNIVERSAL

Tautological Ethic and its connection with Philosophy, either partial or discontinuous. IF the strange idea of an ethical principle that should be formal, in the sense of its not being known exactly what it is and how it is justified, has ever been able to arise, this is due to two erroneous philosophical conceptions, of which one can be called *partial*, the other *discontinuous* philosophy. According to the first conception, man is capable of knowing something of reality, certainly, but not all: he perceives and arranges the data of experience by means of the categories, but he is aware of the limitation of his thought and of the impossibility of attaining to the heart of the real, which he does, it is true, end by attaining in a certain way, but only with the heart, not with thought. This being stated, and coming to the case of Ethic, man hears the voice of conscience in himself, the command of the moral law; he cannot think of any sophism to escape it: but

440

precisely what that law is, he is unable to say; the idea of a divine ordinance of the world which presents itself to his spirit, may also be affirmed by the heart, but never by thought. The second conception is confounded by some thinkers with the first and becomes partial philosophy or agnosticism; but if we observe closely, it is distinct from the other. For here it is not actually asserted that the foundation of morality is unknowable, but it is said to be unknowable in the circle of Ethic, or that such knowledge goes beyond that circle. Ethic establishes the moral law, deduces or arranges beneath it ethical precepts and by means of them judges single actions. Ethic is ignorant as to whether that law really exists, or what may be its precise universal content. It hands this problem over to Metaphysic, or to general Philosophy, which solves it in its own way, or is presumed to be capable of solving it. In this conception, then, there arises a question as to competence and hierarchy between thought and thought, between particular and general philosophy; whereas, in the former, is affirmed the absolute incompetence of thought.

But we do not run the risk of colliding with *Rejection of both these conceptions.* the obstacle placed before us with these philosophical views, because we have constantly rejected them both throughout the whole of our exposition of the Philosophy of the spirit and have demonstrated their falsity. Partial Philosophy is a contradictory concept : thought either thinks all or nothing ; and if it had a limit it would have it as thought and therefore as surpassed. Whoso admits something unknowable, declares everything unknowable, and inevitably falls into total scepticism. Nor is the idea of a discontinuous philosophy divided into a whole and its parts, with the whole outside the parts and the parts outside the whole less inconceivable ; so that, while Ethic is being studied, the whole (complete Philosophy) seems problematical ; and a part (Ethic) can be known to some extent without knowing the whole (the whole of Philosophy). This is a false view, ultimately derived from the empirical sciences, in which it is possible to apprehend one order of phenomena independently of the others ; and to apprehend phenomena without explicitly posing or by dismissing to another occasion the philosophical problem as to their truth. Philosophy is a circle and a unity and every point of it is intelligible only in relation to all the others. The didascalic convenience of exposing a group of philosophical problems separately from others—or also (if it

please others, as it has not pleased us) of
dividing the exposition into particular philosophical sciences, and into general Philosophy
(also called Metaphysic)—should not lead to the
misconception that the indivisible is really being
divided. The whole of Philosophy is at once
enunciated with the first philosophical proposition;
and the others that come after will all be nothing
but explanations of the first.

Therefore, since we have never denied faith *The ethical*
form as
to thought, nor broken in pieces the unity of *volition of*
the universal.
Philosophy, we have no secret to reveal at
this point; not even a poor secret, like the
exponents of discontinuous Philosophy, who
solemnly make known at the end what they have
assumed from the beginning. Our formal ethical
principle is never empty form that must only
now be filled with a content. It is full form, form
in the philosophical and universal sense, which
is also content and therefore universal content.
We have not restricted ourselves to defining the
ethical form as universal form, which would have
resulted in tautologism; but we have defined it
volition of the universal, thus distinguishing it
from the economic form, which is simply
volition of the individual. And if we now ask
ourselves what is the universal, we must reply

that the answer has already been given, and that whoever has not yet understood, whoever indeed has not understood it for some time, will never understand it. The universal has been the object of all our Philosophy of the Spirit, and we have always had to keep it before our eyes, in studying, not only the practical function, but any other function of the spirit; just as we cannot have the idea of the branch of a tree without the idea of the trunk from which it springs and without which there would not be the branch of a tree. That concept, then, is not a *deus ex machina* to appear unexpectedly at the end of the play and hastily bring it to a conclusion, but the force that has animated it from the first to the last scene.

The universal as the Spirit (Reality, Liberty, etc.).

What is the universal? It is the Spirit, it is Reality, in so far as it is truly real, that is, in so far as it is unity of thought and willing; it is Life, in so far as realized in its profundity as this unity itself; it is Freedom, if a reality so conceived be perpetual development, creation, progress. Outside the Spirit nothing is thinkable in a truly universal form. Æsthetic, Logic, Historic, this very Philosophy of the practical, have demonstrated and confirmed this truth in every way. Every other concept brought forward reveals itself (and has revealed itself beneath our analysis), either as a feigned universal, or as something contingent that has been abstracted and generalized, or as the hypostasis of certain of our particular spiritual products, such as mathematical formulæ, or as the negation of the Spirit, on which is conferred positive value (first with metaphor and then with metaphysic).

And the moral individual who wills the universal, or that which transcends him as an individual, turns precisely to the Spirit, to real Reality, to true Life, to Liberty. The universal is in concrete the universal individualized, and the individual is real in so far as he is also universal. He is not able to assert one part of himself without asserting the other (under the penalty of stopping half-way, *dimidiatus vir*, and so of again becoming nothing). But in order to assert them both, he must first posit the one as explicit and the other as implicit, and then make the other also explicit. Man as economic individual, at the first moment (so to speak) of his revealing himself to life and to existence, cannot will, save individually : will his own individual existence. There is no man, however moral he be, who does not begin in this way. How could he ever surpass and finally deny his own individual life, if he had not first affirmed it and did not reaffirm it at every instant? But he who should stop at that affirmation of the individual, regarding the first stage of development as the resting-place, would enter into profound contradiction with himself. He should will, not only his own self individualized, but also that self, which, being in all selves, is their common Father. Thus he promotes the realization of the Real, lives a full life and makes his heart beat in harmony with the universe : *cor cordium.*

The moral individual has this consciousness of working for the Whole. Every action, however diverse, which conforms to ethical duty, conforms to Life ; and if, instead of promoting Life, it should depress and mortify it, for that very reason it would be immoral. Where facts seem to demonstrate the contrary, the interpretation of facts is erroneous, since it affirms as a criterion of judgment a life which is not that true life, which, as we know, we serve even by dying—dying as an individual, as a collectivity, as a social class, or as a people. The most humble moral act can be resolved into this volition of the Spirit in universal. Thus it happens that the soul of a simple and ignorant man, altogether devoted to his rude duty, vibrates in unison with that of the philosopher, whose mind receives into it the universal Spirit: what the one thinks at that moment, the other does, thus attaining by his own path to that full satisfaction, that act of life, that fruitful conjunction with the Real, which the other has attained to by a different path. It may be said that the moral man is a *practical philosopher* and the philosopher a *theoretic actor.*

This criterion of the Spirit, of Progress, of Reality, is the intimate measure of our acts in the moral conscience, as it is the foundation, more or less clearly expressed, of our moral judgments. Why do we exalt Giordano Bruno, who allowed himself to be condemned to the stake for asserting his philosophy? Perhaps for the calmness with which he faced the torture? But many fanatics, even malefactors, are capable of this, and it may sometimes even be a simple sensual desire, of which we have seen examples in history and of which a modern Italian poet has lately sung, exalting the beauty of the flame and the voluptuousness of the pyre. By facing death and refusing to deny his philosophy, Bruno contributed to the creation of a larger form of civilization, and for this reason he is not only a victim, but also a *martyr,* in the etymological

Moral acts as volitions of the Spirit.

sense of the word: witness and realizer of a
demand of the Spirit in universal.—Why do we
praise the charitable man? Perhaps because he
yields to the emotion caused by the spectacle of
suffering. But emotion in itself is neither moral
nor immoral, and thus to yield to it materially
is weakness, that is, immorality. The charitable
man, when he removes or mitigates suffering,
relights a life and reconquers a force for the
common work, which both he and the person
whom he has benefited, must serve.

Critique of
antimoralism.

There is indeed nothing more foolish than antimoralism, so much the fashion in our day; it is an
ugly echo of unhealthy social conditions, of one-
sided theories ill understood (Marxism, Nietzsche-
ianism). Antimoralism is justified, in so far as it
combats moral hypocrisy in favour of effective
morality instead of that of mere words, but it loses
all meaning when it inflates empty phrases or
combines contradictory propositions and preaches
against morality itself. By so doing, it thinks to
celebrate strength, health and freedom, but on the
contrary exalts servitude to unbridled passions,
the apparent health of the invalid and the
apparent strength of the maniac. Morality
(begging pardon of literary immoralists), far
from being a pedantic fiction or the consolation

of the impotent, is *good blood against bad blood*.

We must also declare that this truth concerning the ethical principle understood as will that has for its end the universal or the Spirit, is to some extent confirmed by several of the formulæ that we have criticized, which have erred only in defining it, either confusing altogether the universal and the contingent, or have fallen into tautologism. Those who posit Life, or the interest of the Species, Society or the State, as the end of morality, have in view that Life, that Species, that Society, or that ideal State, which is the Spirit in universal, although they are not able to define it clearly. The same may be said of other formulæ, which often have a better intention at starting than that realized in the development of the relative doctrines, or, on the contrary, a development superior to their bad initial intention. This function of symbol possessed by idealist Ethic, this affirmation that the moral act is love and volition of the Spirit in universal, is to be found above all in religious and Christian Ethic, in the Ethic of love and of the anxious search for the divine presence. This is the fundamental characteristic of religious Ethic, which remains unknown to vulgar rationalists and

Confused tendencies of tautological, material, religious formulæ, etc., toward the Ethic of the Spirit.

The Ethic of the Spirit and religious Ethic.

2 G

intellectualists, to so-called free-thinkers, and to frequenters of masonic lodges, owing to their narrow party passion or lack of mental subtlety. There is hardly an ethical truth (and we have already had occasion to refer to this matter) that cannot be expressed with the words that we have learned as children from traditional religion, and which rise spontaneously to the lips, as the most elevated, the most appropriate and the most beautiful; words which are certainly impregnated with mythology, but are also weighty with profound philosophical content. There is without doubt an exceedingly strong antithesis between the idealist philosopher and the religious individual, but it is not greater than that within ourselves, when, in the imminence of a crisis, we are divided in soul and yet very near to unity and to interior conciliation. If the religious man cannot but see in the philosopher his adversary, his mortal foe, the philosopher, on the other hand, sees in him his younger brother, his very self of a moment past. Hence he will feel himself more nearly allied to an austere, emotional, religious Ethic, troubled with phantoms, than to an Ethic that is superficially rationalistic: for this latter is only in appearance more philosophical than the other, since if it possess the merit of recognizing (verbally only, or with *psittacism*, as Leibnitz would have said) the supreme rights of reason, yet in plucking thought from the soil in which it has grown and depriving it of vital sap, it exercises them very ill.

HISTORICAL NOTES

Merit of the Kantian Ethic. I. IT is the singular merit of Kant to have put an end, once for all, to every material Ethic, by proving its utilitarian character: a merit that is not cancelled by the lacunæ that exist in other parts of his thought, entangling him unawares in the materialism and in the utilitarianism that he had surpassed. It would be antihistorical to desire to judge a thinker by the contradictions into which he falls and so to declare his work to be a failure and of no importance, when it is only imperfect. There are errors in all the works of man, and error is always contradiction; but he who has the eye of the historian discovers where lies the true strength of a thought and does not deny the light, because of necessity accompanied with shadow. Before Kant, ethic was either openly utilitarian or such that although presenting itself in the deceitful form of Ethic of sympathy, or religious Ethic, was yet reducible to utilitarianism. Kant conducted an implacable and destructive war, not only against admitted utilitarian forms, but also against those that were masked and spurious, called by him material Ethic.

In this too, his predecessors are to be found *The predecessors of Kant.* in traditional philosophy of Christian origin, or, if it be preferred, Platonic (opposition of material to formal Ethic can already be observed in the attitude of Aristotle to Plato). If the fathers and the scholastics had been divided as to the question of the relation between moral laws and the divine will, and many of them, especially the mystics, had made that law to depend upon the divine will and upon nothing else, yet views had not been wanting, according to which the power of changing at will the moral laws, that is to say, of changing his own essence, was denied to God, since he could not be *supra se.* Religious Ethic was cleansed of every admixture of arbitrarism and utilitarianism by this solution, accepted by nearly all religious thinkers of the seventeenth and eighteenth centuries (by Cudworth, by Malebranche, and finally by Leibnitz). On the other hand, we cannot but recognize that many other material formulæ used to be understood in an ideal, or, as we have said, in a symbolical manner; and certainly that very eudaemonism of Aristotle, toward which Kant showed himself too severe, was not the pleasure and happiness of the hedonists and utilitarians, and the mediety (μεσότης) proposed as the distinctive character of virtue, although without doubt empty and often incoherent, was already almost a formal principle. The same is to be said of the Stoïc principle of *following nature*; and coming to the immediate predecessors of Kant, of that *perfectio* already mentioned, which Kant, after wavering a little, reduced to happiness, not, however, without stating that it is a more indeterminate concept than any other. With Kant, however, the point was admitted, that the moral law is not to be expressed in any formula, which contains representative and contingent elements.

Defect of that Ethic: agnosticism. The defect of the Kantian Ethic is the defect of his whole philosophy: agnosticism, which prevents his truly surpassing either the phenomenon or the thing in itself, leading him, on the one hand, toward empiricism, on the other toward that transcendental metaphysic, which no one had done more to discredit than himself. He combated the concept of the good or supreme good as the principle of Ethic, and he was right in so far as he understood it as object of any sort, of "a good," as of a "thing." But this did not exempt him from the duty of defining the supreme good as that which is not exhausted in any particular object, or of determining the universal. Now his philosophy was incapable of attaining to the universal.

Hence the involuntary return to utilitarianism, clearly stated by Hegel in his youthful essay upon natural Right. The practical principle of Kant (remarked Hegel) is not a true but a negative absolute ; hence with him the principle of morality becomes converted into immorality : since every fact can be thought in the form of universality, it is never known what fact should be received into the law. In the famous example of the deposit, Kant had said that it is necessary to keep faith as regards the deposit, otherwise there would no longer be deposits.[1] But if there were no more deposits, how would this constitute a contradiction to the form of the law ? There would perhaps be contradiction and absurdity for material reasons, but it is already agreed that this is not to be brought up in the argument. Kant wishes to justify property, but he does not attain to more than the tautology, that property, if it be property, must be property, opening the way to the free choice of conceiving at will as

Critique of Hegel and of others.

[1] *Krit. d. prakt. Vern.* pp. 30-31.

duties these or those contingent definitions of property. The moral maxims of Kant, owing to the empirical determinations that they assume, are contradictory, not only of one another, but of themselves. This inevitable degeneration of the Kantian Ethic was called by Hegel *tautology and formalism.*[1] Other thinkers were also affected by the utilitarianism of the Kantian Ethic: Schopenhauer even declared that his doctrine has no other foundation than egoism, since it can be reduced to the concept of reciprocity, and he protested against the Kantian theory that we should be compassionate to animals, in order to exercize ourselves in the virtue of compassion, judging it to be the effect of the Judæo-Christian views of Kant.[2] Schopenhauer was in some respect right in these observations, although as regards animals we must note that the same attitude is found in Spinoza and in other thinkers and that it derives from material and utilitarian Ethic; and for the rest that it would be very unjust to see nothing but egoism in the categoric imperative of Kant, for this, we repeat, though it constitute its danger, does not constitute its essential character.

[1] *Ueb. d. wissensch. Behandlungsarten d. Naturrechts*, in *Werke*, i. 353; cf. *Gesch. d. Phil.* iii. 533 sqq.
[2] *Grundl. d. Moral*, in *Werke*, ed. cit., iii. 538, 542-543.

Nevertheless, in Kant himself, in this thinker, *Kant and the concept of freedom.* so rich in contradictions and suggestions, was indicated the concept which, when elaborated, was to constitute the principle, not merely of tautological and formalistic, but of concrete and formal Ethic, the concept of *freedom*. By means of this concept Kant enters into the heart of the real and reaches that region of which mysticism and religion had from time to time caught a glimpse and had here and there attained. As the origin of the rigid Kantian ethical conception and of his abhorrence for the material and mundane is to be found in Christianity (and in Paganism), so the origin of the concrete moral idea is to be sought in St. Augustine, and also in St. Paul, in the mystics and in the great French Christians of the seventeenth century; in that virtue of which Pascal wrote as *plus haute que celle des pharisiens et des plus sages du paganisme*, and it operates with omnipotent hand, by means of which alone is it possible *dégager l'âme de l'amour du monde, la retirer de ce qu'elle a de plus cher, la faire mourir à soi-même, la porter et l'attacher uniquement et invariablement à Dieu*.[1] The successors of Kant, especially Fichte and Hegel, closed the circle which he had left open,

[1] *Lettres prov.* l. 5.

and altogether excluding transcendency, they made of God freedom and of freedom reality. Fichte, who expelled the phantom of the thing in itself from theoretical philosophy, removed from the categoric imperative the appearance of *qualitas occulta*, which it had borne in the Philosophy of the practical, illuminating that tenebrous region, ready to receive any sort of phantasm or superstition, such as belief in a moral law arbitrarily imposed by the divinity.[1] Hegel does not recognize duty and the categoric imperative, but freedom only, and as he says, the free spirit is that in which subject and object coincide and freedom is freely willed.

Ethic in the nineteenth century.

II. After the classical epoch of modern philosophy, in the general regression of Ethic, the concept of the concreteness and universality of the practical principle was also lost. Omitting the utilitarians, who no longer have a place here, it must suffice to record how there was a return either to the formalistic principles, which Hegel criticized in Kant (for instance the principle of the Ethic of Rosmini, the *respect for being*, afterwards combated by Gioberti), or directly to those material principles which Kant had already excluded. Such are the *compassion* of

[1] *System d. Sittenlehre*, pp. 49-51.

Schopenhauer, the *five practical ideas* of Herbart, the love of Feuerbach, *benevolence* as the supreme ethical idea of Lotze, the *theological* morality of Baader, the *life* of Nietzsche, and the like. The principles of the first were completed with a religious conception (here too Rosmini may afford an example), and those of the second, when they did not reveal themselves as utilitarian or tautological, showed an obscure tendency toward the Ethic of Freedom. This must not be overlooked in the Ethic of Nietzsche, which despite the rocks and mud that the thought of Nietzsche drags with it, is yet anti-hedonistic and anti-utilitarian and quite full of the sense of Life as activity and power. Positivistic evolutionism is also often unconscious idealism; and the moral actions, united to evolution, can be interpreted as those which correspond to the Spirit in universal. The concepts of the pessimists alone are altogether incapable of idealistic interpretation (for example, Schopenhauer), and those of the semi-pessimist and semi-idealist Hartmann are strangely contradictory. He makes morality to consist of the promotion of civilization, whence so lofty a condition of the spirit can be attained that it will be possible to decree universal suicide by means of the vote of all the world.

The question asked after Kant, whether Ethic should be formal or material, is one that we have made more precise in the other form, whether Ethic should be abstract or concrete, full or empty, tautological or expressive—that is (with even greater precision), whether Ethic can be established before and without a philosophical system and even be reconciled with agnosticism, has no longer been understood, even by its pretended followers, the Neocriticists or Neokantians. These have either believed they had solved it by means of moderate utilitarianism, or by going outside it and denying the most secure result of the Kantian critique of Ethic; or they have discussed it tiresomely, without making a step in advance. Progress indeed was possible on one condition alone: that a philosophical system should be constructed not inferior to that of the postkantian idealists. But this would have been tantamount to demanding the death of neokantianism or neocriticism, which has not only not attempted to surpass the idealistic systems, but has even maintained that we should philosophize without a system, declaring that a system is altogether inconceivable. The Neokantians can thus be recognized as the descendants of Kant, but in the same way as the last descendant of the Hapsburgs in Spain, who was neither emperor, king, soldier, nor man, could be recognized as the descendant of Charles the Fifth, who was man, soldier, king, and emperor: because, like his great predecessor, he possessed the deformed, hanging lip of the Hapsburgs.

THIRD PART

LAWS

I

LAWS AS PRODUCTS OF THE INDIVIDUAL

LAW is a volitional act, which has for content *Definition of law.* a *series* or *class* of actions.

This definition excludes above all from the *Philosophical and empirical* concept of law a determination that is generally *concepts of society.* considered essential to it, the determination of *society*; this amounts to saying that it also extends the concept of law to the case of the *isolated individual.* But in order that there may be no misunderstanding in relation to a point like this of the highest importance, it will be well to show that the word "society" has a double meaning, philosophical and empirical, and if we exclude its empirical sense from the concept of law, it would neither be possible nor our wish, to exclude its philosophical sense. Reality is unity and multiplicity together, and an individual is conceivable, in so far as he is compared with other individuals, and the process of reality is effective, in so far as individuals enter into relations with one another. Without multiplicity there would not be knowledge, action, art or thought, utility or morality; therefore the isolated individual, torn from the reality that constitutes him and that he constitutes, is something abstract and absurd. But he is no longer absurd, when understood in another way, with polemical intention against a false concept; as an individual not absolutely, but relatively isolated, in respect to certain contingent conditions which had wrongly been held essential: in which case the concept of society is conversely itself abstract and unreal. "Society," indeed, is also used to mean a multiplicity of beings of the same species, and it is evident that here an arbitrary element enters into the problem, for the naturalistic concept of sameness of species is arbitrary and approximative; hence the pretended sameness might fail and the society yet exist all the same. A man may not be able to find those who resemble him among a multitude of men and conduct himself as if they did not exist; but this does not prevent his living in the society of beings that are called natural, with his dog, his horse, with plants, with the earth, with the dead and with God. When he is placed in solitude or isolated from the other beings, said to belong to the same species as himself, that other society, or the communion with what remains to him of reality, will always continue, thus enabling him to continue his life of contemplation, of thought, of action and of morality. In order to understand the Spirit in its universality, we must separate it from contingencies, and society in the empirical sense is contingency, which the concept of the isolated individual (isolated from it and not from reality, from the *societas hominum*, not from the *societas entium*), enables us to surpass. The great services which this concept has rendered to Logic, to Æsthetic and especially to Economy, are known, for the latter only began to develop the philosophical spirit in itself, when it conceived economic facts as they take place in the individual, prior to what is called society, thus positing the concept of an isolated economy. Conversely, Economic, Æsthetic, Ethic and all philosophical problems and sciences lost their true nature and became bastardized, when gross *sociologism* replaced among social contingencies those universals, which philosophers had with great labour removed from them and thought in their purity. Defining laws, then, as facts that occur, not only in society, but also in the isolated individual, our intention is simply to concentrate attention upon the concept of *true society*, which is *all reality*, and not allow it to be diverted and confused with accidental determinations, of the kind that may and may not be.

Laws as individual product: programmes of individual life.

No great art is required to find instances of individuals who make laws for themselves, carry them out and change them, grant rewards to themselves and inflict upon themselves punishments; nor is there any need to incommode the worthy Robinson of the economists to this end. Without being obliged to make the effort of imagining ourselves cast upon a desert island and provided only with a sack of corn and the Bible, it suffices to have eyes and to observe our daily life, for numbers of examples of internal legislation to present themselves. Those laws, made for our use and consumption, are called *programmes of life*. Who can live without programmes? Who does not decide that he will desire certain actions and avoid certain others? From youth onward we begin to legislate in this way and this production of internal laws is interrupted only by death. We say, for instance :—" I shall devote my life to agriculture : I shall live in the country every year from June to November; from December

to February I shall come to town, that I may
not lose touch with political or social life; from
March to May I shall travel, for pleasure and
instruction." This programme is subdivided
and completed with other programmes, according to the various conditions and possibilities
taken into consideration; and laws are established as to the way one should conduct oneself
in respect to religion, family, friends, the State,
the Church and also in respect to this or that
individual; for (as is observed by Logic) the
individual conceived as a fixed being, also becomes
a concept, abstraction, group, series, or class. He
who wished it, would be able to establish a parallel
between programmes or individual laws and laws
that are called social : in the individual would be
found fundamental statutes, laws, rules, ordinances,
temporary arrangements, contracts, single laws
and all the other legal forms found in societies.
Now in what conceivable way do the programmes
of the individual differ from those of society?
Are not those laws *programmes*, and are not
those programmes *laws*?

To this interrogation of ours, which does not *Exclusion of*
the character
express a doubt within us, but states what seems *of compulsion*
and critique of
to be an undeniable fact, defying any sort of *this concept.*
contradiction, may be objected (and it is a

common objection) that there is a great difference between individual laws and those of society or of the State: these are compulsory, those are not; and for this reason these are true laws, while the others are mere programmes. But we cannot attach any importance to this objection, at least as thus formulated; because, having now traversed the whole of the Philosophy of the practical, general, and special, we have never met with what is called compulsion in the circle of willing and doing, save in the negative sense of deficiency of will and action. No action can ever be compulsory; every action is free, because the Spirit is freedom; there may not be action in a certain case, but a compulsory action is inconceivable, since it is a question of terms that exclude one another. Does the fact give the lie to our assertion? Let us examine the fact for a little, face to face and without preconceptions. Let us for this purpose take an extreme case: for instance, that of the law of a most powerful despot, who, being in command of police, should order a group of men to bring their first-born to sacrifice to the god in whom he believes, but they do not. Are the men who hear this manifestation of will constrained by it? What menace can make him who wishes to say no, say yes?

That group of men will rebel, will take up arms, will rout the troops of the despot, will put him to death, or render him incapable of harming; and in this hypothesis the law will not reveal any character of compulsion. But in the other hypothesis also, where they do not rebel and in the meantime bow to the will of the despot, either that they may not risk their own lives, or because they defer their rebellion to a more propitious moment and consign their sons to death; they will not have suffered any compulsion, but will have freely willed: they will have willed to preserve their own lives at the expense of their sons'; or to sacrifice some of them in order to have the time to put themselves into such a position that they may be able to rebel with the hope of victory. Thus we find in social laws, now observance, now inobservance of the law; but both occur in freedom. Inobservance may be followed by what is called punishment (that is to say, the legislator who has imposed a given class of actions, will adopt certain definite measures against those who do not obey them; to wit: he will will another class of actions, destined to render possible the first, because the punishment is a new condition of things set before the individual, according to which he must alter his previous mode of action); but the punishment always finds itself face to face with the freedom of the individual. He will be able freely to observe the law in order to avoid the punishment or its recurrence; but he will also be able freely to rebel against it, as in the instance adduced.

Identical characteristics of individual and social laws. If compulsion be wanting to individual laws, this is because it is also always wanting to social laws: while, on the contrary, what is really present in social laws is equally present in the observances and rebellions, rewards and punishments of individual laws.

To return to the former example: the individual who has decided to devote himself to agriculture as programme of life, may be seized all of a sudden with a great desire to devote himself to painting or to music; and what had previously pleased may henceforward displease him: that intimacy with mother earth, with harvests and vintages, which seemed to be the very life for him, his true ideal, may come to seem to him tiresome and repugnant. But if he be a serious person, if he do not will and not will at every moment, if he do not present in his own individuality a complete resemblance to those peoples who change in mid-November the laws made in October and proceed from revolution to revolution, he will examine his situation and will recognize, for instance, that the desire arisen in his soul is a velleity that does not answer to his true vocation and that the first programme must remain intact; hence will take place in him a struggle between that programme and the new rebellious volition. It may happen that in this case the individual will sometimes neglect the programme traced, in order to abandon himself to the temptations of his pictorial or musical dilettanteism; but since this will happen against his individual law, and since force must remain on the side of law, this breach of observance will be followed by special measures, such as the throwing away of brushes and violin, or by his forbidding to himself those moments of recreation in such amusements, which he used to allow himself and which have now become dangerous. In other words, the individual inflicts punishments on himself in case of the non-observance of his law, and these punishments must be held to be such in the strictest sense of the term. And if we accept the other hypothesis, analogous to that made in the case of social laws, should the individual find himself possessed with so vehement a desire of becoming a painter or a musician, as to be compelled to believe that the original programme, the original law of his individuality, did not correspond, or no longer corresponded with his true temperament, he will rebel against the law and destroy it in himself, in the same manner as in the other example the people destroyed the law of the despot, by fighting with him, imprisoning, or slaying him.

Individual laws as in ultimate analysis alone real.

Individual programmes or laws then are laws, and this concept includes the isolated individual as well as society ; and therefore the character of sociality is not essential to the concept of law. Thus, to be more precise, the only laws that really exist are individual laws and it is not possible to conceive of social and individual laws as two forms of the general concept of laws ; unless individual and society be both understood in the empirical sense, thus abandoning philosophical consideration. If the individual be understood in the philosophical sense, in which he is the Spirit concrete and individualized, it is clear that what are called social laws can also be reduced to individual laws ; because, in order to observe a law, we must make it our own, that is to say, individualize it, and in order to rebel against it, we must expel it from our own personality, in which it wished unduly to remain or to introduce itself.

The exclusion of the character of sociality from the concept of law frees philosophy from a series of problems, grafted upon that pretended character. The principal of these was that of the distinction of social laws into political and judicial, on the one hand and merely social on the other; and the further distinction of judicial law into public and private, civil and penal, national and international, into laws properly so called and regulations, and so on. If the concept itself of social law be empirical, then all the distinctions and sub-distinctions of it proposed must also be empirical, and altogether without philosophical value. So true is this that it is impossible to decide for one distinction or definition against another, or to correct those hitherto given by proposing new ones. Whoever undertakes to examine any one of these distinctions, at once realizes the aphilosophical character affirmed of them *a priori*. Thus judicial or political laws have been distinguished from the merely social, with the affirmation that those are compulsory, these conventional; whereas compulsion is impossible in both cases, for the reasons given, and if by compulsion be meant the threat of a penalty, this is to be found in merely social laws, not less than in judicial. The law against

Critique of the division of laws into judicial and social and into their sub-classes. Empiricity of every division of laws.

the falsification of public money is usually
described as judicial : he who falsifies it runs
the risk of undergoing some years' imprisonment.
It is a law called social that we must answer
a salutation with a salutation : he who does not
do this runs the risk of being held ill-bred and
excluded from the society of the well-bred.
What essential difference is there between the
two laws? An attempt has been made to
differentiate them by saying that the former has
emanated from and is sustained by a *supreme
power*, vigilant as to its observance, the second
from particular circles of individuals. But where
is the seat of this supreme power? Certainly
not in a superindividual, who dominates individuals, but in individuals themselves. And in
this case its power and value correspond with the
power of the individuals who compose it ; that
is to say, it is the law of a circle, empirically
considered to be larger and stronger, but whose
volitions are realized in so far as the individuals
composing it spontaneously conform to them,
because they recognize the convenience of doing
so. Monarchs who believed themselves to be
most powerful, have realized at certain moments
that the power did not at all reside in their
persons or title, but in a universal consensus of

opinion, failing which their power vanished, or
was reduced to a gesture of solitary command,
not far removed from the ridiculous. Laws that
seem to be excellent remain unapplied, because
they meet with tacit general resistance, or as is
said, do not accord with custom: this should
suffice to enlighten the mind as to the inseverable
unity of what is called the State and what is
called society. The State is not a being, but
a mobile complex of varied relations between
individuals. It may be convenient to limit this
complex as well as possible, to make a being of
it to oppose other complexes: of this there can
be no doubt; and let us leave to jurists the
excogitation of these and other similar distinctions,
fictitious but opportune; nor let us consider
that their work should be declared in the least
absurd. We only say that it must not be forgotten that the fictitious is fictitious, as is the
claim made to reason about it as rational and
philosophical, and to fill volumes and volumes
with tiresome disquisitions, which are necessarily
vain, though the distinctions that form their
object are not vain in their circle. We who are
not jurists but philosophers, and to whom it is
therefore not permitted to produce and adopt
practical distinctions, must conceive as laws and

include equally in the same category, alike the English *Magna Charta* and the statute of the Sicilian *Mafia*, or of the Neapolitan *Camorra*; the *Regula monachorum* of Saint Benedict and that of the *brigata spendereccia* that was sung in sonnets by Folgore di San Geminiano and Cene della Chitarra and is recorded by Dante in the *Inferno*; the canon law and the military code, and that *droit parisien*, which a certain personage of Balzac had studied for three years in the blue boudoir of one lady and in the rosy drawing-room of another, and which, although no one ever speaks of it, yet constitutes (says the great novelist) *une haute jurisprudence sociale, qui, bien apprise et bien pratiquée, mène à tout.*[1] What more can be said? Even those *literary and artistic laws are laws* which express the will to produce works, possessing this or that other kind of argument and arrangement, as would be the law that drama should be divided into five or three acts or *days*, and that romances must not exceed four or five hundred pages, 16mo, and that a monumental statue must be nude or heroically clad. It is evident that if anybody violate these laws, he may be excluded (and he was indeed excluded) from the academies of

---

[1] Balzac, *Le Père Goriot* (ed. Paris, Calman Lévy, 1891), p. 85.

good taste, which did not prevent his being received for that very reason into the anti-academies of the independents : in just the same way as to have incurred punishments announced by the penal code is a title of admission to certain criminal societies.

These examples that we have selected among the most extraordinary and the most apt to scandalize, help to make it quite clear that the concept of law must be taken in its full logical extension, when we wish to philosophize about it. Among the many obstacles that philosophy meets with is a curious sort of false shame, which looks upon contact with certain arguments as injurious to the dignity of philosophy : a contact which is avoided by arbitrarily narrowing and therefore falsifying philosophical concepts. That of law especially has a tradition of *solemnity*, and brings with it associations that must be broken in pieces. Otherwise it is impossible even to understand what are those *firm and unwritten laws* of the gods, which Antigone opposed to the decrees of men and how they exercise their efficiency ; or *the sayings of Lacedaemon*, in obedience to which fell the three hundred at Thermopylae ; or *the laws of the fatherland*, which, with their irresistible authority, caused Socrates to remain at the

Extension of the concept of law.

moment when others counselled and facilitated his flight. Life is composed of big and little actions, of least and greatest, or better, of a very dense web of very diverse actions; and it is not a too brilliant idea to cut that web in pieces and to throw away some of the pieces as less beautiful, in order afterwards to contemplate in those pieces only that have been thus selected, cut out and disconnected, the web that no longer exists.

II

THE CONSTITUTIVE ELEMENTS OF LAWS. CRITIQUE OF PERMISSIVE LAWS AND OF NATURAL LAW

THE undue restrictions and empirical divisions of the concept of laws having been destroyed, if our attention be now directed to the character that has been determined as properly belonging to them, we have the means of distinguishing them from the other spiritual forms with which they are often confused, partly as the result of the metaphors and homonyms usual in ordinary speech. Laws, as has been said, are *volitional acts* concerning *classes* of actions. Therefore, where the volitional element or the element of class is wanting, there cannot be law, save in name and by metaphor.

The volitional character and the character of class.

So-called *laws of nature* or *naturalistic laws* are not laws, owing to the absence of the volitional element : they consist of simple enunciations of relations between empirical concepts, that is, of rules. This is an instance of what is called a

Distinction of laws from the so-called laws of nature.

natural law: platinum melts at a temperature of 1780 degrees; or this other of a grammatical law: that in the Greek language masculine nouns of the second declension have the genitive in *ου* (with exceptions, in this as in the other case). But they are laws in about the same way as the King of Cups is king; and indeed it is known historically that this denomination was transported by the Stoïcs from the domain of politics, where it had first appeared, to that of nature. Empirical concepts and rules may, as we know, assume an imperative literary form; hence it will be said: "If you wish to melt platinum, heat it to 1780 degrees"; "If you wish to speak Greek, decline masculine nouns of the second declension with an *ου* in the genitive." But the literary form does not change anything of their true nature: those imperatives are hypothetical imperatives, that is, false imperatives, improper laws. Grammatical and chemical laws will remain mere formulæ, instruments of knowledge, and not at all of action, until some one obliges me or I oblige myself to talk Greek, or to open a chemical laboratory where platinum is melted. The jurist who elaborates cases and rules is not the legislator: the latter alone (with a sword in one hand) can endow the excogitations cf the other with the character of law.

Certainly an act of will is necessary in order to construct empirical concepts, formulæ, and rules (as indeed we know), an act of will which is not that of the will implied in every act of thought, but is a special and explicit act which, by manipulating representations and concepts, makes a *quid medium*, which is neither representation nor concept, and although altogether irrational from the theoretical point of view, is of use in the economy of the spirit. But the law in its true meaning is a volitional act, which *assumes* that primary volitional act whence are formed the pseudo-concepts or concepts of class *as already completed*; precisely because it is the will which has for its *object* a *class* of objects. It is not possible to impose speaking according to the rule of the Greek language, or to melt platinum according to its chemical formula, before these rules have been laid down. And here appears very clearly the difference between those two kinds of spiritual products, which the imperative literary form, given to classes and rules, darkens and confuses. This difference can be recognized in concrete cases by means of a most simple expedient: if the rule (as we have already had occasion to prove) can be converted into a statement of class, then the law is inconvertible.

"If you wish to melt platinum, heat it to 1780 degrees" is a proposition that is exactly equal to "platinum melts at 1780 degrees." But the law, "Let there be opened in every city a chemical laboratory where platinum is to be melted," is not to be converted from the imperative to the indicative, whatever efforts we make.

Distinction of laws from practical principles.   If the volitional element be wanting to naturalistic laws, it is certainly present in other spiritual formations also denominated and considered as laws: but not that of *class*, therefore neither are these laws. Such is the case with economic and moral law, and through them, with logical and æsthetic laws. The moral law says, "Will the universal"; that is to say, "Will the good, the useful, the true, the beautiful." Therefore (considered in reality and not in scientific theory, where it appears as the concept of itself) it is a volitional act. But this volitional act has the spirit itself for object, which is and exists, in so far as it wills and affirms itself; it has for object a form or a *universal*, whereas laws have for object something material and at the same time not instantaneous, something more or less fixed, something *general*: a *class*, not an *idea*. Universal laws (that would better be called *principles*) are the Spirit or producer; true and proper laws

are the special product of the spirit; therefore
the first can certainly be called laws, but for
an altogether different reason to the second.

Owing to the absence of the element of *Laws and single acts.*
generality or of class, no one would describe
a single individuated act as law. The resolution
and action by which I do not rise from my
seat at this moment and go eagerly to meet
the friend whose coming at the wrong moment
interrupts me at my work, is a volitional act,
not a law; such as on the other hand would
be the volitional act that I might form within
myself, consisting in the intention or the programme of receiving my friends seated and in
a lukewarm way, whenever they should come
to visit me in the hours before noon, in order
to make them understand by this act of mine
that they disturb me at my work, and that they
should abstain from their inopportune visits,
unless they wish to submit to the penalty of
meeting with anything but a cordial reception
from their friend.

From the general but not universal character *Identity of imperative,*
that we must recognize to the content of laws, *prohibitive, and permissive*
we have the solution of certain controversies of *laws.*
the greatest importance which have been and are
much discussed, hitherto without a satisfactory

or duly demonstrated conclusion. In the first place, we must mention the dispute as to whether or no there exist *permissive* laws, and whether the formula that the law *aut jubet aut vetat aut permittit* is to be accepted. It has generally been admitted that the law *aut jubet aut vetat*, and that the permission is nothing but the removal of a previous inhibition, that is, the partial or total abrogation of a law. But in reality, the law, since it is a volitional act, *jubet* only; to command is to will: to command that a chemical laboratory be opened in every city means to will that one should be opened. And since every willing is at the same time a not-willing, as every affirmation is at the same time a negation, every command is at the same time an inhibition, and every *jubeo* is a *veto* (whether the will be expressed in the literary form of positive or negative, of command or of inhibition, is here without importance).

Permissive character of every law, and impermissive character of every principle. As to permissive laws, these are inconceivable side by side with the imperative or prohibitive, not indeed because no law ever permits, but because by the very fact that those are imperative or prohibitive, they are at the same time permissive : every *jubeo* or *veto* is at the same time a *permitto*. Principles, as universal volitions, never permit, because nothing escapes their command ;

but a single volitional act, affirming itself, does not exclude for that reason the possibility that other volitional acts, indeed infinite acts, should be affirmed; for the singular never exhausts its universal. And laws are volitions of class, they impose groups of single acts—groups that are more or less rich, but always contingent: hence a law always leaves all the other actions and classes of action that can be the object of will unwilled (that is, neither commanded nor prohibited), and, therefore, *permitted*. And even if we take all the laws formulated up to a given moment, all together they do not exhaust the universal; and if new laws be accumulated, one upon the other, be divided and split up " with panting breath," to obtain complete exhaustion, a *progressus in infinitum* will certainly be attained, but never exhaustion, which is unattainable. This amounts to saying that outside law or laws, there is always *the permitted, the lawful, the indifferent, the privilege, the right*, or whatever be termed the concept correlative to that of command, veto, or duty, a duality of terms that expresses the *finitude* of law; hence, when a determined privilege, a determined legal right, a determined right, has been annulled by a new law, when something previously indifferent has been differentiated, privilege, the permitted, the indifferent, right, always arise from the bosom of the new law.

Mutability of laws.

Another contingent character of the content of laws is their *mutability*. Laws are changeable, whereas principles, or laws of the universal content, are unchangeable, and ready to give form to all the most various historical material. Since actual conditions are constantly changing, it is necessary to add new laws to the old, to retouch and correct these, or to abolish them altogether. This is to be seen equally in the programmes of individual lives, as in the programmes of social and political laws.

Empirical concepts as to the modes of change.

The question as to the number of modes of changing that laws possess does not concern us, because, philosophically speaking, there is never but one mode : the free will that produces the new law in new conditions of fact. Involuntary changing can only be a formula for indicating certain changes, always voluntary, that occur in a less solemn way than others ; but from these can never be absent the solemnity of the human will that celebrates itself. Thus, in like manner, the question as to whether we should recognize conservation or revolution as the fundamental concept of practical life, does not concern us ; for every conservative is at the same time a revolutionary, since he is always obliged to adapt the law that he wishes to preserve to the new facts; and every revolutionary is also a conservative, since he is obliged to start from certain laws that he preserves, at any rate provisionally, that he may change others and substitute for them new laws, which he in his turn intends to preserve. Revolution for revolution's sake, the cult of the Goddess Revolution, is an insane effort, which is so none the less because it has sometimes appeared in History and like all insane efforts it ends with suicide. Revolution revolutionizes itself and turns into reaction. Thus when revolutionaries and conservatives are distinguished and opposed to one another, an empirical distinction is made there also, the meaning of which is to be found in the historical circumstances among which it has arisen. Count Cavour was a conservative in respect to certain problems and revolutionary in respect to certain others, to such a degree that he seemed to the Mazzinians to be a conservative and to the clericals and legitimists a revolutionary. Robespierre, if he were a revolutionary for the Girondins and at last even for the neo-moderate Danton, yet to the eyes of Hébert and of Chaumette seemed to be a conservative, enemy of the free development of the rights of man.

Critique of the eternal Code or natural Right. We should on the other hand be very careful as to the demand so often made and also so far as possible put into execution, for *an eternal code, a limit-legislation or model, a universal, rational, or natural* justice, as it has been variously termed. Natural justice, universal legislation, eternal code, claim to fix the transitory and are therefore a contradictory concept: contradictory precisely to the principle of the mutability of laws, which is the necessary consequence of their contingent and historical character. Were natural Right permitted to do what it announces, were God to permit that the affairs of Reality should be carried on according to the ill-assorted ideas of writers and professors, we should witness with the formation and application of the eternal Code, the cessation *ipso facto* of Development, the end of History, the death of Life and the dissolution of Reality.

Natural justice as the new justice. This world-ending does not take place, because, though it be possible to dwell in contradiction, it is impossible to make it concrete and actual : God, that is to say Reality, does not permit this. Thus it happens that under the name of natural justice, two sorts of products have existed in turn, or

sometimes a mixture of those two different products, which have nothing to do with the programme announced. On the one hand, projects
of new laws that seemed better than the old
or good by comparison with these judged more or
less bad, have been proposed as natural or rational
justice, and precisely for this reason the old laws
were called unnatural and irrational and the new
rational and natural. Just as passionate and
erotic temperaments, uninstructed by the experience of their past, swear with the utmost seriousness that their new love will be *constant, eternal
and their last,* so man, when he creates new laws,
is often seized with the illusion that his laws will
not change as did the old ones, forgetting that
the old ones were once young and that they
"satisfied divers" in their heyday, to express
oneself in the words of the old carnavalesque song.
Those natural laws are historical, those eternal
laws are transitory, like all the others. All know
how in certain times and places, religious tolerance, freedom of trade, private property, constitu-
tional monarchy, have been proclaimed eternal;
and in others, the extirpation of unbelievers,
commercial protection, communism, the republic,
and anarchy.

Universal concepts, which were nothing but

Natural justice as philosophy of the practical. the Principles of the philosophy of the practical themselves, have on the other hand had a tendency to be classed as natural justice and to surpass the transitory and contingent. They are certainly eternal and unchangeable, but no longer laws, for they are formal and not material. Thus treatises of natural justice have sometimes become simply treatises (sometimes very valuable) of the Philosophy of the practical and especially of Ethic.—When (as to tell the truth has generally been the case) a practical description has accompanied a general treatment of Ethic, leading to a series of proposals for social, judicial or political reform, there has then occurred a *mingling* of two different productions, which we have mentioned, philosophy and casuistic. But a natural justice has always remained unachieved, because unachievable and contradictory.

Critique of natural justice. In our times, owing to the increase of the historical sense, the constructions of natural justice and of the eternal Code have almost altogether lost the attraction they once exercized. But absurd problems having their origin in those contradictory concepts still persist and absurd methods of treating problems of similar origin legitimate when taken in their true terms. An example of the first of these two kinds of diseased residues is the treating of the *natural rights* of man and the attempt to establish what rights belong to man by nature and what by historical contingencies. Among the first are enumerated the right to life, to liberty, to work, to the family and so on ; and among the second, those that have their origin in the Italian State or in special contracts that have been concluded. But no right of any sort belongs to man outside society (which in this case means outside history), that is to say, considered as spirit in universal, save that of existing as spirit, which indeed is not a right, but necessary reality. Catalogues of natural rights are either tautologies, which repeat that man as spirit has the right (and therefore at the same time the duty) of developing himself as spirit (and he does develop in this manner, if he be man and be alive); or they are arbitrary rationalizations of historical contingencies, such as the right to work, which is nothing but the formula of the workpeople of the *ateliers nationaux* in forty-eight, or of the insurgents of Lyons ; or the right to private property, which was the formula of the burghers against the bonds of feudalism and is again their formula against the modern proletariat movement.

We must recognize examples of the second

Jusnaturalism persisting in judgments and juridical problems.

kind of error in the discussions constantly held as to social or political institutions, when instead of combating them as irrational, or of defending them as rational in historical circumstances, they are defended and combated because they differ from or conform to the true idea of right or to the true idea of those particular institutions, recourse being thus had to abstract reasons, as has very well been said. A reformer will maintain the recognition of the right of women to the administrative or political vote, because women also form part of the State and have general and particular interests, which they wish to guarantee directly, without the interposition of men, whose interests are sometimes at variance with theirs: an argument that a conservative will deny altogether, making appeal to the function of woman, enclosed by eternal law in the circle of the family. A reformer will propose divorce as the natural complement to matrimony, because, where spiritual agreement ends, there too should end every other tie, whereas a conservative will oppose the argument as contradictory to the very essence of matrimony, comparing such a proposal with concubinage, or with what is called free love. And so on.—When such arguments are heard, it is remarked that natural rights are not dead. But the question as to the political vote for women may be serious or ridiculous, according to place and time; as divorce is loftily moral or profoundly immoral, according to time and place, and it is only mental narrowness or ignorance that can place outside humanity, or believe to be living or persisting in immorality, peoples that practise divorce or indissoluble matrimony, or those of to-day, who refuse the vote to women or those of the future who will recognize their right to it, if they do recognize it. But even polygamy or free love is not immoral, irrational and un-natural, once it has been an institution con-sidered legitimate in certain times and places; nor even, we insist upon saying it (however repugnant to our hearts and to our stomachs of civilized Europeans), anthropophagy, for even among the anthropophagi were men (we hope it will be admitted), who felt themselves to be most virtuous in their clearest consciousness of self, and who nevertheless ate their like with the same tranquillity that we eat a roast chicken, without hatred of the chicken, but being quite well aware, for the moment at any rate, that we are not able to do otherwise. The unconscious reasoners on the basis of natural law must have forgotten that page of Cornelius Nepos, which, however, they must certainly have translated in their first years at the gymnasium: *Expertes literarum Graecarum nihil rectum nisi quod ipsorum moribus conveniat putabunt. Hi, si didicerint non eadem omnibus esse honesta atque turpia, SED OMNIA MAJORUM INSTITUTIS JUDICARI, non admirabuntur nos in Graiorum virtutibus exponendis mores eorum secutos. Neque enim Cimoni fuit turpe Atheniensium summo viro, sororem germanam habere in matrimonium: quippe quum ejus cives eodem uterentur instituto; at id quidem nostris moribus nefas habetur. Laudi in Graecia ducitur adolescentulis quam plurimos habere amatores. Nulla Lacedaemoni tam est nobilis vidua quae non ad scenam eat mercede conducta.* . . . And he continues to give further examples.[1] So ancient are the unreasonable tendency to be scandalized and the reasonable defence of the variety of customs made by good sense.

---

[1] *Vitae excell. imper.*, pref.

III

UNREALITY OF THE LAW AND REALITY OF ITS
EXECUTION. FUNCTION OF LAW IN THE PRAC-
TICAL SPIRIT

SINCE law is the volition of a class of actions, it is *Law as abstract and the volition of an *abstract*. But as we already unreal volition.* know, to will an abstract is tantamount to willing abstractly. And to will abstractly is not truly to will, for we will only in concrete, that is, in a determined situation and with a volitional synthesis corresponding to that situation, such that it is immediately translated into action, or better, is at the same time effective action. Consequently it seems that we should declare the volition that is law to be a pretended volition: contradictory, because lacking a single, unique and determined situation; ineffectual, because springing from the insecure ground of an abstract concept; a volition, in fact, that is not willed; a volitional act, not real, but *unreal.*

Such indeed it is. What is really wanted is

Ineffectuality of laws and effectuality of practical principles. not the law, but the single act, done *under* the law, as it is called, that is to say, the *execution* of the law. The single volition is the only one that is carried out : the execution of the law is the only thing really and truly willed and done. When the law has been formulated, life continues ceaselessly to propound its problems, and these either do not enter into the provisions of the law and are solved simply and solely with universal practical principles (economic and ethic), or they do enter into them and then it is necessary *to apply* the law, unless it be held to be more convenient to change it, or (this would be a pathological case) action be not taken against it, although there be consciousness that this is ill done.

But even when we are in the situations foreseen by the law and act in accordance with it, or, as is said, *apply or carry out* the law, we must not allow ourselves to be misled by all these metaphors ; for we must consider that the single situations in which we will and act can never be foreseen by the law, nor is it possible to act in accordance with it, to follow it out and to apply it. Situations are not foreseen, because nothing is foreseen, and the real fact is always a surprise, something that happens once only and we can

only know it as it is after it has happened. For
the new fact a new measure is necessary ; for the
new body a new suit of clothes. The measure
of the law, on the other hand, since it is abstract,
hesitates between the universal and the individual
and is without the strength of either. To carry
out the law? But it is only the pedant of life
who proposes to do such a thing, as it is only the
pedant of art who attempts to apply the rules
of art. The true artist follows the impulse of
his æsthetic conscience, the practical man the
initiative of his practical genius. What is called
the single act, observance and execution of the
law, obeys, not the law, but the ethical or practical
principle, and obeys it individually. The man
who has his head full of laws that he has made
for himself or has accepted from others, makes a
deep reverence to the Ladies' Law when the
time comes for action, and proceeds on his own
initiative.

It is the law that at the age of twenty we *Exemplifi-*
catory
must present ourselves in our district and do *clarification.*
military service for a certain time. Let us for
the moment set aside the case in which those
called upon to serve rebel and, having seized the
power of the government, abolish the law of
conscription, and re-establish that of voluntary

enlistment. And let us likewise set aside the other case, in which the conscripts violate the law by deserting and going abroad, or hide in a cave, like a hero of Padre Bresciani, or (like a good Tolstoïan who applies the principle of non-resistance to evil) allow themselves to be put in prison rather than touch arms. Let us select the case of the peaceful burgess who becomes a warrior that he may not go to prison ; or of the good citizen who recognizes his duty of serving his country and for that reason obeys the law. In presenting himself in his district and in the regiment, he has obeyed, not the voice of the law (which is a voice), but his moral conscience, or simply his economic conscience. This has already been demonstrated and we need not insist upon it. But how can he ever obey the law, which directs him to do military service of precisely this or that nature? Each individual has his own temperament, his own talent, his own particular physical strength, and each one will lend his services entirely in his own way, different from that of another. And (be it noted) he will not do so only more or less well or observing the law more or less, but really in a different way, even when all observe the law with equal diligence and scrupulosity. It may seem as if all

carry out a military exercise at the same moment,
but the fact is that each man moves in a different
way to the others; or that in a parade march all
walk in the same way, but, as a matter of fact, all
(even in the Prussian army) walk in a different
way. If we look at it as a whole and from a
distance, there seems to be uniformity; if we
look at it from near at hand we discover the
difference. If we could make the experiment of
comparing a regiment of fifty years before with
one of fifty years after, leaving military regulations, arms, accoutrements, and everything else
unaltered in the interval, the lack of uniformity of
the apparent uniformity would leap to the eyes, a
lack of uniformity that would have been rendered
possible by the changes that had taken place in
the surrounding life, in the culture, the moral
education, the political conscience, the mode of
nourishment, the dwellings, and so on. But the
experiment is possible, if not in time, then in
space, that is to say, by observing the application of the same military regulations upon two
different populations. Thus one seems to have
in hand one book written in two different
languages; which is literally no longer the same
book, but two different books. Giusti translated into Milanese and Porta translated into

Florentine are no longer Porta or Giusti, but two new poets.

This indubitable truth, as to the impossibility of applying the law and of incorporating it in facts, and as to the necessity of acting in each case, according to historical exigencies, is the true reason for the turning of so many people's heads at different times and in different places, causing them to proclaim nothing less than the inutility of laws and to ask for their abolition. If it be necessary to come eventually to the individual action, and if deliberation and execution must be remitted to the action of the individual, what is the object of binding ourselves with bonds, which it is afterwards necessary to tear off and to break, that we may act? What is the object of laboriously constructing instruments, which we are obliged to throw away when we come to practical action, that we may use our naked hands? Owing to such ingenuous reasonings as these, people have come to long for a society without laws, in which each will do his own share of work, on account of its attractiveness alone, as we find among the Harmonicists of Fourier and in many other anarchical utopias. Or they have sighed for the absolute paternal government of the good old days, for the geniality of a good-hearted tyrant, untrammelled with laws, who will be able to follow the best dictates of his heart. Or, to descend to less strange and more actual examples, it has been proposed that the judge should on each occasion create the law, according to the case before him; that is to say, that he should cease to be a judge (not having a law to apply, and properly speaking not being able to give judgment) and be a free decider of litigation and corrector of customs; or at least that he should free himself from *legal fictions* and judge according to the individual reality of each individual case.

These theories are without doubt unsustain- *Unsustain-*
able, not excluding the last, which has the *ability of such confutations.*
appearance of being moderate; because the so-called judicial fiction is intrinsic to the law and exists even when we think that it is not present, for it is always a fiction to place a concrete case in an abstract category. But defenders of the utility of law have met these erroneous doctrines with the bad argument that law does not admit of individual solutions, and demands strict obedience, because the moment of individuality, of inobservance, and of violation that may be called legitimate, does actually exist in the law and is intrinsic to its very nature. Both adversaries

and defenders of law are therefore philosophically wrong, those who assert its inutility and those who claim for it an impossible utility.

Empirical meanings of those controversies.

And we say "philosophically," for it is well known that in this case, as in so many other disputes of philosophic appearance, are often concealed disputes of a practical and political nature, in which right and wrong are divided and connected in an altogether different manner. The adversaries of laws are often nothing but adversaries of too many laws, or legitimately demand a less pedantic and mechanical office for the judge than that which he often has at present; whereas the maintainers of laws are opposed to revolutionaries, who would wish to abrogate the definite laws, on which civil progress rests, or to discredit all laws, and cause society to enter upon a terrible crisis that would not promise good results. But all this is extraneous to the philosophic problem.

Necessity of laws.

If the defenders of the utility of laws had wished to make use of an argument of good sense against their adversaries, of the sort that imposes, even when it does not rigorously demonstrate their contention, they might have simply noted the demand for laws, for ordinances, for justice, for the State, which appears at all points

of human history.—Better a bad government
than no government at all; better laws that are
mediocre, but stable, than the frantic pursuit for
better and better laws, with the instability that is
the inevitable consequence! And on the other
hand, may God save us from genial despots, from
inspired judges, from tribunals that dive into
treasures of equity!—These are the utterances
that we hear in history. Battles have been
fought for *legality*, and rivers of blood have been
shed for it; for legality are faced the troubles
of litigation, and energetic action is displayed,
which only superficial intellects can consider a
waste of time and trouble; for no trouble is
superfluous when we are protecting our own
rights, and none is more sacred, since it also
guards the offended majesty of the law, the
rights of all. Those who declaim against laws
can well do so with a light heart, for the law
surrounds, protects, and preserves their life for
them. No sooner had all laws disappeared than
they would lose the wish to declaim:

> In such wise as when sometimes in the wood
> The shepherd spies the wolf, and straight has lost
> Spirit and sense, and words die on his tongue;

and he would be obliged to have speedy recourse
to the remedy and make laws of some sort again,

whatever they be, that he may again resume his calm, his work and his gossip.

Passing from consideration *ad oculos* to the philosophical, it is to be said, on the other hand, that the utility of law does not at all reside in its effectuality, which is something impossible, since the single act of the individual is alone effectual; but in this, that in order to will and to carry out the single act, it is usually necessary to address oneself to the general, of which that individual is a single case; that is, to address oneself to the group, of which the individual is a component part, just as in aiming we generally begin by aiming at the region where is the point upon which the aim will be fixed. Law is not a real and effectual volition; it is without doubt an imperfect and contradictory volition, but for that very reason a preparation for the synthetic and perfect volition. Law, in short, since it is the volition of an abstract, is not a real volition, but an *aid* to real volition; as (to employ the usual comparison) wooden bridges and scaffoldings are aids to the construction of a house and have not been useless, because they must be pulled down when the house has been built.

Here the analogy between the constitution of the practical and of the theoretical spirit is again shown to be most exact. We meet with theoretical forms in the latter also, which are not really so and are contradictory in themselves, positing representations that function as universals and universals that are representative: arbitrary forms, in which the will undertakes to command what it is not possible to command, that is to say, representations and concepts, things which precede and do not follow the volitional and practical form. But we know that those fictitious concepts, those formulæ, those laws that are not laws, those admitted falsities, which, therefore, are not falsities, serve as a help to memory, and assist thought in finding its way amid the multiform spectacle of the world, which it must penetrate for itself. We do not think them, but they help us to think; we do not imagine them, but they help us to imagine. Thus the philosopher generally fixes his mind upon the pseudo-concepts, that he may afterwards rise to the universals; and the artist also turns his attention to them that he may find beneath them the individual, the lively and ingenuous intuition that he seeks. The same pseudo-concepts, made the object of volition and changed from formulæ to laws, fulfil an analogous office in the practical spirit, making it possible for the

Analogy between the practical and the theoretical spirit: practical laws and empirical concepts.

will to will in a certain direction, where it afterwards meets the useful action, which is always individuated.

The promotion of order in reality and representation. Another aspect of the analogy is not less important. The pseudo-concepts would not be possible, if reality did not offer the like side by side with the unlike; which is not the universal and necessary, but the general, a contingent (so to speak) less contingent than others, a relatively constant variable. Pseudo-concepts are arbitrary, not because they posit the like where is the unlike, but because they make that variable rigid, which is only relatively constant, making of it something absolutely constant and changing the like into the identical. Now the practical spirit, which creates reality, has need to create not only the unlike, but also the like; not only that which lasts an instant, but also that which endures almost unchanged for a year, a century, a millennium, or a millennium of millenniums; not only the individual, but also the species, not only the great man, but also the people, not only the actions that do not occur again, but also those that return periodically, similar, though not identical. Laws fulfil this function, for they constitute what is called the *social*, or *cosmic order*. This order, how-

ever, is always relative and includes instability
in itself; it is a rectilinear figure, which, on
being closely examined, reveals itself as also
curvilinear. For this reason it is necessary to
make laws, and it is necessary to violate, though
obeying them in their execution.

This function of law as an unreal volition, *Origin of the concept of plan or design.*
aiding nevertheless and preparing the real, throws
light upon a concept that we have had to reject
when exposing the nature and method of function-
ing of the volitional act; that is to say, on the
concept of *plan or design or model*, as proper to the
practical activity, which is said to act by carrying
out a pre-established *design*. We have already
demonstrated that design and the execution of
the design are in reality all one, and that man
acts by changing his design at every instant,
because reality, which is the basis of his action,
changes. And as in the Philosophy of the
practical in general, so in particular in Ethic, the
concept of pre-established design has no place;
because, if it be true than in ethicity the universal
is distinguished from the merely individual action,
it is also true that the universal does not exist
in concrete, save incorporated and individualized
as this or that good action. The universal of
ethicity is not a design and cannot be willed for

itself outside all individuation, in the same way as to fall in love is to fall in love with an individual and not with love. But that concept of design, proposed for action and carried out by its means, though erroneously adopted in Economy and in Ethic, must nevertheless have its legitimate meaning in some special order of facts; otherwise it would not be possible to make even erroneous use of it. This meaning is to be found, as has been seen, in the fact of laws.

IV

CONFUSION BETWEEN LAWS AND PRACTICAL PRINCIPLES. CRITIQUE OF PRACTICAL LEGALISM AND OF JESUITIC MORALITY

NOTHING perhaps better makes clear the true nature of laws than the examination of the very grave errors introduced by their means into the Philosophy of the practical: for, owing to the failure to perceive the character of mere *aid* proper to their function, laws have been confused with practical principles, these being looked upon as laws and those as principles.

Transformation of principles into practical laws: legalism.

We always live surrounded by innumerable laws, although these are always finite in number. The Decalogue also admonishes: " Take not the name of God in vain "; " Honour thy father and thy mother "; " Thou shalt not steal "; " Thou shalt commit no murder "; " Thou shalt not covet thy neighbour's house, nor his wife, nor his man-servant, nor his maid-servant, nor his ox, nor his ass, nor anything that is his "; etc.

Genesis of the concept of the practically licit and indifferent.

The decalogue or hectalogue of prudence admonishes us: "Raise not up against thee too many enemies"; "Mind your own business"; "Conciliate him who is more powerful than thou"; "Hurt him who hurts thee"; etc. Those laws that are so many and so minute easily lead to the false belief that they suffice together to regulate our economic action and our moral life, and that practical principles can be substituted for and be fully represented by a Decalogue or code, which should be the true and proper regulator of human life.

But the Decalogue, the code, the *Corpus juris*, ample and minute though they be, are not, as we know, capable of exhausting the infinity of actions conditioned by the infinite variety of facts. Every law brings with it, as its necessary correlative, as the shadow of its light, actions that are indifferent and indifferentiable, the legally indifferent, the licit, the permissible, the right, the faculty of doing or of not doing. As an inevitable consequence of this, practical principles having been conceived as a series or complex of laws, the concept of the *practically indifferent* must also be posited and the *licit* changed from *legal* to *practical*.

And this is what happens. At every moment

of life we find ourselves face to face with actual *Consequence of this: the* situations, to which the laws that we possess *arbitrary.* either do not apply at all, or apply only in the approximative way that we have seen ; at every moment of life, we find ourselves without the guidance of the law, face to face with the indifferent and the indifferentiated. The practical man knows well that the laws were a mere help, merely a preparatory stage to action, and that he must in each case face the actual situation as it arises, intuite and perceive it in its originality, and perform his own action with originality. But he who has accepted the *legalitarian* conception of the practical activity and has abandoned practical principles as useless or looked upon them as non-existent, now that he finds himself abandoned also by the laws, in which he had put too much trust, has no other guide on which to fall back save his own *will*.

And will is not a guide but *the lack of a guide* ; it is not action but inaction, that is to say, contradictory action ; not activity, but passivity, not prudence and good, but imprudence and evil.

Thus the legalitarian conception of practical principles produces neither more nor less than the death of the practical, installing passivity in the place of activity, evil in the place of good.

The legalitarian theory, which proposes to fix and to determine with precision the true concept of freedom, arrives at just the opposite result : the will.

Ethical legal-ism as simply a particular case of practical legalism. It is opportune to remark here that moral legalism, which has hitherto alone occupied the attention of critics, is nothing but a particular case of general practical legalism, and if the particular and not the general case has been observed, this has depended upon the failure to recognize the economic form in its autonomy, so common with philosophers. But from the examples that we have given, it has clearly resulted that legalism is an error which embraces alike Economy and Ethic, introducing into both the philosophic absurdity of the *practically indifferent*. Even a man without moral conscience, or one deprived of it for a moment, if he conceive the guidance of his utilitarian action in the form of laws, loses the compass of his utilitarianism and falls into the arbitrary, which is the ruin of his own individuality. If (to resume the usual example) I impose upon myself the not drinking of wine as a hygienic law, and it happen to me to find myself at a certain moment in such physiological conditions that a glass of wine can accelerate the beating of the heart and restore to me the strength of which I am in need; and if, through faith in the established law, I forget that the law is conditional and not absolute and that the only absolute law is to do at a given moment what is useful at that moment; it is evident that by so reasoning and acting, I am substituting superstition and therefore the arbitrary for prudence and that I am causing injury to myself.

It is necessary to maintain against the morally and practically indifferent, that it is a concept altogether external to Ethic and Economic and devastates it terribly whenever it penetrates into it, or (what is worse) subtly corrupts it. In Economic as in Ethic, in the true and proper practical field, there is no *faculty* that is not also *obligation*; there is no *right* that is not at the same time a *duty*; there is nothing *licit* that is not *forbidden*; nor *permitted* that is not turned into a *command*. πάντα ἔξεστιν, ἀλλ' οὐ πάντα συμφέρει, said St. Paul,[1] in obscure but suggestive language that has been much discussed—all is allowed to us but we do not allow anything—we should say in explanation; everything can and should be spiritually elaborated by the will and receive the form of freedom. But in order to

Critique of the practically indifferent.

[1] 1 Cor. x. 23.

destroy that paradoxical concept at the roots, it is necessary to reach the point underground where the concept of *practical legalism* is to be found, and to show, as we have done, its origin, in the confusion between *principles and laws.*

Contests between rigorists and latitudinarians and their common error.

In vain have the *rigorists*, becoming aware of the ruin that menaced the theory of Ethic, struggled against the theoreticians of the morally indifferent, or *latitudinarians.* So long as neither party left the legalitarian field, one side was right against the other and both were equally wrong, Pharisees and Sadducees, Jansenists and Molinists. The rigorists clung desperately to the law, refusing to admit that it could be *doubtful* and give rise to the morally indifferent; the law was *certain.* But the law is never really either doubtful or certain: revolving upon empirical concepts, it never limits anything with precision and therefore is not certain; having for its object, not concrete action, but only preparation for it, does not propose to limit the illimitable and so is neither uncertain nor doubtful: it stands on this side or the other of such categories. Thus the rigorists also found themselves face to face with the morally indifferent, and had no way of vanquishing it. They could advise the choice of the most painful and repugnant action, self-denial, self-tormenting; but this too was a kind of wilfulness and evil. The latitudinarians, on the other hand, could enlarge the field of the morally indifferent at their pleasure, placing in evidence the dubiety of law and its consequent impotence as a practical principle; but since they did not recognize any practical principle outside the form of law, they were finally obliged to have recourse to it, that they might have some point of orientation in the guidance of their lives. And since they could not find it in the law itself, recognized as doubtful, they were obliged to place it in the authority of its interpreters; and when these authorities were at variance, in the adding up of authorities (just as is done for the Roman jurists in the law of citation made by Theodosius II.); and since, finally, two or three or four or a hundred authorities, when they are uncertain, are not of greater value than one who is equally uncertain, any sort of authority finally had to suffice them as justification for an action. *Probabilitism*, far from being merely an illegitimate degeneration of legalism, is its logical consequence. Reduced as they were to authority, why should one be of more account than another, when all are estimable people worthy of credence?

Why should the precedence be given to Papinian over Paul or over Ulpian? If Villalobos be of opinion that a priest who has committed a moral sin cannot say mass the same day, Sanchez, on the other hand, opines that he can : why, then, should a priest who finds himself in that case follow Villalobos rather than Sanchez? It is true that if he make a blind choice between Villalobos and Sanchez, he becomes the prey of self-will; but self-will and legalism are indissoluble, and the more carefully he tries to free himself from the bond, the more tightly it winds itself around him.

Jesuitic morality as doctrine of fraud against the moral law.

Practical legalism can also give rise to a monstrously absurd theory, which we shall call *Jesuitic morality*, not because it is peculiar to the Jesuits or to catholicism, but as dutiful homage to the most conspicuous and likewise the most celebrated in literature of its historical incarnations. The theory of Jesuitic morality admits that we can rationally *defraud* ethical law.

Concept of legal fraud.

That the law is *defrauded or eluded* every day, taken in itself, is neither moral nor immoral, since it is an expedient of social strife like another, and in certain cases may be a legitimate act of war and a fraud only in name. A law held to be iniquitous should be combated openly;

but if the imposer of the iniquitous law, or he
who wishes to profit by it, have committed a
mistake in drafting it, so that it can be interpreted
in such a way as to become good, or at least
better, it is very natural that the adversary
should profit by the mistake, if for no other
reason than that he may discredit the law as
equivocal and lacking in precision and compel
society to discuss it again. Who does not
applaud the fraud of Portia, when it is a question
of saving the life of the noble Antonio from a
Shylock? And if even the *ferox animus* of
Shylock has found defenders, as symbol of the
tenacity with which we must make our own
rights respected, yet Portia also will always find
her supporters, as symbol of ingenious rebellion
against an unjust law.

But what is altogether irrational and yet
seems to be admitted by Jesuitic morality, is
the fraud against oneself, and so against one's
own moral conscience. To defraud one's own
conscience, to rebel against it with violence or
with artifice, is contradiction, wilfulness, evil.
It sometimes happens that we exert ourselves
to still what is called the internal voice of admonition, the Socratic demon, or the guardian
angel. This happens in the utilitarian, not less

Absurdity of the fraud against one's self and against the moral law.

than in the moral field; when, for instance, we yield to a pleasure which we know to be harmful and had intended to avoid for that reason, and when by dint of subtleties we try to persuade ourselves that it differs from that which we had recognized as harmful. We attempt, but we never really succeed; we may be able to obscure our conscience for an instant, but we can never permanently and altogether darken it; the effort itself calls for the light that we would avoid.

Jesuitic morality not explainable as mere legalism.

But that pretension of Jesuitic morality cannot on the other hand derive from mere ethical legalism, because legalism produces the contradictions that we have already placed in relief; it generates the morally indifferent and at the same time suppresses it; and when it has suppressed again generates, in order again to suppress it; and so on to infinity, an anxious and sterile doing and undoing. But it never authorizes fraud. Simple legalism will never justify our pretending to ourselves when a definite action is willed or when we have a definite intention, that we will another action and have a different intention; or, as they say, *direction of the intention*: the intention is that which it is and it does not allow itself to be directed at will. To obey the letter of the law with the clear intention of breaking it in spirit will never be justified.

The pretension of Jesuitic morality becomes *Jesuitic morality as* illuminated and transparent to the intellect, only *alliance between legalism* when we make the hypothesis of an alliance *and theological utilitarianism.* between *practical legalism and theological utilitarianism*; that is to say, when not only do we conceive morality as a series or complex of legislative decisions, but when we likewise consider these to be nothing less than the product of the will of God. They are not in themselves moral as such, and to observe them does not arise of intrinsic necessity; but they are obeyed as the lesser evil, through fear of worse or in hope of future advantage. In this case there is a silent struggle between God the legislator and man, a struggle between the weak and the overbearing, in which the strength of the weak lies in ingenuity, their tactic in fraud. Hence the dominant concept of Jesuit morality: to get the better of the divine laws as far as possible, to do the least possible of what they command; and when called upon to give an account of one's own actions before the tribunal of confession, or before the universal judgment, so to subtilize upon the law, that from the interpretation thus put upon it, what has been done seems to belong to the licit and permissive. God forbids man to kill man; but does he intend to forbid this, when the motive for this killing is the glory of God himself? When the slayer acts as though he were the hand of God himself and is all one with him? Without doubt, no: so that it will be lawful for the Jesuit to kill or cause to be killed his Jansenist adversary, who injures divine interests by disclosing the defects of the holy Company, which is the image of God upon earth: that killing, then, is not only lawful, but ordained. But if he want to kill his adversary, not through zeal for the divine glory, but because of the injury that he causes to the personal and immoral interests of the Jesuit? This too is permitted, provided that when killing him, though animated with personal hate, he withdraw his regard from the real motive, and *directing* his intention to the divine glory, thus justify the *means* by the *end*.

Distinction between the doctrine and the practice of the Jesuits.

Such is the monstrous logical product, born of the union between *legalism* and the theory of *theological utilitarianism*; such is the essence of Jesuitic morality, which has justly aroused horror and disgust. And we call it *logical* (or illogical) product, because we wish to make it clear that here as elsewhere we are occupied with theories only and are criticizing them alone. In practical action Jesuitic morality was often better than the theory would imply; even the Padre Caramuel, who put the question as to the right possessed by the Jesuits of slaying the Jansenists, must have been at bottom a good man; because, having almost arrived at an affirmative conclusion to his inquiry by dint of perverting the moral law, he was seized by pity and defrauded his own fraud, concluding negatively that the Jansenists *occidi non possunt quia nocere non potuerunt*, because (said he) they are poor devils, unable to obscure the glorious brilliance of the Company, as the owl does not conceal the light of the sun.[1] And Saint Alphonso dei Liguori, who is usually looked upon as an example of that lurid morality in our day, when he set to work to stir up afresh the ugliness of casuistic in connection with the sixth and ninth commandments, experienced all the repugnance of the gallant gentleman that he was, at such a task, imposed upon him by the traditional mode of treating Ethic, as is to be seen by his declarations, excla-

[1] Pascal, *Prov.* l. 7.

mations, and exhortations: *Nunc aegre materiam illam tractandam aggredimur, cujus vel solum nomen hominum mentes inficit. Det mihi veniam, quaeso, castus lector! . . . Ora studiosos . . . ut. . . . eo tempore saepius mentem ad Deum elevent et Virgini immaculatae se commendent, ne dum aliorum animos Deo student acquirere, ipsi suarum detrimentum patiantur.*[1] If Jesuitism were also moral corruption, this was not due to its abstract theories, but to the education that it practised, which was depressing, servile, and directed to mortify the strength of the will and of the intelligence, to reduce a man to be like *senis baculus,* a docile and passive instrument in the hands of others; and to the confusion in consciences as to the real motives of actions, which it not only preserved but increased, lulling souls to sleep with sophisms and allure-ments of devotion *aisées à pratiquer,* by means of which the gates of Paradise could be unlocked, and with *chemins de velours* on which one could mount to the sky with every indul-gence. The rigorists and latitudinarians are philosophically equivalent; but it is a fact that in practice the rigorists were generally energetic and austere souls; which should not cause us

[1] *Theol. moralis*[7], Bassano, 1773, i. 168.

to forget that the latitudinarians also, amid their distorted theories, sometimes had a lucid vision of the *complications* of reality and felt the necessity of a morality less abstract and less disharmonic in relation to life, however incorrectly they may nevertheless have developed its theory.

V

JUDICIAL ACTIVITY AS AN ACTIVITY GENERICALLY PRACTICAL (ECONOMIC)

Legislative activity, as generically practical. THE will that wills classes of actions, or the activity that makes laws and that we can henceforward term *legislative activity* without fear of misunderstanding, is either moral or merely economic; and therefore, when dialecticized, is either moral or immoral, economic or anti-economic. It is true that this will is abstract and indeterminate; but that does not prevent it from being, and from being obliged to be, either moral or merely economic; and, therefore, abstractly moral and abstractly economic, and so also abstractly immoral and anti-economic. A programme of action will be conceived, as they say, wisely or foolishly, to a good or to a bad end, for mere reasons of utility, or with a lively desire for good. The legislator is a volitional man, and as such to be judged both utilitarianly and morally. The laws that are

his volitional product are useful or injurious,
good or bad. This judgment is also without
doubt abstract, for it is necessary first to see
the legislator engaged in the practical act of
the application of his law, in order to recognize
what he can do and who he is. We know many
(others or ourselves?) who make plans for the
most beautiful lives, legislating admirably for
themselves and for others; yet these show themselves mean and bad in action: and we not
infrequently find the opposite case of men who
calumniate themselves and who, after they have
declared the most dishonest, or at least the
most amoralistic, of intentions, when they find
themselves face to face with the bad action,
ugly with the ugliness of sin, say, as the old
man in the fable said to Death: " I have not
called thee ! "

From these considerations, which seem to *Vanity of*
disputes as to
be most obvious, a not obvious consequence *the character*
of institutions,
is to be drawn ; namely, that it is perfectly *economic or*
ethic : punish-
vain to descant upon the utilitarian or moral *ment, matri-*
mony, the
character of laws, or of these or those laws ; *State, etc.*
to ask oneself, for instance, whether the object
of *punishment* be *deterritio* or *emendatio*; if
matrimony be an exchange of services or a
sacrament, a union of interests or a society

with moral ends; if the *State* be the result
of a contract or of a moral idea, and so on.
These questions have an immense literature
devoted to them, which has been accumulated
for centuries, and although they be vain for us,
yet they cannot be so for one who has not yet
become clear as to the special forms of the
practical activity and as to the nature of law.
For him they are not vain, since they represent
as it were in a concentrated form, the complete
philosophical problem concerning the practical;
although they must of necessity turn out to
be insoluble. Punishment can be conceived
and willed as a mere utilitarian menace, to
prevent others from performing certain classes
of actions, even if they be ethically of the
highest value; or as moral solicitude for the
amelioration of society and the individual himself who has erred, by obliging him to re-enter
himself and change his mind. Even the pain
of death can be directed to this end and death
that has given or restored to the guilty a day,
an hour, an instant of that human life, of that
contact with the infinite, which he had lost,
may be held not to have been in vain. Matrimony may be instituted for the more regular
satisfaction of the sexual instinct and for other

similar interests of utilitarian life; and also to
secure that interpenetration of souls, which is the
great mover of the moral life. The State may
arise from a mere contract which draws together
isolated individuals and groups and unites them
for defence and offence; and also form the
profound moral aspiration of the individuals,
who recognize the universal in themselves and
are attentive to realize it in modes ever more
rich and more lofty. All institutions, all laws
may receive this double form; and although
there be laws that are merely utilitarian, those
that are moral are also, as is clear, utilitarian
or economic, and therefore not useless but
useful. An amoral man will make for himself
amoral laws; and between an amoral man and
an amoral woman no other marriage but that
of interest is possible; and between a hundred
amoral individuals, no other State is possible
but that established by contract; and no other
punishment will be applicable in such a State
save that of mere *deterritio*. It will be objected
that amoral individuals and multitudes do not
exist, and it may be true that they do not exist
in a continuous manner: but they do exist at
certain moments; and this as we know, suffices
to justify, indeed to prove necessary, our theory.

2 M

Legislative activity as economic.

Thus no other answer is possible to the question asked as to whether the legislative activity be moral or merely economic, save that it may be the one or the other, and therefore, that it is not of necessity moral; thus, defining it in its full extension, it must be called *generically practical*, or taken in itself, *merely economic*.

Juridical activity: its economic character.

Passing now from the legislative activity to that of him who realizes and executes the law (an activity that we may call *juridical*, in order not to confound it with the other), and asking whether juridical activity be moral or distinct from morality and if distinct, what is its distinctive characteristic, the answer cannot but be most simple for us who have attained to our present position. So simple indeed, that to give it would seem to be almost superfluous. Not only must the activity of carrying out the law not be intrinsically diverse from the activity of legislating, but as has been seen, it obeys exclusively practical principles, economic and ethic. Hence the juridical activity can be merely economic and it can be moral; and seeing that economicity is the general form that of itself involves the other, the juridical activity is generically practical, or *economic*. As such and in so far as it is such, it is at once distinct from and united with the moral form.

But juridical activity does not merely enter the economic activity; it is exactly identical with it: juridical activity and economic activity are *synonyms*. Legislative activity enters economy and nevertheless distinguishes itself from it, as volition of the abstract, indeterminate volition. The juridical activity is on the other hand concrete and determined, like the other, nor is it distinguished from it by any secondary character. It might be attempted to subdistinguish the economic and juridical activity, while admitting the generic identification, and to look upon the latter as such that although obeying the economic principle, it is yet developed *under the laws*; whereas the former would exist even where *laws were wanting*. But the distinction would be empirical, of undulating boundaries. Strictly speaking, man is surrounded with laws in all his actions, and he always acts under all the laws, and at the same time he effectually acts under none of them, save that of his own practical conscience.

Its consequent identity with the economic activity.

If the identity and synonymity of law, understood as juridical activity with economy, has not been discovered, that too is connected with the lack of recognition of the practical utilitarian category on the part of philosophers and with their considering it, as they erroneously did, either as egotism and immorality, or as an altogether empirical division, to which was added a concept, also empirical, of the juridical activity itself, which should be limited to what are called laws emanating from the State, sometimes graciously including in them social laws, and always altogether ignoring the fundamental form, individual laws.

The failure to recognize the economic form and the meaning of the problem concerning the distinction between morality and law.
But this failure of recognition has not prevented the appearance and persistence of the problem of the *combined unity and distinction of law and morality*, which has been the most frequent though the most complicated mode of affirming the claim of a special Philosophy of economy. A serious beginning of meditation upon law had hardly begun, when something was observed in it that it was impossible to resolve into the concepts of Ethic. Hence the generally admitted recognition of the distinction between law and morality and the many attempts at determining of what the peculiar character of the former exactly consisted.

This character was placed most frequently and with greater insistence in the two deter-

minations of *compulsion* and of *exteriority*. And
it was said that law is distinguished from
morality because it is possible to exercize compulsion in the juridical, but not in the moral
field; or that law deals with the field of external
relations, morality with the internal; or that one
is the *psychical*, the other the *physical* side of
action. But as to the first determination, we
have already shown that it has no meaning at
all when applied to the forms of the spiritual
activity, where nothing is compulsory and everything is at once free and necessary: the juridical
activity, if it be activity, must likewise always be
determined by free agreement. The second,
which is the determination of exteriority, is not
less inconceivable; for it is not given to separate
the external from the internal, since they are
both one, nor the word from its meaning, nor the
body from its spirit. Compulsion and exteriority,
taken strictly as concepts, are therefore, in this
case, void and contradictory formulæ. To fill
them somehow with a thought, it would be
necessary to understand as compulsion certain
modes of action, as opposed to certain other
modes; for instance, compulsion would be the
action by which an accused person was conducted
to prison by two policemen and non-compulsion

Theories of compulsion and exteriority, as distinct- ive characters: critique.

that of him who should be induced to go
and constitute himself a prisoner through the
persuasion of others ; and as exteriority, certain
classes of actions opposed to certain others ; so
that, for example, the deportment of an individual
as communal or provincial councillor would
belong to external life, his relations with his
confessor or with his Æsculapius to internal life.
But compulsion and exteriority, reduced to these
meanings, become gross and empirical concepts,
of which no use can be made in philosophy and
which therefore cannot be of the least value as
qualifying and distinguishing law from morality.

In the same way, no value is to be attached
to such a distinction, when determined from
what is licit to what is commanded, from rights
to duties, from what is permitted to what is
obligatory ; because licit and commanded, rights
and duties, from what is permitted to what is
obligatory, are correlative concepts constituting
an indissoluble nexus and it is not possible to
separate and to oppose them to one another.

*Moralistic
theories of
rights:
critique.*
The difficulty of conveniently fixing the distinction with the characters indicated, leads one
to think of a different sort of tentative, according
to which rights would certainly be distinguished
from ethicity, not placed above or beside it,

but rather in the very sphere of morality itself, as the species in respect to the genus or the part in respect of the whole. Juridical action would be moral, but it would belong to the inferior levels of morality; it would be occupied with the execution of simple *justice*, with the establishment of order, proportion, equality; whereas morality would represent *more than justice*, and would upset the equilibrium of rights with benevolence, generosity, sacrifice, heroism. Rights (it is also said) are limited to the *ethical minimum*, while morality strives for the *maximum*; rights are concerned with strict rights or *perfect* duties, morality with meritorious and supererogatory actions, *imperfect* duties. But these determinations also pretend to separate the inseparable, by drawing an arbitrary line of division between small and great actions, between least and greatest, and they employ concepts that are altogether empirical, as, for instance, that of justice as distinct from benevolence, of the strictly obligatory from the meritorious and supererogatory; and worse still than this, metaphors and symbols, such as equality, order, regularity; or they operate directly with the arithmetical and geometrical proportion of actions. And consciously or unconsciously a return is made to

Ethic pure and simple, with the theories that make juridical activity to consist of the recognition of others as *persons*, or with the search for *general utility* (superindividual). When we act in view of the *person* in other individuals (or in oneself), or of the useful, which is not the useful for the individual, but although it comprehends, yet transcends it:—the merely juridical conscience has already been surpassed, it has been filled with a moral content, that is to say, an ethical form has been given to the practical activity. The double sense of the terms "rights" and "morality" is in this way preserved in words but denied in fact.

Duality of positive and ideal, historical and natural rights, etc.; and absurd attempts at unification and co-ordination. The dual sense of the terms is also affirmed by the very ancient distinction between *positive and ideal, historical* and *natural* rights, *right* and *justice*, or, as it has also been formulated, between the *two different justices*, realistic and idealistic, fruitful in conjunction. Natural rights, with their homonyms just stated, besides the generically practical significations that we have already examined, have also had the narrower one of ethical ideal or morality; and therefore it cannot cause astonishment that it should appear now conjoined with, now detached from positive rights. But how joined and disjoined? For us it is a question of degrees, whence the positivity of both forms is recognized : the second of these is included in the first : the ideal right or morality (if it be right, and not simply abstract excogitation willed by no one, or vague desire) is both positive and historical. But those who posited the distinction without being able to make it definite and so to dominate it were led to conceive one or the other term as negative ; and therefore both as negative between themselves and existing only in a third : which meant to reannul the distinction by reducing it to abstract contradiction. If one of the two were conceived as negative, either the ideal justice (that is, the seriousness of moral strength) was denied and turned to ridicule, or positive justice, that is, the seriousness of volitional strength, was presented as something turbid and impure and at best as a human imperfection, to which it was advisable to resign oneself since it would disappear in a society of perfect men or in a future life of perfection. Juridical activity became something contingent and mortal. Matters were even worse, if it were found impossible to eliminate it with similar religious, apocalyptic, or millenary fancies. The negative was then conceived as positive or co-ordinated with the positive : hence incredible

logical divisions of rights into forms or species of
moral and *immoral* rights, of *just* and *unjust* rights,
in which the species has the function of *negation
of the genus*, almost as though the race of horses
were to be divided into two kinds: *dead* and *living*
horses! Unjust or immoral rights are not rights,
but a contradiction of them, and if we sometimes
describe in this way a real and effective juridical
act (an economic act), it is necessary to observe
that the denomination is given from the point
of view of a superior form of activity. Rights
in themselves as rights, understood positively,
are never immoral, but only *amoral*.

*Value of all
these theories
as confused
perception of
the amoral
character of
justice.*

All these errors, all these sterile tentatives
have their origin, as has been said, in the lively
consciousness of a distinction existing between
right and morality and at the same time of the
impossibility of determining this correctly, owing
to lack of clarity as to the purely economic form
of the practical activity. When the juridical
activity has been identified with the economic
and when juridical (economic) activity has in
consequence been conceived as at once united
with and distinct from morality, we are able to
recognize that these attempts have nevertheless
fulfilled a very useful function; that is to say,
they have more or less energetically asserted and

defended the position that there existed a characteristic distinction between right and morality
and that it was necessary to seek for it. They
are therefore far superior, notwithstanding their
errors, to that confused ethical conception, which
receives rights and morality indistinctly into its
bosom, or to the utilitaristic conception, which
arrives by a different route at the same indistinction. This merit belongs to the theories
of the moral minimum, of justice, of the two
justices and of the contest between positive and
ideal rights ; but in a much greater degree to that
of compulsion, of exteriority, of the licit. With
these last was almost unconsciously set in relief
the fact that right obeys a law different from
that of Ethic, and may be called *compelled and
not free by comparison with it*, because not
founded upon the necessity of the universal ;
that in respect to the supreme *interiority* of
Ethic it can be considered as something *exterior* ;
that in respect to the ethical imperative, it
appears as something indifferentiated or *licit*.
These are without doubt symbols, tautologies,
vague and imprecise phrases, but efficacious in
keeping the attention alert and in promoting
doubt and research.

But the impossibility of absorbing rights into

Confirmations of this character in the ingenuous consciousness. Ethic altogether and without leaving residues is proclaimed or confessed, not only in the theories of philosophers, but by simple thought, and especially by the consciousness we have of the real world being governed, not by abstract morality, but, as is said, by *force*, or by the will in action. " Disarmed prophets " will be efficacious in poetry, but ridiculous in practical reality : *la force prime le droit*, precedes it and is always of greater value than an unreal and contradictory ethical right and aspiration, afterwards dissolved in the empty and arbitrary. We will not recall proverbs, maxims, historical examples, though this would be easy ; that little story of Franco Sacchetti which preserves " a fair speech " of Messer Ridolfo da Camerino, will suffice for all. One of his nephews had been at Bologna studying law for a good twelve years, and when, having become an excellent lawyer, he returned to Camerino, he went to pay a visit to Messer Ridolfo. When he paid the visit, Messer Ridolfo said, " And what didst thou do at Bologna ? " He replied, " My Lord, I have learned *reason.*" Said Messer Ridolfo, " Thou hast spent thy time ill." The young man replied that the saying seemed to him to be very strange. " Why was it ill spent, my Lord ? " And Messer Ridolfo said,

*" Because thou shouldst have learned force, which
is worth two of the other."* The youth began to
smile, and thinking it over again and again, both
he and the others that heard, perceived that what
Messer Ridolfo had said, was true.[1]

And here too we are at last able to establish *Comparison
between right
and language.
Grammars
and codes.*
a parallel between the practical and theoretic
activity, between the problems of the Philosophy
of right and those of Logic and Æsthetic.
The comparison of right and language has been
several times attempted, with very great correction of thought, although necessarily defective
execution, since it was customary to conceive
both language and right in an abstract and empirical manner. Whoever should wish to take
up the inquiry again would do great service, were
he to insist upon the fact that since it has
been impossible to understand what language
really is, so long as grammars and vocabularies
were taken as its reality, so it is impossible to
understand anything of rights, so long as the eye
is fixed upon laws and codes, or what is even
worse, upon the commentaries of jurists, or upon
the abstract volitional fact, or altogether upon
what is not a true and proper volitional fact, but
the elaboration of formulæ and of general concepts.

---

[1] *Novelle*, xl.

Logic and language; morality and rights.

Only when rights appear as individual and continually new work of individuals, only when the attention is directed to the spectacle of real life and not to the abstractions of legislators and dispenses with the dissertations of jurists, is it possible to state the problem: how does this juridical work coincide with, and how does it differ from moral work? And here too the comparison with language is fitting, although language be not logicity, yet logical thought cannot become concrete, save in speaking; so moral activity cannot live, save by translating itself into laws and institutes, and in the realization of laws and institutes, that is, in the juridical and economic activity.

Finally, just as the history of a language is always arbitrary and abstract, so long as it is considered alone, outside the works in which the language is incarnate and the true history of a language is its poetry and literature, so *the true history of the rights of a people* (of the rights that have really been executed and not merely formulated in laws and codes, be often proved to be a dead letter) cannot but be altogether one with *the social and political history of that people*: an altogether juridical or economic history; a history of *wants* and of *labour*.

VI

HISTORICAL ANNOTATIONS

I. THE history of the distinction between morality and rights is very important, precisely because, as has been said, it is the manifestation of the very strongly - felt desire to posit in some way a philosophy of the aethical or amoral practical form: a manifestation which is the most conspicuous of all those that we have had occasion to note on the subject (theory of politics, theory of the inferior appetitive faculty, theory of the passions, etc.).[1] And owing to the impossibility of satisfying that exigency with the intellectual data possessed, the problem of the relation between rights and morality has become anything but an amusing puzzle, a theme for true vain eloquence.

Distinction between morality and rights, and its importance for the history of the economic principle.

Emmanuel Kant in the *Critique of Pure Reason*, wishing to give a characteristic example of the difficulty of definitions, found nothing

[1] See above, pp. 286, 287.

543

better to record than that jurists were always seeking a definition of rights, but had never succeeded in finding one.[1] And a jurist philosopher of our times (Jhering) has called the definition of rights, in their difference from morality, the "Cape Horn," or the Cape of tempests (or shipwrecks?) of juridical science.

Indistinction up to the time of Thomas. The problem of that distinction is on the other hand relatively recent and therefore the history of the Philosophy of rights has rightly been placed not further back than the end of the seventeenth century, or not much beyond Christian Thomas.[2] Up to that time, it is not possible to speak strictly of a Philosophy of rights. Treatises of jurisprudence, of rights and of the State, in regard to what of philosophical they contained, were nothing but treatises of Ethic; not indeed because the two sciences were (as they were) materially united in the same books, but precisely because the two concepts were indistinct. The speculations of antiquity for this part also of the Philosophy of the practical have the character of ingenuousness already noted. It would be incorrect to reconstruct a moralistic philosophy from the rights of Plato, founding it,

---

[1] *Krit. d. rein. Vern.* (ed. Kirchmann), p. 572.
[2] Lasson, *System der Rechtsphilosophie* (Berlin, 1882), p. 2.

for example, upon the theory developed in the *Gorgias* as to the eagerness to purge his punishment that should exist in the criminal, similar, in this respect, to the sick man, who knows that the medicine will free him from his disease.[1] The researches of Aristotle also as to justice (perhaps the best the classical world has left us on the subject), look upon justice in a narrow sense, as a virtue among virtues,[2] which should not intrinsically possess any greater reason for distinguishing itself from the other virtues than they for distinguishing among themselves. The pompous definitions of the Roman jurists, still the joy of schools of jurisprudence and of judges' rhetoric, have no philosophical weight and would in any case confirm the identity of rights with Ethicity, if not absolutely with the entire knowable and practical universe. There is hardly a ray of the distinction to be traced in the discussions as to whether rights exist by nature or by convention and in the concept of a ἁπλῶς δίκαιον, opposed to that of πολιτικὸν δίκαιον found in Plato, and more explicitly in Aristotle,[3] and rendered popular by Cicero when speaking of the *recta ratio, naturae congruens, diffusa in omnes,*

---

[1] *Gorgias,* 476-478.
[2] *Eth. Nicom.* 3, v. c. 1-2.
[3] *Ibid.* v. c. 7, 9 ; *Magna Moralia,* i. c. 34.

constans, sempiterna; of rights not drawn from
the Twelve Tables or from the pretorian Edict,
but *ex intima philosophia*; and of rights that on
the other hand are *varie et ad tempus descriptae
populis*, whence they have the name of laws
favore magis quam re.[1]

This rough distinction between natural and
positive, absolute and relative rights; this concept of an ideal right placed face to face with
real rights, or of which the real should be
an imperfect and partial translation, also reappears in St. Thomas Aquinas and in other
scholastics. And there is nothing more than
this in those thinkers who founded what was
called natural rights in the seventeenth century,
such as Grotius and his followers. It is true that
the boast of having distinguished rights from
morality and religion has usually been attributed to
that historical period. But it is hardly necessary
to repeat that what was meant by these formulæ
were the great social and political questions which
took the form of wars of religion in the Europe
of the sixteenth and seventeenth centuries; that
so-called distinction, therefore, the result of long
strife, though it have great practical value as a
sign of social transformation, has no doctrinal

---

[1] *De republ.* iii. c. 22 ; *De legibus*, ii. c. 5.

value. The idea of autonomy, proper to the juridical activity, is absent even in the profound treatise of Vico on universal rights, for this contains only an altogether empirical distinction between *virtus* and *justitia*; of these the first *cum cupiditate pugnat*, and the second *utilitates dirigit et exaequat*; and both derive their origin from the *vis veri* or *ratio humana*; and as all the virtues are connected and none of them can exist alone (*nulla virtus solitaria*), so *virtus* and *justitia* are at bottom one.[1] The work of Vico, which gives a new conception of the relation between ideal and history and most original applications of Roman history, turns out to be nothing but Ethic, when considered beneath the aspect of Philosophy of Rights. Nor on the other hand could the problem of the nature of rights truly form the object of enquiry on the part of utilitarians (Hobbes and others); with whom, if the absorption of rights in morality was not found, this did not arise because the one was distinguished from the other, but because morality itself was denied in what was proper to itself: the problem of the distinction disappeared, because its terms disappeared.

II. Thomas provided the apple of discord, or *Thomas and his followers.* as might also be said, cast the leaven of progress

---

[1] *De imo univ. jur. princ.* §§ 41, 43, 86.

into the treatment of rights, when he distinguished three forms of the *rectum* : the *justum*, the *honestum*, the *decorum*, placing the first in opposition to the other two, the *forum externum* to the *internum*, and attributing to rights and justice the character of coercibility.[1] The formula had a rapid and unsuspected fortune, and became current in the schools. Gundling, for instance, defined right as the "ordering of external relations."[2]

Kant and Fichte. It was completely developed and reasoned out, with all the strictness that its erroneity permitted, in the doctrines of Kant and Fichte, who were the greatest of Thomas's scholars for this part of the study. Kant opposed *legality* to morality ; the juridical imperative is expressed with the formula, " act externally " (*handle äusserlich*) ; right is conjoined with the faculty of compulsion (*zwingen*). Hence his doctrines are often amoralistic or economic as regards individual juridical institutions, and this is especially the case when he deals with the State, with matrimony, and with punishment ; these were followed by Fichte, who made some reservations for matrimony alone, considering it an institution not only juridical, but

---

[1] *Fundamenta juris nat. et gentium* (1705).
[2] Windelband, *Geschichte d. Phil.*[2] p. 424.

also natural and moral.[1] On the other hand rights were for Kant something that surpassed the individual will and utility; it was the sum of the conditions by means of which the will of the one can be united with the will of another, according to a universal law of liberty.[2] Fichte in like manner conceived of rights as altogether free of every admixture of morality; as an objective order, arising from the fact of the individual who coherently affirms himself and his own liberty, thus also affirming other individuals and their liberty.[3] Both philosophers thus preserve the moralistic concept of the legal and the *justum*; rights, although armed with compelling power, are never force alone, but the external ordering of freedom, namely, justice.   For this reason, Kant explicitly excludes force, in so far as it is constitutive of rights and speaks of a "force without law"; and both he and Fichte make coercibility to flow, not from the nature of the volitional force itself, but from the violation of order.   It is just, says Kant, to repel force with force, when it would interfere with liberty.   The right of coercion (repeats Fichte) is founded solely upon the violation of the original right.   But it remains obscure

---

[1] *Grundl. d. Naturr.* (1796), append., sect. 1.
[2] *Metaphys. d. Sitten*, 1797 (ed. Kirchmann), pp. 31-35.
[3] *Grundl. d. Naturr.* pt. i. sect. 1.

what this poor legality, justice, coexistence, and harmony of wills may be; what force may be and why and how it is connected with the preceding definition is not investigated. The distinction of the juridical from the moral sphere is announced and proclaimed more loudly than perhaps was ever done before or since; but to announce and to proclaim is not to carry out. If rights be changed into an ordinance more or less rational, to be identified with the concept of justice, one does not see how they can exist independently of morality. Kant and Fichte were prevented from conceiving the juridical function free from every element of morality or immorality, by the function which they assigned to compulsion (symbol of law), submitting it to ethical exigencies. In this uncertainty, there cannot be wanting and there is not wanting the thought that rights are not indeed an eternal category, but a historical and transitory fact; and as Spinoza had already said, *si cum humana natura ita comparatum esset ut homines id quod maxime utile est maxime cuperent, nulla esset opus arte ad concordiam et fidem*; Fichte thus looked upon the juridical State simply as a *State of necessity* opposed to the *State of reason*: and when perfection has been attained and there is complete accord of all in the common end, " the State " (he said) "disappears as a legislative and compulsive force."[1]

In the ulterior phase of his thought, Fichte *Hegel.* afterwards took further steps toward a closer union between morality and rights. But the complete resolution of the first in the second is effected in the system of Hegel, though it is customary to blame this philosopher for the opposite fault, namely, that he resolves morality in right. Above all, Hegel would hear nothing of the concept of force in right : facts of force and of violence, as, for instance, the relation between a slave and his master, appertain, according to him, to a circle, which lies on this side of right, to the subjective spirit, to a world in which wrong can still be right. The fact that violence and tyranny are met with in positive rights is an accidental thing and does not affect its real nature. For Hegel, as for his predecessors, co-operation arises only as reaction from the violation of what is just, and is violence preservative of liberty, suppression of the previous violence. " To define abstract and rigorous rights as law which we can be compelled to obey, means" (writes Hegel) " to see them as a consequence of

[1] Spinoza, *Tract. pol.* c. 6, § 3 ; Fichte, *System d. Sittenlehre*, § 18 *in fine.*

what takes place only by the cross road of wrong."
But there is more : abstract rights, which form
the first moment of the Philosophy of the practical
in Hegel, are unreal; he opposes to them the
second moment, morality, which also is abstract
and unreal, consisting of the good intention,
which has not yet been incorporated in action
and life : thus concrete reality is realized only in
the third moment, in the ethos, which synthetizes
the abstract rights and the abstract morality of
the intention in social life.[1] From this it is clear
that the purely juridical moment does not possess
effective spiritual autonomy for Hegel; so much
so, that it is placed by him upon the same plane
as abstract and unreal morality.   In consequence
of his identification of rights with ethicity, Hegel
is opposed to Kant and Fichte in his definitions
of single rights; he rejects the compulsory and
contractual theory of the State and (the Kantian)
theory of matrimony as a strict contract made
between individuals as to the reciprocal use of
their bodies.[2] The compulsory theory of punishment seemed to him to reduce the latter to a
mere economic fact, by means of which " the
State as judging power, opens a business with

---

[1] *Phil. d. Rechts*, passim, concerning force and violence, §§ 3, 57, 94.
[2] *Op. cit.* § 158, *sqq.* 161, 258.

goods called crimes exchangeable for other goods, and the code is *the list of prices.*" [1]

Herbart too denies the originality of the *Herbart and Schopenhauer.* character of compulsion in the idea of rights, and this is one of his five practical ideas, or, " the agreement of many wills, thought as a rule that eliminates strife." But even in this superficial moralistic reduction, force reappears all of a sudden, one knows not how : society has need of an external bond, in order to subsist ; force and power (*Macht*) are added to society and *the State* arises.[2] The same contradictions are to be found in Schopenhauer : after he has posited the two virtues of justice and benevolence, he makes a chapter of morality out of the pure doctrine of law. The science of rights in the specific sense borrows this chapter in order to study its opposite : all the limits that morality looks upon as not to be passed without intention of wrong-doing, on the contrary are considered by the science of rights as limits, of which violation by others is not to be tolerated and from which one has the right to expel others. Thus the distinction between internal and external is in this way reproduced in all its unmaintainability under the denomination of *rights and their opposite.* But the bridge of asses

---

[1] *Werke*, I., p. 371.   [2] *Allg. prakt. Phil.* pp. 48, 126-128.

is always the junction of rights with force, that is to say, with the element extraneous to Ethic; and in this connection Schopenhauer has nothing better to offer than a comparison. "As there are certain chemical substances never to be found pure and isolated, but always in some sort of combination with another element, which gives to them the necessary consistency; so rights, when they must set foot in the real world and dominate it, have need of a small adjunct of will and force, in order to be able (notwithstanding its nature, which is really ideal and therefore ethereal) to operate and persist in this real and material world, without evaporating and flying to heaven, as was the case with Hesiod."[1]

Rosmini and others.

Rosmini presents the two elements not well harmonized, as the eudæmonological and the ethical. Rights for him are not mere eudæmonism, but a eudæmonistic fact, produced by moral right and receiving form from it; hence the science of rights "stands between Eudæmonology and Ethic, so that one of its ends extends to the one and the other to the other." It would not be easy to explain and to justify what he calls a mediate science, composed of Eudæmonology and Ethic; and it would be far less easy to explain how this

[1] *Werke*, i. 441-445; cf. v. 259-260.

science comes to be "completely distinct" as regards its components. If rights have a moral form,
they are moral and not eudæmonological. Owing
to this difficulty Rosmini was led to introduce the
concept of the licit as criterion of differentia-
tion, defining right as "a personal faculty and
power of enjoying, acting and being able to act,
a lawful good that must not be impeded by
others."[1] Juridically understood this constitutes
a tautology, ethically something worse. Other
Catholic authors (Taparelli, for example) deplore
the separation of *ethos* from *jus*, introduced (they
say) by Protestant doctrines and the limitation
of right to what a man can externally exact from
others according to law; "whence it happens
that in the enumeration of laws, actions are
sometimes posited that are real moral faults in
the agent"; maintaining on the contrary the
necessity of treating morality and rights together,
"for rights are part of morality in the same way
that trigonometry and conic sections are a part
of geometric theories."[2]

III. If Catholic doctrines deserve mention for *Stahl, Ahrens,*
Trendelenberg.
their conservativism, it is necessary to record the
names of Stahl, Ahrens, and Trendelenburg, for

[1] *Fil. d. diritto* (Napoli, 1844), i. 20-21, 88-89, 94-97.
[2] *Saggio teor. d. dir. nat.* (Palermo, 1857), *in princ.*

no other reason than the great popularity that they enjoyed in the schools. Stahl divides the ethical action of man into two domains, differing in content and character. This dualism is founded upon the double relation of human existence, individual and social, which gives rise to two forms of imperatives: to the imperative of the individual will, of religion, and of morality, and to that which aims at moulding social life and is the imperative of rights. This theory, which has a varied terminology, can be reduced to the theory of exteriority (sociality, rights), and interiority (individuality, morality). In a very similar way Ahrens includes law in the science of the good or Ethic—the fundamental science. He remarks that good intention, virtue, are not sufficient to secure to man that complex of material and spiritual goods of which he has need, and therefore there must be a second mode of effecting in the good, which what is of importance would be, not the motives of the will, but the pursuit of the good and its real existence in life. Trendelenburg (who regrets the classical concept of the identity of Ethic and Law and looks upon the time when they began to be distinguished as a beginning of degeneration) discovers three sides to rights: the *logical*, the *ethical*, and the *physical* (compulsion),[1] of which none, as we see, is truly judicial.

For the reasons already indicated, it is not necessary to pause over the juridical ideas of the utilitarians of the eighteenth and nineteenth centuries, whose last celebrated representatives were, in England, Bentham, Austin and Spencer. The German Kirchmann is to be identified with the utilitarian tendency. He reduces morality to the *respect* inspired, not by the law, but by the *person* of the legislator, a respect afterwards converted into respect for the law "owing to a peculiarity of human nature, as the result of long custom and exercise." According to this view, rights are defined as "a union of pleasure and morality, whether the first calls the second to its aid or the second the first, in cases when the isolated efficacy of either should prove insufficient." Thus rights are declared to be, not an original principle, but the simple union of two different elements. Jhering failed to surpass utilitarianism, notwithstanding his profound juridical knowledge and his lively intellect. He attempted to impart an original character to his utilitarian theory, by declaring that it was

Utilitarians.

---

[1] Stahl, *Rechts- u. Staatslehre*[2] (Heidelberg, 1845), b. ii. ch. 1 ; Ahrens, *Naturr.* (It. tr., Napoli, 1860), i. 219 *sq.* ; Trendelenburg, *Naturrecht auf d. Grunde d. Ethik* (Leipzig, 1860).

objective in respect to the usual utilitarian theories, but he always remained under the obligation that he had undertaken, of showing how the purest ideality of Ethic could be fortified with such a conception. The distinctions drawn by Jhering between recompense, compulsion, duty, and love, since they lack a foundation, vacillate and prove but little convincing.[1]

Recent writers of treatises.

IV. Running rapidly through other recent philosophers of Rights, we do not meet with original thoughts that compare with those of Kant, of Fichte, and of Hegel. Lasson conceives of the philosophy of Rights as a part of Ethic and co-ordinates with it three other parts—the philosophy of custom, of morality or doctrine of the virtues and the doctrine of the ethos or of the ethical personality. Rights are the first of these three ethical moments and is concerned with the willing of man as a willing still essentially natural; reason joins it as a force essentially determining and limiting, at first only external; the object of rights is to guarantee the conditions of the common life, in so far as it is the condition for all human ends.—Steinthal recognizes that rights undoubtedly "possess an exteriority altogether

---

[1] Kirchmann, *Begr. d. Rechtes u. d. Moral*[2] (Berlin, 1873), pp. 107-114; see Jhering, *Der Zweck i. Recht* (i.[2], 1883; ii.[3], 1886).

opposed to the interiority of Ethic; hence, if they be not apprehended in their profound nature, they may easily be repugnant to moral feeling": they are "the system of modes of compulsion, by means of which are secured social ethical ends." But (we repeat) since the external cannot be separated from the internal, we do not see in what way ethical ends can be distinguished from their modes of realization. Steinthal also says that "Ethic is like a river and Rights like the bed of the river": a comparison that can be variously interpreted, like all comparisons and which for our part we should be disposed to find excellent, were it admitted that as the bed of the river, when it runs dry, yet remains always the bed of a possible river, so Rights can remain without Ethic and yet be always Rights. But the signification in which Steinthal employs that comparison is simply the same as the diad of external and internal; that is to say, he in his turn wishes to distinguish the indistinguishable, so that it would on the contrary be necessary to reply that the bed of the river and the river are not two things but one, because a river without a bed cannot exist and a bed without a river is not the bed of a river.—Schuppe denies that Rights and the State can claim what is immoral, but affirms that all the same they are inferior to the exigencies of morality, because Rights and the State concern individuals in their spatial-temporal concretion, but do not attain to the profundity afforded by conscience in universal. The ethical concept of rights preponderates in Wundt, for he does not conceive of any other object of rights, subjective and objective, save morality. Cohen, in like manner, does not admit other independence to the science of rights save that of writing in concepts, and of organizing as a system of concepts the rights that is eternally unwritten, the moral law.[1]

As we see, if the names of the writers and sometimes their phraseology change, the thoughts that alternate or combine are always the same. Rümelin, who undertook to criticize a series of definitions of rights, from that of Kant onwards, reproved Kant for having drawn too great a distinction between rights and morality, and others (Ahrens, Stahl, Trendelenburg) for having drawn too little. Finally, he gives his definition in a provisional and tentative manner : "juridical ordinance has the task of assuring to a people

---

[1] Lasson, *op. cit.* ; Steinthal, *Allg. Ethik* (Berlin, 1885), pp. 135-8 ; Schuppe, *Ethik u. Rechtsphil.* (Breslau, 1881), pp. 283-4 ; Wundt, *Ethik*[2] (Stuttgart, 1892), p. 565 *sq.* ; Cohen, *Ethik d. reinen Willens* (Berlin, 1904), p. 567.

that part of the good adapted for realization by a social force, according to universal norms." Jellinek distinguishes the norms of rights from those of religion, of ethicity and of custom, by a triple character: (*a*) because they are norms for the external conduct of men among themselves; (*b*) because they derive from a recognized external authority; (*c*) because their obligatoriness is guaranteed by external powers. —Stammler attaches secondary importance to the element of compulsion, and although he does not explicitly identify justice and morality, assigns to them the same territory, where they should act with different methods, since the perfection-ment of the soul, the character and the thought are distinct from right behaviour. And adopting the turn of phrase of a famous proposition of the *Critique of Pure Reason,* he ends by formulating the following statement: "Justice without love is empty; compassion without a right rule is blind." The Frenchman Duguit transports with greater frankness the centre of rights into morality: he conceives of rights as altogether different from force; not as *political,* but as *limit* of force; as consciousness of human solidarity, beneath whose rule we are all placed, State and individual, strong and weak, governors

and governed. French philosophers of rights
generally oppose the German school, in which
the character of force is prominent, so that
French juridical philosophy sometimes assumes
(for example, in Fouillée) an attitude analogous
to that assumed, as we know, by the "generous"
French economic school toward the English
economists. And merely that some Italian
name should not be absent from this review
of recent writers, we will record Miraglia, who
repeats the old Kantian division, making it
yet more empirical: "Morality and rights are
part of Ethic, because the good can be chiefly
developed in the intimate relations of the conscience, or on the contrary can be developed
by preference in the external relations between
man and man and between man and thing";—
and Vanni, who mixes a little positivistic evolutionism with this empirical reduction, affirming
that rights are not originally distinct from morality,
but that afterwards they were gradually differentiated, and rights now have the special function
of guardianship and guarantee: "that is to say,
the ethical minimum alone has been guaranteed,
that much of the ethical field as is most directly
necessary for the maintenance of life in common,
leaving to other forces the task of regulating

what is most individual in life." And so on, though it seems that this is enough.[1]

Such are the contradictions in which the *Strident contradictions. Stammler.* Philosophy of rights has struggled for about two centuries. Rights do not seem to be identical with Ethic, but they also do not seem to be simply different ; they seem to be at once identical and different, but yet it has been found impossible to fix the element of difference with the concepts of external, of compulsion and others such. The thought of a difference between the two forms of activity has not been further eliminated ; but neither has it been transformed and absorbed. This is a morbid condition, of which the gravest symptom is the logical absurdity of the aforesaid two rights and two justices. Rümelin talks of the pure ideal justice, which selects from the evidence and judges on the basis of immediate impressions of feeling ; and of a realistic, rational, empirical, disciplined and developed justice : two justices that must however act together.[2] Others, seeking relations between those two concepts from a single fact and

---

[1] Rümelin, *Reden u. Aufsätze*, new series (Freiburg i. B., 1881), p. 342 ; Jellinek, *Allgemeine Staatslehre* (Berlin, 1900), p. 302 *sq.* ; Stammler, *Lehre v. richtig. Rechte* (Berlin, 1902) ; Duguit, *L'État, le droit objectif et la loi positive* (Paris, 1901) ; Fouillée, *L'Idée moderne du droit en Allem., en Angl. et en France* (Paris, 1876) ; Miraglia, *Fil. d. dir.* (Napoli, 1903), p. 80 ; Vanni, *Lez. d. fil. d. dir.* (Bologna, 1904), pp. 113-114.

[2] Rümelin, *op. cit.* pp. 176-202. Cp. Lasson, p. 215 *sq.*

failing to conquer the difficulty, force logic by distinguishing between *concept* and *ideal* of rights,
or (as Varini said) between *logical* concept and
concept of the *rational exigencies* of rights: as
though a concept could be truly logical, if it
do not derive from rational exigencies, and
as if these can be valid, if they be not the
concept itself. Worse still, Stammler affirms
the identity of rights with moral rights, and of
rights alone with immoral rights, arriving at the
already criticized division of effective rights
(*Gesetzes*) into two classes. It "is either right
rights (*richtiges Recht*) or not; and right rights
are effective, whose content of will possesses the
property of being *right*. Hence, right rights
stand to effective rights as *species to genus*."[1] To
meditate upon this plan of division is more than
sufficient to produce the conviction of the failure
of the Philosophy of rights, as it has been developed
and as it could be developed with the practical
presuppositions hitherto admitted. As the result
of the direction of studies, from Thomas to
the most recent, there remains nothing but the
problem itself, as originated by the definitions of
Thomas, and become certainly more acute and

---

[1] *Op. cit.* p. 22. Cf. Bergbohm, *Jurisprudenz u. Rechtsphilosophie*
(Leipzig, 1892), i. 141-147 *n.*

difficult, owing to later disputes and inquiries, but never solved.

V. Less attention has been bestowed upon *The value* the concept of *law*, upon which it was impossible *of law.* to obtain full light, on the one hand before the theory of abstract concepts had been developed (representative of class) in their difference from the universal, and on the other before preconceptions as to the necessary social and political character of laws had been discarded.

But the difficulties contained in that concept *In antiquity.* had several times been observed in antiquity. In a dialogue between Alcibiades and Pericles, preserved in the *Memorabilia*, it is asked if all laws be laws, or only those that are just; and it is shown that it does not suffice that a law should be a law, in order to ensure its observance.[1] No true solution, however, was reached in this, as in many questions discussed at this period by Greek philosophy. The *Crito* is rather a stupendous work of art than a philosophical thesis, for it shows to the life the state of soul of Socrates, and the importance that he attributed to the laws and to the social order: the reason alleged for obedience to them, being placed in the fact that we have tacitly or explicitly agreed

[1] *Mem.* i. 2. 40 *sq.*

to remain within the boundaries of a given state, has in it something of the sophistical. Even in antiquity was seen the necessity of tempering the rigidity of laws by means of the equable, τὸ ἐπιεικές, which Aristotle defined as the correction of the law where it sins through its character of generality (ἐπανόρθωμα νόμου ᾗ ἐλλείπει διὰ τὸ καθόλου).[1] But it was not possible to escape from empiricism by means of the concept of equity. The law sins, not once, but always, through abstractness, or better, it never sins at all, because its function resides precisely in that abstractness.—In modern times Diderot felt and expressed all the gravity of the conflicts that arise, alike from the observance and from the inobservance of the law, and he expresses this in his *Entretien d'un père avec ses enfants sur le danger de se mettre au-dessus des lois.* "*Mon père* (remarks one of the sons at the end of the dialogue), *c'est qu'à la rigueur il n'y a pas de lois pour le sage. . . . Parlez plus bas. . . . Toutes étant sujettes à des exceptions, c'est à lui qu'il appartient de juger des cas où il faut s'y soumettre ou s'en affranchir.—Je ne serais pas trop fâché* (concludes the father), *qu'il y eût dans la ville un ou deux citoyens, comme toi;*

---

[1] *Eth. Nicom.* Bk. v, c. 11.

*mais je n'y habiterais pas, s'ils pensaient tous de
même."* [1]

The attitude of rebellion to the laws showed *Romanticism.*
itself in German thought and literature in the
preromanticism of the *Sturm und Drang* (for
instance in the *Räuber* of Schiller), and in
Romanticism properly so called, when among
others appeared the theories that limited the
State, such as those of Wilhelm von Humboldt,
and theories of sexual relations, such as those
of Friedrich Schlegel. In the *Lucinde* is displayed great horror for *bourgeois* customs and for
every sort of constraint, sexual relations being
advocated with woman, family, love and fidelity,
but without matrimony.

Jacobi represents this attitude in several of *Jacobi.*
his writings, with great elevation of soul, and
especially in the *Woldemar* (1779, 1794-96), the
most lively protest that has ever been made
against law in the name of the individual. Here
the question treated is precisely whether we
should follow the inspirations of our own conscience or the laws of our own people. Sides
are taken against "the compulsion and violence
exercised by usages, customs, habits, and against

[1] *Œuvres,* edit. Assézat et Tourneux, v. (Paris, Garnier, 1875), pp.
307-8.

those who do not think, save by means of those laws, holding them sacred, with resolute soul and mind inert"; and "that audacious heroic spirit is celebrated, which raises itself above the laws and common morality that it may produce a new order of things." "His heart alone tells man immediately what is good; his heart alone, his instincts only, can tell him immediately: to love it is his life. Reflection teaches him to know and to practise what leads to good. Habit assures and makes his the wisdom that he has acquired." "But this individual initiative," he observes, "may be the cause of abuse and mis-understandings." "Without doubt," replied Jacobi, "but what cannot be misunderstood has little meaning, and what cannot be abused has but little force in use." Men may be divided into two classes; the one exaggerates fear, the other hope and courage. The former are circumspect, always in doubt, they fear the truth because it may be misunderstood, they fear great qualities, lofty virtue, because of the aberrations to which it may give rise; and they have evil always before their eyes. The latter are the bold (who could be called the irreflective in the Platonic sense) and they behave with less exacti-tude; they are not so perplexed, they trust

rather to the voice of their heart than to any
word from without; they build rather upon
courage than upon virtue, which generally keeps
them waiting too long. They sometimes ask
themselves with Young: Is virtue then alone
baptized and are the passions pagan? "If," says
Jacobi, "I must keep to one of these classes, I
choose the second." "Yes," he exclaims elsewhere, opposing the abstractness of Kant,—"yes,
I am atheist and impious, yes, I will to lie, in
opposition to the will that wills nothing, as
Desdemona lied when dying, I will to lie and to
deceive like Pylades, when he slew himself for the
sake of Orestes; I will to slay like Timoleon; to
break laws and oaths like Epaminondas and
John de Witt; to commit suicide like Otho;
to despoil the temple like David; to pluck
ears of corn on the Sabbath day, if only
because I am hungry and the law is made for
man, not man for the law. By the sacrosanct
conscience that I have within me, I know that the
privilegium aggratiandi for such crimes against
the pure letter of the law, rational, absolute and
universal, is the sovran right of man himself,
the seal of his dignity, of his divine nature."[1]
But it must be remarked upon reading these

---

[1] *Woldemar*, passim.

effusions (most sincere, as all that came from the pen of Jacobi), that they are rather manifestations of states of the soul than theories, and therefore, strictly speaking, not to be theoretically censured, as is the case with all affirmations that place in relief one side of reality, without denying the others by doing so.

Hegel. Hegel discovered this, observing in relation to our last extract: " Neither of the two sides can be wanting to moral beauty, neither its liveliness as individuality, by which it does not obey the dead concept, nor the form of concept and of law, universality and objectivity, which is the side exclusively considered by Kant, by means of the absolute abstraction to which he submitted liveliness, thereby suffocating it. The passage cited as to the liveliness and freedom of the moral life does not exclude objectivity, but does not express it either." Hence the danger of the romantic attitude, which had no need of exhortations such as those of Jacobi, for it already too much preferred *magnanimous* to *honest, noble* to *moral* action; and was much inclined to free itself of the law itself under the pretext of freeing itself from the *letter* of the law. Meeting empirical with empirical observations, Hegel also remarked that the

examples of the violation of laws due to the
divine majesty of man, adduced by Jacobi, were
conditioned by the natural temperament, by
actual situations, and especially by circumstances
of supreme misfortune, of supreme and rare
necessity, in which few individuals find themselves. "It would be very sad for liberty if
it could only prove its majesty and become
actual in extraordinary cases of cruel laceration
of the moral and natural life and in extraordinary
individuals. The ancients, on the other hand,
found the highest morality in the life of a well-
ordered State." Hegel admitted that the affirmation of Jacobi, "The law is made for man,
not man for the law," contained a great truth,
when it was intended to allude in this way to
the positive or statutory law. But the opposite
was also true, when the allusion was to the
moral law, taken as universal, outside of which,
when the individual was separated from it, there
was nothing but appetites and sensible impulses,
which can only be means for the law.[1]

But we must not fail to recognize that Hegel
does not avail himself of this most exact distinction in his philosophy, for there the dominating
motive is respect for the laws and the tendency

[1] *Werke*, i. 52 *sq.*; xvi. 21 *sq.*

to attack individual initiative. Hegel repeats many times with complacency the saying of the Pythagorean, that the best way of educating a young man is to make him citizen of a State ruled by good laws; and he remarks that Herculeses belong to primitive and barbarous times, and that individual valour has but a small field in times of culture. He was most averse to criticism of and rebellion against the authority of the State; for these did not seem to him to correspond to the reality of the spirit. That surface is not the reality; at bottom all desire order; and it is necessary to distinguish apparent political sentiment from that which men really will, for within them they will the thing, but hesitate as to particulars, and enjoy the vanity of censuring.[1] Men believe that the State exists and that in it alone are particular interests realized; but habit makes invisible to them that upon which our entire existence depends. There is in short in Hegel, besides the philosopher, a politician and moralist regretful of the excesses of revolutionaries and of unbridled romanticism; and there is also in him the desire for an exact inquiry into the function and limits of positive law.[2]

---

[1] *Phil. d. Rechts,* sect. II. *passim* ; cf. pp. 150, 153.
[2] *Op. cit.* § 268, *Zus.*

In recent times there have been many and *Recent doctrines.* very various manifestations connected with the concept of this function and of its limits, and it would occupy much space to enumerate and to illustrate them all. We shall mention three, very distant and different. The first, which belongs to the political and social field, is the doctrine of anarchy and is opposed to laws of all sorts; it is a not purely philosophical doctrine, though it involves philosophical questions.[1] The other two, which more properly belong to the juridical field, are the assertion of the importance of laws and of the duty of defending their existence, even where their violation by others does not interfere with our individual interests, or when their defence costs individual sacrifices (this was the argument of a vigorous little book by Jhering);[2]—and by way of contrast the demand for a free creation of the law by the judge (*die freie Rechtsfindung*), which has given rise to discussions that are yet burning, more directly provoked by a little book of Kantorowicz (Gnaeus Flavius).[3]

VI. If then there has not been a great gain

---

[1] An ample exposition of such doctrines is to be found in E. Zoccoli, *L' Anarchia*, Turin, 1907.

[2] *La Lotta pel diritto*, It. tr., Milan, 1875.

[3] *La Lotta per la scienza del diritto* (It. tr., Palermo, 1908); cf. *Critica*, vi. pp. 199-201.

Natural rights and their dissolution. The historical school of rights. in clearness of fundamental concepts, as regards this part of the subject, there has on the contrary been an indubitable advance in consciousness acquired as to the mutability of laws and as to the consequent contradictoriness of the idea of natural Rights. This, with its complement, the catalogue of innate natural and inalienable rights of man, had great success in the seventeenth century for political and social reasons, attaining its highest development in the century following. But it may be said that the doctrine of innate rights was liquidated by Kant in the *Metaphysic of Custom*, when he wrote the proposition that liberty is the only original and innate rights, which belong to man through his very humanity,[1] at the very moment when it was most energetically affirmed in a practical form in the *Declaration of the Rights of Man*. In the system of Hegel the constructions of natural rights began to lose their rigidity; becoming indeed historical categories of Ethicity or *Sittlichkeit*, determinations of the spirits of various peoples (*Volksgeister*), which are in their turn determinations of the Absolute or of the Idea. Owing to this view (without taking into account his error of wishing to philosophize and to make dialectical what is

[1] *Metaphys. d. Sitt.* p. 40.

historical and empirical), Hegel connected himself closely with the historical school of rights
(Hugo, Savigny, etc.).   This, notwithstanding
the exaggeration by which he seemed to deny
the value of the ideal demands made of rights,
had the merit of shaking the old conception of
natural rights.   This has retained its place in
treatises from that time onward in a more or
less worm-eaten and unstable condition by the
force of inertia; or it has been preserved by
Catholic writers (by Rosmini not less than by
the Padre Taparelli), whose conception is of
necessity but little historical; or it has re-
appeared in those curious Catholics and anti-
historians, the positivists (Spencer, Ardigò).
But that natural rights are nothing but *new*
historical rights in the struggle of their becoming,
is a conviction that has penetrated the general
consciousness.

We also owe to the historical school the *The compari-*
son between
comparison between the life of rights and the life *rights and*
language.
of language ; this was prepared by the discoveries
of comparative linguistic, which although substantially correct, yet had, as we have observed,
the defect of limiting itself to the *grammatical*
form of both facts, not to their genuine and
direct reality.   Jacobi, in the already quoted

effusions of *Woldemar*, had recourse to the same comparison, for other reasons and with a more exact understanding of its terms; speaking there of the moral infraction of laws, he wrote: "For such exceptions, for such *licences of lofty poetry*, the grammar of virtue has no definite rules and therefore does not mention them No grammar, least of all the general and philosophical, could contain in itself all that appertains to a living language, and teach how, in every epoch, every dialect must be formed. But it would be unwise to affirm that every one may speak as they feel inclined." And again, "Virtue is free art; and as artistic genius gives laws to art by its creations, so moral genius gives laws to human conduct: just, good, noble, excellent, is what the just, good, noble, and excellent man practises, achieves and produces in conformity with his character; he *invents virtue*, procures and generates adequate expression for human dignity."[1]

The concept of law, and the studies of comparative Rights and of the general Doctrine of Rights. VII. The study of the concept of law is also progressing, and henceforth is not confined to so-called juridical laws and to legislations and codes. Researches into primitive rights and into those of savage and barbarous peoples, known as

---

[1] *Woldemar*, pp. 111, 416, and *passim*.

juridical Ethnography or comparative rights, have greatly contributed to destroy many prejudices; as also the attention that has been directed to facts called social, that is to say, not strictly political. A school that has had independent yet partly similar manifestations in England (Austin, Sumner Maine, etc.) and in Germany, where it has taken the name of school of *the general Doctrine of Rights* (*allgemeine Rechtslehre*, according to the denomination given to it by Adolph Merkel), studies in particular the concept of law in its various classes and subclasses; and from it there cannot but issue a more correct understanding of the concept of law, as from the refinement of political Economy into pure Economy has come, first Psychology and then the Philosophy of economy. Meanwhile (and as far as we know) the literature of the school, dominated as it is by the needs of jurisprudence, maintains an empirical or *intellectualistic* character; and jurists, rather than philosophers themselves, are those that most cultivate it. The distinctions and subdistinctions of the laws are conducted with subtlety, but are without solid foundation, because the concept posited as basis of law is uncertain and arbitrary. Limiting ourselves to a single example, let us mention Bierling, perhaps the most philosophical of those various writers. Bierling first of all excludes from the concept of law the modes of man's conduct toward God, toward himself, and toward animals; but he gives no serious reason for this. He then arrives, by a mere arbitrary act, at the limiting of the concept of law to the manner of men's conduct among themselves, and defines rights in the juridical sense (as he calls it: "in general, all that men living together in any sort of community reciprocally recognize as a norm and rule of this living together"). He then introduces into the concept thus defined, not by deduction, but as the result of a second arbitrary act, the concept of exteriority, adding that, "the object of law is a definite *external* procedure of man toward man."[1] In all this is evident the bad influence of jurisprudence and of its empirical preoccupations.

Legalism and moral casuistic. VIII. Ethical legalism became a bitter question for Christianity, precisely because of the contest between lofty Christian morality and its legalitarian form, chiefly inherited from Judaism. In the ancient world there is almost no trace of the question, just because the struggle was never acute.[2] Hence the difficulties debated among the

[1] Bierling, *Juristische Prinzipienlehre* (Freiburg i. B., 1894–98, 2 vols.).
[2] Sidgwick, *History of Ethics*, London, 1892, p. 111 *sq.*

patristics and the scholastics as to derogability from divine laws and the consequent distinctions between a perfect and an imperfect moral life, between precepts and counsels ; and as recourse is had to precedents in judicial questions, so here with these ethical problems concerning exceptions made by God to the moral law, to the precepts of the Bible (where some were not beautiful).[1] The practical needs of confession give origin to books on casuistic, of which collections exist dating from the fourteenth and fifteenth centuries. The Reformation manifested aversion to these treatises : Luther said that moral theologians had first extinguished in men the fear of God and had then placed soft cushions beneath their hands and feet; and Melanchthon lamented that the Christian Republic was honoured *theologastrorum sententiis de conscientiae casibus, inestricabilibus, ubi nunquam non ex quaestione quaestio nascitur*, and called them *conscientiarum cauteria*.[2]

The inconclusiveness of legalism was con-*Probabilitism and Jesuitic morality.* verted into a most powerful poison by the Jesuits, with their *probabilitism*, of which precursors were not wanting in the Middle Ages, but it received

[1] A. Bonucci, *La derogabilità del diritto naturale nella Scolastica*, Perugia, 1906.

[2] Hist. remarks in dissert., *De casuisticae theologiae originibus, locis atque praestantia* (together with De Ligorio, *Theol. mor.*, ed. cit., pp. xxiv-lxxvi).

definite form from the Dominican Bartolomeo Medina in 1577. From that time onward probabilitism began to be surrounded with a copious literature, which continually increased in the course of the seventeenth century, to decline in the century following. The opposition originated by the Jansenists, whose capital literary document, the *Provinciales* of Pascal also dates from the seventeenth century (1656), was the period of the greatest vigour of the doctrine. But if the most perfect and most Christian moral conscience dwelt in the Jansenists and in Pascal and if the absurd consequences to which probabilitism led became clearly evident in that polemic, yet it cannot be said that philosophically the error was finally superseded. Ere this could have happened, it would have been necessary, on the one hand to destroy all possibility of theological utilitarianism (which was impossible to carry out in a religious and transcendental Ethic, owing to its mystical and irrationalistic character) and on the other to destroy legalism. Pascal himself (and St. Augustine, to whom he appeals) was always confined in the legislative conception of morality; hence he speaks of the laws of "not slaying," which it was necessary to obey strictly, save in the cases established by God or when he gives particular orders to put certain persons to death. The Catholic Church, always astutely political, condemned without hesitation the extreme *rigorists*, who wish that the law should always be followed and the extreme *latitudinarians*, who think that any sort of reasons, however slight and improbable, suffice for not observing the law; allowing intermediate sects to discuss among themselves until they were out of breath, that is to say, *the moderate rigorists, the probabiliorists or tutiorists, the equiprobabilitists and the probabilitists.* Sant Alfonso dei Liguori adhered to these last, who were of opinion that it is always permissible to do what we wish, provided always that there be probable reasons, though less probable than those that militate in favour of the law. In his *Dissertatio de usu moderato opinionis probabilis,*[1] he thus exposed the principal argument of his thesis : *Peto ab adversariis ut indicent (si possunt) ubinam legem hanc esse scriptam invenerint, quod teneamur inter opiniones probabiles probabiliores sequi ? Haec lex quidem, prout universalis, deberet omnibus esse nota et certa : at quomodo ista lex certa dici potest, cum communis sententia doctorum, saltem longe major illorum pars, post tantum discrimen absolute*

---

[1] In *Theol. mor.* i. 10-24.

asserant, hanc legem non adesse? Usque dum igitur de tali lege dubitatum, opinio quod adsit haec lex sequendi probabiliora, quamvis alicui videatur probabilior, nunquam tamen lex dici potest, sed appellanda erit mera opinio, utpote ex fallibili motivo deducta, quae vim nequaquam habet, ut lex, obligandi. This doctrine still retains in our day very firm supporters among the Jesuits (Cathrein,[1] Lehmkuhl,[2] etc.).

Critique of the concept of the licit. But if the destruction of theological utilitarianism has been brought about by the criticism of the transcendental and by idealistic Ethic, that of legalism, with its expression as the licit, the permissible, or morally indifferent, appears in Fichte and in Schleiermacher. Kant did not treat the question explicitly and, as observed, we can deduce from certain of his utterances that he did not altogether abandon the concept of the licit.[3]

Fichte. But Fichte, in a note to his *Natural Rights*, wrote: "A right is evidently something of which a man can avail himself or not; and is therefore the result of a law that is merely permissive. . . . The permission is not expressly given by the law and is deduced by interpretation from its

[1] Cathrein, *Moralphilosophie*,[4] i. 428-437.
[2] *Probabilismus vindicatus* (Freiburg, Bk. i., 1906).
[3] See above, p. 405 ; cf. also *Krit. d. rein. Vern.* pp. 10-11 *n.*

limitation. And the limitation of a law is shown by the fact of its being something conditioned. It is not absolutely apparent, therefore, that a permissive law which commands in an unconditioned manner and therefore extends to all, can be deduced from the moral law."[1]

What was a mere mention in Fichte became *Schleiermacher.* an ample demonstration in the celebrated memoir of Schleiermacher, *On the Concept of the Licit* (1826), which resolutely drove the licit out of the field of Ethic, by demonstrating its altogether juridical nature: "The original seat of this concept cannot be the domain of Ethic, in which it is not admissible: it appertains to the domain of law and of positive law; and there is something originally licit in civil life, precisely in this sense that there is something half-way between what is commanded and what is forbidden, the proper object of law."[2]

Rosmini, owing to having ignored this origin *Rosmini.* of the lawful, proceeded to divide human actions into four classes: the prohibited, the licit, the commanded, and the superogatory; the last three were all innocent, but the licit was simply innocent, while the commanded and the super-

---

[1] *Grundl. d. Naturr.* introd. § iii. *n.*

[2] *Werke*, sect. iii., vol. ii., pp. 418-445; cf. G. Mayer, *Die Lehre vom Erlaubten in der Gesch. d. Ethik seit Schleiermacher*, Leipzig, 1899.

ogatory were also furnished with moral value.
Hence arose grave errors in his Ethic and
in his Philosophy of law and definitions that
it is impossible to grasp, such as the following
relating to superogatory actions: "The obligatory
consists in preserving the moral order, but
the superogatory consists in preserving the
said order in a more excellent and perfect
manner, with fuller, more frequent, and more
ardent acts of the will. These second not only
preserve the moral order, but augment it, almost
creating a part of it themselves with their activity ;
they make themselves not only followers of the
good, but authors of the good itself." Rosmini
also considered that the posing of the question of
probabilitism represented progress in Ethic; that
is, upon "what man should do, if he found himself
in doubt as to performing or omitting to perform
an action." But the solution of the question that
he gave on his account amounted (be it said to
his honour) to the annihilation of legalism, since
for him a doubtful law does not oblige when
it is positive Rights, but it does oblige when it is
moral law, that is, when there is a fear of offending against the supreme and necessary law, which
wills absolutely to be always fulfilled.[1] In other

---

[1] *Compendio di Etica*, pp. 48, 96, 284-285.

terms, the true practical law is never (even when it appears to be so) positive law ; and the concept of law, which always has a positive meaning, is extraneous to Ethic and to the Philosophy of the practical : a result to which Rosmini does not attain, or at least is not conscious of attaining.

CONCLUSION

The Philosophy of the Spirit as the whole of Philosophy. WITH the Philosophy of the practical terminates the exposition that we had proposed to give of the Philosophy of the Spirit; and the exposition of the whole of Philosophy also terminates, because the Spirit is the whole of Reality.

Here at the end, this proposition has no need of such proof or verification as is customary in calculation. Because the proof of Philosophy is intrinsic to it and consists of the reciprocal confronting of the development of thought and its demands, between the System and Logic. And Logic, as we know, if it be in a certain sense the whole of Philosophy (philosophy in brief or in idea or in potentiality), is also a part among the parts of the philosophical system; so that the confrontation of the System and of Logic, of thought in act and thought in idea, between thought and the thought of thought, has been continuously present and active in the course of the exposition, and the coincidence of the two processes and

586

their confluence into one has been clearly
demonstrated.

Logic affirms the thinkability of the real and *Correspondence between Logic and System.*
the inconceivability of any limit that could be
put to thought, of every excogitation of the
unknowable. And Philosophy, examining every
part of the real, has not found any place in
which to lodge the unknowable in thought.
Logic posits as the ideal of the concept, that it
should be universal and not general, concrete and
not abstract ; that it should be pure of intuitions
such as those of mathematics and differ from
them in being necessary and not conventional ;
fruitful in intuitions like those of the empirical
sciences, but differing from them by its infinite
fecundity which dominates every possible manifestation of the real. And the system has
effectively shown that this desideratum of Logic is
not a chimæra and that the Spirit is indeed that
concept which corresponds to the ideal of the
concept : there is nothing that is not a manifestation of the Spirit (an effectual manifestation,
not conventional or metaphorical). Logic, rejecting all dualism or pluralism, wills that the
philosophical concept shall be a unique concept
or of the One, and does not suffer heterogeneous
concepts at its side. And the system has con-

firmed that the concept of the Spirit alone fulfils
the logical condition of the concept; and that
the concept of Nature, far from being a concept
of something real, is the hypostasis of a manner of
elaborating reality, not philosophical but practical;
thus the concept itself of Nature, in so far as it is
effectual, is nothing but the product of a function
of the Spirit.

On the other hand, the Logic of the idea of
the concept deduces that it must be a synthesis
of itself and of its opposite. For its opposite,
far from being heterogeneous and different, is
flesh of the flesh and blood of the blood of the
concept itself, as negation is of affirmation. And
the system has led us before the Spirit or Reality
as development, which is the true reality of the
real and synthesis of opposites. Logic deduces
that the concept is synthesis of itself and of the
distinct from itself, of the universal and of the
individual, and that therefore Philosophy must
flow into History, and mediate its comprehension.
And the system shows the capacity of its principles
for interpreting the complex reality of History,
and above all the history of philosophy itself, by
solving its problems. Logic does not admit
other distinctions of the concept than those that
are the outcome of its own nature, such as the

relations of subject - object and of individual-universal; and the system has confirmed these distinctions, duplicating itself as Philosophy of knowledge and Philosophy of action, of theory and of practice; subdividing itself as to the first, into Æsthetic and Logic; as to the second, into Economic and Ethic. And since the demand of the concept has been entirely satisfied, when these divisions have been exhausted, we have not found the possibility of new subdivisions, for example into various æsthetic or into various ethical categories among the particular sub-forms of the Spirit.

Some are seized as with a sense of dissatisfaction and delusion when they arrive at the end of the philosophical system and at the result that there is no reality save the Spirit and no other Philosophy save the Philosophy of the Spirit; and they do not wish to resign themselves to accepting that and nothing else as Reality, although obliged to do so by logical necessity. A world beyond which there is no other seems to them poor indeed; an immanent Spirit, trammelled and far inferior by comparison with a transcendental Spirit, an omnipotent God outside the world; a Reality penetrable by thought, less poetical than one surrounded

Dissatisfaction at the end of every system, and its irrational motive.

with mystery; the vague and indeterminate, more beautiful than the precise and determined. But we know that they are involved in a psychological illusion, similar to his who should dream of an art so sublime that every work of art really existing would by comparison appear contemptible; and the dreamer of this turbid dream, should not succeed in achieving a single verse. Impotent are those poets most refined; impotent those insatiable philosophers.

Rational motive: the inexhaustibility of Life and of Philosophy. But precisely because we know the genesis of their psychological illusion, we know that there is in it (and there could not fail to be) an element of truth. The infinite, inexhaustible by the thought of the individual, is Reality itself, which ever creates new forms; Life is the true mystery, not because impenetrable by thought, but because thought penetrates it to the infinite with power equal to its own. And since every moment, however beautiful, would become ugly, were we to dwell in it, so would life become ugly, were it ever to linger in one of its contingent forms. And because Philosophy, not less than Art, is conditioned by Life, so no particular philosophical system can ever contain in itself all the philosophable; no philosophical system is *definite*, because Life itself is never *definite.* A philosophical system solves a group of problems historically given and prepares the conditions for the posing of other problems, that is, of new systems. Thus it has always been and thus it will always be.

In such a sense, Truth is always surrounded with mystery, an ascending to ever higher heights, which are without a summit, as Life is without a summit. At the end of one of his researches every philosopher just perceives the uncertain outlines of another, which he himself, or he who comes after him, will achieve. And with this *modesty*, which is of the nature of things themselves, not my personal sentiment; with this modesty, which is also confidence that I have not thought in vain, I bring my work to a conclusion, offering it to the well disposed as an *instrument of labour.*

THE END

Æsthetic as Science of Expression and General Linguistic

TRANSLATED FROM THE ITALIAN OF
BENEDETTO CROCE

BY

DOUGLAS AINSLIE, B.A.

Price 10s. net.

SOME PRESS OPINIONS

SPECTATOR.—"Mr. Ainslie translates the whole of the *Theory of Æsthetic*, and in a very useful 'Historical Summary' gives a synopsis of the historical portion of the original. The translator is an enthusiast for his subject, as is evident from the introduction, but on the whole we do not think he makes extravagant claims for Croce. This *Æsthetic* is really a most remarkable performance, and an English translation is a real boon."

HIBBERT JOURNAL.—"Every recognition is due to Mr. Ainslie for having made the volume, full, when all is said, of the most suggestive and original views, accessible to English readers."

JOURNAL OF PHILOSOPHY (AMERICA).—"A book which has aroused more interest than any other recent work on æsthetics. . . . Croce's work is valuable not simply for the theory which it presents, but for the many suggestive views which the author puts forward on most of the subjects related to æsthetics. His criticisms of other æsthetic doctrines are very outspoken and usually adverse, nevertheless they are stimulating and valuable."

MORNING POST.—"The translation is most felicitous and readable. . . . Our gratitude to Mr. Ainslie for having made Croce's 'Æsthetics' accessible to English readers can only be enhanced if we realise the courage required to undertake the translation of a work full of such original and unwonted theories."

TIMES.—"Signor Croce's destructive criticism is deadly. No one after reading his book has any excuse for believing any kind of nonsense about art, either the nonsense that pretends to be mystical, or the nonsense that pretends to be scientific; and when he comes to construction, his main ideas are usually supported by reasoning at once close and candid. Those ideas, we believe, are of great importance, though the conclusions to be drawn from them could only be set out in a book as long as his own. The translation is usually very clear, and Mr. Ainslie has done a valuable service in making it."

ATHENÆUM.—"Signor Croce's work will appeal to many. It is in the grand manner, simple, severe, spaceless and timeless as any classic. Italy may well be proud of him."

MACMILLAN AND CO., Ltd., LONDON.

By DOUGLAS AINSLIE

JOHN OF DAMASCUS

Third Edition.   Price 6s.

SOME PRESS OPINIONS

MORNING POST.—" Mr. Ainslie, in this third edition of his suggestive poem, has given to the world in swift spontaneous verse the mature expression of the conception in which his thoughts have long been centred.   With a singular deftness of touch he has contrived to weave so many fresh arguments in the woof of the old material as to produce the effect of a work almost wholly new.   Not only do these additions help to knit the thread of the narrative more harmoniously together, they redound as well to the reader's ease in keeping in touch with it.   Nay, they do something more than this ; they go far both to enlighten the student and charm the partisan.   Pre-eminently is this the case in the stirring pages which deal with the story of Muhammad's life and the conquests of the doughty warriors who fought after him. . . . Everybody whom the advice may concern would be wise to allow Mr. Ainslie's revised and enlarged version to take the place of its forerunners on his shelves. . . . His new readers will be many, for *John of Damascus*, having 'stretched his limbs,' now wears a resolute air to extend from day to day the circle of his influence and his friends."

OUTLOOK.—" Perhaps no more authentic expression of the Oriental spirit has appeared in English poetry since FitzGerald translated the quatrains of Omar than is to be found in Mr. Douglas Ainslie's *John of Damascus*. . . . In this day of snippety ' occasional verse ' it is a welcome change to come upon a solid sustained effort on a great theme written by a man in love with his subject.   Long as the poem is, it is neither oppressive nor dull.   Mr. Ainslie writes easily and naturally. . . . His diction is musical and fluent, and lures the reader along by constant variety and happy turns of expression. . . . The fascination of the East, which is casting its spell more and more over our literature, has taken hold of the author's mind and communicates itself to his verse."

LIVERPOOL POST.—" One cannot but be glad to see such a book as *John of Damascus*, by Douglas Ainslie, in its fourth edition.   This fact shows that there are readers who find recreation in a high class of literature."

CONSTABLE AND COMPANY Ltd.

10 ORANGE STREET LEICESTER SQUARE LONDON W.C.

By DOUGLAS AINSLIE

THE SONG OF THE STEWARTS

PRELUDE

Price 7s. 6d. net

SOME PRESS OPINIONS

DAILY TELEGRAPH.—"Mr. Ainslie's volume will without doubt afford a good deal of pleasure to Stewart devotees."

SCOTSMAN.—"Every lover of this kind of poetry should read it with both interest and admiration.'

OBSERVER.—"The author has a distinct sense of rhythm, and writes with a cultured fervour and distinction."

MORNING LEADER.—"His poetry has tremendous vigour, and its force alone is a notable quality . . . it never lacks point and definiteness."

BYSTANDER.—"Mr. Ainslie is obviously in love with his subject, and the verse is worthy of the theme."

CATHOLIC FIELD.—"Few who take up the book will lay it down without reading to the end, and none but will be stirred and stimulated by the strong human strokes that on every page strike fire from the bedrock of our common sympathies."

MOMENTS

Price 1s. net ; Cloth, 2s. 6d. net.

SOME PRESS OPINIONS

T. P.'S WEEKLY.—"Nearly every poem has thought that was worth expressing, and the expression is musical and distinguished."

TRUTH.—"A charming little booklet of verse. . . . The Stewart poems seem to us specially stirring and raise high expectations."

DAILY EXPRESS.—"Mr. Ainslie is another real poet. . . . His verse is musical and full of happy phrases and imagery."

MORNING POST.—"He certainly has qualities which will not fail to find appreciation. He has distinctly original ideas."

GLASGOW HERALD.—"The verse runs on like a brook, so that its rippling almost makes one shut the ears to its subtlety or depth of suggestion. Delicate in texture, it is often packed with significance. . . . Betokens a writer with the true lyric gift and genuine poetic insight."

CONSTABLE AND COMPANY Ltd.

10 ORANGE STREET LEICESTER SQUARE LONDON W.C.

By DOUGLAS AINSLIE

MIRAGE

Price 3s. 6d. net

SOME PRESS OPINIONS

EVENING STANDARD.—"The work of a scholar, these poems are beautifully made. Form, a little despised by some of our young individual poets, is treated with respect : a pretty sight."

GLASGOW HERALD.—"Of Mr. Ainslie's qualifications as a poet there can be no question ; as little can there be of the high quality of his verse. At his best he attains a singular clearness, the clearness of primary colour, of pure water, or of crystal, the clearness of sure vision which is the condition of completed imaginative effort."

NATION.—"Mr. Ainslie's poetry is interesting. . . . we do feel the presence in it of a determination to use poetry for some vital purpose, some attempt, not to escape from modern life into cells of exquisite beauty, but to interpret into poetic form and feeling at least the consciousness of human destiny."

TIMES.—"These are the poems of a man of taste and culture, always interesting."

MORNING POST.—"Mr. Ainslie is 'the perfect Phyllistine.' Phyllis is wooed with sapphics at Versailles, Oenone with album-verses in Mayfair, Violet with Neapolitan quatrains, and Daphne with diamonds."

DAILY CHRONICLE.—"Mr. Ainslie is a good story-teller ; but he uses the ballad as his vehicle, instead of dramatic blank verse. There is a rhythm and a swing in his ballads that carries us along, and a power of narration."

LONDON : ELKIN MATHEWS, VIGO STREET, W.

THE SONG OF THE STEWARTS

CANTO I.

The first Canto takes up the narrative where the Prelude leaves off, and deals with the most luminous events of the reigns of Robert II. and of David II., the first Stewart Kings of Scots.

The system of a series of poems in different metres, such as was carried out in the Prelude, is here again adopted, and the first Canto will be issued in a form similar to that of the Prelude.

[*To be published shortly.*